Growing Apart

Interests, Identities, and Institutions in Comparative Politics

Series Editor:
Mark I. Lichbach, University of California, Riverside

Editorial Advisory Board:
Barbara Geddes, University of California, Los Angeles
James C. Scott, Yale University
Sven Steinmo, University of Colorado
Kathleen Thelen, Northwestern University
Alan Zuckerman, Brown University

The post–Cold War world faces a series of defining global challenges: virulent forms of conflict, the resurgence of the market as the basis for economic organization, and the construction of democratic institutions.

The books in this series take advantage of the rich development of different approaches to comparative politics in order to offer new perspectives on these problems. The books explore the emerging theoretical and methodological synergisms and controversies about social conflict, political economy, and institutional development.

Democracy without Associations: Transformation of the Party System and Social Cleavages in India, by Pradeep K. Chhibber

Gendering Politics: Women in Israel, by Hanna Herzog

Origins of Liberal Dominance: State, Church, and Party in Nineteenth-Century Europe, by Andrew C. Gould

The Deadlock of Democracy in Brazil, by Barry Ames

Political Science as Puzzle Solving, edited by Bernard Grofman

Institutions and Innovation: Voters, Parties, and Interest Groups in the Consolidation of Democracy—France and Germany, 1870–1939, by Marcus Kreuzer

Altering Party Systems: Strategic Behavior and the Emergence of New Political Parties in Western Democracies, by Simon Hug

Managing "Modernity": Work, Community, and Authority in Late-Industrializing Japan and Russia, by Rudra Sil

Re-Forming the State: The Politics of Privatization in Latin America and Europe, by Hector E. Schamis

Protest and the Politics of Blame: The Russian Response to Unpaid Wages, by Debra Javeline

Growing Apart: Oil, Politics, and Economic Change in Indonesia and Nigeria, by Peter M. Lewis

Growing Apart

*Oil, Politics, and Economic Change
in Indonesia and Nigeria*

PETER M. LEWIS

THE UNIVERSITY OF MICHIGAN PRESS
Ann Arbor

Copyright © by the University of Michigan 2007
All rights reserved
Published in the United States of America by
The University of Michigan Press
Manufactured in the United States of America
⊛ Printed on acid-free paper

2010   2009   2008   2007   4   3   2   1

A CIP catalog record for this book is available from the British Library.

Library of Congress Cataloging-in-Publication Data

Lewis, Peter, 1957–
    Growing apart : oil, politics, and economic change in Indonesia
and Nigeria / Peter M. Lewis.
        p.   cm. — (Interests, identities, and institutions in
comparative politics)
    Includes bibliographical references and index.
    ISBN-13: 978-0-472-09980-1 (cloth : alk. paper)
    ISBN-10: 0-472-09980-9 (cloth : alk. paper)
    ISBN-13: 978-0-472-06980-4 (pbk. : alk. paper)
    ISBN-10: 0-472-06980-2 (pbk. : alk. paper)
    1. Indonesia—Economic conditions—1945–   . 2. Nigeria—
Economic conditions—1970– . 3. Indonesia—Economic policy.
4. Nigeria—Economic policy.   I. Title.

HC447.L47   2007
330.9598—dc22   2006025449

For Tamara

Contents

Acknowledgments

This has been a long project, spanning several continents, and I have naturally incurred a great many debts, personal and professional. Much of the initial research and conceptualization was concluded during a year as a National Fellow at the Hoover Institution, Stanford University. At Stanford, I especially appreciated the collegiality and interest of David Abernethy, Bruce Bueno de Mesquita, Larry Diamond, Thráinn Eggertsson, Terry Karl, Richard Roberts, Hilton Root, and Barry Weingast. Thomas Henriksen and Wendy Minkin made the program as rewarding and pleasant as one could have hoped for.

The bulk of the writing was subsequently completed as a Fellow at the Woodrow Wilson International Center for Scholars. Bob Hathaway was a generous host in the Asia Program, and Lee Hamilton a remarkably congenial and engaging presence in leading the institution. Special thanks go to Arlyn Charles, Lindsay Collins, and Rosemary Lyon for creating a supportive, productive, and enjoyable setting for scholarship.

Large portions of the draft manuscript were read and perceptively critiqued by Deborah Brautigam, Pierre Englebert, John Heilbrunn, and Nic Van de Walle. They have been good friends and valued colleagues, for which I am very thankful. Two anonymous reviewers for the University of Michigan Press also provided incisive comments that have significantly improved the book. Any remaining flaws are obviously mine to claim.

Various pieces of this study have been presented at Stanford, the University of California, Berkeley, the University of Ibadan, the Center for Strategic and International Studies in Jakarta, Johns Hopkins School of Advanced International Studies, American University, and several professional meetings. I particularly benefited from comments by Robert Aten, Robert Bates, Charles Cadwell, Evan Lieberman, Bob Price, Michael Ross, and Ben Ross Schneider. A number of mentors and friends also deserve thanks. Nancy Bermeo, Henry Bienen, Atul Kohli, and John Waterbury were inspiring teachers. Glenn Adler, Eva Bellin, Cathy Boone, Tom Callaghy, Gyimah Boadi, Mike Bratton, Lou Goodman, Jon

Kraus, Carl Levan, Lynne Rienner, Don Rothchild, Howard Stein, Steve Stedman, and Carol Wise and have been great friends and colleagues.

A special set of thanks must go to the Indonesian and Nigerian mafias, those groups of collaborators that illuminate these large and often impossibly complex places. The help and advice of various Indonesia specialists have been much appreciated. Don Emmerson, Bill Liddle, Ross McLeod, and Jeff Winters have been particularly generous with their insights and time. Andrew MacIntyre offered invaluable early counsel on fieldwork in Indonesia, and as we have followed parallel intellectual paths, my debt to his work is evident. I have also benefited from extended discussions with Harold Crouch, Robert Hefner, Suzaina Kadir, Jamie Mackie, and Adam Schwarz. In Washington, Edward Masters has been tremendously helpful. If they judge that I have gotten the story even half right, I should be satisfied.

In Indonesia, thanks must first go to Dr. Hadi Soesastro, who has hosted me at the Center for Strategic and International Studies and has offered keen insights and invaluable assistance. Clara Joewono and Mari Pangestu have been equally generous and intellectually engaging. Mohammed Sadli was a witty and energetic discussant. Radius Prawiro, Emil Salim, and Ali Wardhana were also forthcoming and helpful to a newcomer, and their graciousness is acknowledged. Kwik Kian Gie, Miranda Goeltom, Dorodjatun Kuntjoro-Jakti, and Thee Kian Wie furnished essential analysis of the nature of the economy and problems of reform. Faisal Basri and Sri Mulyani Indrawati offered needed perspective during a turbulent period of transition. I also benefited greatly from conversations with James Castle, Andrew Ellis, Paul Deuster, Ben Fisher, Dennis Heffernan, Blair King, Douglas Ramage, Joseph Stern, David Timberman, and James Van Zorge. Eric Bjornlund and his family briefly adopted me and helped wend my way through the byways of Jakarta.

I have found a personal and professional home mainly among the Nigeria crew, and I must give all due recognition. Henry Bienen, Tom Biersteker, Larry Diamond, Richard Joseph, Paul Lubeck, Mike Watts, and Ernie Wilson provided enthusiastic support for my entry into the daunting enterprise of studying Nigeria, and they have remained friends and collaborators. Pauline Baker, Tony Carroll, Peter Ekeh, Tom Forrest, Darren Kew, Princeton Lyman, Steve Morrison, Ebere Onwudiwe, John Paden, Pearl Robinson, Barnett Rubin, Richard Sklar, Patrick Ukata, and Crawford Young have been welcome colleagues in this continuing enterprise.

In Nigeria, the list is long. My good friends and guides include Kenneth Adeyemi, Ukaha Amogu, Judy Asuni, Tunde and Kemi Durosinmi-

Etti, Lukman Durosinmi-Etti, Uma Eleazu, the late Emeka Ezera, Nnamdi Ezera, Kayode Fayemi, Udy Kalu, Ojo Maduekwe, Ugo Okarafor, Femi Segun, and Pat Utomi. Early support and assistance came from Tade Akin Aina, Philip Asiodu, Alaba Ogunsanwo, and Oyeleye Oyediran. I have benefited greatly from the views of Said Adejumobi, L. O. Adekunle, Olisa Agbakoba, Olu Ajakaiye, the late Claude Ake, Allison Ayida, Seyi Bickersteth, Usman Bugaje, Innocent Chukwuma, Pascal Dozie, Wale Edun, Emma Ezeazu, Obi Ezekwesili, Olu Falae, Rasheed Gbadamosi, Jibrin Ibrahim, Attahiru Jega, Kalu Idika Kalu, Dimieari von Kemedi, Abiodun Kolawale, Dick Kramer, O. A. Kuye, A. B. Mahmoud, Arthur Mbanefo, Clement Nwankwo, Ayo Obe, Femi Ojudu, Ngozi Okonjo-Iweala, Festus Okoye, Akin Olanaiyan, Adekunle Olumide, Abdul Oroh, Adeto Peterside, Nasir el-Rufai, Ernest Shonekan, Rotimi Suberu, Bola Tinubu, and Ishola Williams.

A squad of invaluable research assistants have helped at various stages of the project. Many thanks go to Nida Al-Ahmad, Victor Brobbey, Michael Gonzales, Heidi McGowan, Mvuselelo Ngcoya, David Plotz, and Kevin Warr, with a special appreciation for Bea Reaud, who saw the manuscript to completion.

Friends and family have been the deepest source of encouragement and support. Arthur Allen, Margaret Talbot, Steve Tucker, and Eileen St. George are great friends who have shared the rigors of writing and travel. My parents, Robert and Barbara Lewis, and my brother Jim have lived with various writing projects for nearly as long as they shared a house with me. My children, Daniel and Claire, have put up with absences and distraction, while providing a constant source of happiness. And for Tamara, who has been patient, supportive, and compelling in every way, I give my love and gratitude.

CHAPTER 1

Introduction

What types of institutional arrangements are essential for economic growth in poor countries? What are the political conditions that foster the development of growth-inducing institutions? Although there is a good deal of consensus about the institutions generally needed for prosperity over the long term, we have much less certainty about the conditions for economic progress in poorly performing states, or in circumstances of political instability. Some of the answers can be supplied theoretically, but wider empirical knowledge of economic change is indispensable for understanding the interplay of institutions, politics, and economic performance. These central questions in comparative political economy are animated by divergent performance among particular regions in the developing world. Many countries in East and Southeast Asia have achieved lengthy periods of rapid growth, leading to general inferences about the institutional foundations of "late" development. The strongest contrast to Asia is found in the widespread, persistent stagnation of sub-Saharan Africa, where economic revitalization remains stubbornly elusive. This book seeks to illuminate the sources of institutional variation and comparative economic performance by comparing the paths of two broadly comparable states, Indonesia and Nigeria.

In May 1998, Indonesia's President Soeharto, beleaguered by street protests, rising social unrest, and a deepening economic crisis, resigned after thirty-two years in office. Power hastily transferred to Vice President B. J. Habibie, a long-standing member of the regime's inner circle. Amid speculation about his intentions for reform, Habibie put into place a program of democratic transition while attempting to stabilize the failing economy. A year later his government supervised elections that, despite many shortcomings, were broadly accepted by the Indonesian public and international observers. Habibie stepped aside, permitting an independent presidential candidate, Abdurrahman Wahid, to assume power.

Three weeks after Soeharto's fall, Nigeria's military ruler, Sani Abacha, whose regime was beset by social instability and a declining economy, died of a reported heart attack.[1] He was quickly replaced by an insider from the ruling council, General Abdulsalami Abubakar. Despite suspicions about his intentions, General Abubakar outlined a program of transition to democracy while attempting to stabilize the flagging economy. Within a year his government supervised elections that were accepted by domestic and international observers, notwithstanding serious flaws. An independent candidate, Olusegun Obasanjo, was elected, and the military stepped aside for civilian rule at the end of May 1999.

In the wake of these pivotal moments, Indonesia and Nigeria currently show remarkable parallels as they struggle with formidable challenges of political reform against a background of economic malaise and social violence. Each country recently emerged from a long era of authoritarian rule to embark on a tenuous process of democratic change. Repeated elections have been held and competitive political structures set in place. Yet the new institutions are weak and inchoate, political elites appear divided and self-serving, popular legitimacy is fragile at best, and these fledgling regimes face numerous challenges including detrimental economic conditions. Indonesia suffers lingering effects of the economic crisis of 1997–98, in which the economy plummeted by 13 percent in a single year. Nigeria's economy is beset by a secular decline lasting decades. Slow growth, joblessness, slack investment, institutional disarray, and fitful policy change have deepened popular discontent in each country. These pressures contribute to mounting trends of ethnic, religious, and local conflict. Privation and political insecurity have sharpened sectional identities, resulting in confrontation among ethnic, regional, and religious communities and the central state. Questions of national unity and stability are fundamentally at issue in these plural societies.

The parallel course of recent events highlights the comparison among these large, regionally dominant states. Both are populous countries, embodying broad cultural diversity along with a history of communal tension and conflict. As major oil exporters, resource wealth has shaped their position in global markets and the contours of their domestic political economies. Each country has a fraught history of democratic experimentation and previous failure. Following major political upheavals in the 1960s, both were dominated politically by the military for much of the ensuing three decades. Authoritarianism has tentatively given way to nascent democratic regimes.

---

1. Abacha's death has been clouded by mysterious circumstances, as sources both in Nigeria and the United States have alleged that Abacha was poisoned, most likely by elements within the military. See Tim Weiner, "U.S. Aides Say Nigeria Leader Might Have Been Poisoned," *New York Times,* July 11, 1998, section A, 4.

The recent signs of convergence in the political and economic fortunes of these states would appear to alter three decades of disparate performance. In spite of important similarities in size, social makeup, resources, economic composition, regimes, and political history, Indonesia and Nigeria displayed strikingly different paths of governance and economic performance from the late 1960s through the 1990s. Indonesia achieved substantial growth, structural change of its economy, a reduction in poverty, and diversified integration in world markets, all in a context of general political stability. During the same period, Nigeria reflected minimal growth, an inert economic structure, chronic poverty, and growing marginality in the global economy, amid circumstances of political volatility.

The concurrence of political instability, economic stasis, and social violence might indicate similar destinies in the two countries. However, while both states have experienced similar short-term crises and dislocations, the legacy of earlier developmental efforts will strongly influence distinctive political and social development over the longer term. Deeper alterations of economic and social structure—the result of prior institutional choices and political strategies—have created fundamentally different conditions as each country grapples with the challenges of reform.

From a broader comparative vantage, these cases are important outliers in the context of low-income developing countries and resource-exporting states. Indonesia is distinguished by its impressive accomplishments and abrupt decline, Nigeria for the depth and persistence of its economic failure. How can we account for these paths? Why was Indonesia able to make such strides in social and economic development despite inauspicious beginnings? Why did an apparently strong model of development collapse so suddenly? What accounts for the downward spiral of Nigeria's economy and its persistent malaise? In view of the uncertain outcomes of political and economic reform, what will determine the course of change in these states?

Given their size, regional predominance (in Southeast Asia and West Africa, respectively), and significance in international energy markets, the processes of economic and political restructuring in these two countries are of considerable importance. Moreover, the comparative experiences of Indonesia and Nigeria hold lessons for other large, diverse, resource-producing states such as Russia, Brazil, or Mexico. The study carries broader theoretical significance as well. By comparing outcomes in two countries with similar political legacies, social composition, and economic structures, this study aids our understanding of the general political conditions for economic development, particularly the institutional dimensions of economic change.

Observations and Propositions

This book examines the relationships among politics, institutional change, and economic growth in Indonesia and Nigeria. An explanation for their economic divergence and subsequent convergence centers on political factors, specifically the interests arrayed around economic policy-making and the nature of institutional development. Each state embodies different capacities to forge alliances with private economic actors and generally to foster capital formation.

Sustained economic growth relies upon the state's provision of credible commitments to investors and producers. If private economic actors are to make investments in productive activities they require assurances of policy predictability, secure property rights, and the effectiveness of contracts.[2] Governments play a critical role in securing these collective goods by providing them directly and facilitating coordination among market actors. These insights from institutional economics have strongly influenced recent analyses in comparative political economy.[3] Yet the shortcomings of institutional approaches point to a research frontier. We need a stronger appreciation of institutional variation—the necessary and sufficient conditions that enable growth in different political and economic systems—as well as better accounts of how institutions develop over time. This calls for elaboration of the political dimensions of economic change.

Institutional perspectives furnish an explanation for the path of development in Indonesia and Nigeria. Indonesia's economic achievements under the New Order (1966–98) arose from credible commitments to private economic actors, reflecting a stable coalition between the state and crucial producer groups. These arrangements arose from precarious crafting of institutions and incentives under a personalized authoritarian regime. However, the political balancing act underlying Indonesia's developmental regime was brittle, and a combination of external and domestic

2. Leading analyses include Oliver Williamson, *The Economic Institutions of Capitalism* (New York: Free Press, 1985); Douglass North and Barry Weingast, "Constitutions and Commitment: The Evolution of Institutions Governing Public Choice in Seventeenth Century England," *Journal of Economic History* 49, no. 4 (1989): 803–32; and Thráinn Eggertsson, *Economic Behavior and Institutions* (Cambridge: Cambridge University Press, 1990). For a more recent review see Philip Keefer, "A Review of the Political Economy of Governance: From Property Rights to Voice," World Bank Policy Research Working Paper No. 3315 (2004).

3. Adam Przeworski, *States and Markets* (New York: Cambridge University Press, 2003), 11; John McMillan, *Reinventing the Bazaar: A Natural History of Markets* (New York: Norton, 2002), 11. See also Bruce Bueno de Mesquita and Hilton L. Root, eds., *Governing for Prosperity* (New Haven: Yale University Press, 2000).

pressures caused the system to fracture in the late 1990s. Credibility dissipated, the dominant coalition collapsed, and the country succumbed to institutional disarray and economic distress.

In Nigeria, social divisions and distinct political incentives have hampered the formation of a stable pact between state elites and private capital. Under the pressures of competitive patronage, Nigerian regimes have not furnished credible signals for private investment, but instead a weak, fragmented business class has gravitated toward diffuse rent seeking rather than productive accumulation. The pattern of expedient distributional politics deteriorated rapidly as petroleum revenues waned and a series of predatory military rulers seized power. By the time of Abacha's death, institutional decay, political uncertainty, and social polarization severely degraded the economy.

These cases also yield insights that refine institutional theory and related perspectives on development. The divergence among the two economies highlights the institutional conditions necessary for investment and capital formation, which allows a better understanding of institutional effects in particular settings. The comparative experiences of Indonesia and Nigeria suggest inferences about the political requisites of institutional change and economic development. This comparison suggests a set of propositions.

(1) *States with weak formal institutions may provisionally achieve substantial economic growth.* Economic transformation is generally associated with a stable rule of law. This study, however, shows that regimes in early stages of development can provide inducements for investment prior to the emergence of a fully effective legal and procedural framework. Governments can help to coordinate the expectations of investors and producers even under circumstances of political uncertainty, and when capabilities for the enforcement of rules are relatively weak.[4] In settings with a weak rule of law, special commitment devices and informal guarantees are needed to compensate for uncertain institutional safeguards. There are limits, however, to such expedient management of the economy. Informal signaling and coordination can be sufficient in early phases of economic development, but states are unlikely to sustain capital formation and eco-

---

4. Stephen Haber, Armando Razo, and Noel Maurer, *The Politics of Property Rights: Political Instability, Credible Commitments, and Economic Growth in Mexico, 1876–1929* (Cambridge: Cambridge University Press, 2003), 351. See also Andrew MacIntyre, "Investment, Property Rights, and Corruption in Indonesia," in J. E. Campos, ed., *Corruption: The Boom and Bust of East Asia* (Manila: Ateneo University Press, 2001), 16.

nomic expansion if they fail to strengthen the formal institutions that reduce transaction costs and provide for the enforcement of essential rules.

Indonesia provides the main illustration. Soeharto's regime furnished credible commitments to investors through a combination of formal policies and informal patronage, even though many state institutions remained weak throughout his rule. The failure to construct a more effective institutional architecture rendered the system vulnerable as the economy expanded and integrated more extensively into global markets. In the wake of Soeharto's rule, institutional failure has been a central impediment to economic recovery.

(2) *The political organization of rent seeking and corruption has varying effects on economic performance.* The political allotment of economic gains, and the corruption that accompanies state patronage, generally create adverse economic conditions. Collusion between state officials and private clients gives rise to inefficiency, capital flight, inequality, widespread mistrust, and uncertainty. These conditions are usually antithetical to credible commitments and incompatible with capital formation, yet they are not always obstacles to growth, as was evident in much of East and Southeast Asia from the 1970s through the 1990s.[5] The political organization of rent distribution influences the degree to which rent seeking and corruption are a hindrance to economic growth. Such activities can either be coordinated, centralized, and regulated, or else anarchic and dispersed. In some settings, leaders have sufficiently disciplined rent seeking and corruption to enable productive investment. Furthermore, general macroeconomic conditions influence the use of such gains, determining whether rents are invested in the domestic economy, circulated among nonproductive activities, or sent abroad.[6] A favorable policy context can facilitate productive investment even when capital is obtained through collusive or illicit means.

Economies with high levels of rent seeking and corruption can be unstable. In the absence of reliable institutional guarantees, abrupt political changes or economic shocks disrupt collusive relations among the state and private interests, with adverse consequences for investment and growth. Indonesia and Nigeria both exemplify these tendencies. In

---

5. David C. Kang, *Crony Capitalism: Corruption and Development in South Korea and the Philippines* (Cambridge: Cambridge University Press, 2002), 182–83.

6. This point is stressed by Andrei Shleifer and Robert W. Vishny, "Corruption," *Quarterly Journal of Economics* 108, no. 3 (1993): 600. On the reinvestment of gains see Guy J. Pauker, "Indonesia in 1980: Regime Fatigue?" *Asian Survey* 21, no. 2 (1981): 236.

Indonesia, comparatively well-organized corruption and stable macroeconomic conditions proved compatible with economic expansion for three decades. Despite strong performance, however, the syndrome of patronage politics deepened the effects of the 1997–98 crisis and has since undermined Indonesian efforts at reform. Nigeria's contentious, divided elites and unstable politics have fostered an anarchic realm of rent distribution. The macroeconomic setting has also been unfavorable. In Nigeria, corruption has dissipated resources, obstructed growth, and stymied economic remediation.

(3) *In systems with few formal checks on leaders, the devolution of policy authority and the use of institutional lock-in measures can bolster credibility.* Developmental regimes often face a contradiction: assertive leaders can galvanize a project of economic growth, but excessive discretion by the executive can also undermine credibility.[7] In circumstances where rulers have few formal checks on their authority, investors and producers may question the reliability of nominal commitments by the government. Credibility can be encouraged by devolving authority to a strong economic policy team and by selectively employing lock-in mechanisms that incur high penalties for policy deviations. The existence of strong countervailing influences in the economic bureaucracy can assuage the arbitrary authority of the executive. Lock-in mechanisms (e.g., an open capital account) signal costs for adverse policy decisions, thereby fortifying general confidence in the credence of government commitments.[8]

Indonesia's New Order regime was more personalized and centralized than most Nigerian governments, though both countries have been governed by presidential systems in which rulers have few institutional limits on their discretion. Soeharto reduced the uncertainties surrounding his personal control by according influence to a team of capable economic technocrats and by locking in policies through a balanced budget rule, an open capital account, and close cooperation with donors. Nigerian economic management has been erratic and ineffective, as leaders have changed unexpectedly and technocratic groups have not had a dominant role in decision making. Political instability and adverse policies have undermined credibility. The consequences can be seen in low savings and investment, massive capital flight, and diffident responses to economic policy reforms.

7. This is emphasized by Andrew MacIntyre, *The Power of Institutions: Political Architecture and Governance* (Ithaca: Cornell University Press, 2003), 18–19.
8. Avinash Dixit, *The Making of Economic Policy* (Cambridge: MIT Press, 1996), 65.

(4) *Developmental leadership is framed by particular sets of political challenges and opportunities.* Structural factors alone cannot explain economic outcomes, making it essential to account for the incentives and strategies of rulers.[9] While developmental leadership is often serendipitous and difficult to anticipate, rulers with a strong economic agenda arise in specific circumstances.[10] Leaders commonly embark on a developmental course in response to economic crisis, domestic instability, or particular types of security threats.[11] Political strategies toward the economy are influenced by the nature of challenges as well as the available coalitions among elites.

The developmental direction of Soeharto's rule in Indonesia contrasts with the growing predation among Nigerian leaders. The difference is best captured by Mancur Olson's distinction between "stationary" and "roving" bandits.[12] Stationary bandits seek to provide a stable setting for economic activity so that they may tax a steady (or growing) stream of income. Roving bandits prefer the "smash and grab": heavily discounting the future, they have little interest in long-term income flows, and they prey upon the economy with indifference to negative effects. Although patronage and corruption have been integral to both countries, Soeharto ruled as a stationary bandit, while Nigerian executives acted as roving bandits, to use Olson's terms. It is impossible to explain Indonesia's economic achievements since 1965 without a focus on Soeharto. His outlook, personality, motives, and actions shaped the country's economic and political development for more than three decades. Yet Soeharto's ascent, and the choices he exercised, occurred in a particular context. Indonesian leaders in the 1960s faced a broad-based security challenge arising from powerful social forces mobilized by a large domestic communist party, radical mobilization in the rural areas, and the offsetting forces of popular Muslim organizations. The need to grapple with economic crisis and to assuage class-based political tensions encouraged a developmental

9. Richard Samuels examines the distinctive contributions of developmental leadership in *Machiavelli's Children: Leaders and Their Legacies in Italy and Japan* (Ithaca: Cornell University Press, 2003).

10. Jeffrey A. Winters, *Power in Motion: Capital Mobility and the Indonesian State* (Ithaca: Cornell University Press, 1996), 49.

11. Edgardo Campos and Hilton L. Root, *The Key to the Asian Miracle: Making Shared Growth Credible* (Washington, DC: Brookings Institution, 1996), 31; see also Kang, *Crony Capitalism,* 29.

12. Mancur Olson, "Dictatorship, Democracy, and Development," *American Political Science Review* 87, no. 3 (1993): 568; see also Mancur Olson, *Power and Prosperity* (New York: Basic Books, 2000), 4–11.

approach to the economy. The choice of strategy was facilitated by the presence of effective technocrats and a producer group that would enter into a political alliance with rulers.

Several Nigerian leaders (notably Yakubu Gowon, Murtala Muhammed, Olusegun Obasanjo, Ibrahim Babangida, and Sani Abacha) have shaped the country's path of economic change. This roster illustrates the lack of stable leadership over the past four decades. Elite division and communal competition have created a fragmented political arena, leading to pervasive uncertainty and a frequent turnover of regimes. Nigerian leaders, increasingly insecure and facing short time-horizons, fashioned strategies of political survival that relied on dispersed clientelist politics. The main security challenges faced by state elites arose from tensions among sectional groups, which were addressed through selective patronage and populist redistribution. In the wake of the petroleum boom, moreover, rulers perceived little in the way of fiscal constraints, which further impelled patronage strategies. While segments of the private sector could potentially serve as the basis for a producer coalition, communal rivalries thwarted a stable compact between regimes and investors.

(5) *Developmental states rest upon an organizational basis for elite coordination.* Developmental states—those political systems capable of fostering economic growth and transformation—reflect political resolve as well as organizational capacity.[13] The quality and effectiveness of institutions varies widely among these systems. There is no single source of institutional strength common to all developmental regimes, but these systems are commonly stabilized by some organization capable of reconciling elite interests. Political parties, the military, the bureaucracy, and selective elements of civil society (such as business or professional associations) are instrumental in fortifying consensus around a policy regime and accompanying strategies of accumulation.[14]

13. See Peter Evans, *Embedded Autonomy: States and Industrial Transformation* (Princeton: Princeton University Press, 1995), 50, and Atul Kohli, *State-Directed Development: Political Power and Industrialization in the Global Periphery* (New York: Cambridge University Press, 2004), 381.

14. The role of the bureaucracy is emphasized by Chalmers Johnson, *MITI and the Japanese Miracle* (Stanford: Stanford University Press, 1982). See also Meredith Woo-Cumings, "Chalmers Johnson and the Politics of Nationalism and Development," in Meredith Woo-Cumings, ed., *The Developmental State* (Ithaca: Cornell University Press, 1999). An assessment of the relative role of business interests is provided by Karl Fields, "Strong States and Business Organization in Korea and Taiwan," in Sylvia Maxfield and Ben Ross Schneider, eds., *Business and the State in Developing Countries* (Ithaca: Cornell University Press, 1997), 149–50.

Indonesia's economic success derived from a durable coalition among military, the bureaucracy (especially the peak economic agencies), and key producer groups. The New Order sought, with limited success, to extend this coalition through the formation of a corporatist party structure.[15] The regime nonetheless established organizations that could coordinate elites toward a coherent set of political and economic strategies. This presents a striking contrast to Nigeria's increasingly factionalized military, its evanescent, often sectional political parties, and a politicized, turbulent bureaucracy. Nigeria's social divisions, and the absence of an organizational framework of elite accommodation, have consistently posed hindrances to economic performance.

(6) *In culturally diverse societies, inclusive alliances between the state and private producers are needed for sustained development.* Culturally diverse societies face especially sharp tensions between the goals of growth and distribution. Stable coalitions among state elites and private producers are essential for long-term economic growth. In diverse societies, growth coalitions are likely to be insecure unless salient distributional concerns are also addressed. In circumstances where a producer alliance is narrowly constituted among a particular ethnic or regional group, political and social polarization can disrupt the compact, especially in periods of economic distress.[16] This presents a special political challenge for economic development, as governments must strike a careful balance between furnishing benefits to producers and providing gains for the wider public. In heterogeneous states, given the realities of uneven development, it is inevitable that dynamic entrepreneurial groups will be found among particular segments of the population, usually a cultural minority.[17] The government must credibly commit to this set of producers and investors in order to foster capital formation, while furnishing assurances and support for other groups. In the absence of such equilibrium, economic growth is politically fragile.

The comparison of Indonesia and Nigeria highlights these dilemmas. Indonesia's New Order regime forged a narrowly constituted growth

15. Donald K. Emmerson, "The Bureaucracy in Political Context: Weakness in Strength," in Karl D. Jackson and Lucian Pye, eds., *Political Power and Communications in Indonesia* (Berkeley: University of California Press, 1978), 99–100.

16. This is provocatively argued by Amy Chua, *World on Fire: How Exporting Free Market Democracy Breeds Ethnic Hatred and Global Instability* (New York: Anchor Books, 2004).

17. Anthony Reid, "Entrepreneurial Minorities, Nationalism, and the State," in Daniel Chirot and Anthony Reid, eds., *Essential Outsiders* (Seattle: University of Washington Press, 1997), 34.

coalition, drawn largely from the ethnic Chinese minority and small set of *pribumi* (indigenous) cronies, in alliance with foreign capital. While this compact achieved impressive growth for an extended period, distributional concerns, amid a sharp economic downturn, contributed to a collapse of the coalition. In Nigeria, ethnic and regional competition has hampered the formation of a stable growth coalition between the state and private producers. Political elites have turned instead to populist strategies and diffuse rent distribution among a fragmented and polarized business class. The populist option proved short-lived when oil revenues dwindled, while the residual rentier alliances were unstable, resulting in economic stagnation and disarray.

Politics, Institutions, and Economic Change

The analysis presented here centers on the provision of credible commitments to private economic actors. Economic performance is crucially affected by the state's ability to furnish a reliable setting for investment and production. In order to foster investment in productive assets, the sine qua non of economic advancement, states must provide not just sound policies but also stable property rights and a conducive setting for private contracting. Credibility, then, is used in the institutional sense to refer to more than the reliability of policies, encompassing also the organizational and cognitive environment for economic transactions. The state has the pivotal role in providing these collective goods. To an important degree, credible commitment can be viewed as a particular institutional arrangement. This prompts questions about the political sources of institutional change.

Appropriate economic policies are clearly necessary for economic success, but they are not sufficient. Institutional conditions provide the decisive factor in long-term performance. Successful economies in the developing world have reflected a basic set of policies including low inflation, realistic exchange rates, fiscal discipline, investments in physical infrastructure and education, price incentives for producers and investors, and engagement in international trade. These minimal guidelines are compatible with a range of economic strategies, from relatively interventionist approaches (as in South Korea) to more liberal stances (as in Hong Kong).[18] While policy packages may vary significantly within a bounded

18. The range of strategies among late industrializers is discussed by Stephan Haggard, *Pathways from the Periphery* (Ithaca: Cornell University Press, 1990). Robert Wade also observes that economic theory offers no precise guidelines for policy; see Robert Wade, *Governing the Market: Economic Theory and the Role of Government in East Asian Industrialization* (Princeton: Princeton University Press, 1990), 349.

range of options, the determining factor in economic performance is the state's capacity to implement chosen policies.[19] State capacity depends upon coordination among the state and private economic actors, and the influence (and intervention) of government on the market environment.[20] Governments cannot remake institutions de novo, but the state essentially has a veto on the adoption or persistence of growth-enhancing institutions. Although governments face constraints from inherited institutions, social forces, and aspects of the international environment, rulers hold the decisive role in providing public goods and encouraging or inhibiting market arrangements.[21]

"Developmental" states have successfully provided the collective goods for high growth and international competitiveness. Comparative analyses of the archetypal developmental state, modeled on the dynamic economies of East Asia, emphasize a distinctive combination of growth-oriented leadership, capable economic bureaucracies, and selective enforcement capabilities.[22] Consultation among public officials, private sector elites, and key societal groups enhances the flow of information and bolsters the legitimacy of regimes.[23] States in the high-growth Asian economies have been particularly able in fulfilling coordination roles, and

19. Hilton Root, *Small Countries, Big Lessons: Governance and the Rise of East Asia* (New York: Oxford University Press, 1996), 5.

20. Variations in the character of state interaction with market actors are covered by Wade, *Governing the Market;* Andrew MacIntyre, "Power, Prosperity, and Patrimonialism: Business and Government in Indonesia," in Andrew MacIntyre, ed., *Business and Government in Industrializing Asia* (Ithaca: Cornell University Press, 1994), 262–63; Evans, *Embedded Autonomy,* 78–81; Campos and Root, *Key to the Asian Miracle;* Sylvia Maxfield and Ben Ross Schneider, "Business, the State, and Economic Performance in Developing Countries," in Maxfield and Schneider, eds. *Business and the State in Developing Countries;* and Pranab Bardhan, "The Nature of Institutional Impediments to Economic Development," in Mancur Olson and Satu Kahkonen, eds., *A Not-So-Dismal Science: A Broader View of Economies and Societies* (Oxford: Oxford University Press, 2000).

21. Bruce Bueno de Mesquita, Alastair Smith, Randolph M. Siverson, and James D. Morrow, *The Logic of Political Survival* (Cambridge: MIT Press, 2003), 7–8. For illustrations of how predatory rulers undermine institutions, see Joel Migdal, *Strong Societies, Weak States: State-Society Relations and State Capabilities in the Third World* (Princeton: Princeton University Press, 1988), 140–41, and William Reno, *Warlord Politics and African States* (Boulder: Lynne Rienner, 1999).

22. The general features of the developmental state have been evaluated by Haggard, *Pathways from the Periphery;* Alice Amsden, *Asia's Next Giant: South Korea and Late Industrialization* (New York: Oxford University Press, 1989); Woo-Cumings, *Developmental State;* and Kohli, *State-Directed Development.*

23. Consultation among the state and business is extensively treated by Evans, *Embedded Autonomy;* Campos and Root, *Key to the Asian Miracle;* and Maxfield and Schneider, eds., *Business and the State in Developing Countries.*

so resolving the principal collective action problems that impede economic transformation.[24] Public authorities were able to credibly convey incentives to investors and producers while also holding them accountable for performance. They fostered an administrative and policy regime that provided guidance for market activity. The experiences of these countries underscore the importance of effectively aligning expectations among the state and market actors.

However, the archetype of the strong developmental state has been increasingly questioned. Not only are there relatively few successful examples, but recent evidence also suggests that the images of autonomy and political insulation presented in earlier accounts of East Asian development were overdrawn.[25] The Asian financial crisis brought to light the substantial role of collusion, rent distribution, corruption, and policy uncertainty in ostensibly "strong" developmental systems such as South Korea, while highlighting these liabilities in such countries as Malaysia and Thailand.[26] This suggests a change of perspective on the comparative analysis of economic development. Typically, countries at lower levels of development embody weak formal institutions. Senior policymakers and agencies in these states are susceptible to political pressures, while their bureaucracies lack professionalism and cohesion, and their legal systems and enforcement capabilities are frail. Many countries also reflect erratic macroeconomic policy, insecure terms and enforcement of property rights, few legal or regulatory guarantees for contracting, and scarcity of information. They therefore face the problems of establishing credibility among market actors, which alters private orientations and behavior toward investment and growth.

24. See Dietrich Rueschemeyer and Peter Evans, "The State and Economic Transformation: Toward an Analysis of the Conditions Underlying Economic Transformation," in Peter Evans, Dietrich Rueschemeyer, and Theda Skocpol, eds., *Bringing the State Back In* (Cambridge: Cambridge University Press, 1985), 45; and Kiminori Matsuyama, "Economic Development as Coordination Problems," in Masahiko Aoki, Masahiro Okuno-Fujiwara, and Hyung-Ki Kim, eds., *The Role of Government in East Asian Economic Development: Comparative Institutional Analysis* (Oxford: Oxford University Press, 1996), 135.

25. See, for instance, Danny Unger, *Building Social Capital in Thailand: Fibers, Finance, and Infrastructure* (Cambridge: Cambridge University Press, 1998); Kang, *Crony Capitalism*, 2; and MacIntyre, *Power of Institutions, 25*.

26. Meredith Woo-Cumings, "The State, Democracy, and the Reform of the Corporate Sector in Korea," in T. J. Pempel, ed., *The Politics of the Asian Economic Crisis* (Ithaca: Cornell University Press, 1999), 117; and Stephan Haggard, *The Political Economy of the Asian Financial Crisis* (Washington, DC: Institute for International Economics, 2000), 52, 61. See also Mushtaq H. Khan and K. S. Jomo, eds., *Rents, Rent-Seeking, and Economic Development: Theory and Evidence in Asia* (Cambridge: Cambridge University Press, 2000).

We are led to consider the political conditions that permit states to shift from weaker to stronger developmental orientations. Under conditions of pervasive uncertainty, private economic actors are inclined to preserve mobility of assets (largely through speculative activities and capital flight) and to engage in rent-seeking activities or other collusive relations with government officials. These strategies, while rational from the perspective of individual entrepreneurs, undermine the economy as a whole by diverting resources to nonproductive endeavors or by draining them abroad.

Governments face basic coordination challenges in shifting private expectations and encouraging widespread investment in fixed, productive assets. Policy reform often fails to provide reliable incentives, since market participants evaluate government initiatives in light of reputation and institutional considerations. Private economic actors may discount price signals or other formal inducements, since they fear expropriation by arbitrary bureaucratic action, unpredictable macroeconomic conditions, sudden political changes, or social violence. Political authorities must augment policy measures with institutional demonstrations of commitment. Commitment devices constitute ex ante arrangements to limit government discretion, providing guarantees of policy reliability and property rights.[27] In some instances, exogenous enforcement mechanisms can serve to limit the discretion of political leaders in areas of economic policy.[28] An independent central bank, for instance, limits control over monetary measures, while international trade compacts reduce latitude on trade issues. Other measures, called lock-in mechanisms, enforce high penalties for policy deviation.[29] An open capital account, to take another example, will penalize governments for fiscal indiscipline through reduced currency flows and adverse movements in the exchange rate. In addition, governments may also take elective actions such as widening exposure to competitive pressures, disciplining business performance, measures to stem official corruption, and consultation with business groups, entrepreneurs, and external donors.

27. Joel M. Diermeier, Timothy Frye, and Steven Lewis, "Credible Commitment and Property Rights: The Role of Strategic Interaction between Political and Economic Actors," in David L. Weimer, ed., *The Political Economy of Property Rights: Institutional Change and Credibility in the Reform of Centrally Planned Economies* (Cambridge: Cambridge University Press, 1997).

28. Paul Collier, "Africa's External Economic Relations: 1960–90," *African Affairs* 90, no. 360 (1991): 339.

29. Dixit, *Making of Economic Policy,* 65.

The problems of commitment and coordination suggest different strategies depending on the level of economic development, the nature of the political system, and the historical setting of policy reform. During early phases of economic development, and in periods of political transition, weak or insecure governments can foster growth through a carefully crafted use of commitment devices and informal signaling. Over the longer term, economic performance relies upon a more regular framework of expectations, requiring administrative and regulatory development, the establishment of a stable and efficacious legal regime, and the growth of important private institutions such as stock exchanges and financial reporting systems.[30]

Explaining Institutional Change

Much of the early analysis from the new institutional economics offers a functionalist model of institutional change: rational economic actors, when confronting inefficient institutions, will eventually contract with each other and/or the state for more efficient arrangements. This model largely excludes political explanations for institutional development, which explicitly account for conflict and competition among divergent interests. In my analysis, the emergence of a developmental regime is regarded as a contingent process that is principally influenced by three factors: the nature of leadership, the composition of social coalitions, and regional setting.

Political leaders have a decisive influence on government's role in economic change. Successful developmental regimes have been led by executives with sustained commitment to economic growth and a pragmatic approach to policy and economic management. Such leaders, whether governing in authoritarian or democratic settings, commonly hold extended time-horizons and fashion conscious strategies linking their political legitimacy to the benefits of an expanding economy. They focus on the provision of general benefits for large portions of society, rather than narrow distribution to particular supporters and cronies. A hallmark of effective economic management is the willingness of senior leaders to delegate policy authority to a capable technocratic team and to strengthen and protect institutions within the economic bureaucracy such the central bank, ministries of finance, planning, or trade, and independent regula-

---

30. Robert Barro, *Determinants of Economic Growth: A Cross-Country Empirical Study*, Cambridge: MIT Press, 1997.

tory units.[31] These groups and agencies, in turn, can pose limits on the discretion of the executive. Because leadership is often idiosyncratic and unpredictable, there is a temptation to view this factor as random. Yet a variety of structural and institutional factors influence the selection of leaders, their orientation in office, and their circumstances of succession. Leadership selection is not merely accidental, and executives in power face particular sets of incentives and choices. The appearance of a significant cluster of developmental leaders in East and Southeast Asia, contrasted for instance with the prevalence of predatory rulers in sub-Saharan Africa, should remind us of the bounded nature of leadership accession and motives.

The experiences of Indonesia and Nigeria tell us something about the role and context of leaders. Rulers may be impelled to adopt developmental goals as a political survival strategy when faced with major challenges to stability including security threats, domestic challenges to social order, or economic crises. When relatively cohesive regimes face broadbased distributional pressures from class or sectoral groups, there is a greater propensity to meet these demands through economic expansion. Where elites are divided, and distributional demands emanate from segmented groups such as ethnic or regional communities, there is a greater likelihood that leaders will employ patronage and piecemeal distributional strategies.

The relation between leaders and support constituencies raises a general question about the social foundations of economic change. Institutions have distributional consequences, and particular institutional arrangements give rise to different constellations of societal interests. Consequently, economic models are impelled and sustained by social coalitions, and transformation requires a shift in the underlying support base. The establishment of an implicit compact among the regime and a support constituency is integral to the process of economic change.[32] In order to forge an effective reform coalition, governments must win the confidence of critical producer groups and offer a wider set of opportunities and

31. Haggard, *Pathways from the Periphery,* 45–46.
32. Jennifer Widner, "The Political Economy of Reform in Southeast Asia and Sub-Saharan Africa," in David L. Lindauer and Michael Roemer, eds., *Development in Asia and Africa: Legacies and Opportunities* (San Francisco: International Center for Economic Growth, 1994). The elements of coalition formation are discussed in Bruce Bueno de Mesquita and Hilton L. Root, eds., *Governing for Prosperity* (New Haven: Yale University Press, 2000).

benefits.[33] An alliance between the state and a narrow set of producers can yield growth, but it is likely to be fragile—especially in culturally polarized states—if large segments of the population feel excluded or systematically disadvantaged by the market.[34] Distributional access, if not equity, is an important condition for gathering commitment to reform.

It is important to recognize the international context of economic change. Apart from the encompassing effects of global markets and institutions, we should place special emphasis on the regional dimension of economic strategy. Regions often reflect similar orientations and policy choices, creating a "neighborhood effect" that provides an important indicator of the reform propensities of different countries.[35] The neighborhood effect suggests that countries within a geopolitical region tend to hold similar positions in the international economy, by virtue of historic market situation and parallel policy choices.[36] There are three central aspects, the first of which is the demonstration effect of adjacent regimes and economies. Policy ideas often have regional cachet, and leaders or policy elites are frequently drawn to adopt the policies of influential or successful neighbors. A second element is the direct linkages among regional neighbors. Close relations of trade, investment, labor migration, or aid may have a decisive influence on the policy direction of proximate states. Third, the reputation of regions within global markets affects investment and trade. The herd instincts of investors and bankers constitute powerful forces in the global economy, and regional prospects are significantly shaped by perceptions toward particular areas and markets. Neighborhood effects can be witnessed in the cycles of populism, structuralism and orthodox reform in Latin America, the concentration of high-growth export-oriented economies in East Asia, or the prevalence of statist and nationalist strategies in sub-Saharan Africa. There are variations and outliers within each region but also substantial affinities among neighboring states.

---

33. See Tun-jen Cheng, "Political Regimes and Development Strategies: South Korea and Taiwan," in Gary Gereffi and Donald Wyman, eds., *Manufacturing Miracles: Paths of Industrialization in Latin America and East Asia* (Princeton: Princeton University Press, 1990), and Haggard, *Pathways for the Periphery,* 34.

34. Amy L. Chua, "Markets, Democracy, and Ethnicity: Toward a New Paradigm for Law and Development," *Yale Law Journal* 108, no. 1 (1998), 6–7.

35. Barbara Stallings, ed., *Global Change, Regional Response: The New International Context of Development* (Cambridge: Cambridge University Press, 1995).

36. Thomas Callaghy, "Political Passions and Economic Interests: Economic Reform and Political Structure in Africa," in Thomas Callaghy and John Ravenhill, eds., *Hemmed In: Responses to Africa's Economic Decline* (New York: Columbia University Press, 1994), 475–76.

Understanding Indonesia and Nigeria

The developmental experience of Indonesia and Nigeria can be summarized in light of these analytical categories. Both countries have embodied weak formal institutions, yet the Indonesian state has been comparatively successful in providing a necessary threshold of collective goods and making credible commitments to market participants.

The Soeharto regime fostered credibility by delegating macroeconomic policy to a technocratic team, bolstering a small cluster of economic agencies, imposing fiscal discipline, and assuring capital mobility, a combination of commitment devices that created assurances for market participants. In addition, leaders furnished ad hoc protection of property rights for specific producers, notably members of the ethnic Chinese minority and the president's family, thereby using informal signals to bolster certainty for particular actors. These arrangements elided, and hampered, the establishment of a broader rule of law. Under the New Order, the Indonesian state moved in a developmental direction and created sufficient conditions for productive accumulation. The military-backed regime forged an elite consensus around national stability and economic growth, and it sustained this orientation through a combination of formal incentives and informal guarantees. The system unraveled, however, as the dominant coalition narrowed, leadership incentives shifted toward the protection of particular benefits for the ruling circle, and Indonesia became increasingly integrated into global markets that responded unfavorably to domestic institutional weakness.[37]

Indonesia's economic governance in this period had several noteworthy elements. Probably most important, the government pursued a stable and comparatively liberal macroeconomic policy, facilitated by a small but influential team of economic technocrats close to the president. A few peak centers of competence emerged within the economic bureaucracy. In addition the government furnished guarantees to important market actors. President Soeharto established an effective alliance with key producers through provisional assurances of property rights and contracts. As the authoritarian regime gained stability, these informal clientelist arrangements instilled growing confidence among investors. The government provided collateral guarantees through the maintenance of an open capital account, which served as a barometer of economic stability and an outlet for quickly exiting the system in times of uncertainty. The dispersal of benefits in the system was unquestionably skewed toward cronies and core support groups, but

---

37. MacIntyre, "Investment, Property Rights, and Corruption in Indonesia," 17.

the regime's measures to increase incomes and expand social provisions served to encourage wider acquiescence toward the regime.

A growth-oriented leadership emerged in Indonesia following a period of severe political and economic crisis. President Soeharto sought to legitimate the authoritarian government and assuage social conflict by promoting broad-based economic development. The New Order was able to extend its core coalition over time to incorporate critical producers and the beneficiaries of redistributive policies. This strategy was undoubtedly facilitated by Indonesia's position in Southeast Asia, where the country benefited from regional trade and investment linkages, as well as the region's broader international reputation. The sources of success, however, also proved to be the key points of vulnerability.

Over time, Soeharto's personalized authoritarian rule became increasingly narrow and myopic. The regime's coalition diminished as a few prominent cronies, chiefly linked with the president's family, monopolized economic resources and opportunities. As the country integrated more extensively into global markets, the opaque character of domestic finance and corporate governance created new liabilities. This culminated with the crisis of 1997–98, when the neighborhood's troubled reputation sparked a general reaction among investors, sweeping aside the insubstantial foundations of Indonesia's commercial edifice. In the wake of the crisis, the prospects for economic revitalization turned upon the emergence of a developmentally oriented leadership, the convergence of a new reform coalition, and the institutional changes that might ensue from new political alliances and commitments.

Turning to Nigeria, we see an economic malaise that reflects the absence of a coordinating authority. Political elites have been divided by multiple cleavages, and it has proven difficult to consolidate a stable coalition among the country's disparate interests and groups. The leading power-centers in the military, the bureaucracy, and political parties have been fragmented and unstable. Consequently, a central organization has not emerged to provide national integration or guidance.

This configuration of interests has evolved into a classic social dilemma, in which actors have few incentives for cooperation to provide collective goods, and the state cannot enforce cooperation. In consequence, actors compete for preferential access to public agencies and resources, and the state is enmeshed in a chaotic web of distributional contention. This is not a depiction of the model "predatory" state in which self-aggrandizing rulers systematically plunder societal resources.[38]

38. Evans, *Embedded Autonomy,* 45. See also Paul Hutchcroft, "Oligarchs and Cronies in the Philippine State: The Politics of Patrimonial Plunder," *World Politics* 43, no. 3 (1992).

Rather, state and private actors compete over the distribution of influence and assets. Military and civilian governments have pursued erratic macroeconomic policies with strong populist and nationalist orientations. Technocratic groups have not held influence within policy-making circles for any considerable length of time, while the economic bureaucracy has limited professional competence or political weight. The institutions of enforcement, including regulatory agencies, the civil service, the police, and the judiciary, are weak and politicized, thereby compounding the uncertainties that flow from central policies.

This setting has given rise to insecure property rights, uncertain contracting, and pervasive information asymmetries, all creating high risks of expropriation for market actors. The response has been weak investment and a premium on asset mobility. In a setting of unstable and fragmented clientelist politics, there is little possibility of forging relationships with state actors for the protection of assets; thus the sort of impromptu guarantees that were evident in Indonesia are absent in Nigeria. In consequence, political leaders have not established a viable producer coalition, nor have they stabilized a distributional compact. Nigeria's leaders have vacillated in their stance toward economic development. During the oil boom, military rulers evinced aspirations for economic transformation. The civilians governing the Second Republic were consumed by distributional competition, and their military successors displayed a brief but pronounced reformist impulse. Eventually, however, the slide toward personal autocracy gave rise to a predatory style of domination. Democratization poses major challenges for economic change. An attenuation of Nigeria's social dilemma will require the emergence of distinctive leadership, the mobilization of new constituencies, and a concerted process of institutional transformation.

Reform entails both political direction and institutional change. The fundamental question for Indonesia and Nigeria, in the wake of their political transitions, is whether these new regimes can make credible commitments to investors and producers in the near term, and engender a rule of law over the longer term. In both countries, the challenges are formidable and the prospects of success relatively narrow, but different initial endowments do suggest separate trajectories of reform. The legacy of institutional crafting, economic diversification, and social change in Indonesia suggests a different post-crisis path from that of Nigeria. Nigeria's institutional weakness, concentration of fiscal resources, and deep social divisions will continue to exert basic influences on the course of attempted reform.

The argument advanced here suggests that effective economic change will rely upon a selective devolution of decision making, more inclusive social coalitions, and integration in particular international institutions and markets. Both countries face the challenge of dismantling rentier coalitions and fostering new constellations of interest around a more competitive and equitable economy. As the fledgling democratic regimes seek to restructure their economies, greater political inclusion and a wider dissemination of benefits will be integral for stabilizing new institutional arrangements.

Comparative Questions

At a more general level, this study engages a set of issues at the center of contemporary debates over politics and development, including the necessary political conditions for economic growth, the tensions among political and economic reforms in developing countries, and the available strategies for negotiating the challenges of the global economy.

These issues are brought to the fore by the recent experiences of Indonesia and Nigeria. The study covers a forty-year span in which both countries, starting initially from similar levels of development, encountered fundamental challenges of building the institutional capabilities for economic growth. Indonesia has a stronger record of policy-making, manifest in superior economic performance for much of the period. In the wake of the recent financial implosion, the country faces a crisis of reputation among investors and a stark deficit in essential institutions. Nigeria, by comparison, has faltered badly in economic performance, as central policies and institutions have largely failed to provide incentives for capital formation.

These states reflect notable differences in the depth and timing of economic decline, a disparity partly explained by different propensities to adjust to external shocks. Indonesia has had a comparatively sustained experience with liberal macroeconomic policy, while Nigeria's efforts at reform have been sporadic and inconsistent. Until the mid-1990s, Indonesian leaders were comparatively responsive to shocks and willing to undertake policy adjustments, but Nigerians proved far less flexible and largely failed to respond to unfavorable external circumstances. Consequently Indonesia's abrupt downturn in 1997 was a singular event triggered by the Asian "contagion," while Nigeria was gripped by chronic decline beginning in the early 1980s. Although the genesis of economic descent has varied, these countries now face comparable difficulties in regularizing macroeconomic policy and providing credible commitments to investors and producers.

In both Indonesia and Nigeria, uneven processes of economic adjustment have been joined by rapid changeovers to democratic rule, giving rise to problems of managing economic and political reform. The collapse of the authoritarian regime in each instance was linked to poor economic performance, and the fledgling democracies face widespread popular demands for economic opportunities and improved distribution. Democratization gives rise to greater political contestation over reform measures, which slows needed changes and often disrupts the continuity of economic policy. Poor economic performance affects the legitimacy and stability of the new democratic regimes. Old elites have preserved influence, populist constituencies are important, and pressures from parties, elite interests, and popular sectors encumber the policy process. The uneven course of economic reform poses significant challenges for the consolidation of democracy.

The pattern of political conflicts over economic policy is quite similar in both cases. Central areas of reform such as financial restructuring and privatization have been slowed by legislative resistance and sectional lobbying. Some policymakers seek to avoid the political capture of reform by well-placed elites, while at the same time, factional rivals struggle over the distribution of gains. The resulting political stalemates hamper key initiatives to resolve banking and corporate distress, and to divest moribund state ventures. In addition, distributional demands from ethnic and regional groups in resource-producing areas have risen to the top of economic policy debates. Pressures for fiscal autonomy and revenue allocation pose challenges for national cohesion and constitutional design.

Turning to the questions noted earlier, both of the countries under consideration have confronted substantial difficulties in coming to terms with economic globalization. There is, first, the question of integration into the global market system and, second, the dilemma of managing domestic social pressures under conditions of rapid economic change. In the 1980s Indonesia successfully promoted a strategy of export-oriented growth, diversifying its economy from petroleum and entering into new markets. In addition the country maintained an open capital account and, in the 1990s, attracted large flows of portfolio investment. Thus Indonesia has been heavily integrated into global product and financial markets and is a destination for direct foreign investment.

By contrast, Nigeria's engagement in the world economy has narrowed over the past two decades. The economy has not diversified from the oil and gas sector, foreign direct investment in nonoil activities has dwindled, and restrictive financial rules (along with pervasive uncertainty) have precluded portfolio investment. The two countries currently face problems of establishing a reputation in domestic and international markets and attracting investment in the real sectors of the economy. Different endowments from the past three decades, however, suggest that these challenges will be resolved in different ways.

The pressures of globalization have placed domestic social compacts under severe stress in these countries. Indonesia has been credited with sharing the dividends of growth, and indeed the New Order regime significantly diminished absolute levels of poverty and improved many social conditions. President Soeharto's government, however, came under increasing criticism in the 1990s for the narrow distribution of economic benefits, notably the diversion of opportunities to a small circle of family and cronies. The financial crisis carried severe social costs, and the new democratic government confronts the challenge of incorporating broad sections of the public into a model for economic recovery.

Nigeria must fundamentally come to terms with the global economy. Lacking any recent experience of high growth, the country has suffered deepening poverty and deteriorating quality of life. The new civilian leadership has been eager to reverse the country's global economic isolation so as to enlist trade and investment as catalysts of economic revitalization. Against a background of worsening inequality, there is much contention over the distribution of costs and benefits associated with liberalization. Furthermore, Nigeria, like Indonesia, has engaged in creditor-led adjustment programs that significantly reduce fiscal discretion.

The Logic of Comparison

This study is structured as a paired-case comparison. These two states are significant not only for their size and relative regional positions, but also because they embody attributes—cultural diversity, natural resources, authoritarian rule, and democratic transition—that are shared to some degree by a number of other large, socially plural, democratic countries around the world. Thus the comparison yields insights that are especially relevant to developing democracies.

Comparative historical analysis provides a narrative account of the cases, and it works inductively to derive broader generalizations about the political foundations of economic development. Some of the propositions in the study, drawn from institutional approaches in political economy, are generated deductively. The analysis does yield conditional generalizations that may be tested through longitudinal evidence from the cases and comparative evidence from other countries and regions. It should be frankly acknowledged that many of the explanatory concepts in comparative political economy present difficulties of measurement (e.g., techno-cratic delegation, reputation, credibility, state capacity), and the conclu-sions are necessarily imprecise and suggestive.

The cases reflect strong similarities on a number of structural and his-torical variables including social composition, economic structure, politi-cal regimes, major economic shocks, political violence, and regime change. These likenesses allow us to control for important explanatory factors in shaping the analysis. The study attempts to explain disparities in economic performance among the cases. By seeking uniformity (or limited variance) on a number of potential independent variable(s), and large variance on the dependent variable, the study follows a "most similar systems" design.[39] In other words, I am attempting to understand different out-comes in comparable political, social, and economic contexts.

If we hold constant leading background factors and historical condi-tions in these countries, we can more readily assess the importance of strat-egy and choice in the process of economic development. In the analysis presented here, institutional variation is the intervening variable that best accounts for economic performance, while state elites, social coalitions, and international factors are determinants of institutional stasis or change. The framework allows us to specify more clearly the role of agency and contingent elements in economic change, as well as the relative importance of structural factors.

The approach used here draws on two theoretical traditions that often pose contending approaches to studies of political economy. Comparative historical sociology focuses on the interaction of large social forces, macrolevel institutions, and historical conditions as a basis for explaining economic outcomes. Macrosociological analysis commonly frames theo-ries in interpretive terms and relies on inductive approaches to derive and verify central propositions.

Institutional analysis, particularly as embodied in the field of new institutional economics, is more formal in its approach to explanation, deriving theories in a deductive fashion and presenting them as testable hypotheses. Furthermore, institutional methods are actor-oriented, seek-ing to understand how institutional settings influence particular incentives and strategies. This mode of analysis considers the microfoundations of political and economic action. Each of these theoretical traditions can offer important tools and insights, and this study seeks to bridge the tradi-

---

39. Adam Przeworski and Henry Teune, *The Logic of Comparative Social Inquiry* (New York: Wiley-Interscience, 1970), 32–33.

tional gap between them by constructing an eclectic account of governance and economic performance.

The literature on institutions and transaction costs, which has developed significantly within the past decade, offers an essential perspective on the necessary and sufficient conditions for economic change. A transaction-cost framework helps us to understand the effects of particular institutional arrangements on the scope, density, and content of economic exchange, and it has been particularly important in illuminating problems of collective action and coordination in economic life. This approach has important applications to such critical issues as industrial transformation, the transition to a market economy, the comparative role and genesis of corruption, and the competitiveness of different economies. Recent analyses have also sought to shed light on processes of economic policy choice, especially the relative propensity to adjust to shocks.[40]

As is evident from the more influential works in rational choice–inspired institutional analysis, microlevel approaches cannot stand apart from the influences of social structure and must account for contextual factors including culture and historical specificity. It is no surprise, then, that strong contributions have come from economic historians, anthropologists, and political scientists.[41]

The tradition of political sociology has also provided fundamental contributions to comparative political economy. Many of the important recent works on the politics of industrialization and economic reform have been grounded in this approach and elaborated through comparative historical analysis.[42] Sociological approaches consider the role of state orga-

40. Lee J. Alston, Thráinn Eggertsson, and Douglass C. North, eds., *Empirical Studies in Institutional Change* (Cambridge: Cambridge University Press, 1996); Dixit, *Making of Economic Policy;* Weimer, *Political Economy of Property Rights.*

41. Major contributions include Douglass North, *Institutions, Institutional Change, and Economic Performance* (Cambridge: Cambridge University Press, 1990); Douglass North and Barry Weingast, "Constitutions and Commitment: The Evolution of Institutions Governing Public Choice in Seventeenth Century England," *Journal of Economic History* 49, 1989: 803–32; Jean Ensminger, *Making a Market: The Institutional Transformation of an African Society* (Cambridge: Cambridge University Press, 1992); Jack Knight, *Institutions and Social Conflict* (Cambridge: Cambridge University Press, 1992); Avner Greif, "Reputation and Coalitions in Medieval Trade: Evidence on the Maghribi Traders," *Journal of Economic History* 49, no. 4 (1989); Avner Greif, Paul Milgrom, and Barry Weingast, "Coordination, Commitment, and Enforcement: The Case of the Merchant Guild," *Journal of Political Economy* 102, no. 4 (1994).

42. Amsden, *Asia's Next Giant;* Haggard, *Pathways from the Periphery;* Wade, *Governing the Market;* Stephan Haggard and Robert Kaufman, *The Political Economy of Democratic Transitions* (Princeton: Princeton University Press, 1995); Evans, *Embedded Autonomy;* David Waldner, *State Building and Late Development* (Ithaca: Cornell University Press, 1999); Woo-Cumings, *Developmental State;* Kohli, *State-Directed Development.*

nizations and the institutional foundations of economic management, while also accounting for the social constituencies underlying particular models of growth and change. In sum, there is a strong convergence of interest in these two theoretical fields and grounds for a fruitful dialogue between them.

Plan of the Book

In this chapter I have presented the basic research questions guiding the study, the basis of comparison among the cases, and an overview of the analytical framework. The following chapter elaborates the theoretical grounding for the study, offering a review of important trends in comparative political economy and proposing a synthesis of approaches for understanding the role of institutional change in economic development. The discussion sets out key definitions and assumptions, and it details a framework for analyzing the political basis of economic change. Chapter 3 moves from the general to the particular, elaborating the comparison and providing an analysis of the cases. The developmental experiences of Indonesia and Nigeria are summarized in light of the conceptual scheme.

The next two chapters offer a fuller overview of politics and development in each of these countries. Chapter 4 focuses on the political context of economic policy in Indonesia from 1966 to the eve of the Asian financial crisis. The discussion opens with a summary of historical origins and colonial experience, then concentrates on postindependent development, noting key political events and detailing macroeconomic patterns. The overview covers the initial democratic regime, political upheaval in the 1960s, the era of the petroleum boom, the cycles of crisis and reform in the 1980s, and the early 1990s, in which Indonesia successfully pursued an outward-oriented economic strategy. Chapter 5 covers similar themes and periods in Nigeria, with special attention to the sources of state weakness and economic decline in the 1990s. Chapter 6 provides a brief overview of the economic data at the heart of the comparison, examining comparative indicators of performance for the period 1965 through 2004.

Both countries have recently experienced democratic transitions and embarked on new episodes of economic reform, and chapters 7 and 8 examine these liberalization processes. Each chapter examines the sources of breakdown in the former authoritarian regime and the institutional framework of political transition. I then consider how institutional reform and distributional politics have driven economic outcomes in these states, with particular focus on issues of state restructuring and the formation of new support coalitions. The chapters conclude with some propositions about the requisites for successful reform in Indonesia and Nigeria. In chapter 9, I conclude with a summary of the analysis, reflections on transitions and crisis management, and comparative observations.

CHAPTER 2

The Political Economy
of Development

This study is concerned with the effects of institutional arrangements on economic growth and the political factors leading to institutional change. The central argument is that differences in long-term economic performance are determined by variations in the ability of states to make credible commitments to market participants. Such commitments include policy stability, secure property rights, and a conducive setting for contracting, which together enable capital accumulation.

This study takes issue with the prevailing functionalist assumptions in much of the new institutional economics that cast institutional change as an evolutionary process arising from changes in relative prices or other economic exigencies. Instead, I regard alterations in important economic institutions as a process of political conflict in which actors and interests contend for preferred institutional arrangements.[1] The analytical framework emphasizes the role of leadership, social coalitions, and international effects as decisive sources of institutional change.

This chapter clarifies basic assumptions about the nature of institutions, the relationship of institutions to economic outcomes, and the causal relations among political factors, institutional change, and economic performance. The following discussion differentiates approaches in comparative political economy, considering in turn neoclassical policy reform, the new political economy, sectoral analysis, state-centered analysis, and institutional theories.

1. Peter A. Hall and Rosemary C. R. Taylor, "Political Science and the Three New Institutionalisms," *Political Studies* 44, no. 5 (1996): 952. Joel M. Diermeier,Timothy Frye, and Steven Lewis, "Credible Commitment and Property Rights: The Role of Strategic Interaction between Political and Economic Actors," in David L. Weimer, ed., *The Political Economy of Property Rights: Institutional Change and Credibility in the Reform of Centrally Planned Economies* (Cambridge: Cambridge University Press, 1997), 36. For a rationalist account, see Jack Knight, *Institutions and Social Conflict* (Cambridge: Cambridge University Press, 1992), 40–41.

Neoclassical Policy Reform

Neoclassical economists have framed an influential view of economic performance stressing the importance of policy selection and the need to delimit the economic role of government. This perspective is associated with the Washington Consensus emanating from the Bretton Woods institutions (the International Monetary Fund and the World Bank), along with like-minded economic and development agencies of the U.S. government. This perspective reflects an orthodoxy concerning the relation of government and markets and the ensuing prescriptions for economic reform.[2]

Neoclassical analysis stresses the primacy of market mechanisms in efficiently allocating resources, citing excessive and inappropriate state interference in the economy as a leading constraint on growth in developing countries. This perspective favors a circumscribed role for government, generally limited to the maintenance of property rights and the provision of such public goods as law and order, a stable currency, selected regulatory roles, limited elements of infrastructure, and important services such as education. In addition to favoring broader leeway for private economic activity, the orthodox package calls for greater integration with the world economy plus a pronounced outward orientation in trade and investment policy.

The orthodox position also holds that economic policies are the strongest determinants and the best predictors of development outcomes. Neoclassical analysts place primary weight on the incentives and constraints provided by formal economic policies. Policy regimes that distort prices, impose political direction on factor or product markets, and impede the initiatives of investors and producers are liable to crises and slow growth. Approaches that encourage competitive markets, equilibrium prices, and the free movement of factors are more likely to produce efficient outcomes. Consequently, comparative analysis must primarily consider the policies chosen by different regimes.[3]

2. Miles Kahler, "Orthodoxy and Its Alternatives: Explaining Approaches to Stabilization and Adjustment," in Joan Nelson, ed., *Economic Crisis and Policy Choice* (Princeton: Princeton University Press, 1990), 35–36. John Williamson, *The Progress of Policy Reform in Latin America* (Washington, DC: Institute for International Economics, 1990). Moises Naim, "Fads and Fashions in Economic Reforms: Washington Consensus or Washington Confusion?" *Third World Quarterly* 21, no. 3 (2000), 505.

3. World Bank, *Accelerated Growth in Sub-Saharan Africa* (Washington, DC: World Bank, 1981); World Bank, *Sub-Saharan Africa: From Crisis to Sustainable Growth* (Washington, DC: World Bank, 1989); World Bank, *Adjustment in Africa: Reforms, Results, and the Road Ahead* (New York: Oxford University Press, 1994). David Sahn, ed., *Adjusting to Policy Failure in African Economies* (Ithaca: Cornell University Press, 1994).

This perspective has inspired previous examinations of developmental performance in Indonesia and Nigeria.[4] A recent comparative study provides extensive description and analysis of the policies undertaken in these two countries and their respective economic outcomes through the early 1980s. The authors conclude: "The comparison of Nigeria and Indonesia provides dramatic evidence that policies matter."[5] This account reflects both the contributions and the shortcomings of neoclassical policy analysis.

Policy differences are undoubtedly important for many aspects of comparative economic performance, though the absence of a clear political dimension in orthodox policy studies weakens its insights. It is widely accepted that policy choices influence economic outcomes, but this basic premise is inadequate to explain variations in economic change.[6] An emphasis on policies and their selection begs three crucial questions: How are "good" policies chosen by leaders? How can governments implement the "right" policies? And how can appropriate policies be politically sustained? What is strikingly absent from the neoclassical approach is a model of reform that accounts for political actors, groups within the political system, and the institutional framework of policy change.[7]

The neoclassical position proffers an implicit political rendering of reform, based upon assumptions of rational action, volition, and interest group behavior. From this vantage, political leaders *should* have a rational stake in pursuing orthodox policies, since these measures promise to alleviate economic distress and improve popular welfare. In choosing to pursue economic reform, leaders admittedly face problems of time inconsistency and coalition building.

Time inconsistency refers to the tension between popular expectations

4. Brian Pinto, "Nigeria during and after the Oil Boom: A Policy Comparison with Indonesia," *World Bank Economic Review* 1, no. 3 (1987). David L. Bevan, Paul Collier, and J. W. Gunning, *The Political Economy of Poverty, Equity, and Growth in Nigeria and Indonesia, 1950–86* (Washington, DC: World Bank, 1999).

5. Bevan, Collier, and Gunning, *The Political Economy of Poverty, Equity, and Growth in Nigeria and Indonesia, 1950–86,* 424.

6. William Easterly and Ross Levine, "Africa's Growth Tragedy: Policies and Ethnic Divisions," *Quarterly Journal of Economics* 112, no. 4 (1997): 1241; Vladimir Popov, "Shock Therapy vs. Gradualism: The End of the Debate (Explaining the Magnitude of Transformational Recession)," *Comparative Economic Studies* 42, no. 1 (2000): 1.

7. Peter A. Hall, *Governing the Economy: The Politics of State Intervention in Britain and France* (Oxford: Oxford University Press, 1986). See also Christopher Ellison and Gary Gereffi, "Explaining Strategies and Patterns of Industrial Development," in Gary Gereffi and Donald Wyman, eds., *Manufacturing Miracles: Paths of Industrialization in Latin American and East Asia* (Princeton: Princeton University Press, 1990), and Stephan Haggard and Steven Webb, *Voting for Reform: Democracy, Political Liberalization, and Economic Adjustment* (Washington, DC: World Bank, 1994).

of reform and the actual distribution of results. Economic reform carries distributional consequences, producing differential mobilization among affected groups. In most instances, the costs of liberalization are quickly evident. A variety of entrenched interests are threatened by currency devaluation, subsidy cuts, privatization, retrenchment, and reduced trade protection. The groups that might be expected to benefit from liberalization, however, may be unsure of their prospective gains, which are realized only after a significant lag in time.[8] Faced with short-term mobilization by a politically salient group of "losers" from reform, political leaders confront the challenge of crafting a coalition among putative "winners."

In much of the literature from the Washington institutions, these collective action problems can be resolved through the "political will" of leaders to press ahead with reform even in the absence of a clear support constituency.[9] Ultimately, a combination of executive resolve and shifting interests will presumably stabilize a reform project. These suppositions have proven inadequate to account for the actual dynamics of reform in many countries.

The New Political Economy

Lacking a political model of economic change, neoclassical policy analysts have generally failed to apprehend the reform process or to anticipate particular outcomes.[10] Advocates of orthodoxy have often been vexed by the failure of reform, a problem commonly attributed not only to the resistance of political leaders but also to diffidence by private sector elites. One approach to explaining these dynamics, the "new political economy" (NPE), gained prominence in the 1980s. Rooted in neoclassical economics, this perspective depicts the economic bases of political coalitions and government decision making and the reciprocal effects of political coalitions on economic performance. The "new" element of the NPE is the application of neoclassical theory to the study of political-economic interactions, emphasizing the microfoundations of policy choice and coalition formation.

8. Raquel Fernandez and Dani Rodrik, "Resistance to Reform: Status Quo Bias in the Presence of Individual-Specific Uncertainty," *American Economic Review* 81, no. 5 (1991): 1147.

9. John Waterbury, "The Political Management of Economic Adjustment and Reform," in Joan Nelson, ed., *Fragile Coalitions: The Politics of Adjustment* (New Brunswick: Transaction Books for the Overseas Development Council, 1989), 54–55. Jeffrey Herbst, "The Structural Adjustment of Politics in Africa," *World Development* 18, no. 7 (1990): 949.

10. Miles Kahler, "External Influence, Conditionality, and the Politics of Adjustment," in Stephan Haggard and Robert R. Kaufman, eds., *The Politics of Economic Adjustment* (Princeton: Princeton University Press, 1992), 128.

This mode of analysis addresses two conundrums of reform: the frequent preference of governments for "irrational" or growth-retarding policies, and the political resistance to reform, even in the face of failed status quo policies. In responding to these questions, the NPE literature seeks to model the sources of state intervention in markets and the political impediments to economic change.

The core of the new political economy is provided by the analysis of rent seeking, broadly defined as the competition for politically mediated economic gains. In the seminal discussion of rent seeking by Krueger, government restrictions on markets (principally through trade bans, quotas, and foreign exchange rationing) create opportunities for special premiums above the level that would obtain in circumstances of full competition.[11] Scarcity rents are disbursed at the discretion of government officials, and market actors lobby for preferential access to these resources.

Two effects follow. First, rent seeking creates substantial inefficiencies within the private sector, as businesses devote resources to securing extramarket benefits rather than improving competitiveness or investing in value-creating activities. Second, state elites (who capture their own rents through payments and favors for collusion) are inclined toward economic intervention, so as to enhance their discretion over resources and market access. An expanded treatment of this problem by Bhagwati looked beyond trade policies to encompass collusion over a broader set of state subsidies, licenses, and regulatory discretion, all of which give rise to "directly unproductive, profit-seeking activities" (evocatively called DUP) in which public and private actors conspire around the allotment of particular benefits.[12] The account provided by Mancur Olson holds that the consolidation of strong "distributional coalitions" with the capacity to lobby for particular benefits will eventually stultify growth and competitiveness, as governments become enmeshed in rent-seeking interests, thereby losing the flexibility to respond to changes in technology or market structure.[13]

The essential proposition of NPE is that collusion between state and private actors over the provision of divisible (or excludable) benefits creates a number of impediments to economic performance. Political leaders have incentives to favor policies that increase their discretion over

11. Anne O. Krueger. "The Political Economy of the Rent-Seeking Society," *American Economic Review* 64, no. 3 (1974): 291–303.

12. Jagdish N. Bhagwati, "Directly Unproductive, Profit-Seeking (DUP) Activities," *Journal of Political Economy* 90, no. 5 (1982): 988–1002.

13. Mancur Olson, *The Rise and Decline of Nations* (New Haven: Yale University Press, 1982).

resources. This creates a bias toward political intervention in markets rather than measures to encourage competition and the dispersal of economic power. In many instances, the self-interest of state officials contributes to an erosion of institutional capacity, as atomized rent seeking and corruption undermine the cohesion and purpose of public agencies. Competition for rents also influences the formation of social coalitions and political constituencies. Business groups develop vested interests in protection, clientelism, and other collusive practices, creating a rent-seeking coalition among groups in the public and private sectors.

The NPE framework sheds light on some important problems in the study of development. The application of microeconomic reasoning, with its emphasis on individual motivation, provides further insight into the questions of why some states behave in a predatory fashion, why governments resist certain types of reform, and how societal interests coalesce around particular policy regimes and institutions. This perspective also provides a necessary focus on problems of opportunism in political and economic interactions—a range of self-interested behaviors including collusion, corruption, and cheating that undermine the performance of state institutions and foster distortions in the operations of markets.

This approach has significant flaws. The methodological individualism of the NPE is inherently pessimistic about the possibilities for collective action to enhance developmental performance. By viewing actors as self-seeking utility maximizers, this approach essentially casts state agents as fragmented rent-seekers, state institutions as malign predators, and economic interest groups as supplicants for state preferences.[14] Following this theoretical logic, social dilemmas and predatory behavior would be the norm in developing countries. On both conceptual and empirical grounds, these assumptions are too narrow to furnish a convincing model of political-economic relationships. The spectrum of actual policy choices, reform processes, and political configurations in the developing world indicate that economic outcomes are contingent. Some states behave in a developmental rather than predatory fashion, giving priority to growth and capital accumulation over consumption or redistribution. While rent seeking and collusion frequently create dynamics that impair growth or change,

14. Paul Mosley, Jane Harrigan, and John Toye, *Aid and Power: The World Bank and Policy-Based Lending,* vol. 1 (London: Routledge, 1991), 13–14. Merilee Grindle, "The New Political Economy: Positive Economics and Negative Politics," in Gerald M. Meier, ed., *Politics and Policy Making in Developing Countries: Perspectives on the New Political Economy* (San Francisco: ICS Press, 1991), 43. Peter Evans, *Embedded Autonomy* (Princeton: Princeton University Press, 1995), 23–24.

state predation is neither predetermined nor immutable.[15] A clearer conception of political contention and institutional effects can improve our understanding of economic change.

Sectoral Analysis

The analysis of sectoral effects on politics and economic change provides another approach. The focus here is the composition of economic sectors and their influence on politics and economic performance. Sectoral approaches proceed from a common assumption that important economic sectors give rise to distributions of social and political power. Sectoral configurations privilege some social groups over others and provide different bases of state revenues.[16] These fiscal and coalition patterns affect the capacity of public institutions and the interests of state elites. They also determine the interests and cohesion of societal groups and the bases of accommodation between state and society. To a significant degree, leading sectors define political and economic development.

Sectoral analysis is especially relevant to the understanding of resource-exporting states.[17] In the case of oil exporters (and more generally countries with a prominent mineral export sector), fiscal effects are especially salient in structuring government institutions and interests. Mineral exports provide rents directly to sovereign states, effectively dissociating their revenue base from domestic production and taxation. The analysis of rentier or petro-states presents a general model of fiscal autonomy and minimal accountability. Large revenues under the direct discre-

---

15. The linkages between state character, intervention, and economic outcomes are discussed in Peter Evans, "The State as Problem and Solution: Predation, Embedded Autonomy, and Adjustment," in Stephan Haggard and Robert Kaufman, eds., *The Politics of Economic Adjustment* (Princeton: Princeton University Press, 1992); Sylvia Maxfield and Ben Ross Schneider, eds., *Business and the State in Developing Countries* (Ithaca: Cornell University Press, 1997); and Atul Kohli, *State-Directed Development: Political Power and Industrialization in the Global Periphery* (Cambridge: Cambridge University Press, 2004).

16. Peter Gourevitch, *Politics in Hard Times: Comparative Responses to International Economic Crises* (Ithaca: Cornell University Press, 1986). Ronald Rogowski, *Commerce and Coalitions: How Trade Affects Domestic Political Alignments* (Princeton: Princeton University Press, 1989). D. Michael Shafer, *Winners and Losers: How Sectors Shape the Developmental Prospects of States* (Ithaca: Cornell University Press, 1994).

17. Shafer, *Winners and Losers;* Alan Gelb, "Adjustment to Windfall Gains: A Comparative Analysis of Oil Exporting Countries," in J. P. Neary and S. van Wijnbergen, eds., *Natural Resources and the Macroeconomy* (Oxford: Basil Blackwell, 1986); Richard M. Auty, *Sustainable Development in the Mineral Economies: The Resource Curse Thesis* (London: Routledge, 1993); Terry Lynn Karl, *The Paradox of Plenty* (Berkeley: University of California Press, 1997); Michael Ross, "The Political Economy of the Resource Curse," *World Politics* 51, no. 2 (1999).

tion of political leaders give rise to fiscal centralization. At the same time, state elites are less accountable to producer groups and civil society. This disposes rulers toward statist economic policies, as they seek to maximize their control over resources. State leaders, endowed with independent revenues, are inclined to disregard the effects of economic policies on domestic output and international competitiveness. These regimes—particularly the "capital scarce" countries with large populations relative to revenues—seek political legitimacy through strategies of selective distribution. The largesse wielded by the central state helps to secure popular quiescence through populist or patrimonial systems.

Accounts of the rentier state emphasize a number of consequences. In the political sphere, weak accountability gives rise to authoritarian regimes and corruption. Rent seeking becomes the central avenue for accumulation, as elites in both the public and private sectors lobby for allotments of state revenues and preferential access to government-regulated markets. This affects the formation of coalitions, prompting business groups to converge around rent distribution rather than improvements in productivity, and leading other popular sectors to lobby for subsidies and social provisions. Political competition focuses chiefly on leverage or control over the state where resources are vested, thus aggravating political instability and patronage politics. Pervasive rent seeking, endemic corruption, and distributional contention have corrosive effects on the policy autonomy and institutional capabilities of governments, essentially weakening the state as an agent of development. Mineral exporters are also liable to a number of pitfalls in economic policy, including profligate spending, high levels of indebtedness to smooth revenue cycles, and shortsighted planning induced by a bonanza mentality. An array of policy distortions, combined with myopic behavior, tend toward economic crises in these systems. Paradoxically, windfall revenues undermine the capacity of petro-states to foster economic growth.

Sectoral analysis has identified generic challenges in mineral export economies including structural distortions, policy errors, institutional liabilities, and perverse incentives for political leaders and societal interests. This perspective has not accounted for varying outcomes within sectoral groups. When differences are evident among a set of structurally similar cases, there is a need to revise our method of explanation.

State-Centered Analysis

State-centered analysis is chiefly concerned with the macrolevel effects of institutions, governing elites, and social formations on economic change.

This view assumes that economic development is conditioned by the interests and capacities of the state, defined as the apparatus of institutions and personnel exercising sovereign authority over a particular territory. State theorists hold that the collective goods provided by the state are integral to economic transformation and that governments are necessary progenitors of growth and accumulation.[18]

Broad variations in state performance hold consequences for economic outcomes. "Developmental" states arise from a confluence of leadership, institutional development, and interests within the political system.[19] These states are effective in promoting capital accumulation, industrialization, and international competitiveness through a combination of direct interventions and complementary measures to organize markets.[20] These regimes make critical investments in physical infrastructure and human capital, they mobilize finance, and they frequently underwrite key areas of production or technology. The provision of government-structured incentives, guarantees, and sanctions conveys credible signals to private actors, offering a crucial dimension of calculability in the setting for markets.[21] Politicians and officials in these systems adopt a long-term vantage in emphasizing goals of national development. Economic policy is commonly the province of a capable team of economic advisers who enjoy insulation from wider political pressures.[22] The delegation of authority to technocratic groups affords a degree of autonomy from particularistic influences and improves the ability to select appropriate policies. These states also conform more closely to the Weberian form of legal-rational bureaucracy.

Developmental regimes embody a degree of accountability and reciprocity between state and society. Political parties, corporatist organiza-

18. Alice Amsden, *Asia's Next Giant: Korea and Late Industrialization* (Oxford: Oxford University Press, 1989); Peter Evans, *Embedded Autonomy;* Kohli, *State-Directed Development.*

19. Bruce Cumings, "Webs with No Spiders, Spiders with No Webs: The Genealogy of the Developmental State," in Meredith Woo-Cumings, ed., *The Developmental State* (Ithaca: Cornell University Press, 1999), 64–65.

20. Robert Wade, *Governing the Market: Economic Theory and the Role of Government in East Asian Industrialization* (Princeton: Princeton University Press, 1990), 297–98; Evans, *Embedded Autonomy,* 77–81; T. J. Pempel, "Developmental Regime in a Changing World Economy," in Woo-Cumings, ed., *Developmental State,* 139–42.

21. Thomas Callaghy, "The State and the Development of Capitalism in Africa: Theoretical, Historical, and Comparative Reflections," in Donald Rothchild and Naomi Chazan, eds., *The Precarious Balance: State and Society in Africa* (Boulder: Westview, 1988).

22. Guillermo O'Donnell, *Modernization and Bureaucratic-Authoritarianism* (Berkeley: Institute of International Studies, 1973); John Williamson, ed., *The Political Economy of Policy Reform* (Washington, DC: Institute for International Economics, 1994).

tions, and ad hoc consultative arrangements provide for interchange between government and economic groups.[23] In addition, the benefits of growth are widely dispersed, and the comparatively good equity record of developmental states has been vital to securing the social contract in these societies.[24] Developmental regimes create social compacts conferring legitimacy, subject to performance. The construction of a social coalition supporting the regime's transformative goals provides the political security necessary to pursue an enduring strategy of growth.

Conversely, many systems are inimical to economic growth and transformation. These states are characterized by weak formal institutions, personalized authority, pervasive corruption, and a large scope of discretion among public officials. Whether categorized as "predatory" states or "neopatrimonial" systems, the analytical conclusions are similar: a range of states create hindrances to economic development by bleeding or monopolizing resources, fostering arbitrary political constraints on economic activity, and dissipating wealth through expedient distribution to allies and clients.[25] These political circumstances largely preclude market calculability, thereby discouraging private actors from commitment to fixed assets, which engenders asset mobility and capital flight, and gives rise to economic stagnation.

State theory challenges other salient approaches in comparative political economy. Replying to the admonitions of neoclassical analysis for market-oriented policies, research on the state highlights the importance of political capabilities as well as policy choice, while emphasizing the need for government engagement to facilitate, encourage, and regulate market forces. This perspective also offers a riposte to the new political economy, disputing the latter's assumption that state involvement in the economy necessarily leads to predatory rent seeking. State-centered analysis holds that it is possible (indeed necessary) for governments to exercise collective action for the purposes of economic development and, moreover, that collaboration between public officials and market actors does not inevitably produce opportunism and collusion.

23. Hilton L. Root, *Small Countries, Big Lessons: Governance and the Rise of East Asia* (Oxford: Oxford University Press for the Asian Development Bank, 1996), 13; Stephan Haggard, Sylvia Maxfield, and Ben Ross Schneider, "Theories of Business and Business-State Relations," in Sylvia Maxfield and Ben Ross Schneider, eds., *Business and the State in Developing Countries* (Ithaca: Cornell University Press, 1997).

24. Edgardo Campos and Hilton L. Root, *The Key to the Asian Miracle: Making Shared Growth Credible* (Washington, DC: Brookings Institution, 1996), 44–49.

25. Christopher Clapham, *Third World Politics* (Madison: University of Wisconsin Press, 1985), 48–52; Paul Hutchcroft, "Oligarchs and Cronies in the Philippine State: The Politics of Patrimonial Plunder," *World Politics* 43, no. 3 (1993).

Although there is much attention to the macrolevel effects of institutions on economic performance, there is less careful analysis of how alternative institutional arrangements influence the decisions of individuals or firms, which are the microfoundations of economic change. We have an archetype of the strong developmental state, as well as its dysfunctional opposite, but we are less clear about the factors that lead from weaker to stronger developmental orientations within particular settings. What is required is a better account of the elements influencing leadership choices, the political interests fostering developmental roles, and the key features of institutional reform.

Institutional Analysis

The study of institutions holds promise in bridging the gap between macrolevel organizational analysis and an understanding of microlevel behavior among individuals and firms. This area of research also addresses the relation between structure and agency by examining the interactions of institutional arrangements and the choices of actors. Two streams of theory inform the present analysis: the new institutional economics and sociological institutionalism. Although these are often regarded as being alternative or even antithetical approaches, I view them as complementary.

The new institutional economics is concerned with the organizational features of the economy, especially pertaining to the problems of collective action and coordination accompanying the operation of markets. A cornerstone is the idea that "institutions matter" for the ways that markets work.[26] The simplifying assumptions of "frictionless" markets in neoclassical theory leave out crucial features of economic activity as it is actually conducted.[27] An institutional approach introduces the idea of transaction

26. Seminal statements include Douglass C. North and Robert P. Thomas, *The Rise of the Western World: A New Economic History* (Cambridge: Cambridge University Press, 1973); Douglass C. North, *Structure and Change in Economic History* (New York: W. W. Norton, 1981). Relevant applications include Kathryn Firmin-Sellers, *The Transformation of Property Rights in the Gold Coast* (Cambridge: Cambridge University Press, 1996); David L. Weimer, ed., *The Political Economy of Property Rights: Institutional Change and Credibility in the Reform of Centrally Planned Economies* (Cambridge: Cambridge University Press, 1997); and Stephen Haber, Armando Razo, and Noel Maurer, *The Politics of Property Rights: Political Instability, Credible Commitments, and Economic Growth in Mexico, 1876–1929* (Cambridge: Cambridge University Press, 2003).

27. Oliver Williamson, *The Economic Institutions of Capitalism* (New York: Free Press, 1985), 19; Kenneth Arrow, "The Organization of Economic Activity: Issues Pertinent to the Choice of Market versus Nonmarket Allocation," *Public Expenditures and Policy Analysis: The PPB System*, vol. 1. U.S. Joint Economic Committee, 91st Congress, 1st session (Washington, DC: U.S. Government Printing Office, 1969), 48; Douglass North, *Structure and Change in Economic History* (New York: W. W. Norton, 1981), 9.

costs, observing that most market actors lack full information, and that information asymmetries create problems in securing contracts and surmounting other forms of market failure.[28] The costs of transacting—gauging the reliability of others, assessing performance, and guarding against cheating, reneging, or free riding—constitute an additional dimension of economic activity that influences the conduct of actors and the dynamics of markets.[29] Institutions provide a nonmarket outlet for overcoming these problems by establishing rules and procedures that can regularize expectations and constrain individual behavior. By structuring choice and regulating exchange, institutions reduce transaction costs, allowing for a broader scale and scope of economic activity.[30] Economic performance depends on the nature of comparative institutions and how well different systems perform these economizing functions.

This mode of analysis draws upon three central concepts: the rationality assumption, the nature of contracting, and the definition of property rights. Institutional economists assume that actors (individuals, firms, or interest groups treated as unitary actors) are self-interested utility optimizers who behave in an instrumental and strategic fashion.[31] For any economic system the incentives and strategies of actors are affected by the milieu of contracting and the nature of property rights. In both market and nonmarket spheres, transactions are regulated by contracting, that is, by negotiated agreements among actors about the terms of their relationship. The relative ease and reliability of contracting determines the organization of firms, the movement of factors, and the scope of markets.[32] A related concern is the nature of property rights, defined as rules for the ownership and disposition of assets. The delineation of property rights and the nature of their enforcement set further parameters for economic activity. Regardless of the particular definition of property rights, superior

28. Williamson, *Economic Institutions of Capitalism,* 20–23. Douglass North, *Institutions, Institutional Change, and Economic Performance* (Cambridge: Cambridge University Press, 1990), 27.

29. Mancur Olson, *The Logic of Collective Action* (Cambridge: Harvard University Press, 1965); Robert Bates, "Social Dilemmas and Rational Individuals: An Assessment of the New Institutionalism," in John Harriss, Janet Hunter, and Colin M. Lewis, eds., *The New Institutional Economics and Third World Development* (London and New York: Routledge, 1995); Oliver Williamson, *Market and Hierarchies* (New York: Free Press, 1975); Elinor Ostrom, *Governing the Commons: The Evolution of Institutions for Collective Action* (New York: Cambridge University Press, 1990).

30. North, *Institutions, Institutional Change, and Economic Performance,* 35.

31. North, *Structure and Change in Economic History,* 4; Thráinn Eggertsson, *Economic Behavior and Institutions* (Cambridge: Cambridge University Press, 1990), 7–8.

32. Williamson, *Economic Institutions of Capitalism,* 15–18.

outcomes arise in circumstances where rights are clearly specified, reliably applied, and consistently enforced.[33]

Institutional economics seeks to provide an account of how alternative organizational arrangements affect the behavior of market participants, and more generally economic performance. By taking into consideration the broader setting for markets, the institutional approach departs from the conventional neoclassical assumptions that price signals and other nominal incentives are sufficient to shift economic behavior. The problems of economic change in particular settings are related to the legal framework, public administration, industrial organization, social groupings, and even cultural norms. Institutional studies help to elaborate the microfoundations of economic performance while providing new accounts of particular forms of market failure and institutional response.[34]

New institutional economics nonetheless reflects limitations. This perspective does not adequately account for variations in institutional design, nor does it provide a satisfactory model of institutional change. In any given setting, there is a range of possible institutional choices, including alternative arrangements that might yield comparable levels of efficiency and welfare. Yet the broadly construed concepts of contracts and property rights do not offer much leverage in understanding the particular institutional arrangements that arise in specific situations.[35] With regard to institutional development, economic reasoning commonly holds that change is driven by a pervasive impulse toward greater efficiency, portraying a world in which rational actors contract for new institutional arrangements to improve their welfare, thereby furnishing positive collective outcomes. This functionalist argument largely omits the political dimension of institutional choice, which is rife with conflict and contingency.[36] Institutional change commonly gives rise to contention over the distributional consequences of alternative arrangements, and such controversies are often resolved through the dominance of particular group interests or the coer-

33. North and Thomas, *Rise of the Western World,* 6–7; North, *Structure and Change in Economic History,* 17–18.

34. John Toye, "The New Institutional Economics and Its Implications for Development Theory," in Harriss et al., eds., *New Institutional Economics and Third World Development,* 49–68.

35. Robert Bates, "Social Dilemmas and Rational Individuals: An Assessment of the New Institutionalism," in Harriss et al., eds., *New Institutional Economic and Third World Development,* 41; Fritz W. Scharpf, "Institutions in Comparative Policy Research," *Comparative Political Studies* 33, no. 6–7 (2000): 762–90.

36. Mark Granovetter, "Economic Institutions as Social Constructions: A Framework for Analysis," *Acta Sociologica* 35, no. 1 (1992): 3–11; Bates, "Social Dilemmas and Rational Individuals," 44; Hall and Taylor, "Political Science and the Three New Institutionalisms," 952.

cive power of the state.[37] Depending upon the political context, struggles over institutional change may yield an outcome that preserves the status quo or fosters suboptimal results, rather than providing Pareto-superior outcomes.

Sociological and historical approaches to institutionalism offer different perspectives on institutional development.[38] Comparative historical sociology treats institutions as organizational forms associated with particular social arrangements, economic systems, and governing structures.[39] These studies draw inductive conclusions about comparative political and economic organization from an examination of historical cases and patterns. When analyzing economic change, they emphasize shifts in social power, alterations in ideology and culture, and innovation in institutions. In this account, institutional change occurs in a broader social context, driven not just by utilitarian imperatives for greater efficiency, but by the ascendance of interests and ideas.[40] From a definitional perspective this research tradition adopts a relatively concrete treatment of institutions, including firms, private associations or organizations, political parties, systems of law and legal administration, large-scale bureaucracy, and the sovereign state. The central virtue of this approach is a focus on the formation and evolution of institutions and an explicit consideration of how institutions operate in particular social and cultural domains.

37. Adam Przeworski, *Democracy and the Market: Political and Economic Reforms in Eastern Europe and Latin America* (Cambridge: Cambridge University Press, 1991); Knight, *Institutions and Social Conflict,* 188–91.

38. Important contributions include Mark Granovetter, "Economic Action and Social Structure: The Problem of Embeddedness," *American Journal of Sociology* 91, no. 3 (1985): 481–510; Peter A. Hall, *Governing the Economy: The Politics of State Intervention in Britain and France* (Oxford: Oxford University Press, 1986); Sven Steinmo, Kathleen Thelen, and Frank Longstreth, eds., *Structuring Politics: Historical Institutionalism in Comparative Analysis* (Cambridge: Cambridge University Press, 1992); Richard F. Doner, "Limits of State Strength: Toward an Institutionalist View of Economic Development," *World Politics* 44, no. 3 (1992): 398–431. Useful discussions include Hall and Taylor, "Political Science and the Three New Institutionalisms"; Karen Remmer, "Theoretical Decay and Theoretical Development: The Resurgence of Institutional Analysis," *World Politics* 50, no. 1 (1997): 34–61; and Ellen Immergut, "The Theoretical Core of the New Institutionalism," *Politics and Society* 26, no. 1 (1998): 5–34.

39. Emile Durkheim, *The Division of Labor in Society* (New York: Free Press, 1984); Otto Hintze, *The Historical Essays of Otto Hintze,* ed. Felix Gilbert (New York: Oxford University Press, 1975); Max Weber, *Economy and Society* (2 vols.) (Berkeley: University of California Press, 1978); Anthony Giddens, *Central Problems in Social Theory: Action, Structure, and Contradiction in Social Analysis* (Berkeley: University of California Press, 1979).

40. Max Weber, *General Economic History* (New York: Collier Books, 1961); Max Weber, *The Protestant Ethic and the Spirit of Capitalism* (New York: Scribner, 1976); Albert O. Hirschman, *The Passions and the Interests: Political Arguments for Capitalism before Its Triumph* (Princeton: Princeton University Press, 1997).

Sociological and historical approaches assume that institutions retain a degree of autonomy from societal actors. Rather than emerging from voluntary, atomistic contracting within economic or political markets, institutions are socially and politically constituted arrangements of power. Institutions impose constraints and determine prospects for elements of society, influencing not only an instrumental calculus of utility but also fundamental beliefs and attitudes. Institutions are social products reflecting shared interests, common norms, cultural orientations, and historical exigencies. Institutions cannot produce regular compliance without a substantial degree of acquiescence. In other words, institutions are "embedded" in particular social configurations, and they derive much of their potency from their relative legitimacy and efficacy. A further insight is that institutional configurations reflect the dominance of particular interests. Institutional change is not merely a rational response to market failure or collective action problems, but rather an expression of contending interests and groups, the outcome of which is historically determined. While recognizing asymmetries of social power and the tendency toward "path dependence" arising from inherited institutions, the outcome of social and institutional struggles is a contingent process.[41]

The sociological tradition supplements a purely actor-oriented mode of analysis with an account of structural factors. Its attention to culture and ideas speaks to the formation of preferences, rather than taking preferences as constant and given. The consideration of power and inequality poses an alternative to the simple assumptions of instrumental contracting as a basis for institutional arrangements. And finally, the adoption of a historical perspective, incorporating conflict and contingency, moves us away from evolutionary images of institutional change and avoids the emphasis on comparative statics inherent in economic theory.[42]

Institutions and Economic Change

Economic development may be defined by three criteria: growth, structural transformation, and poverty reduction. Strong aggregate growth (for most developing economies, at least 6 percent annually in real terms) is a requisite for real increases in average income, as well as for levels of savings and investment needed to sustain future growth. Sustained economic

41. Granovetter, "Economic Action and Social Structure," 504–5.
42. Kathleen Thelen, *How Institutions Evolve: The Political Economy of Skills in Germany, Britain, the United States, and Japan* (Cambridge: Cambridge University Press, 2004). See also Kathleen Thelen, "Historical Institutionalism in Comparative Politics," *Annual Review of Political Science,* vol. 2 (Palo Alto: Annual Reviews, 1999).

expansion is almost invariably accompanied by a transformation in the structure of economies, by which is meant a diversification of activities as well as increases in efficiency. It is possible to have episodes of high growth (for instance, during commodity booms or after civil wars) not linked to structural change, but these conditions are more fleeting and volatile.

Structural transformation entails diversification toward manufacturing, services (including information technologies), increased productivity, and higher returns. A more productive agricultural sector also raises incomes, frees labor for other activities, and generates greater surplus for investment. Decreases in absolute poverty and the enhancement of average living standards are integral to the development process, not least because they enhance productivity and savings, and bolster political legitimacy. Together, these indices constitute benchmarks for economic progress.

Consistently strong investment in fixed, value-producing assets is the foundation of economic development. The bulk should arise from domestic investors and producers. Direct foreign investment can provide critical resources in certain strategic activities or particular moments, but it is often insufficient for structural change and broad improvements in income. Portfolio investment may furnish important financial resources, yet, as recent global experience demonstrates, international financial markets are too volatile to offer a reliable catalyst of development. Foreign capital can be regarded as an important adjunct for development, but a vigorous, diverse investment response by domestic actors is usually essential for economic transformation. Private investment is the leading element of capital formation.[43] State resources and interventions are rarely sufficient to meet the investment needs of a diversified, competitive economy. Economic development arises from complementary investments by state and market actors in value-creating activities, yet the driving element in growth is private investment in productive enterprise, and such investment will most likely be forthcoming when credible commitments are furnished by the state.

It follows that development requires a political setting offering sufficient inducement for private investment in productive assets. Economic agents behave in accordance with their assessment of risk; the ability to judge future conditions and calculate returns shapes the character of investment and entrepreneurship. When time horizons are long and the actions of government officials and other market participants can be fore-

---

43. The centrality of private capital is emphasized by Jeffrey Winters, *Power in Motion: Capital Mobility and the Indonesian State* (Ithaca: Cornell University Press, 1996), 3.

seen with relative confidence, holders of capital are inclined to enter into more extended and complex commitments. These conditions are more likely to facilitate the expansion of productive capital, which often entails lumpy investments, long gestation periods, diverse exchange relations, and specialization.[44] In circumstances of relative calculability, we expect greater investment in assets such as machinery and physical plant, productivity-improving measures such as irrigation, land improvement, research or technological innovation, sophisticated economic arrangements requiring multiple exchange relations and forward contracting, and a higher degree of specialization among firms. By contrast, when the behavior of government and private actors is uncertain or suspect, economic actors are prone to emphasize liquidity, diversified portfolios, short-term transactions, collusion with public officials, extralegal actions, and a limited scope of contracting or exchange relations. These strategies emphasize speculative activities and mercantile endeavors (e.g., real estate, currency arbitrage, general trading, and distribution) rather than productive investment, and recourse to rent seeking, corruption, and capital flight.

Many factors influence calculability including government policies, administrative performance, political stability, external shocks, and levels of social trust. A core concern is the problem of *expropriation*, defined as susceptibility to the loss of assets, generally occurring through the actions or deficiencies of the state. Expropriation can take the form of a simple property grab through nationalization or confiscation. More commonly, assets are lost or eroded through inflation, excessive taxation, a sudden termination of subsidies or protection, the retraction of contracts, licenses, or permits, regulatory changes rendering an enterprise unviable, arbitrary legal revisions, biased judicial action, pervasive criminal activity, or cataclysmic social violence (i.e., riots or warfare). These are nonmarket risks arising from government policy, the operations of public agencies, and deficits in governing institutions (such as an inability to instill order).[45]

The relative risk of expropriation reflects the security of property rights and the certainty of contracting. Where the hazard of expropriation is high, economic actors are risk averse, resorting to strategies of capital mobility, hedging, informality, and collusion. Productive accumulation is likely in circumstances where the hazard of expropriation is limited, and

---

44. Robert Bates, *Prosperity and Violence: The Political Economy of Development* (New York: W. W. Norton, 2000); Mancur Olson, *Power and Prosperity* (New York: Basic Books, 2000); Margaret Levi, *Of Rule and Revenue* (Berkeley: University of California Press, 1998).

45. Hilton Root, *Small Countries, Big Lessons: Governance and the Rise of East Asia* (Oxford: Oxford University Press for the Asian Development Bank, 1996). Haber, Razo, and Maurer, *Politics of Property Rights.*

private agents rely primarily on market calculus rather than concerns for political and policy risks. The problem of development turns on the political structure of markets and the ability of states to guarantee a conducive setting for private accumulation. This is the principal issue in credibility: whether market agents can accept policy signals and plan economic activity with minimal concern for expropriation. Credible commitments denote more than the acceptance of government pronouncements, implying a broader assessment of institutional performance. Tax policy can hardly be effective if taxes are rarely collected, tariff levels lose much of their relevance in circumstances where duties are commonly settled by bribing customs officials, and nominal interest rates may be immaterial when inflation fears are high or large parallel markets operate. If the state cannot furnish basic assurances of reliable governance, there is little possibility for authorities to influence market behavior positively. Credible commitments enable the use of public policy for the goals of national development.

Institutions are treated here as arrangements for the elaboration and enforcement of rules. Institutions lend regularity to human activities by setting out expectations, imposing restraints, and providing guidelines for collective interactions. Institutional arrangements not only provide incentives and limits for individuals but also indicate the range of behavior that can be anticipated from others.[46] In addition, institutions commonly define norms and shape public values and perceptions. This allows for a greater degree of certainty in political, social, and economic life.

To summarize, credible commitments constitute assurances of the transparency of policy incentives, as well as guarantees against arbitrary state action or untoward conduct by other market participants. They are essentially pledges against predatory or opportunistic behavior. While governments may use informal signaling to bolster credibility, the most effective types of commitment arise from formal institutional arrangements. This requires prior (ex ante) measures that limit or preclude the possibility of arbitrary actions at a later date and that reduce the risk of expropriation.[47] Authorities can buttress confidence in government behavior by limiting the discretion of officials. Especially important are con-

46. North, *Institutions, Institutional Change, and Economic Performance*, 25; Immergut, "The Theoretical Core of the New Institutionalism," 54; John M. Carey, "Parchment, Equilibria, and Institutions," *Comparative Political Studies* 33, no. 6–7 (2000): 737.

47. Avinash Dixit, *The Making of Economic Policy* (Cambridge: MIT Press, 1996); Andrew MacIntyre, *The Power of Institutions: Political Architecture and Governance* (Ithaca: Cornell University Press, 2003), 21.

straints on the executive arising from legal provisions, oversight by government agencies, or checks and balances among different units.

In addition, governments can enter into arrangements that call forth high costs for deviant actions, thus "locking in" stated commitments.[48] This might be achieved through such measures as currency convertibility, open financial markets, or membership in international organizations and regimes.[49] These arrangements indicate that a significant departure from expressed policy will trigger sanctions to the detriment of government. Finally, states can insulate market agents against expropriation by signaling state action (through legislative oversight, procedural requirements for policy change, formal consultative arrangements with economic groups, or the barometer of financial markets) and by providing for capital mobility, thus permitting an exit option in times of uncertainty. The establishment of competent, neutral regulatory and enforcement agencies is a longer-term effort that can improve the security of property and contracts, thus increasing certainty and trust among market agents. The tool kit of appropriate measures is diverse.

The Politics of Institutional Change

Why do some political systems successfully converge around growth-enhancing institutional arrangements, while others fail to solve the collective action problems surrounding economic development? How can countries move from predatory to developmental systems? What types of interests, strategies, and historical endowments are conducive to institutional reform? These questions guide the contemporary study of development. My framework highlights the role of leadership, the nature of social coalitions, and the effects of regional position in explaining institutional change and economic performance.

The motives, capacities, and organization of leadership are critically important for many systems. In developing countries and states undergoing rapid political transition, the role of leadership looms large in shaping the institutional landscape. Where formal institutions are weak or insecure, the discretion of leaders is necessarily heightened, and they may wield decisive influence in fostering certain types of institutional arrangements or precluding alternatives. Leaders work under constraints posed

---

48. Pranab Bardhan, "The Nature of Institutional Impediments to Economic Development," in Mancur Olson and Satu Kahkonen, eds., *A Not-So-Dismal Science: A Broader View of Economies and Societies* (Oxford: Oxford University Press, 2000).

49. Paul Collier, "Africa's External Economic Relations: 1960–90," *African Affairs* 90, no. 360 (1991): 339–56.

by inherited institutional arrangements, available resources, and interests within the political system, but they also possess considerable leeway in shaping the course of institutional development. State elites may accept limits on their discretion and seek to build stronger institutions of administration and economic management, or they can undermine and weaken institutions in order to enhance their own prerogatives.[50]

When leaders possess broad latitude in a setting of weak countervailing structures or groups, the hazard of predatory behavior creates an inherent problem for establishing credible commitments. Rulers in systems with weak institutions face few constraints against self-aggrandizement or arbitrary economic intervention. This poses a danger that the executive will seize resources or otherwise take capricious policy actions that undermine the economy. The consequent risk of expropriation can have adverse effects on investment and growth. Those rulers concerned with economic development face the problem of crafting organizational and policy arrangements that attenuate the hazards of arbitrary action or violations of property. Predation is only a possibility, not an ineluctable outcome. The different approaches that leaders adopt toward the economy reflect their innate values and perceptions as well as the pressures and incentives arising from the political system. Executives make a political calculus regarding their governing strategy and the salience of economic concerns. Some leaders embrace an agenda of economic growth as a means of political consolidation, while for others the political logic of rule conflicts with the needs of development, leading to economic distress or despoliation.[51]

Predatory behavior may take different forms. Here, Mancur Olson's distinction between stationary and roving bandits is illuminating.[52] Stationary bandits (e.g., crime syndicates) seek to provide stable elements of governance within their territories, so as to feed off the proceeds of a viable economy. By contrast, roving bandits plunder with abandon, lack-

50. Joel S. Migdal, *Strong Societies and Weak States* (Princeton: Princeton University Press, 1988); Evans, "State as Problem and Solution"; David Waldner, *State Building and Late Development* (Ithaca: Cornell University Press, 1999).

51. Thomas Callaghy, "Lost between State and Market: The Politics of Economic Adjustment in Ghana, Zambia, and Nigeria," in Joan Nelson, ed., *Economic Crisis and Policy Choice* (Princeton: Princeton University Press, 1990), 263, and Callaghy, "Political Passions and Economic Interests: Economic Reform and Political Structure in Africa," in Thomas Callaghy and John Ravenhill, eds., *Hemmed In: Responses to Africa's Economic Decline* (New York: Columbia University Press, 1994), 470.

52. Mancur Olson, "Dictatorship, Democracy, and Development," *American Political Science Review* 87, no. 3 (1993): 567–76; Mancur Olson, *Power and Prosperity* (New York: Basic Books, 2000), 6–12.

ing any stake in the community they prey upon. The distinction is whether rulers seek to maximize short-term gains or to exploit the benefits of a protracted stream of income.[53] Soeharto's rule provides an exemplary picture of the stationary bandit, as the New Order fostered a developmental regime in which the ruler and his circle also enjoyed fabulous gains through corruption and rents.[54] By contrast, Sani Abacha, like his Congolese counterpart Mobutu Sese Seko, behaved as a roving bandit, appropriating a large proportion of national income and despoiling the economy while sending much of the proceeds abroad.

Apart from the personal inclinations of rulers, what circumstances dispose regimes to predation or growth? The choices of leaders are contingent, yet ruling strategies are hardly random. Opportunities and constraints within the political system influence the nature of governance. These factors, while not strictly deterministic, shape the calculus of rulers. External shocks and domestic economic crises frequently stimulate shifts in development strategy. Apart from these proximate challenges three factors are important: the nature of security challenges, the pattern of distributional politics, and the composition of the ruling coalition.

State security problems can exert pressure on leaders to make better use of resources, resolve distributional problems, improve extractive capacities, or pursue rapid growth. Historically, evidence shows that external security challenges can induce leaders to pursue strategies of intensive resource mobilization and extraction as a means of bolstering state power.[55] In the high-performing economies of East Asia (notably South Korea, Taiwan, and Singapore) the proximate threat of a large neighboring state had a bracing effect in moving leaders in a developmental direction.[56] Domestic challenges are also important. In Latin America, the rise of local radicalism in the 1960s and 1970s created threats to elite property rights, contributing to the emergence of bureaucratic-authoritarian

53. Levi, *Of Rule and Revenue,* 42–47; Olson, *Power and Prosperity,* 4–5; Bruce Bueno de Mesquita and Hilton L. Root, "When Bad Economics Is Good Politics," in Bruce Bueno de Mesquita and Hilton L. Root, eds., *Governing for Prosperity* (New Haven: Yale University Press, 2000), 1–16.

54. R. William Liddle, "The Relative Autonomy of the Third World Politician: Soeharto and Indonesian Economic Development in Comparative Perspective," *International Studies Quarterly* 35, no. 4 (1991): 403–27; John Bresnan, *Managing Indonesia: The Modern Political Economy* (New York: Columbia University Press, 1993), 288–92.

55. Charles Tilly, *Coercion, Capital, and European States, AD 990–1990* (Cambridge, MA: Basil Blackwell, 1990).

56. David C. Kang, *Crony Capitalism: Corruption and Development in South Korea and the Philippines* (Cambridge: Cambridge University Press, 2002), 29.

regimes that sought to reform the economy.[57] Communist challenges in Southeast Asia, notably the Indonesian Communist Party's strength in Indonesia, contributed to leaders' desire for better economic performance as a means to reduce social tensions and bolster political stability.

Distributional politics also play a role. When distributional pressures are rooted in broad social classes rather than particular group interests, leaders are more likely to adopt encompassing growth strategies as a means of securing stability and legitimacy. By contrast, demands from segmented minorities (usually reflecting communal or local concerns) or discrete sectoral groups are more easily resolved through strategies of patronage, selective redistribution, or repression. In general, predatory clientelist systems are most likely in countries with fragmented communities and weak societal organizations.[58]

The hazard of expropriation is heightened to the degree that the executive operates without restraints. By dispersing responsibility for economic management, leaders can attenuate the liabilities of excessive discretion. Clear delegation of important policy and implementation roles to technocratic groups and the bureaucracy serves to increase confidence in nominal commitments by the government. Effective delegation improves the quality of policy decisions, provides a check on the executive's impulses, and signals greater predictability of state action to market participants. At a minimum, the presence of capable, politically insulated technocratic groups presents an important countervailing force to the caprices of a strong leader.[59]

The contingent choices of elites are best understood in relation to social groupings and alliances, as I have suggested. Effective institutions rest upon a degree of self-enforcement, drawing their influence from voluntary compliance rather than coercive enforcement by political authorities. It follows that the relative capacity and stability of institutional arrangements derive substantially from their degree of popular legitimacy. Economic models are associated with particular compacts that support

57. Karen L. Remmer and Gilbert Merkx, "Bureaucratic-Authoritarianism Revisited," *Latin American Research Review* 17, no. 2 (1982): 3–40; Guillermo O'Donnell, "Reply to Remmer and Merkx," *Latin American Research Review* 17, no. 2 (1982): 42; Robert R. Kaufman, "Industrial Change and Authoritarian Rule in Latin America: A Concrete Review of the Bureaucratic—Authoritarian Thesis," in David Collier, ed., *The New Authoritarianism in Latin America* (Princeton: Princeton University Press, 1979), 190.

58. Joel S. Migdal, *Strong Societies and Weak States* (Princeton: Princeton University Press, 1988); Easterly and Levine, "Africa's Growth Tragedy," 1203–51.

59. Adrian Leftwich, "Bringing Politics Back In: Towards a Model of the Developmental State," *Journal of Development Studies* 31, no. 3 (1995): 400–427.

political regimes and assent to institutional rules. Countries with well-performing economies draw upon more inclusive coalitions of interest.[60] In political systems that foster productive accumulation, the provision of important public goods creates a basis for broad popular support of the state, its central rules, and core policies. Among society at large, economically important groups abide by formal institutions and policy incentives. This cooperation is founded upon an essential social compact. Developmental states, founded upon comparatively expansive social coalitions, are better able to solve the coordination problems inherent in the market economy, thereby engendering investment and growth.[61]

By contrast, predatory systems embody narrow coalitions and a weak basis for institutional development. Personalized authoritarian governments are sustained by a circle of military elites, government retainers, political allies, business cronies, and constituencies of support among client groups. In these circumstances, the informal rules of clientelist politics—an instrumental relation of loyalty in return for largesse—dominate the political and economic system.[62] These regimes provide few public goods, instead furnishing discrete benefits on a contingent and often arbitrary basis. The vagaries of the institutional setting preclude investment and productive accumulation.

A central challenge in effecting economic change is to weaken or dismantle social coalitions associated with predatory or rent-distributing systems, and to forge new alliances around productive investment and competitive markets. In the strategic interaction of state and society, the political regime is clearly the dominant element in fostering such change. Institutional reform is often supplied by the state, as regimes attempt to restructure government functions and to shift their base of support in favor of a reform agenda. Successful reform projects usually bear the stamp of a strong executive with a sustained commitment to change, and leaders seek to refashion societal interests in the pursuit of new economic strategies. Absent a basic commitment to change on the part of state elites, the possibilities for introducing new institutional arrangements are highly constrained.[63] The pressures arising from social groups and the accommodation of popular sectors can also be important in achieving a new com-

60. Bruce Bueno de Mesquita, Alastair Smith, Randolph M. Siverson, and James D. Morrow, *The Logic of Political Survival* (Cambridge: MIT Press, 2003), 101.

61. Donald K. Crone, "State, Social Elites, and Government Capacity in Southeast Asia," *World Politics* 40, no. 2 (1988): 252–68.

62. Clapham, *Third World Politics,* 55.

63. Nicolas van de Walle, *African Economies and the Politics of Permanent Crisis, 1979–1999* (New York: Cambridge University Press, 2001), 50.

pact. In many instances, popular groups create demands for better economic governance, and institutions arising from private associations or market arrangements can fill organizational deficits.[64]

Regimes seeking to expand the economy naturally seek to enlist the confidence of those groups most likely to evoke a supply response, particularly foreign firms, large domestic manufacturers, and the financial sector. In forging a producer coalition, states make credible commitments to dynamic groups or sectors. While these alliances can produce growth in the near term, they raise problems of distributional equilibrium. Small entrepreneurs, farmers, urban workers, and particular ethnic or regional communities are often excluded from—or disadvantaged by—arrangements that favor a narrow producer coalition. When the gains for producer groups are dissociated from the distributional demands of the population at large, economic downturns have a large potential to undermine the system. Producer coalitions may yield growth, yet development strategies are likely to be politically fragile in the absence of a stable distributional compact.[65]

The propensity for institutional reform and changes in economic performance is also influenced by international factors. Here I am not referring to the myriad effects of globalization, which carry general import across many countries, nor am I chiefly concerned with national position in a global division of labor, which is usually a particular circumstance. Instead, I wish to emphasize the relevance of regional position in the process of economic development. States within geopolitical regions commonly reflect similar historical experiences, international market relationships, and sometimes social structures or political regimes. These features, and the effects of transactions among neighbors, have important influences on policy choice, institutional design, and economic outcomes.[66]

The regional factor can be considered as a *neighborhood effect* that has different elements.[67] First, there is a demonstration effect within regions. Similar cultural referents, ideological origins, or nationalist identities foster likenesses in outlook among leaders and policy elites within regions. In addition, many regimes learn from the programs or strategies of their

64. Doner, "Limits of State Strength," 429.

65. Joel S. Hellman, "Winners Take All: The Politics of Partial Reform in Postcommunist Transitions," *World Politics* 50, no. 2 (1998): 233–34.

66. Barbara Stallings, ed., *Global Change, Regional Response: The New International Context of Development* (Cambridge: Cambridge University Press, 1995).

67. Peter Katzenstein, "Regionalism in Comparative Perspective," *Cooperation and Conflict* 31, no. 2: 123–59.

neighbors, especially those countries that embody particular developmental success. When trying to explain the trajectory of countries and regions, the enduring power of demonstration effects and policy learning can help to make sense of why countries adhere to particular policies or adopt certain innovations.

Second, intraregional linkages influence the choices and capacities of neighboring states. In addition to trade, they include labor migration, direct foreign investment, flexible production networks, financial flows, and membership in regional organizations. The rise of regionalism in economic and security affairs increasingly shapes behavior among proximate groups of countries. Regional market arrangements and security organizations affect the establishment of norms, the adherence to common rules and standards of conduct, and the resources available to member states in pursuit of policy goals. Where regional transactions are dense and organizations strong, states face inducements to conform to particular strategies, and they have access to supporting resources. When intraregional linkages are sparse and organizations weak, incentives for change are limited.

Finally, regions embody reputation in international markets. Transnational firms and financial and equities markets make decisions based on perceived risks and returns in particular areas. Given the problems of information in international commerce, market actors commonly make assessments based on the general reputation of a region. A favorable regional reputation can float a country's standing in international markets, even when domestic problems are apparent, while a poor regional reputation is likely to penalize even stable and conscientious states. Reputation accounts for "stickiness" in the behavior of markets and for much of the path dependence of particular regions in the world economy.

Two pertinent examples illustrate neighborhood effects. In Southeast Asia, development strategies have been significantly influenced by the successes of export-led growth models in Japan, South Korea, and Taiwan, as well as the local performance of Singapore. Japan has been a hub of investment and aid for many countries of the region, and intraregional trade accounts for a substantial proportion of the total external transactions for many states. The rise of ASEAN and more recently of APEC has provided important security and economic resources for participant states. The region benefited through much of the 1980s and 1990s from a buoyant international reputation, which brought direct investment and financial flows, and was equally buffeted by the abrupt loss of confidence in 1997, leading to the financial "contagion" and ensuing crash.

This stands in contrast to West Africa, where nationalist ideologies evoke widespread suspicion of the global economy and domestic market forces. Even in countries that have fostered market activities, such as Côte d'Ivoire, the political regime has controlled access to markets and sectors. Transactions within the region, especially recorded trade and investment, are negligible, notwithstanding a large realm of smuggling, labor migration, and other informal cross-border linkages. The principal regional organization, the Economic Community of West African States (ECOWAS), was launched as an economic integration scheme, yet it has never functioned effectively as an agent of policy coordination or regional development. Furthermore, since the 1980s a downward spiral of political instability and economic stagnation has increased the region's marginality in global markets. Poor reputation continues to hinder investment and trade, even in the face of local reforms and international initiatives to improve the region's global integration.

In sum, neighborhood effects include a set of policy and institutional options for countries, as well as the organizational and financial resources available to support particular choices. For different regions, these effects may facilitate institutional change and improved economic performance, or create hindrances to reform and revitalization.

CHAPTER 3

Growing Apart

Divergent Political Economies

Comparing Indonesia and Nigeria

Indonesia and Nigeria offer natural comparisons as well as marked contrasts. With populations currently estimated at 242 million and 134 million, respectively, they are large countries with crucial positions in their subregions. Indonesia encompasses an archipelago of some 16,000 islands stretching over 3,000 miles from the Pacific to the Indian Oceans. The country accounts for about 40 percent of the total population among the ten members of the Association of Southeast Asian Nations (ASEAN). Nigeria occupies a contiguous territory roughly 750 miles by 600 miles in West Africa, fronted by the Gulf of Guinea in the Atlantic Ocean. Within the sixteen countries in the Economic Community of West African States (ECOWAS), Nigerians are somewhat more than half the regional population.

Both countries reflect impressive cultural diversity, with postcolonial boundaries incorporating a wide array of ethnic, linguistic, and religious communities. Indonesia encompasses approximately two hundred distinct ethnic or language groups as well as three broad religious traditions: Islam, Christianity, and Hinduism. In many respects the country reflects a dominant cultural character, since its people are primarily speakers of Bahasa Indonesia (a Malay derivative) and about 87 percent are Muslim. At least 45 percent of Indonesians are Javanese, a proportion that far exceeds the next largest group (the Sundanese, about 14 percent). The concentration of regional, linguistic, and religious identities should not obscure the important role of minority communities in the country's political and social affairs, especially such areas as Aceh (north Sumatra), Riau (central Sumatra), East Timor, Irian Jaya (West Papua), the Moluccas, and Bali. A perennial tension has been evident between Jakarta, the Javanese seat of power and the hub of economic growth, and the outer islands where many essential resources and economic activities are based.

These strains have been aggravated in no small degree by the high degree of political centralization during the New Order government. By the late 1990s, pressures for autonomy or independence accumulated in several areas (notably in Aceh, Irian Jaya, and East Timor) alongside several local concentrations of religious and ethnic conflict.

Nigeria's social map is even more diverse. Estimates of Nigeria's cultural communities vary greatly, though most accept the figure of 250 ethnolinguistic groups as a benchmark. Given the problems of sketchy census data and difficulties of categorization, some observers reckon as many as 400 distinct cultural identities in Nigeria. In terms of ethnicity and language there is significant dominance by three principal groups, who together make up about two-thirds of the national population. The Hausa-Fulani (commonly regarded as a commingled or "hyphenated" identity), concentrated in the northwestern area of the country, constitute about 29 percent of population: the southwestern Yoruba account for 21 percent: and the southeastern Igbo, roughly 18 percent.[1] Historically these major groups form ethnic and regional identities that shape important features of national politics. Many cultural minorities are politically assertive as well. Smaller communities such as the Tiv, Edo, Ijaw, Ibibio-Efik, Kanuri, and Nupe have attained greater weight through administrative and constitutional changes.

In terms of religious identity, it is commonly estimated that perhaps half Nigeria's population is Muslim, with the greatest concentration in the northern part of the country. About 45 percent are nominal Christians, with the southeastern portions of the country being almost exclusively Christian and the Yoruba people reflecting an equivalent balance among the two religious traditions.[2] A residual 5 percent of Nigerians are regarded as practicing "traditional" (i.e., animist) religion, though it must be noted that areas of faith are often ambiguous. Ethnic lines of cleavage have frequently dominated the popular imagination in Nigeria, though ethnicity and language often merge with regional identities. Religious divisions, spurred by various factors, have become increasingly prominent within the past two decades. Nigeria, like Indonesia, has in recent years experienced a flurry of diverse local conflicts with multiple sources of contestation.

The obvious distinctions in demography and cultural patterns between the two cases should not detract from a basic comparative obser-

---

1. Larry Diamond, "Nigeria: The Uncivic Society and the Descent into Praetorianism," in Larry Diamond, J. Linz, and S. M. Lipset, eds., *Politics in Developing Countries: Comparing Experiences with Democracy,* 2d ed. (Boulder: Lynne Rienner, 1995), 420.
2. David Laitin, *Hegemony and Culture* (Chicago: University of Chicago Press, 1986), 8.

vation that Indonesia and Nigeria constitute heterogeneous societies with substantial distributional pressures from disparate communities and groups. This is manifest in conflicts over fiscal policy, development spending, and other economic measures, along with institutional choices about the constitution, administration, and electoral systems. Minority representation in the central government is fundamentally at issue in both countries, as are the relations of the central state and diverse subnational communities.

A third important parallel between the countries is their global position as resource exporters. Prior to the 1970s these were primarily agrarian economies, with the largest portion of national output coming from the rural sector, and the bulk of exports composed of unprocessed agricultural products. In the era immediately following independence, they embodied an "open economy" in which primary commodities generated essential revenues, most manufactured and intermediate products were imported, and trade taxes provided the fiscal engine of the state. With the oil price increases of 1973, petroleum production transformed both economies. Hydrocarbon activities quickly became the major source of hard currency and state revenues, while the magnitude of these resources grew precipitously. Indonesia's oil and gas sales grew from about 10 percent of export proceeds in 1965 to 75 percent a decade later, and from 21 percent of public revenues in 1971 to 62 percent in 1981.[3] For Nigeria, oil increased from 26 percent of total exports in 1965 to 93 percent by 1974 and has persisted at this level or higher until the present day. Petroleum exports contributed 7 percent of government revenues in 1965, growing to 82 percent in 1974.[4] This sector has subsequently provided at least two-thirds of public revenues.

Both countries are important global energy exporters, with their economies highly sensitive to trends in world oil and gas markets. Indonesia and Nigeria may also be likened by political regime, as both countries were dominated by authoritarian governments for most of the period under consideration. General Soeharto's assumption of executive powers in March 1966 was almost concurrent with Nigeria's first coup in January of that year. The New Order regime in Indonesia evolved from a military government into a nominally civilian system with institutionalized military participation. Notwithstanding the efforts to contrive a multiple-party system and an electoral schedule, the Soeharto regime was funda-

---

3. Hal Hill, *The Indonesian Economy since 1966* (Cambridge: Cambridge University Press, 1996), 46.

4. Scott R. Pearson, *Petroleum and the Nigerian Economy* (Stanford: Stanford University Press, 1969), 73; Tom Forrest, *Politics and Economic Development in Nigeria,* 2d ed. (Boulder: Westview, 1995), 134.

mentally nondemocratic, as they restricted competition and fundamental political rights.

In Nigeria, following the initial coup d'état, the country had a succession of military governments, save for a brief civilian interregnum from 1979 through 1983 under the Second Republic. Over the four decades covered by this study, Nigeria experienced six successful coups and several attempted seizures by military factions. Some of the resulting military governments were relatively collegial, while several, notably those of Generals Ibrahim Babangida and Sani Abacha, were highly personalized. Nigeria's authoritarian regimes varied with regard to civil and political rights, although all suspended the constitution and recessed most elected civilian institutions. Once again, the peculiarities of the two cases do not efface the decades-long experience of military involvement in politics, restrictions on competition and participation, and nonaccountable executive power.

Finally, the regional preeminence of the two countries forms an important point of comparison. These countries loom large in the fortunes of their subregions, and their course of economic and political development is consequential for their neighbors. The geographic and demographic positions have already been noted, to which may be added the relative size of their economies. In terms of raw proportions, Indonesia would seem to be less prominent, as it provided about one-fifth of ASEAN's combined 1999 output, while Nigeria generated half of the gross domestic product among ECOWAS states. These figures are not especially revealing, since they tell little about the array of linkages within regional economies. Indonesia is embedded in a nexus of trade, investment, and labor migration with its neighbors. Its economic performance and political stability are of significant concern not only within Southeast Asia but also for Asian trade and investment partners such as Japan.

Nigeria is an anchor for the West Africa subregion, as it dwarfs its neighbors in population, economic magnitude, and political influence. Nigeria appears far less integrated with its ECOWAS neighbors, as there is a limited degree of recorded trade or investment among these countries. Again, the formal record is deceiving because it overlooks the substantial unrecorded transactions in West Africa, not only in trade but also labor migration and investment. Nigeria's widely recognized dominance in regional security affairs also bolsters the country's standing.

Historical Junctures

These structural features—population, diversity, resources, political regime, and international position—do not exhaust the comparison. The two countries also show likenesses in their historical evolution, especially a series of important junctures that have marked their odyssey since independence. As a starting point, the legacy of colonial rule is worthy of mention. Many aspects of the colonial experience evidently differed among the two countries, as will be seen in greater detail. The Netherlands was engaged in Indonesia for three and a half centuries and held sway as colonial ruler for 150 years. Independence was formally attained in 1949 through a four-year armed struggle.

British control in Nigeria was not fully consolidated until the early twentieth century, and colonial rule ended five decades later through a brief process of negotiation culminating in 1960. There are, nonetheless, important similarities in the character of colonial rule, notably the weak foundations for postindependent economic development. In both countries, the colonial powers established a commodity export regime based upon local small-scale producers, along with plantation agriculture and foreign-operated mining activities. Colonial rule brought modest expansion of productivity in agriculture, a middling growth of manufacturing, and only a limited development of physical infrastructure and human capital. In contrast to the legacy of Japanese colonialism in South Korea and Taiwan, which significantly expanded productive capabilities and export capacity in those economies, European rule had a much less propitious developmental impact in Indonesia and Nigeria.[5]

In postindependent Indonesia and Nigeria, the collapse of fledgling democratic governments in the mid-1960s was accompanied in both cases by large-scale political violence, creating a pivotal moment in the development of each country. Sukarno's "Guided Democracy" broke down in 1965 amid an economic shambles and a rising tide of ideological and sectarian conflict. A spasm of political violence claimed roughly half a million victims, mainly those associated with the Indonesian Communist Party, within a matter of months. Authoritarian rulers under the New Order inaugurated a system of dual power among military and civilian institutions. The regime terminated the radical populist experimentation of Sukarno and adopted a more orthodox macroeconomic stance.

Nigeria's parliamentary First Republic weathered a series of crises in the early 1960s, each punctuated by growing unrest and violence, until military officers stepped in at the dawn of 1966. The initial coup was followed

5. Anne Booth, *The Indonesian Economy in the Nineteenth and Twentieth Centuries: A History of Missed Opportunities* (New York: St. Martin's Press, 1998), 5–7; Atul Kohli, "Where Do High-Growth Political Economies Come From? The Japanese Lineage of Korea's Developmental State," in Meredith Woo-Cumings, ed., *The Developmental State* (Ithaca: Cornell University Press, 1999).

by a countercoup and rising ethnic violence, cresting with the attempt by Igbo rebels to secede under the banner of Biafra in 1967. In the ensuing civil war, at least a million people died from combat and starvation. The conflict, ending in 1970, had two important legacies. First, it essentially precluded secessionist challenges in subsequent decades and demonstrated the resolve of Nigeria's elites to maintain the political unity of the federation. Second, it strengthened a group of senior technocrats who favored selective state intervention in the economy and an assertive nationalist economic stance. In short, Indonesia and Nigeria almost simultaneously weathered political and economic transitions.

The oil boom was another pivotal experience for the two countries. As noted earlier, the OPEC-inspired price hikes of 1973–74 provided a windfall for the leading petroleum exporters, recasting both the scale and structure of their economies. The gross domestic product of Indonesia and Nigeria nearly doubled (in nominal terms) from 1973 to 1975, and more than doubled again by 1980. Government spending accelerated at an even faster rate. The proportion of public investment in Indonesia's GDP rose from 5.3 percent in 1973 to 10.5 percent in 1981, and showed a sixfold increase in Nigeria (from 2.6 percent to 15.4 percent) during the same period.[6] The new resources dramatically shifted goals and prospects, as leaders perceived an opportunity to rapidly modernize their economies. Both governments embarked on ambitious agendas of state-sponsored industrialization, infrastructure expansion, and the delivery of social provisions. These programs were framed by a widespread expectation that oil could serve as an enduring source of economic growth.

The resource windfalls also gave rise to many liabilities. A syndrome of fiscal changes, price distortions, and institutional effects that commonly afflict resource-exporting states came into play in both Indonesia and Nigeria. Resource rents accrued directly to the central government, fostering a marked centralization of fiscal policy and a growth in the economic role of the state. Furthermore, government revenues were essentially divorced from a domestic tax base, which reduced accountability and dampened incentives to promote local production. In the "Dutch disease" effect, large resource windfalls cause a shift in relative prices as the value of domestic nontradables (e.g., construction, services) increases relative to tradables accompanied by an appreciation of the exchange rate.[7] The

6. World Bank, *Accelerated Growth in Sub-Saharan Africa* (Washington, DC: World Bank, 1981).

7. J. Peter Neary and Sweder van Wijnbergen, "Natural Resources and the Macroeconomy: A Theoretical Framework," in J. Peter Neary and Sweder van Winjbergen, eds., *Natural Resources and the Macroeconomy* (Oxford: Basil Blackwell, 1986), 16–17; Alan Gelb,

result is a shift in resources from the tradable sectors to nontradables, with consequences for productive activities such as agriculture and manufacturing. A real appreciation of the currency tends to discourage nonoil export activities while providing stronger incentives to import, thus aggravating problems in the balance of payments.

Apart from the syndrome of statism (or *dirigisme*), price effects, and resource shifts, oil windfalls are also associated with a number of common problems including fiscal instability, poor financial oversight, wasteful expenditure, growing indebtedness, and heightened corruption. Resource-exporting economies are often slow to adjust to exogenous shocks, as spending commitments are relatively inflexible, and expectations lingering from the windfall can blind policymakers to the possibility of significant drops in revenue. These challenges influenced both countries under study during the boom era, although in differing degrees.

Just as the oil boom of the 1970s lifted both economies on a tempestuous wave, the recession in oil markets and the growth of debt pressures in the 1980s prompted an economic slump. Beginning in 1982 international petroleum prices declined substantially, as did OPEC's market share in the face of new exporters. This shock was more acute for Nigeria than for Indonesia, although both countries witnessed significant reductions in revenue during the course of the 1980s. In addition, previously incurred debt obligations accumulated rapidly, as new price shocks raised the nominal value of foreign obligations. Indonesia's foreign debt comprised 27 percent of its GDP in 1982, climbing to 69 percent in 1987. Nigeria's debt burden rocketed during the same period from 24 percent to 124 percent of GDP.[8] In both countries decreasing revenues and rising debt service led to abatement of expenditures, compression of imports, and a slowdown in growth. Nigeria's crisis was earlier and deeper, but Indonesia also experienced sagging performance. The downturn created substantial pressure for immediate macroeconomic stabilization and longer-term structural reforms. The two countries showed different propensities to adjust to adverse shocks during this period, but both grappled with orthodox stabilization measures and broader initiatives to liberalize their economies.

Finally, transitions to democracy have recently unfolded in parallel

---

"Adjustment to Windfall Gains: A Comparative Analysis of Oil Exporting Countries," in Neary and Wijnbergen, ed., *Natural Resources and the Macroeconomy,* 76–77; Michael Ross, "The Political Economy of the Resource Curse," *World Politics* 51, no. 2 (1999): 306–7.

8. World Bank, *World Debt Tables 1989–90: External Debt of Developing Countries,* 2d supp. (Washington, DC: World Bank, 1990): 38, 54.

fashion. The departure of authoritarian leaders set into motion an almost identical sequence of events. Both were succeeded by transitional figures drawn from the old regime. In each instance, the successors eased restrictions on political and civil liberties, released prominent detainees, and embarked upon a program of transition to democratic rule. Though initially greeted with considerable distrust, leaders in each country gradually attained credibility and presided over a schedule of party reform, electoral revisions, legal changes, and balloting for local and national offices. The incumbents both stepped aside from the presidential race, allowing independent candidates to win the executive. The political transition processes were monitored by international and domestic observers who sanctioned the outcome of elections. The new democratic governments have been burdened by the institutional legacies of preceding regimes, and they face acute challenges of economic revitalization and national stability.

Explaining Divergence and Convergence

A number of different explanations help to account for the comparative developmental performance of Indonesia and Nigeria. Three middle-range approaches have been applied to these cases. In previous work by economists and political scientists, they have been compared as hydrocarbon exporters.[9] From this perspective, economic outcomes are influenced by the structure of the economy and by a set of political consequences ensuing from the energy sector. Energy exporters commonly experience fiscal centralization, rapid growth in discretionary state revenues, changes in relative prices, and a lagging performance of nonoil productive activities. Politically, the analysis holds that oil revenues reduce the accountability of state elites and dispose them toward strategies of distribution rather than capital formation. Windfalls induce shortsightedness among policymakers, and the sudden influx of resources undermines institutions of economic management and revenue extraction outside the energy sector.[10] In consequence, governments are poorly positioned to counteract

9. Brian Pinto, "Nigeria during and after the Oil Boom: A Policy Comparison with Indonesia," *World Bank Economic Review* 1, no. 3 (1987); Alan Gelb, *Oil Windfalls: Blessing or Curse?* (Oxford: Oxford University Press for the World Bank, 1988); Terry Lynn Karl, *The Paradox of Plenty* (Berkeley: University of California Press, 1997); and D. L Bevan, Paul Collier, and J. W. Gunning, *The Political Economy of Poverty, Equity and Growth in Nigeria and Indonesia, 1950–86* (Oxford: Oxford University Press for the World Bank, 1999).

10. Karl, *The Paradox of Plenty;* D. Michael Shafer, *Winners and Losers: How Sectors Shape the Developmental Prospects of States* (Ithaca: Cornell University Press, 1994); and Ross, "Political Economy of the Resource Curse," 320–21.

the adverse economic effects of oil exports, and they commonly adopt policies that limit growth and competitiveness.

Sectoral analysis helps shed light on important structural problems and policy challenges in Indonesia and Nigeria, but it is insufficient to explain their divergent economic performance. The burgeoning role of hydrocarbon exports was the dominant theme in the economic development of both states during the 1970s and 1980s, and major economic shocks during this period arose from the energy sector. In addition, both countries showed some of the expected effects of resource windfalls, notably centralization, growing corruption, an expanding state sector, and vulnerability to external market fluctuations. Indonesia, however, is an outlier among oil exporters, as it sustained a realistic exchange rate, controlled inflation, invested in agriculture, encouraged manufacturing, and achieved considerable economic diversification, all of which contributed to a trajectory of growth. The Indonesians adopted policy measures to counteract some of the liabilities of energy exports, choices reflecting a developmental impulse within the state elite. By the 1990s, when manufactured exports exceeded oil and gas as a source of revenue, it was no longer the case that hydrocarbons were the economy's "leading sector." Consequently, Indonesia does not fit neatly within models of the Dutch disease or the dysfunctional "petro-state."[11]

Nigeria, on the other hand, presents a textbook case of the petroleum syndrome in both its economic and political dimensions. In one multi-country study of windfall effects, Nigeria ranked among the economies with the greatest distortions from the resource boom.[12] Many observers have linked Nigeria's poor economic record to the perverse effects of the oil sector.[13] The variation in economic performance among these countries, and the changing economic structure among the cases, suggest that a focus on resource exports does not fully capture their comparative experience.

Another vantage is to see these countries in terms of distributional politics. As populous, heterogeneous states they confront distinctive problems of equity and legitimacy that bear significantly on their propensities

11. Karl, *Paradox of Plenty;* Kiren Aziz Chaudhry, *The Price of Wealth: Economies and Institutions in the Middle East* (Ithaca: Cornell University Press, 1997).

12. Gelb, "Adjustment to Windfall Gains," 81.

13. A representative sample includes Forrest, *Politics and Economic Development in Nigeria;* Eghosa Osaghae, *Crippled Giant: Nigeria since Independence* (Bloomington: Indiana University Press, 1998); Michael Watts, "Agriculture and Oil-Based Accumulation: Stagnation or Transformation?" in Michael Watts, ed., *State, Oil, and Agriculture in Nigeria* (Berkeley: Institute of International Studies, 1987); and Sayre Schatz, *Nigerian Capitalism* (Berkeley: University of California Press, 1977).

for growth. Several writers have argued that distributional pressures in large plural countries may impede growth.[14] Ethnic and regional groups often constitute effective distributional coalitions, since cultural affinities and networks help to surmount the collective action problems necessary for effective lobbying. Further, governments in heterogeneous societies with large inequalities are especially concerned to avoid destabilizing conflicts over distribution. Consequently, communal groups have significant leverage in pressing for public allocations and the provision of rents.[15] These competing interests create disparate claims on economic policy and reduce the capacity of government to carry out long-term policies for growth. Distributional pressures impel governments toward populist policies as well as the use of patronage, which dissipate resources through expedient disbursements and current consumption rather than marshaling capital for investment and productive expansion. Resource exporters with sizable populations have no special advantages in meeting distributional demands, since the per capita value of any revenue windfall is fairly low. Indonesia and Nigeria are both "high absorbers" of capital (contrasted with such "capital surplus" economies as Saudi Arabia or Libya).[16]

Still, the large autonomous revenue base afforded by mineral rents does increase the discretionary resources available to rulers, fostering a greater propensity toward patronage politics and populist measures as means of securing legitimacy. Abundant external revenues also tend to intensify the focus of rent-seeking groups on the state. The centralization of state largesse arising from revenue windfalls clearly aggravates the problems of distributional politics.

The framework of distributional politics calls attention to basic problems in the political economies of Indonesia and Nigeria, and it offers a window into the hazards of economic policy-making under democratic regimes. Once again, however, the distinctive experiences of the two countries suggest that this perspective has limited explanatory value. During

14. William Easterly and Ross Levine, "Africa's Growth Tragedy: Policies and Ethnic Divisions," *Quarterly Journal of Economics* 112, no. 4 (1997): 1203–51; Mancur Olson, *The Rise and Decline of Nations* (New Haven: Yale University Press, 1982); Richard A. Joseph, *Democracy and Prebendal Politics in Nigeria: The Rise and Fall of the Second Republic* (Cambridge: Cambridge University Press, 1987); Pranab Bardhan, *The Political Economy of Development in India* (Delhi: Oxford University Press, 1984).

15. Robert Bates, "Modernization, Ethnic Competition, and the Rationality of Politics in Africa," in Donald Rothchild, ed., *State versus Ethnic Claims: African Policy Dilemmas* (Boulder: Westview, 1982).

16. Terry Lynn Karl characterizes such populous resource-exporting states as "capital deficient"; see Karl, *Paradox of Plenty*, 18–19. See also Michael Watts, "Introduction," in Watts, ed., *State, Oil, and Agriculture*, 9.

the period under study, Indonesian rulers pursued a strategy through which economic expansion was broadly compatible with improved distribution. The New Order regime sustained strong growth for at least two decades while significantly diminishing poverty and maintaining one of the more equitable patterns of income distribution in the developing world.[17] Under the authoritarian government, leaders were able to politically contain some distributional pressures, notably demands from communities in the outer islands; entreaties from *pribumi* (indigenous) interests for greater equity, viz., the ethnic Chinese minority; and periodic upheavals among students and the urban poor. These tensions were resurgent in the wake of the economic crisis and democratic transition.

Nigeria, by contrast, vividly embodies the tension between growth and distribution. The country had anemic growth during this period along with increasing poverty and worsening inequality. Ethnic competition and the palliative strategies of political leaders form a prominent theme in Nigeria's developmental failure. The contention among the three large ethnolinguistic groups has been augmented by rising demands from selected minorities and lobbying by organized labor and domestic manufacturers. Nigerian governments have responded to these pressures with subsidies and restrictive pricing policies, ad hoc distributional programs, patronage politics, and endemic corruption, all of which have deadening effects on economic performance. Distributional contention has been more freewheeling and volatile under democratic politics, and more concentrated (as well as more predatory) under military rulers. The recent return to democratic rule opens the door to pressures from social groups and sectional lobbies, raising once again the specter of policy impasse and slow growth. Nigeria's high level of inequality suggests that distributional politics could be more corrosive of democratic stability than in Indonesia, though this is a proposition that awaits further evidence.

A third analytical approach emphasizes the nature of state and regime in these countries as a guide to developmental outcomes. In particular, Weberian models of patrimonialism have been applied to analyses of politics and governance in each case.[18] In the classic model of patrimonial rule, power is concentrated and personalized, as the state becomes an extension of the ruler's household.[19] With few formal restraints on the pre-

17. Edgardo Campos and Hilton L. Root, *The Key to the Asian Miracle: Making Shared Growth Credible* (Washington, DC: Brookings Institution, 1996).

18. Joseph, *Democracy and Prebendal Politics in Nigeria;* Harold Crouch, *The Army and Politics in Indonesia* (Ithaca: Cornell University Press, 1978).

19. Marc Bloch, *Feudal Society,* vol. 1 (Chicago: University of Chicago Press, 1961), 241–42; Max Weber, *Economy and Society,* vol. 1 (Berkeley: University of California Press, 1978), 231–36.

rogatives of the executive, decision making is often arbitrary and opaque, and the ruler exerts discretionary control over resources and institutions. The distinction between public and private resources is effaced, as leaders have broad leeway in appropriating or dispensing state funds, providing employment and contracts, or otherwise regulating market opportunities.

Contemporary analysts have used the term *neopatrimonialism* to distinguish the historical forms of "pure" patrimonial rule discussed by such writers as Weber and Bloch from current forms of personal domination in many developing countries.[20] Neopatrimonial regimes maintain formal aspects of constitutional order, bureaucratic organization, and legal procedure (often inherited from a colonial regime), yet beneath this institutional veneer power is personalized and discretionary. The executive constitutes the regime through a web of personal allies and retainers, governing through patron-client ties, loyalist networks, and the disbursal of largesse. This arrangement can provide considerable stability to a regime, as is evident from the longevity of such rulers as Mobutu, Somoza, Marcos, or Stroessner. Yet these systems are largely incapable of fostering economic development, as they furnish lax management of public finances, pursue capricious political interventions into markets, fail to provide a rule of law, and generally lack constraints on the predatory impulses of rulers.

Bringing in the concept of neopatrimonialism raises two questions: How well does the model fit the case? And how well does the model explain economic performance? The concept of neopatrimonial rule certainly captures essential features of the Soeharto regime in Indonesia. Under the New Order, power was progressively centralized in the hands of the executive, and Soeharto steadily cleared away hindrances to his authority. Although the military held a prominent institutional position in the regime, ABRI did not impose accountability on the ruler. Other leading institutions, especially the party system and the legislative bodies, developed as props for the regime rather than independent elements of government. The judiciary had no independence or capacity to challenge the leadership, and the civil service was enlisted as a political arm of the regime. Soeharto cultivated a network of allies, loyalists, and cronies, initially drawn from the military, the ethnic Chinese community, and other

20. Christopher Clapham, *Private Patronage and Public Power: Political Clientelism in the Modern State* (New York: St. Martin's Press, 1982), 198; Clapham, *Third World Politics* (Madison: University of Wisconsin Press, 1985), 48–49; Michael Bratton and Nicolas van de Walle, "Neopatrimonial Regimes and Political Transitions in Africa," *World Politics* 46, no. 4 (1994); Peter M. Lewis, "Economic Statism, Private Capital, and the Dilemmas of Accumulation in Nigeria," *World Development* 22, no. 3 (1994): 439–40.

elites, and increasingly centered on his own family. The president lavished resources and commercial opportunities on his inner circle, and he accumulated a family fortune estimated in the billions (or tens of billions) of dollars. In the wake of Soeharto's rule, a palpable breakdown of institutions attests to the personal character of governance and the brittle organizational foundations of the New Order state.

For much of the period under review here, Nigeria reflected the neopatrimonial model less perfectly, as many regimes tended to be less personalized and more decentralized. Furthermore, Nigeria arguably retained greater institutional constraints on the executive through an independent judiciary and the structures of federalism. Nigeria is frequently described in terms of pervasive corruption and diffuse clientelist politics, a pattern captured in Richard Joseph's discussion of prebendalism.[21] The appropriation of state offices and revenues by rival communal elites gives rise to a weak institutional framework that undermines formal rules and organizations. Until the mid-1980s, however, the system did not reflect the hallmarks of individual dictatorship. This changed under successive military rulers, Ibrahim Babangida and Sani Abacha, who consolidated personal domination and largely swept aside formal restraints on their power. These leaders fomented the degeneration of major state institutions such as the military, the civil service, the judiciary, and the educational system.[22] They narrowed their ruling circles, wielded more ruthless tactics against perceived opponents, and amassed enormous personal fortunes. Although neither leader achieved longevity in office, the effect of these regimes was to move Nigeria closer to a "typical" neopatrimonial system of governance.

This observation raises concerns about analytical utility. Does this perspective on the state and the nature of governance account for variations in economic performance? Here we encounter a puzzle, as the model of neopatrimonialism predicts a high degree of state predation, with correspondingly poor developmental outcomes, yet Indonesia's experience appears to belie these expectations. There is little question that the Soeharto regime in Indonesia reflected the political elements of neopatrimonial rule, yet the New Order presided over considerable growth and struc-

21. See, for instance, Diamond, "Nigeria: The Uncivic Society"; Joseph, *Democracy and Prebendal Politics in Nigeria;* Gavin Williams and Terisa Turner, "Nigeria," in John Dunn, ed., *West African States: Failure and Promise* (Cambridge: Cambridge University Press, 1978); Forrest, *Politics and Economic Development in Nigeria;* and Osaghae, *Crippled Giant.*

22. Peter M. Lewis, "From Prebendalism to Predation: The Political Economy of Decline in Nigeria," *Journal of Modern African Studies* 34, no. 1 (1996): 79–103.

tural transformation of the economy. The economic dissipation anticipated by the model of neopatrimonialism did not come about, at least not
for a considerable period. This evident contradiction points to some limitations in analyses of the predatory state.

The model of neopatrimonialism accurately depicts the interaction of
formal and informal institutions in particular regimes, and it portrays a
consistent political logic in these systems. Outcomes, however, can only be
regarded as probabilistic. Personalized regimes have a high degree of discretion in making institutional and policy choices, and the lack of formal
restraint on rulers creates a permissive setting for self-aggrandizing
actions. This outcome is not inevitable, however, and a given ruler might
choose a strategy of encouraging growth as a means of enhancing his
power and legitimacy. Most neopatrimonial rulers do not choose this
course, but incentive structures and temperament obviously vary in different contexts. One consequence implied by the model is that economic
growth will be fragile in the absence of strong formal institutions. The
Indonesian experience thus reveals the boundaries of developmental
achievement under neopatrimonial rule, as well as the difficulties of sustaining growth through a regime transition.

With reference to Nigeria, it is evident that personal dictatorship,
while often linked to predatory behavior, is not the only source of economic failure. The country's economy foundered under a series of governments, both military and civilian, personal and collegial. It is noteworthy,
however, that the ascendance of rulers in the neopatrimonial mold
inspired a marked deterioration of both policy and institutions, with
severe consequences for growth, poverty, and equity. A chain of decline is
evident, as weak institutions facilitated the rise of personal predatory
rulers, who in turn despoiled public institutions and the economy. Nigeria's decline in the 1990s was largely contrary to the trend toward stabilization in sub-Saharan Africa. The depredations of public finances, state
institutions, and international reputation create a burdensome inheritance
for future economic performance.

Analyzing Indonesia and Nigeria

Leading middle-range theories in comparative political economy fail to
account for disparate patterns of economic performance in Indonesia and
Nigeria. I adopt an institutionalist approach to the study of economic performance in these countries. A better explanation of politics and economic
development in two salient cases can yield inferences with broader comparative application.

In the course of three decades, regimes in Indonesia and Nigeria pursued increasingly divergent economic policies, and the two countries achieved markedly different economic performance. These variations are noteworthy in light of similarities in their economic endowments, social structure, and political regimes. The divergence in economic outcomes can be attributed to the different abilities of these states to credibly commit to investors and producers through assurances of policy continuity and the provision of essential public goods, especially guarantees of property rights. The discrepancy in state roles is traced to distinctions in leadership, social coalitions, and the regional context of development strategy. A brief overview of politics and development in each country highlights these factors.

Indonesia

By most measures, Indonesia's economic achievements under the New Order regime (1966–98) were impressive. In 1965, the year in which the Sukarno regime collapsed and the country was engulfed by political violence, Indonesia registered per capita income of about 600 dollars, virtually no economic growth, a poverty rate approaching 60 percent of the population, and inflation in excess of 1,100 percent. Over the next three decades, the economy grew by more than 6 percent a year on average, and per capita income expanded by nearly 5 percent annually in real terms. Average inflation was below 20 percent, remaining under 10 percent for the most part since the early 1980s. Less than a sixth of the population was below the poverty line on the eve of the 1997 economic crisis.[23] This was not only a remarkable recovery from the collapse of the 1960s, but a distinctive record of growth and poverty reduction within the developing world.

The personal role of Soeharto weighs heavily in explaining this course of development. As the apex and architect of the New Order, Soeharto asserted priorities, fostered coalitions, backed policies, and nurtured institutions that made possible these sustained economic accomplishments.[24] He adhered to a core vision of economic change and for many years played a crucial role in setting goals and allowing for course corrections in eco-

23. Asep Suryahadi, Sudarno Sumarto, Yusuf Suharso, and Lant Pritchett, *The Evolution of Poverty During the Crisis in Indonesia, 1996–99,* Policy, Research Working Paper no. WPS 2435 (Washington, DC: World Bank, 2000), 27.

24. Hamish McDonald, *Suharto's Indonesia* (Victoria: Fontana/Collins, 1980); Michael Vatikiotis, *Indonesian Politics under Suharto* (London: Routledge, 1993); Hal Hill, ed., *Indonesia's New Order: The Dynamics of Socio-Economic Transformation* (Sydney: Allen and Unwin, 1993).

nomic management. Yet he also had an uneven relationship with the economic team that authored central policies, often displaying ambivalence about economic strategy and oversight.[25] Moreover, Soeharto's regime created imbalances and problems in Indonesian development that were pivotal in the collapse of the New Order's economic model. An understanding of his motives and tactics is essential to Indonesia's economic saga.

In his spare autobiographical comments, Soeharto professed that his concern for development arose from his childhood in rural Java.[26] This idiosyncratic explanation raises the obvious question of why other leaders with rural origins—in Indonesia as well as other countries, including most of sub-Saharan Africa—should reflect less devotion to the agrarian masses. Another line of explanation has emphasized leadership cohesion and stability, which presumably extended the perspective of policymakers and allowed for more ambitious development planning. Since these features of the regime emerged over time, however, it is important to avoid post hoc analysis in accounting for the initial stance of the New Order as well as the sources of continuity in policy and institutions. Along with his internal aims and convictions, the set of opportunities and challenges in which Soeharto operated had a crucial impact on the course of his leadership.

The New Order emerged from the political and economic collapse of the Sukarno regime. During the period of Guided Democracy (1957–65), Sukarno's political experimentation, hybrid coalitions, and radical populist measures culminated in ideological polarization, policy stalemate, institutional disarray, and rapid economic decline. In October 1965 a coup was attempted by officers with the apparent backing of the Indonesian Communist Party (PKI). The revolt was quelled, and General Soeharto emerged at the head of the prevailing military command. Over the next several months the new leadership presided over the virtual liquidation of the PKI (then the world's largest nongoverning communist party), in the course of which at least a half million people were killed, mainly on Java and Bali. Soeharto assumed de facto executive powers in March 1966, steadily consolidating his control over the government and the state during the next two years.[27]

25. William R. Liddle, "The Relative Autonomy of the Third World Politician: Soeharto and Indonesian Economic Development in Comparative Perspective," *International Studies Quarterly* 35, no. 4 (1991): 403–27.

26. McDonald, *Suharto's Indonesia;* Soeharto, *Soeharto: My Thoughts, Words, and Deeds* (Jakarta: PT Citra Lamtoro Gung Persada, 1991).

27. Adam Schwarz, *A Nation in Waiting: Indonesia in the 1990s* (Boulder: Westview, 1994); John Bresnan, *Managing Indonesia: The Modern Political Economy* (New York: Columbia University Press, 1993); M. C. Ricklefs, *A History of Modern Indonesia since c. 1300* (Palo Alto: Stanford University Press, 1981).

The features of this initial crisis shaped the contours of the regime. Soeharto displayed an abiding concern for economic instability, especially the reappearance of hyperinflation, along with deep antipathies toward communism, radical challenges emanating from the countryside, and separatist pressures from the outer islands. The PKI as an organization was eliminated, yet the demands of a diverse, impoverished, and mobilized population were not as easily suppressed. After moving quickly to stabilize the economy, the new government charted a course of economic policy that would revive investment, spur growth, and furnish benefits for broad segments of the countryside and the regions. Economic development was integral to the strategy of political consolidation.

Through the New Order, Soeharto crafted a system of authoritarian capitalism in which political centralism and coercion were intertwined with efforts to expand the economy and incorporate popular sectors.[28] The regime restricted political space, employed high levels of repression, centralized authority, expanded its bureaucratic reach and penetrative capabilities, aggressively sought to establish policy credibility, encouraged an important sphere of market activity, and provided incentives for investment. This strategy was facilitated by a relatively coherent and secure leadership group within ABRI (the Indonesian armed forces) and most importantly by an alliance with a small circle of U.S.-trained Indonesian economists who became known as the Berkeley mafia. These advisers had the confidence of the president, a mandate for engineering economic recovery, and insulation from political pressures and demands.[29] A strong core coalition and effective technocratic delegation were early features of the New Order.

Institutionally, the regime employed an assortment of commitment devices through both formal and informal means. Among the earliest efforts to mark a new direction in economic policy was the meeting of donors and creditors through the Inter-Governmental Group on Indonesia (IGGI), in which the government presented its strategy and sought reciprocal pledges from international actors. Soeharto's assumption of executive powers established a new locus of policy authority, which reduced the possibility of reversals. The regime's initial stabilization program included a "balanced budget" rule governing state expenditures, a devaluation of the rupiah, and full currency convertibility. The government abruptly lifted major restrictions on trade, investment, and capital move-

28. Jeffrey Winters, *Power in Motion: Capital Mobility and the Indonesian State* (Ithaca: Cornell University Press, 1996).

29. Bresnan, *Managing Indonesia;* Liddle, "Relative Autonomy of the Third World Politician."

ments, signaling a decisive shift from the statist and nationalist stance of the Sukarno regime and employing lock-in mechanisms for fiscal and monetary policy as assurances of intent. Furthermore, rules on capital mobility and foreign exchange furnished a rapid exit option, offering a hedge against uncertainty.[30]

These policies were accompanied by a more uneven process of institutional development. The senior technocrats presided over key government departments including the Ministry of Finance, the Foreign Investment Board, the central bank (Bank Indonesia), and Bappenas, the central planning agency. These peak institutions of economic management developed into centers of competence within the state sector. Another relatively effective organization was Bulog, the state logistics agency responsible for inputs and marketing in the agricultural sector. Despite these important changes, it is important to keep in mind the limitations of institutional development under the New Order. The bureaucracy remained relatively inefficient and corrupt, while the judiciary and the legal system were similarly compromised.[31] The military's territorial organization permitted surveillance, control, and local access for soldiers to economic rents, but it was not a channel for improving administrative performance or the provision of services. Yet the islands of organizational change facilitated capable management at the macroeconomic level and bolstered overall confidence in policy commitments.

The coalition assembled under the New Order was essential to the early success of the regime's economic strategy.[32] Within the state, the alliance between the military and the economists provided the mainstay of policy-making. The early New Order regime was organized along bureaucratic-authoritarian lines, similar in many respects to counterparts in Latin America. The military-led government delegated economic policy authority to a small technocratic circle, who pursued an orthodox stabilization program. The regime sharply circumscribed the political arena,

30. Bruce Glassburner, "Indonesia's New Economic Policy and Its Sociopolitical Implications," in Karl D. Jackson and Lucien W. Pye, eds., *Political Power and Communications in Indonesia* (Berkeley: University of California Press, 1978); Wing Thye Woo, Bruce Glassburner, and Anwar Nasution, *Macroeconomic Policies, Crises, and Long-Run Growth: The Case of Indonesia, 1965–90* (Washington, DC: World Bank, 1995), 30.

31. Fiona Robertson-Snape, "Corruption, Collusion, and Nepotism in Indonesia," *Third World Quarterly* 20, no. 3 (1999), 592; Bresnan, *Managing Indonesia,* 154–59; Vatikiotis, *Indonesian Politics under Suharto,* 49–52.

32. See Richard Robison, *Indonesia: The Rise of Capital* (Sydney: Allen and Unwin, 1986), and Andrew J. MacIntyre, "Power, Prosperity, and Patrimonialism: Business and Government in Indonesia," in Andrew MacIntyre, ed., *Business and Government in Industrializing Asia* (Ithaca: Cornell University Press, 1994).

providing political insulation for the technocrats to implement anti-inflationary measures, fiscal retrenchment, and rationalization of external accounts. The political role of the military was elevated through the doctrine of *dwifungsi* (dual function), and their position was entrenched through two institutional mechanisms.[33] The armed forces had a quota of nonelected seats in the national legislature (DPR) and the consultative assembly (MPR). In addition, the territorial organization of ABRI served as the armature for a shadow military authority down to the village level. This arrangement, ironically Leninist in form, served the regime's initial priority of consolidating internal security while also enhancing its political reach and providing patronage outlets for military personnel. The regime also placed civil servants under the virtual control of Golkar, the central political party that became a corporatist vehicle for the government.[34]

From an economic perspective, however, the most important alliance was the relationship between Soeharto and the ethnic Chinese community.[35] Sino-Indonesians make up about 3 percent of the national population, and they have historically been an insecure minority, subject to resentment, beset by recurrent social violence, and largely excluded from political power. They have attained a disproportionately large role in the economy, however, through a strong entrepreneurial tradition and the use of extensive social networks. Beginning in the period of anticolonial resistance, segments of this community established a special relationship with the fledgling national army. Amid scarce resources, regional commanders often resorted to self-financing through the local economy, and commercial links cultivated between military leaders and ethnic Chinese entrepreneurs in the 1940s and 1950s came to the fore under the New Order.

In the *cukong* relationship between ABRI officers and ethnic Chinese entrepreneurs, the military furnished political access and security of property in return for a stake in burgeoning economic activities. Soeharto's connections with several key associates constituted the model for these affiliations.[36] A producer alliance with ethnic Chinese business elites and foreign capital provided the driving element in growth throughout much

33. R. William Liddle, "Soeharto's Indonesia: Personal Rule and Political Institutions," *Pacific Affairs* 58, no. 1 (1985): 68–90.

34. Donald Emmerson, "The Bureaucracy in Political Context: Weakness in Strength," in Karl D. Jackson and Lucien W. Pye, eds., *Political Power and Communications in Indonesia* (Berkeley: University of California Press, 1978), 108–9; Schwarz, *Nation in Waiting,* 31–32.

35. J. A. C. Mackie, "Changing Patterns of Chinese Big Business in Southeast Asia," in Ruth McVey, ed., *Southeast Asian Capitalists* (Ithaca: Cornell University Southeast Asia Program 1992), 177–82; Robison, *Indonesia: The Rise of Capital,* 271–322.

36. Harold Crouch, *The Army and Politics in Indonesia* (Ithaca: Cornell University Press, 1978), 285–87; see also Schwarz, *Nation in Waiting,* chap. 5.

of the New Order period, especially the export push and financial expansion of the 1980s and 1990s. These interests were dominant in large-scale manufacturing and banking, building diversified conglomerates with national and international presence. By the time of the crisis, it was generally estimated that Chinese interests controlled perhaps 160 of the 200 leading conglomerates and nearly two-thirds of assets in the large-scale formal sectors of the economy.[37]

The formation of social coalitions under the New Order embodied both cooperation and coercion. The authoritarian regime established a governing compact based upon the delivery of economic benefits and improved social provisions, in return for expectations of social peace and political quiescence. Popular sectors, including peasants and urban labor, were incorporated within Golkar as "functional groups," or through separate corporatist organizations certified by the regime. These organizations of control effectively constrained participation and denied a political voice for much of the population. Soeharto engineered an electoral system that set clear limits on pluralism and competition. The party system offered token (and largely symbolic) representation for Muslim interests, the ethnic Chinese community, and reform elements. Responding periodically to areas of dissatisfaction and dissent, Soeharto courted the Muslim community and sought to mollify concerns arising from indigenous capitalists, students, and regional interests. Underlying efforts at bargaining, cooptation, and incorporation, however, was a formidable security apparatus and a readiness to employ repression.

The economic strategy of the New Order was influenced and encouraged by Indonesia's regional position. Soeharto quickly distanced himself from the foreign policy stance of his predecessor, which had emphasized radical nationalism and regional confrontation. In light of Indonesia's geostrategic and economic importance, the turn toward a conservative external position yielded substantial dividends. Amid the escalating Cold War tensions in Southeast Asia, Indonesia's foreign overtures were eagerly greeted by Western donors and regional economic interests. Japan, the former occupying power, maintained significant links through aid, investment, and trade. The new regime also participated in a revival of

37. Thee Kian Wie, "Reflections on Indonesia's Emerging Industrial Nationalism," Working Paper no. 41 (Perth: Murdoch University Asia Research Centre, 1994), 7; Schwarz, *Nation in Waiting,* 99; J. A. C. Mackie, "The Indonesian Conglomerates in Regional Perspective," in Hal Hill and Terence Hull, ed., *Indonesia Assessment, 1990,* Political and Social Change Monograph 11 (Canberra: Australian National University, Research School of Pacific Studies, 1990); Hill, *Indonesian Economy since 1966,* 109–11; Bresnan, *Managing Indonesia,* 255–60.

regional organization with the establishment of the Association of Southeast Asian Nations in 1967. In the course of the next two decades, the spectacular progress of Singapore and the subsequent export-led economic ascent of Malaysia and Thailand served as both example and admonition for economic policymakers in Indonesia. The success of neighboring economies also helped to enhance the region's international reputation and to heighten Indonesia's visibility. This process was accelerated by the formation of the Asian Pacific Economic Cooperation (APEC) forum in 1989 and the subsequent transformation of global financial markets.

By the middle of the 1990s, Indonesians and foreign observers could reflect on a remarkable record of growth, structural transformation of the economy, and substantial improvements in popular incomes and welfare.[38] This legacy served to enhance the credibility of official commitments and the country's international reputation as an emerging market. Large inflows of portfolio investment and rising direct foreign investment fostered buoyant attitudes in Jakarta despite misgivings about lingering protectionism, inefficient state investments, pervasive corruption, and a looming problem of political succession. With the onset of financial crisis in October 1997, the system quickly unraveled. The reasons for this economic and political collapse are to be found in many of the same factors that explain the New Order's earlier success.

The New Order was a neopatrimonial regime revolving around the personal authority and prerogatives of Soeharto.[39] The president operated with few checks on his power, whether from state institutions, countervailing groups within the elite, or societal interests.[40] He employed patronage as a central mechanism of elite control and economic inducement, a strategy of rule that gave rise to corruption and institutional weakness. The process of capitalist expansion in Indonesia, vigorous as it was, was politically mediated and controlled by the executive.[41]

For many years, these problems were offset by Soeharto's overriding concerns for economic development, as well as fortuitous resource wind-

---

38. A. Battacharya and M. Pangestu, *The Lessons of East Asia: Indonesia Development Transformation and Public Policy* (Washington, DC: World Bank, 1993); Hal Hill, *Indonesia's Industrial Transformation* (Singapore: Institute of Southeast Asian Studies, 1997).

39. Harold Crouch, "Patrimonialism and Military Rule in Indonesia," *World Politics* 31, no. 4 (1979): 571–87: Andrew MacIntyre and J. A. C. Mackie, "Politics under the 'New Order,'" in Hal Hill, ed., *Indonesia's New Order: The Dynamics of Socio-economic Transformation* (Sydney: Allen and Unwin, 1994), 1–53.

40. Hilton Root, *Small Countries, Big Lessons: Governance and the Rise of East Asia* (Oxford: Oxford University Press for the Asian Development Bank, 1996); Liddle, "Relative Autonomy of the Third World Politician."

41. Robison, *Indonesia: The Rise of Capital;* Schwarz, *Nation in Waiting,* chaps. 5 and 6.

falls and the support of external donors. The president proved adept in charting a course for the government, building institutions of economic management and political control, balancing the fluid, often contentious interests among elites and popular sectors, and enlisting necessary international support. Viewed through the lens of principal-agent analysis, Soeharto served as a principal for state and private sector agents, requiring a modicum of investment and output in exchange for largesse and opportunity. Prodigious corruption was nonetheless bounded by expectations of performance. This form of accountability however, was highly circumstantial, lacking any basis in a rule of law. Eventually, the weakness of formal institutions and the question of executive succession raised basic questions about the durability of the New Order's economic model.

By the late 1980s there was a perceptible shift in the regime's priorities. The twilight of the Cold War substantially removed the threat of communism, and there were few salient concerns for domestic security apart from separatist pressures in East Timor and spotty regional tensions, which were for many years successfully contained by the military. After decades in power, the regime's sphere of control was well established. Economic development was less clearly associated with security imperatives than had been the case in the earlier periods. The success of the economy also bred a degree of complacency, particularly as foreign financial flows and direct investment continued to grow in spite of lingering policy problems and structural weaknesses. Most important, however, were the accumulating economic interests of Soeharto's immediate family and his key business allies in the Sino-Indonesian community. The holdings of the inner circle were largely synonymous with the leading sectors of the Indonesian economy, and Soeharto became increasingly absorbed with protecting these interests and providing further rents. The president's advancing age and myopic perspectives arising from political isolation must also have played a role. The ruler's changing concerns weakened the focus on economic management. Although the fundamentals of macroeconomic policy were preserved, the influence of the technocrats clearly waned, and there was less effective delegation to a coherent policy team. Sectoral and trade policies were rife with special preferences and arbitrary interventions. A bottleneck was apparent in advancing reform of the economy.

The changing role of leadership was accompanied by an alteration in coalitions. The regime's social base narrowed in the 1980s as the claims of the president's family and business associates gained increasing salience, along with those of loyalists in the military and the ruling party. In the early 1990s the regime sought to bolster support among the Muslim community, which had shown signs of increasing disaffection. The government also contended with growing pressures from *pribumi* (indigenous) business interests for greater equity and less favoritism toward the ethnic Chinese minority.[42] Students furnished a perennial source of dissent against corruption, inequality, and autocracy. A burgeoning middle class had a substantial stake in the stability and prosperity afforded by the New Order, yet they comprised a more assertive and outward-looking constituency that could challenge the political restrictions and economic imbalances of the regime.

In sum, the early sources of strength in Soeharto's regime—a developmentally effective elite coalition and a broadly constituted framework of popular incorporation—weakened in the decade prior to the financial crisis. Although these tensions were widely recognized at the time, few observers took them as portents of a systemic collapse.[43] Fortified by a structure of coercion and control, political maneuvers by the executive enabled the regime to weather strains in the system. The remarkably favorable trends in international markets also provided a crucial source of stability during this period.

Economic globalization, however, was also the root of vulnerability for the New Order. Indonesia's rapid export expansion and the country's integration into global capital markets not only facilitated a new economic boom but also introduced sources of instability and reduced the capacity of government for managing the system. The economy was susceptible to the 1997 contagion arising from the collapse of neighboring financial markets. Once nervous investors reconsidered the Indonesian terrain in light of regional problems, the country's weak formal institutions, opaque banking sector and corporate financial relations, and long-standing ambiguities of public finance triggered a rapid retreat from the market.[44] Eco-

42. Schwarz, *Nation in Waiting,* chaps. 5 and 6; Linda Y. C. Lim and L. A. Peter Gosling, "Strengths and Weaknesses of Minority Status for Southeast Asian Chinese at a Time of Economic Growth and Liberalization," in Daniel Chirot and Anthony Reid, eds., *Essential Outsiders: Chinese and Jews in the Modern Transformation of Southeast Asia and Central Europe* (Seattle: University of Washington Press, 1997), 297–300.

43. Hal Hill, *The Indonesian Economy in Crisis: Causes, Consequences, and Lessons* (New York: Palgrave Macmillan, 1999); and Ross McLeod, "Indonesia," in Ross H. McLeod and Ross Garnaut, eds., *East Asia in Crisis: From Being a Miracle to Needing One?* (London: Routledge, 1998), 31–32.

44. Stephan Haggard, *The Political Economy of the Asian Financial Crisis* (Washington, DC: Institute for International Economics, 2000), 15–20; Andrew MacIntyre, "Political Institutions and the Economic Crisis in Thailand and Indonesia," in T. J. Pempel, ed., *The Politics of the Asian Economic Crisis* (Ithaca: Cornell University Press, 1999), 143–47; Steven C. Radelet and Wing Thye Woo, "Indonesia: A Troubled Beginning," in Wing Thye Woo, Jeffrey D. Sachs, and Klaus Schwab, eds., *The Asian Financial Crisis: Lessons for a Resilient Asia* (Cambridge: MIT Press, 2000), 170–72.

nomic crisis, in turn, fractured the implicit governing compact of the regime and undermined a wavering support base. As students took to the streets, the middle class essentially defected, and the military signaled its ambivalence, Soeharto abruptly fled power. A rapid transition ensued from neopatrimonial rule to electoral democracy amid a miasma of uncertain authority and institutional collapse.

Nigeria

If we consider the baseline year of 1965, Nigeria's initial conditions were more propitious than those of Indonesia. In the early years after independence, the Nigerian economy expanded at about 5 percent on average, and growth in 1965 was a moderate 4.9 percent. Per capita income stood at $624, slightly above that of Indonesia, and inflation was negligible at 4.1 percent.[45] Nigeria was a low-income agrarian economy, though it boasted a range of primary agricultural commodities (cocoa, palm produce, groundnuts, and rubber) with stable terms of trade, alongside solid mineral exports (including coal, limestone, and tin) that bolstered export income.

During the next thirty years, the economy fluctuated drastically. Over the course of the 1970s, recovery from the civil war and the advent of oil wealth created impressive gains, although this was offset by poor management and uneven revenues. The economy grew at an average rate of about 5 percent during the boom decade. This was followed by several years of decline in the early 1980s as oil markets slumped and debt increased. Even with hesitant stabilization, net growth from 1981 through 1990 averaged only 1.33 percent, and the economic growth rate little more than doubled for the 1990s. With population growth virtually unchecked, per capita income eroded during much of the period in question, increasing merely 0.57 percent when averaged over thirty years. Indeed, by the middle of the 1990s, real per capita GDP, at about $940, was a third *less* than it had been two decades earlier, and estimates of poverty ranged as high as 70 percent.[46]

The failure of Nigerian development stems above all from the absence of a political and institutional center to serve as a principal of economic change. Nigeria's elites, divided along communal and factional lines, have not consolidated stable political regimes or fostered capable state organi-

45. Data on growth, inflation, and poverty are from the World Bank, *World Development Indicators,* http://devdata.worldbank.org/dataonline/. Data on per capita income are from Penn World Tables, http://pwt.econ.upenn.edu/.

46. World Bank, *World Development Indicators,* http://devdata.worldbank.org/dataonline/; Penn World Tables, http://pwt.econ.upenn.edu/.

zations. Insecure leaders employ patronage and ethnic cooptation as a basis of rule, mirroring a fractious social groundwork. Ruling groups have been unable to cement a producer coalition or to resolve central pressures for distribution. Military and civilian governments construct bases of support through clientelism, rent seeking, and the disbursement of largesse.[47] In a setting of weak formal institutions and myriad conflicts over distribution, the Nigerian state has succumbed to a social dilemma: individuals and groups focus on particular gains at the expense of collective goods and general welfare.[48] Nigeria embodies a striking absence of central authority, whether arising from a strong leader, a governing party, the military, or the bureaucracy, to furnish public goods and enforce institutional prerogatives. The inability of the state to establish credible commitments has vitiated economic policy and undermined capital formation. Nigeria's poor economic performance is linked to this central problem of collective action.

The late 1960s proved to be a watershed in Nigerian development, as it was for Indonesia, although with markedly different results. The failure of Nigeria's democratic regime, the First Republic, arose from tensions between federal institutions, parliamentary rule, and invidious communal competition. A string of political crises led to erosion of civil order and a violent coup d'état in January 1966. Within months, a bloody counter-coup ousted the first military regime, setting in motion a chain of social conflicts that culminated in the attempted secession of Igbo nationalists in 1967.[49] The civil war was resolved by the beginning of 1970, and the end of hostilities permitted a rapid increase in petroleum production, centered in the areas previously claimed by the Biafran rebels.[50]

This protracted crisis had a crucial influence on ruling strategies and the path of economic change. The political upheavals of 1966 spurred an enduring sense of insecurity among Nigerian elites. General Gowon consolidated executive control and subsequently achieved a federal victory in

47. Lewis, "Economic Statism"; Joseph, *Democracy and Prebendal Politics in Nigeria.*

48. Elinor Ostrom, "A Behavioral Approach to the Rational Choice Theory of Collective Action: Presidential Address, American Political Science Association, 1997," *American Political Science Review* 92, no. 1 (1998): 1.

49. Larry Diamond, "Nigeria: Pluralism, Statism, and the Struggle for Democracy," in Larry Diamond, Juan J. Linz, and Seymour Martin Lipset, eds., *Democracy in Developing Countries: Africa* (Boulder: Lynne Rienner, 1988); Robin Luckham, *The Nigerian Military: A Sociological Analysis of Authority and Revolt, 1960–67* (London: Cambridge University Press, 1971).

50. Douglas Rimmer, "Development in Nigeria: An Overview," in Henry Bienen and V. P. Diejomaoh, eds., *The Political Economy of Income Distribution in Nigeria* (New York: Holmes and Meier, 1981), 49–50.

the civil war, but his regime was nonetheless shadowed by uncertainty. Gowon initially promised a timely return to civilian rule but lingered in office until he was toppled by a military successor. His regime's indecisive role as political caretaker created an institutional limbo for the armed forces and politicians alike.[51] The civil war helped to redefine the security perceptions of the military establishment and its response to distributional problems. Leaders viewed the sectional demands of Igbo rebels as a particular grievance rather than a general consequence of weak economic performance. In the aftermath of the conflict, which largely foreclosed further separatist pressures, military rulers pursued social and political stability through stopgap measures of redistribution. Successful management of the wartime economy also reinforced the nationalist and statist tendencies in economic policy.[52] The emergency accentuated the influence of a group of senior civil servants (the "super" permanent secretaries, or super permsecs) who advocated a strong tutelary role for the state, and insulation of domestic markets and producers from foreign competitive pressures.

These strategic choices were soon reinforced by an additional factor, the revenue windfall from oil.[53] Petroleum production, which had begun in earnest just prior to the outbreak of conflict, accelerated rapidly in the early 1970s, and the OPEC-created price hikes of 1973 yielded a steep rise in income. The growth of central resources removed many of the perceived constraints on development spending and redistribution, as a surfeit of revenues and a surge of foreign investment masked many of the liabilities of poor policies and weak administration.

These events entrenched a pattern of unstable leadership and distributional politics that persisted for more than three decades. Gowon was ousted in 1975 by General Murtala Muhammad, a populist reformer, in a move that prolonged military control while accentuating the internal divisions of the armed forces. Murtala was assassinated nine months later in a failed coup attempt, and his second in command, General Olusegun Obasanjo, assumed control. Obasanjo supervised a planned transition to civilian rule in 1979. The Second Republic, afflicted by corruption, political rancor, and policy immobility, survived little more than a single term

51. Anthony Kirk-Greene and Douglas Rimmer, *Nigeria since 1970: A Political and Economic Outline* (London: Hodder and Stoughton, 1981), 4–8.

52. Allison Ayida, "Development Objectives in the Seventies," in Allison Ayida, ed., *Reflections on Nigeria Development* (Ibadan: Heinemann Educational Books, 1987), 90–93.

53. Williams and Turner, "Nigeria," 153; Peter Lewis, "Development Strategy and Public Enterprise in Nigeria," in Barbara Grosh and Rwekaza Mukundala, eds., *State-Owned Enterprise in Africa* (Boulder: Lynne Rienner, 1993), 67–69.

before officers stepped in once again in the final hours of 1983. Twenty months later, General Muhammadu Buhari was ousted by General Ibrahim Babangida, who also pledged lasting political and economic reform. Babangida ruled for eight years, repeatedly postponing a promised democratization program, until elections were finally convened in 1993. After annulling the results, Babangida resigned and handed authority to a civilian caretaker committee that lasted only ten weeks before being shouldered aside by General Sani Abacha. Abacha sought to extend his rule indefinitely, but he died in June 1998. His successor, General Abdulsalami Abubakar, carried through a new transition to civilian rule, which concluded in May 1999.

The litany of political succession—six successful coups, numerous failed revolts, two abortive democratic regimes, three inconclusive democratization programs—illustrate essential problems of leadership and institutional development in Nigeria.[54] The armed forces are fractured not only by ethnoregional identities but increasingly by factions and personal alliances, as political ambition and rivalry have grown to dominate the organization. The civilian political elite, a roiling array of partisan, communal, and factional elements, have been chronically insecure about their position under both authoritarian and democratic regimes.[55] The political landscape fosters short time-horizons among rulers, encouraging narrow goals for the stabilization of regimes. A few leaders have shown initiative for reform—notably during Murtala's brief rule and General Babangida's early years—but these were truncated by political instability and the exigencies of preserving power. Rather than setting out conditions for investment and capital formation, rulers commonly emphasize short-term inducements for political accommodation.

Frequent turnover of regimes also hinders effective delegation to policy specialists. Nigerian executives pursue strategies of political consolidation requiring discretion over policies and resources, leading them to resist devolution of authority to specialist advisers or agencies. Following the purge of the Super Permsecs in the wake of Murtala's coup, no government has sustained a cohesive and capable economic policy team.[56] Repeated cabinet changes, shake-ups in the civil service, and an ever-changing array of advisory arrangements reduce the quality of policy advice and implementation capabilities while allowing broad leeway for the executive. Effective cabinet officials or advisory groups periodically

54. Eghosa Osaghae, *Crippled Giant.*
55. Diamond, "Nigeria: The Uncivic Society and the Descent into Praetorianism," 473–75.
56. Forrest, *Politics and Economic Development in Nigeria,* 253.

attain some leverage, yet they do not operate from a stable institutional position. Contending policy ideas, including structuralist, populist, and orthodox perspectives, are also influential. In sum, unstable elite coalitions and a lack of technocratic delegation have eroded the capabilities of the state to manage the economy.

The nature of coalitions also shapes institutional change. Nigerian regimes have relied upon rent distribution and fiscal perquisites to secure stability and control.[57] These strategies are influenced by the bargaining structure of groups and the fiscal organization of the state. Nigerian leaders face strong distributional demands from ethnic or regional communities, but few broad pressures from organized class strata. Governments respond to these disparate claims through piecemeal efforts at redistribution, a strategy facilitated by petroleum revenues and the growth of central resources. The pattern of rent distribution is affected by regime type: civilian governments use state-mediated rents to cement political allegiances, build party coffers, and afford an economic base for an emergent political class.[58] Military rulers disburse economic favors, business opportunities, and political sinecures to cultivate support within the armed forces and to secure cooperation from politicians and business elites.[59] These practices are centralized and concentrated under military regimes, and more dispersed in civilian systems. A diffuse arena of distributional politics defines the system. State elites and private sector interests have converged around patron-client relationships and rentier activities, largely skirting formal institutions and competitive markets.

The distribution of assets and political power hampers the formation of an effective producer coalition. The most politically salient communal groups (principally the northern Hausa-Fulani, the southwestern Yoruba, the southeastern Igbo, and a few smaller minorities) embody different economic interests and endowments. Southern groups have achieved a dominant position in the modern sectors of the economy, drawing upon comparatively strong educational attainments, closer proximity to major centers of commerce, and international linkages. Northern elites, while economically less competitive, have proven adept at forming political coalitions and have frequently controlled the central government.

Herein lies a central problem for economic policy and institution building, as competing elites—invariably representing a sectional minority

57. Forrest, *Politics and Economic Development in Nigeria,* 256; Joseph, *Democracy and Prebendal Politics in Nigeria;* Lewis, "Economic Statism."

58. Larry Diamond, "Class Formation in the Swollen African State," *Journal of Modern African Studies* 25, no. 4 (1987): 567–96.

59. Lewis, "From Prebendalism to Predation."

or a weak central coalition—fear that concentrations of economic power among other sections of the country might translate into political leverage and control.[60] Rulers are averse to broad economic growth, preferring to regulate economic allocations by expanding state prerogatives and controlling economic activity. Property rights are administered chiefly by political fiat. Immigrant entrepreneurs and foreign investors were largely expropriated in the 1970s and have since remained wary of the market. Domestic business interests must contend with unpredictable policies, erratic institutions, and insecure relations with state officials.[61] The disposition of property rights, in a context of political instability and shifting alliances, precludes credible commitments to entrepreneurial groups. Uncertainty hampers the expansion of fixed assets and productive activities, yielding deficits in capital formation.

The relation between elites and the mass public is another element of coalition formation. The frequent turnover of regimes and the fractiousness of ruling groups work against the establishment of a stable governing compact. Nigerian regimes have limited capacities for meeting popular needs or framing public purpose, leading to shallow and contingent political legitimacy. Especially during the period of the oil boom, governments pursued populist measures to foster support, including price controls and subsidies, burgeoning public employment, extensive social provisions, protection and assistance for local entrepreneurs, and expansive fiscal, monetary, and borrowing policies to finance growth.[62] The strategy garnered a degree of political acceptance, but it was economically unsustainable and collapsed in the early 1980s as oil revenues declined. Military governments have also sought to control organizations for labor, women, students, and academics as a means of co-opting these groups. Nigeria's authoritarian rulers, however, have not shown the ideological coherence or organizational capacity to build a stable corporatist compact.

As is the case in intraelite bargaining, political leaders commonly address popular demands through informal dispensations and bargaining

60. Michael Watts and Paul Lubeck, "An Alliance of Oil and Maize? The Response of Indigenous and State Capital to Structural Adjustment in Nigeria," in Bruce Berman and Colin Leys, eds., *African Capitalists and African Development* (Boulder: Lynne Rienner, 1994).

61. Pat Utomi, *Managing Uncertainty: Competition and Strategy in Emerging Economies* (Ibadan: Spectrum Books, 1998), 320.

62. Michael Watts and Paul Lubeck, "The Popular Classes and the Oil Boom: A Political Economy of Rural and Urban Poverty," in I. William Zartman, ed., *The Political Economy of Nigeria* (New York: Praeger, 1983); and Henry Bienen, "Oil Revenues and Policy Choice in Nigeria," in Henry Bienen, ed., *Political Conflict and Economic Change in Nigeria* (London: Frank Cass, 1985).

among sectional groups. Regimes commonly look to some form of multi-ethnic coalition as a basis for political consolidation. Electoral alliances or other public compacts have been fragile, leading different governments to pursue elite co-optation, patronage politics, and, in the case of dissident minorities, intermittent repression.[63] Distributional politics in Nigeria has reinforced a particular path of institutional development characterized by high levels of political discretion, a low salience of formal institutions, and widespread pressures on state elites for preferential benefits.

The regional context should also be noted. Nigeria operates in a difficult neighborhood. Surrounded by small, low-income states, Nigeria dwarfs the other economies of the region, yielding limited options for trade and investment from neighboring countries. Regional economic linkages are diverse but limited in scale and scope. Flows of commerce and migration are substantially unrecorded. The Economic Community of West African States was established in 1975, largely with Nigerian backing, to advance regional economic integration. The organization has barely effected initial steps toward trade reform.[64] Nigerian trade is overwhelmingly oriented toward Europe and North America. Prolonged regional economic crisis, beginning with the second oil price shock of 1979, aggravated problems of marginality in global markets. Chronic political instability sullies the region's international reputation. In terms of policy diffusion, West Africa reflects a fairly narrow range of statist policies and development strategies, with few compelling examples of reform in the wake of the economic crisis. Nigeria's position in West Africa provides few inducements for policy change and limited resources to support reform.

Despite the generally poor record of Nigeria's economic performance, there has not been a straight-line trajectory of decline. The economy has fluctuated with trends in petroleum markets and the nature of governance. During the 1970s, buoyant revenues fostered an ambitious agenda of state-led capitalist growth and populist social policies. In the wake of the civil war, military rulers sought to construct a social pact through economic expansion. The sudden expansion of state activities overwhelmed capacities for monitoring or effective management. Public institutions were prey to widespread corruption and misallocation of resources. After 1981, the collapse of international oil markets largely nullified a populist

63. Rotimi Suberu, *Federalism and Ethnic Conflict in Nigeria* (Washington, DC: United States Institute of Peace, 2001), 7–16.
64. Carol Lancaster, "The Lagos Three: Economic Regionalism in Sub-Saharan Africa," in John W. Harbeson and Donald Rothchild, eds., *Africa in World Politics* (Boulder: Westview, 1991).

strategy. The downturn in revenues occurred during the civilian Second Republic, whose leaders were ill-equipped to respond to adverse shocks. Economic adjustment was hampered by sectional competition and patronage politics. The resultant crisis dissolved the tenuous foundations of the democratic regime.

In the wake of the Second Republic, authoritarian stabilization measures had limited effect. In the middle of the 1980s, the Buhari regime pursued a stringent austerity program accompanied by restrictive political measures. These policies were poorly informed by economic realities, and economic decline quickly soured the public on the autocratic leader. His successor, General Babangida, initially promised a fresh breeze of political openness and economic revitalization, and he displayed some early success in enlisting the support of many elements of Nigerian society. Babangida included competent figures in his policy team, and his early initiatives for economic reform yielded some success in reversing decline.

In the face of military factionalism and lingering economic problems, however, the regime soon turned inward. Babangida personalized power, increased his predatory actions toward the economy, and expanded repression to maintain stability. General Abacha modeled his rule on Babangida's later years, fashioning a closed neopatrimonial system that plundered the economy and browbeat much of the population into submission.[65] The regime's slender foundations proved a growing liability, especially as social violence escalated and the economy spiraled downward. With Abacha's passing, military elites sought to arrest further degeneration of the state and the economy.

The vicissitudes of changing regimes and policies reveal consistent patterns. The polarization of Nigerian elites arises from a circulation of civilian and military regimes and factionalism within ruling groups. Ethnoregional contention is particularly evident in the disaffection of communities such as the Yoruba and the minorities of the Niger Delta, defensive responses by northern and eastern groups, and ubiquitous social violence. In addition, social inequalities bred by the boom period and the long era of stabilization give rise to caustic social divisions. Societal dissension is set against an increasingly autocratic trend in governance. From the 1980s, military rulers personalized their control and accentuated the use of coercion. The tendency toward autocracy narrowed the social foundations of rule, as elite coalitions diminished and popular support dissipated. In the domain of mass politics, organizational weaknesses and communal division worked against the emergence of forceful or coherent

65. Lewis, "From Prebendalism to Predation."

strata of civil society. Authoritarian rule also fostered discord and mistrust among society.

Predatory rule has fomented the degeneration of state capabilities and essential institutions. Political decay is bound up with economic decline during the past two decades. The economy has been plagued by imprudent policies and poor management, outlandish corruption, capital flight and widening criminality, declining investment and production, and growing marginality in the international system. The braids of political and economic crisis reveal a social dilemma in which elites and nonelites contend for access to politically mediated resources, in a setting of weak regimes and unstable social compacts. Central authorities and institutions lack the coherence to organize the rudiments of economic life, with ruinous consequences for development.

Having elaborated the comparative framework, the following two chapters discuss in greater detail the evolution of politics, institutions, economic policy, and performance in each of the two countries at the center of our concern.

CHAPTER 4

Indonesia

Crisis, Reform, and Growth

Between 1966 and 1996 a widening gap appeared in the relative economic performance of Indonesia and Nigeria. Much of the variation can be explained by distinct economic policies that evolved in different political and institutional settings. This chapter and the next one summarize the critical periods of political and economic change for each state. After providing a brief historical prelude for each country, the discussion focuses on the context of choice and the evolution of policy over three decades. Chapter 6 compares their economic performance, and chapters 7 and 8 take up the subsequent periods of crisis and political transition for each country.

The divergence in economic outcomes among these two countries is all the more striking given similarities in their initial endowments, economic structure, and external shocks. Neither country had a relative advantage in economic development arising from colonial rule. In the initial period after independence, both were open economies exporting an array of agricultural commodities and solid minerals, with comparatively low levels of industrialization and limited development of indigenous human capital. Political instability and weak state institutions hampered effective policymaking and development administration.

The energy markets of the 1970s transformed both economies. Rising oil production elevated their presence as global suppliers, and the OPEC-induced price rises of 1973 dramatically increased revenues. In each case the scale and scope of the economy increased exponentially, accompanied by dramatic changes in the structure of production. Indonesia and Nigeria shifted virtually overnight from predominantly agricultural economies to hydrocarbon exporters. Revenues wavered during the course of the decade, but a second price rise in 1979 conferred another major windfall on both governments. The oil boom fostered similar dynamics in both states. First, the rising importance of resource exports created a rentier political economy based upon the proceeds from petroleum which accrued directly to the government. Foreign revenues eclipsed the domestic tax base, giving the state broader discretion over central resources. Second, the oil windfall fostered statist economic strategies that were also substantially inward-looking. Third, the resource boom fomented extensive corruption in official life and in the private sector. Fourth, large oil rents gave rise to fiscal indiscipline and accumulation of external debt. Fifth, shifts in relative prices (notably rising inflation and appreciation of the exchange rate) undermined other productive sectors of the economy and hindered competitiveness. Finally, the growing reliance on oil and gas introduced new sources of economic volatility. Petroleum receipts were unpredictable, and fluctuating revenues affected the balance of payments, domestic output, and incomes. The two governments differed, however, in the speed and regularity with which they responded to these problems. Indonesian leaders made efforts to correct macroeconomic distortions and to mitigate problems in public sector performance, while Nigeria reflected growing policy distortions and institutional deficiencies.

The oil boom ended abruptly in the 1980s. Two negative price shocks, in 1982 and 1986, undermined the performance and international position of these economies. In the first shock, adverse energy markets and rising external debt caused downturns in both countries. International recession, diversification of global energy production, and divisions among the OPEC cartel caused a drop in world oil prices from the historic pinnacle of 1980–81. In the meantime, producer countries had rapidly accumulated foreign debt, and the nominal value of debt obligations grew sharply as a result of rising interest rates and currency shifts. When the 1982 Latin American defaults ignited a general debt crisis, a number of OPEC producers were further distressed by the sudden withdrawal of international credit. Along with other countries, Indonesia and Nigeria suffered from budget shortfalls, worsening balance of payments, and a slowdown in growth. A second shock came in 1986, when a steep reduction in oil prices sent revenues plummeting. During this period, the differences in policy and performance intensified between the two countries. Indonesia responded to the shocks of the 1980s with incremental but effective adjustment. A series of reforms in trade, investment, and finance increased competitiveness and restored rapid growth. The macroeconomic situation stabilized, output in the nonoil sectors of the economy increased, and Indonesia moved into new export and financial markets. Despite the persistence of politically induced restraints on competition, Indonesian leaders displayed a substantial measure of flexibility and adaptation in economic policy.

The early 1990s were characterized by a remarkable expansion of global investment and capital flows, accompanied by widening attention to the emerging markets of the developing and postsocialist countries. Indonesia was well positioned to take advantage of these conditions in light of its earlier reforms and regional location. Growth increased significantly, fueled by copious inflows of direct and portfolio investment and spurred by the activities of domestic investors. Local and foreign observers harbored misgivings about the persistence of excessive regulation, an opaque business environment, weaknesses in the banking system, bureaucratic corruption, and political favoritism. These concerns, however, were generally quelled by exuberance over a lively market in a global zone of growth. With these general observations in mind, we can turn to a more detailed consideration of Indonesia's developmental experience.

Indonesia's Historical Legacy

Like many former colonies, contemporary Indonesia was formed by European powers from diverse political systems, peoples, and cultures. Centralized states were present in the region, notably on Java, Sumatra, and Bali, for several centuries prior to the encroachment of European rule. Economic life throughout much of the archipelago was influenced by long-distance and interisland trade. Trade and migration were vehicles for the influence of major religious and cultural traditions from South and East Asia. Numerous states reigned on Java and Sumatra in the millennium following the sixth century. Java was ruled by the Sailendra dynasty and its successors, the Mataram, Kediri, and Singhasari states, whose control extended east to Bali, Kalimantan (Borneo), and parts of Sulawesi.[1] The height of Javanese power was attained under the Majapahit empire in the thirteenth and fourteenth centuries. Sumatra's most prominent rulers included the early commercial empire of Srivijaya and the sixteenth-century Muslim state of Aceh. The Malay trading empire of Malacca waxed during the fifteenth century, with wide linkages throughout the island chain.[2] Commercial and cultural influences from India were crucial, and the rise of Islam in India spread to Southeast Asia during the fifteenth and sixteenth centuries, where it supplanted Buddhism and Hinduism as the dominant religious tradition.

1. D. R. SarDesai, *Southeast Asia, Past and Present,* 4th ed. (Boulder: Westview, 1997), 44–50.

2. M. C. Ricklefs, *A History of Modern Indonesia since c. 1300,* 2d ed. (Stanford: Stanford University Press, 1993), 19–21.

Colonialism and Nationalism

European involvement in the area began in the sixteenth century. The Portuguese established the earliest ventures in the archipelago, followed by Dutch and then British undertakings. The European presence grew over two centuries, starting from various trading outposts in Java, Sumatra, Flores, Timor, the Moluccas (Spice Islands), and peninsular Malaya. The Dutch East Indies Company (VOC) expanded its influence in the eighteenth century, and by the 1770s the Netherlands was the dominant power throughout most of the Indonesian territory. Dutch authority was well established in Java by the early nineteenth century, while control of Sumatra and many of the outer islands was subsequently consolidated in the course of several decades. The Diponegoro revolt in Java during the 1820s and the Acehnese War in northern Sumatra in the 1870s were important episodes of resistance to foreign control, and Dutch suppression of the rebellions marked decisive moments in the consolidation of colonial control.

In the nineteenth century, colonial economic policy aimed at maximizing the extraction of revenues, principally through the coercive development of export crops. Under the "culture" system (*cultuurstelsel*), centered mainly on Java, colonial authorities dramatically expanded the production of cash crops such as coffee, sugar, indigo, and tobacco through heavy exactions on peasant cultivators. The system was based on the imposition of cash land taxes, diversion of peasant lands for large plantations, and the expansion of infrastructure, largely using forced labor. The *cultuurstelsel* generated large revenues for the colonial state and substantial gains for the Javanese elites who administered the system.[3] It also created enormous hardships for cultivators and induced dislocations in the rural economy that contributed to famines in the 1840s. The system was eventually curtailed in response to mounting economic problems in the colony and opposition among the Dutch public.

At the turn of the century, reformist impulses led to the introduction of the so-called ethical policy that placed greater stress on local economic and social progress. This prompted a development of education, economic facilities, and enterprise, along with greater inclusion of Indonesians in the colonial bureaucracy and nominal representation in the local legislature. The reformist turn of the colonial regime had lasting effects. The educational and economic initiatives were limited in scope, yet they contributed to the emergence of new elites who challenged Dutch rule. The introduc-

3. Ricklefs, *History of Modern Indonesia*, 122–23; SarDesai, *Southeast Asia*, 96–97.

tion of tens of thousands of indigenous people into the bureaucracy (albeit mainly in the lower tiers) broadened administrative experience. Most important, the state's developmental role was generally expanded and elaborated.[4]

Modern Indonesian nationalism contained distinctive ideological and cultural strands. The organizations Sarekat Islam and the Muhammadiya defined an influential Islamic tendency in the nationalist community. These movements contended with a secular nationalist trend that emerged in the 1920s, mainly through the Indonesian Nationalist Party (PNI), whose leaders included the young Sukarno. Finally, the Indonesian Communist Party (PKI) attained prominence in the late 1920s before being suppressed by authorities, only to reemerge in the period after World War II.[5] The Japanese occupation of Indonesia in 1942 effectively ended Dutch control. During the brief period of Japanese rule, the expedient cooperation of the PNI allowed Sukarno, Mohammad Hatta, and other nationalist leaders to build a following and sustain their organization. The local Japanese-organized militia also created the foundation of the national armed forces. When the Netherlands attempted to restore colonial authority in 1945, an armed struggle for independence ensued. The nationalist forces led by Sukarno declared independence and established a constitution. The PNI leadership promulgated the principles of *pancasila,* calling for a plural, secular state, and promoted such unifying elements as the Malay-derived lingua franca, Bahasa Indonesia. The Dutch relented in 1949, ceding full independence to the nationalists.

Independence and the Era of Sukarno

Sukarno's rule framed development in the 1950s and 1960s, influencing the context of choice for the later New Order regime. Challenges of national identity and territorial unity loomed large among the many urgent problems faced by the new government. Nationalist forces engaged in contentious debate over the governing formula for the new nation, with advocates of a centralized unitary state prevailing over those urging a federal system. This political settlement remained contentious, and lingering restiveness gave rise to dissent and violence. The newly established national armed forces fought a string of regional rebellions and army

4. Anne Booth, *The Indonesian Economy in the Nineteenth and Twentieth Centuries: A History of Missed Opportunities* (New York: St. Martin's Press, 1998), 154–55.

5. Robert Cribb and Colin Brown, *Modern Indonesia: A History since 1945* (London: Longman, 1995), 12–13; Ricklefs, *History of Modern Indonesia,* 241.

mutinies during the 1950s, including episodes in Aceh and other parts of Sumatra, West Java, Ambon, South Sulawesi, and elsewhere.[6] A sense of nationhood gradually took hold across much of the archipelago as the revolts were subdued and the regime encouraged common symbols and ideas. Serious tensions remained in two particular directions: the pervasive historical friction between Jakarta and the outer islands, and the lasting dissension between secular and Islamic visions of the political order.[7] Another major challenge arose from intensifying struggles among ideological groups. Nationalist, Communist, and Islamic parties, each allied to mass organizations, engaged in intense competition for control of the government and public ideology. The army was another central force that contained diverse political loyalties.[8] As the leadership sought to balance and placate the various interests within this restive political arena, the country was immersed in a growing mood of crisis.

Sukarno's economic policies moved in an increasingly radical direction, emphasizing nationalism and the growth of the state. Anticapitalist sentiments could be found across the political spectrum, as many Indonesians associated the market economy and private enterprise with European colonialism.[9] Article 33 of the 1945 national constitution called for the state to hold a dominant role in the economy. Ironically, the activist role of the colonial regime also created a potent legacy of government economic intervention.[10] Newly independent Indonesia faced inherent structural problems, many of which were aggravated by poor economic management under Sukarno. Years of conflict had depressed production and decimated much of the country's infrastructure. During the Japanese occupation, habits of corruption deepened among the weak, overextended bureaucracy. Sukarno faced sharp differences among his ministers over economic strategy, and strife within the cabinet, along with the president's regular reshuffles, fostered inconsistent policies that were often harmful to growth.[11] The government nationalized foreign firms after 1957 and pursued discriminatory policies toward the ethnic Chinese community, both

6. Ricklefs, *History of Modern Indonesia,* chap. 18.

7. Adam Schwarz, *A Nation in Waiting: Indonesia's Search for Stability,* 2d ed. (Boulder: Westview, 2000), 7–15.

8. Harold Crouch, *The Army and Politics in Indonesia* (Ithaca: Cornell University Press, 1978), 27–36.

9. J. A. C. Mackie, "The Indonesian Economy, 1950–1963," in Bruce Glassburner, ed., *The Economy of Indonesia: Selected Readings* (Ithaca: Cornell University Press, 1971), 43–44.

10. Booth, *Indonesian Economy,* 155.

11. Bruce Glassburner, "Economic Policy-Making in Indonesia, 1950–57," in Bruce Glassburner, ed., *The Economy of Indonesia: Selected Readings* (Ithaca: Cornell University Press, 1971), 70–98.

of which undermined investment and output.[12] Sukarno's combative international stance and the nationalization of foreign enterprise deepened the country's economic isolation. In addition, restrictive trade regulations and the maintenance of an overvalued exchange rate reduced exports.[13] The penchant for external borrowing aggravated problems in the balance of payments. The budget swelled from extensive subsidies, investment in state-owned enterprises, and spending on defense and public works. Growing fiscal deficits were financed by expanding the money supply, thereby fueling inflation, which accelerated out of control during the early 1960s.[14] Not long after independence, economic growth stalled and poverty worsened as the economy suffered rising volatility and international marginality.[15]

Guided Democracy, Guided Economy

Major political forces became stalemated during the 1950s over electoral contention and constitutional debates. The antipathy between Muslim and Communist blocks was especially threatening. The PKI, pressing land redistribution issues, made increasing inroads in rural Java and Sumatra, where they typically challenged more conservative Muslim organizations and landowners.[16] Sukarno's efforts to contain these tensions through eclectic ideology, national symbols, and personal politicking became increasingly strained.[17] The military grew restive over social instability and the disarray of civilian politics.

In 1957, elements of the army and the Muslim parties joined a regional rebellion in Sumatra. Sukarno reacted by declaring martial law. Over the next several years, backed by the central army leadership, Sukarno articulated his conception of Guided Democracy, which provided for broad

12. Herbert Feith, "Politics of Economic Decline," in T. K. Tan, ed., *Sukarno's Guided Indonesia* (Brisbane: Jacaranda Press, 1967), 54.

13. Wing Thye Woo, Bruce Glassburner, and Anwar Nasution, *Macroeconomic Policies, Crises, and Long-Run Growth: The Case of Indonesia, 1965–90* (Washington, DC: World Bank, 1995), 26–28.

14. Feith, "Politics of Economic Decline," 52–53.

15. Sukarno's poor apprehension of economic realities, and the worsening reputation of the regime, are summarized in John Bresnan's *Managing Indonesia: The Modern Political Economy* (New York: Columbia University Press, 1993), 53–54.

16. Ricklefs, *History of Modern Indonesia,* 274.

17. Clifford Geertz, "The Integrative Revolution: Primordial Sentiments and Civic Politics in the New States," in Clifford Geertz, ed., *Old Societies and New States* (New York: Free Press, 1963), 133; and Benedict R. O'G. Anderson, "The Idea of Power in Javanese Culture," in Benedict R. O'G. Anderson, ed., *Language and Power: Exploring Political Cultures in Indonesia* (Ithaca: Cornell University Press, 1990), 29–30.

executive powers and sharply curtailed the influence of the political parties and popular organizations. The emerging doctrine of a "Middle Way" for joint civilian-military governance was advanced by influential senior officers, bolstering the political role of the armed forces. In practical terms, the army exercised control through its territorial organization, which included parallel political-administrative units down to the village level. In addition, new military-controlled units were created to liaise directly with mass organizations and separate them from the political parties.[18]

The period of Guided Democracy was characterized by a personalized, presidential system of governance. Sukarno gathered power and ruled through his cabinet in a patrimonial manner with few checks from the parties, the national consultative assembly, or the mass public.[19] His alliance with the military bolstered central authority, but he nonetheless struggled to maintain control by counterbalancing rival political groups. As Sukarno drew closer to the left, strains intensified between the PKI, the armed forces, and the executive.[20] The regime's formula called for a grand coalition dubbed "Nasakom," bringing together nationalists, religious groups, and communists. Popular organizations, the military, and other social sectors were incorporated as "functional groups" in the integrative formula. This attempt to offset different ideological tendencies belied the deep antipathy among major parties and their supporters. Popular organizations were formally subordinated by the regime, but as social mobilization intensified, the political environment grew more volatile.

The fragile equilibrium of Guided Democracy (and the associated features of the Guided Economy) ultimately gave way to economic degeneration and political collapse. The capricious ideological nature of Sukarno's rule only deepened the tensions among the left, the military, and the Muslims. The course of economic decline accelerated as a consequence of erratic policies and virtual repudiation of the international economy. The nadir came in 1965 as inflation approached 1,000 percent annually, output and trade sagged, investment dwindled, and popular hardships mounted.[21]

In October, the skein of Sukarno's regime unraveled.[22] A military faction apparently instigated a coup d'état in which several senior officers

18. Cribb and Brown, *Modern Indonesia,* 79–80; Crouch, *Army and Politics in Indonesia,* 24–34.

19. Schwarz, *Nation in Waiting,* 16–17; Anderson, "Concept of Power in Javanese Culture," 46–48.

20. Crouch, *Army and Politics in Indonesia,* 69.

21. Cribb and Brown, *Modern Indonesia,* 89–90; Bresnan, *Managing Indonesia,* 55.

22. Bresnan, *Managing Indonesia,* 7–28.

were killed. The revolt was quickly put down, and Major General Soeharto of the army's strategic reserve command emerged at the helm of the
surviving army leadership. The military hierarchy attributed the revolt to
the PKI, and over the next few months the new leadership presided over a
massive, violent purge of the party and its supporters. With the collapse of
Sukarno's authority, Nasakom disintegrated, and a variety of disaffected
Muslims, Nationalists, and others turned on the Communists and their
perceived allies.[23] Anticommunist massacres took place across large portions of Java, Bali, Sumatra, and in other parts of the country. The army
participated in some of the killings, facilitated others by assisting local
militias and vigilante groups, or simply overlooked local rampages. It is
commonly estimated that half a million people died in this cataclysm.

Although Sukarno ostensibly remained in office following the coup,
his power was badly diminished and he was soon shouldered aside by Soeharto, who assumed de facto executive powers in March 1966. As he
fortified his control, Soeharto began to set in place the contours of his New
Order. The army moved into key positions of political authority, isolating
Sukarno's supporters and creating their own organizations of political
control. The earlier notion of a Middle Way in civil-military relations
evolved into a doctrine of *dwifungsi* (dual function), establishing the political role of the military as an institutional principle. Antileftist purges were
conducted in the military and the civil service. These measures consolidated the authority of conservative officers, fostered greater cohesion
among the leadership, and buttressed the political reliability of state agencies. In 1967 Soeharto was named acting president, and the following year
he was elected in military-controlled elections.

Politics and Policy under the New Order

As Soeharto extended his personal authority and consolidated the regime,
the central goals of the New Order came into focus. The military leadership attributed the political and economic maelstrom to the excesses of
Sukarno's rule. Concerned with the integrity and stability of the nation,
they sought an end to the disruptive political divisions, uncontrolled mobilization, ideologically driven policies, and international confrontation that
they blamed for the 1965 crisis.

The military, faced with the need to build a new foundation of power,
allied their political goals to a general vision of development. They were

23. Robert W. Hefner, *Civil Islam: Muslims and Democratization in Indonesia* (Princeton:
Princeton University Press, 2000), 63–65.

preoccupied with economic turmoil and the explosive social tensions in the countryside and the outer islands. The core of the emerging strategy called for a restoration of economic growth and a broad dispersal of benefits. Politically, the army also moved to deepen its political control while suppressing challenges from the left and other autonomous popular groups. The emergent New Order articulated an authoritarian model of reform with greater emphasis on market forces, spurred by an expectation that improved economic performance would furnish essential stability and legitimacy for the regime.

After assuming executive authority, Soeharto's position was augmented in several respects. His formal powers were expanded, his leadership group within the army attained greater cohesion and stability, and the regime established political control over major social forces. The military moved in the early months of 1966 to sideline Sukarno's cabinet and establish a new governing team, in which the Sultan of Yogyakarta presided over economic affairs. This signaled a decisive shift in economic strategy.[24]

The regime turned for its economic plan to a core group of economic technocrats, establishing a pattern of policymaking that was to become a central feature of the New Order. This coterie of economists had received training in the United States (mainly at the University of California, Berkeley) and was affiliated with the University of Indonesia's faculty of economics. The advisers, who came to be known colloquially as the Berkeley mafia, were a close-knit group with similar credentials and a neoclassical outlook on economic policy.[25] In a series of public seminars and policy statements early in 1966, they analyzed the failures of Sukarno's economic program and outlined a strategy for stabilization and development. A pivotal meeting with Soeharto and other military leaders at the army's staff college in Bandung brought the economic team together with central figures in the government. From this period forward, the technocrats enjoyed privileged access to Soeharto and carried substantial weight in economic policy matters. In the ensuing decades, members of the economic team held key positions in the cabinet and peak agencies, and as influential advisers.

24. The actions of the new policy team are detailed by H. W. Arndt and J. Panglaykim, "Survey of Recent Developments," *Bulletin of Indonesian Economic Studies* 2, no. 4 (1966): 1–35.

25. Bruce Glassburner, "Political Economy and the Suharto Regime," *Bulletin of Indonesian Economic Studies* 14, no. 3 (1978): 32–34; David B. H. Denoon, *Devaluation under Pressure: India, Indonesia, and Ghana* (Cambridge: MIT Press, 1986), 91. An account from a member of the Harvard advisory group is provided by William C. Hollinger, *Economic Policy under President Soeharto: Indonesia's Twenty-Five Year Record* (Washington, DC: United States-Indonesia Society, 1996), 10–11.

Stabilization and Credibility

Stabilization of the economy was the main priority for the new policy team. Sukarno's economic policies had been strongly biased against foreign trade and the private sector, including restrictions on production, prices, and commerce. Public finances were in a shambles, and there were severe deficits in the external account. A first order of business was to gain control of inflation, improve basic macroeconomic performance, and restore incentives for investment and exports. The technocrats led this endeavor in coordination with the International Monetary Fund and other donors.[26]

In a series of public statements and policy decrees throughout 1966, Soeharto's group broke with Sukarno's economic program and introduced a broad set of reform measures.[27] The rupiah was sharply devalued and the arcane multiple exchange rate system then in place was pushed toward a common rate. Subsequent reforms unified the exchange rate, made the rupiah convertible, and effected further devaluation. In addition, the capital account was fully opened in 1970. Much of the import licensing system was abolished, removing a critical bottleneck on trade and production while reducing the corruption and inefficiency of these bureaucratic controls.[28] The trading environment was opened further by devaluation and the relaxation of export regulations, which boosted export activities in Java and the outer islands.

The government also sought to balance the budget through changes in both revenue and spending. Revenues were increased by enhanced tax administration and growing trade. On the expenditure side, budgetary austerity and foreign aid produced rapid improvements in fiscal balances. Subsidies were cut, off-budget spending curtailed, and major capital projects suspended. These fiscal measures were accompanied by a tight money and credit policy. Interest rates rose, and banking regulations were changed to direct more resources to the private sector. At the end of the year a "balanced" budget was presented to parliament, and a balanced budget rule was set forth by government.

The reform program aimed at reintegrating Indonesia with the world economy, including special efforts to instill foreign confidence in the new policies. The government sought to reposition Indonesia internationally

---

26. David Denoon, *Devaluation under Pressure,* 96–97; H. W. Arndt, "Five Years of New Order," in H. W. Arndt, ed., *The Indonesian Economy* (Singapore: Chapman, 1984), 33.

27. Bresnan, *Managing Indonesia,* 55–65.

28. Bresnan, *Managing Indonesia,* 65; see also D. H. Penny and Dhalan Thalib, "Survey of Recent Developments," *Bulletin of Indonesian Economic Studies* 3, no. 6 (1967): 1–2.

by rejoining the United Nations, the International Monetary Fund, and the World Bank, ending the confrontation with Malaysia, and convening external meetings with major noncommunist creditors. In addition, many foreign firms nationalized by Sukarno were returned to their former owners, and a new investment law substantially protected investors from nationalization. In September 1966, Indonesian representatives at a creditors' meeting in Tokyo outlined the new policy regime and sought assurances regarding debt restructuring and foreign aid. Three weeks later the government unveiled a comprehensive stabilization program. Once key policies had been implemented, a follow-up Paris meeting in December produced more comprehensive debt rescheduling and substantial commitments of new assistance. The process of external engagement was formalized in February 1967 with the establishment of the Inter-Governmental Group on Indonesia (IGGI), which brought together the chief donors and trading partners on a regular basis. This mechanism facilitated debt workouts, concessional lending, and foreign assistance, while furnishing a catalyst for private investment. External aid commitments grew from $167 million in 1967 to more than $600 million by 1970.[29]

These measures achieved impressive stabilization of the economy. More transparent and rigorous budgeting, restraint on money and credit, and large inflows of foreign assistance served to quickly bring down inflation. In early 1966, prices were increasing at a rate of more than 1,000 percent on an annual basis; this was reduced to a little over 100 percent in 1967, and only 15.5 percent by 1969. Greater price stability and higher interest rates fostered a surprisingly rapid return of flight capital from abroad.[30] As policies toward the private sector became more encouraging, there was a substantial revival of investment in export activities as well as domestic manufacturing.

Economic growth attained momentum after 1967. The economy expanded by an average of 8.7 percent a year from 1968 through 1971, or 6.2 percent on a per capita basis. By contrast, growth in the last five years of Sukarno's Guided Economy averaged slightly less than 2 percent. With population growing at nearly 3 percent, this meant declining per capita income. A much-remarked achievement of the post-1966 stabilization was the success in suppressing inflation and achieving fiscal balance without diminishing popular consumption or increasing unemployment.[31] In part,

29. Woo, Glassburner, and Nasution, *Macroeconomic Policies,* 47.
30. Woo, Glassburner, and Nasution, *Macroeconomic Policies,* 47; Denoon, *Devaluation under Pressure,* 91.
31. Arndt, "Five Years of New Order," 34–35; Woo, Glassburner, and Nasution, *Macroeconomic Policies,* 30.

this was because of the boost given to the export sector, which absorbed substantial labor. Another important dimension, however, was the commitment to stabilize prices for key commodities, notably rice and textiles.[32] A considerable proportion of foreign assistance went to market supports for these goods, along with large-scale public projects for the rehabilitation of infrastructure. The new regime inherited an economy spiraling downward and isolated from world markets, yet they were able in a remarkably short period to shift incentives and elicit a significant investor and supply response. A combination of policy changes and political factors came into play during this transformation.

The balanced budget rule and the opening of the capital account furnished two crucial lock-in mechanisms to bolster confidence in the new policies. The balanced budget rule decreed that fiscal deficits could not be financed by the central bank, thus placing inherent limits on both spending and the money supply. The formal pledge of fiscal discipline placed a major constraint on policymakers and signaled a clear anti-inflationary principle in economic affairs. This mandate, however, contained a crucial loophole, since the development portion of the budget—including large capital projects—was funded by foreign aid, and assessed separately from other expenditures.

Despite this contrivance, the new policies departed from the preceding regime's opaque, expansionary fiscal practices.[33] While the balanced budget principle offered a commitment to fiscal responsibility, it was not a fully binding constraint on government, especially as executive power grew. An open capital account, however, could impose further costs for budgetary indiscipline, since large fiscal deficits or excessive growth of the money supply would quickly trigger erosion in the value of the currency. This provided a clear barometer of macroeconomic management, as well as an exit for holders of capital in times of uncertainty. Policymakers therefore faced high costs for irresponsible policies.

In addition to formal lock-in measures, the new regime engaged with outside institutions and accepted external constraints as a means of bolstering credibility. The renewal of Indonesia's membership in international organizations and the multilateral financial institutions symbolized a new attitude toward the outside world, but even more important was the acceptance of common standards and external scrutiny of the government's policies. The formation of the Tokyo Club and the IGGI bolstered

---

32. Bresnan, *Managing Indonesia,* 64–65.
33. Hal Hill, *The Indonesian Economy since 1966* (Cambridge: Cambridge University Press, 1996), 59.

this process, effectively introducing a consultative element into domestic policymaking. Indonesia's participation in the 1967 formation of the Association of Southeast Asian Nations (ASEAN) signaled a further set of strategic and economic alignments. The rapid increases in external resources—loans, aid, direct investment, and a reversal of capital flight—demonstrated the efficacy of these initiatives.

At a less formal level, the new leadership cultivated relations with important groups of investors and producers. While the overtures to foreign capital were important, the burgeoning alliance with ethnic Chinese entrepreneurs was pivotal for the regime's goal of reviving growth. Sino-Indonesians were already preeminent in domestic trade, light manufacturing, and other commercial endeavors, yet they held a precarious footing in social life and political affairs. Making up about 3 percent of the population, this community was economically conspicuous, culturally distinct, and frequently subject to resentment and violence (including several outbursts in the years after Sukarno's fall).

Soeharto and other senior officers, however, had long-standing commercial relations with ethnic Chinese entrepreneurs, and these networks attained greater importance in the early years of the regime. The economic interests of the military converged with their broader goals of economic growth, and a set of collusive relations developed to spur investment and entrepreneurship.[34] With the implicit protection of the executive and the army elite, along with access to protected markets, public contracts, and other opportunities, Sino-Indonesians became a leading force in the economy.

During this period the regime also built a system of political control. Soeharto sought to regularize his rule by elaborating an electoral machine and creating organizations to incorporate key elements of state and society. In 1967 the military made Golkar a central political vehicle. Although designated as a collection of "functional groups" rather than a formal party, Golkar quickly became the regime's electoral machine and framework for political incorporation. Organizations for labor, students, women, farmers, business, and others were affiliated with Golkar, along with the civil service organization KORPRI, which public employees were required to join. In the early years of the New Order, several political parties were permitted to operate under tight restrictions, but they were dissolved in 1973 and replaced with the Muslim-oriented Development Party (PPP) and the Democratic Party (PDI), which attracted many Christians and ethnic Chinese. Operating in the shadow of the military's territorial

34. Crouch, *Army and Politics in Indonesia,* 273–74.

organization, these parties and groups framed an authoritarian corporatist system that channeled or limited popular participation. Following Soeharto's 1968 victory at the polls, the new electoral mechanism largely assured his tenure.

In view of our main concern for the political sources of policy credibility, it is important to bear in mind the degree of uncertainty and choice in this phase of economic stabilization. The policy innovation and political maneuvering that revitalized the economy were hardly foreordained. Soeharto's government, which included different groups and tendencies, required time to find its footing, solidify a program, and articulate new institutions.[35] Public perceptions, the essence of credibility, changed only incrementally in response to initiatives from the state. Yet important foundations were established in this period.

The early years of the New Order witnessed a number of political struggles and contested areas of control. Although Sukarno's position eroded rapidly after the 1965 crisis, the erstwhile president continued to maneuver weakly for influence for more than a year following Soeharto's assumption of power. The military leadership also faced dissent and pressure from a variety of social forces, especially students concerned with corruption and foreign economic influence. The signals and lock-in measures that fostered a shift in investment behavior did not take hold immediately. Key measures such as the removal of capital controls and currency convertibility were undertaken several years into the period of stabilization. The increasing flow of foreign capital, a potent indicator of international confidence in the government, materialized over several years. The informal alliance with domestic business groups was a cumulative process of policy shifts and growing mutual confidence. By the early 1970s, as stabilization measures gained momentum, a new round of economic shocks, social pressures, and political contention altered the course of economic change.

From Stabilization to Windfall

Although the New Order's economic program accorded a substantial role for market mechanisms and the private sector, the shift in policy was not as sweeping as it might have appeared in some quarters. The technocrats pushed macroeconomic policy in a liberal direction, yet the state retained a dominant position in the economy and intervened extensively at the sectoral level. Macroeconomic liberalization coexisted with an essentially

---

35. Arndt and Panglaykim, "Survey of Recent Developments," 1–3.

dirigiste microeconomic approach. Further, there were intense ideological differences among the heterogeneous national elites. Advocates of neo-classical policies were based in the universities, the senior bureaucracy, and segments of the business community, with the support of Soeharto and a few key officers. These elements contended with other elites including military leaders, many bureaucrats, politicians, and even large portions of the private sector, who were leery of "free-fight" capitalism, sympathetic to socialist ideas, and strongly nationalist in outlook. The leaders of the New Order also set about constructing extensive networks of patronage as a means of consolidating power and bolstering political control. Several crosscurrents thus shaped the tides of Indonesian economic policy: market and anticapitalist impulses, nationalism and outward orientation, liberalism and intervention, pragmatism and patronage.[36] Domestic political rivalries and external shocks influenced the balance among these competing tendencies.

Even as the orthodox program gained ground, alternative approaches could be discerned among the regime's policies. The first five-year plan, Repelita I (1969–74), looked beyond immediate stabilization and outlined measures for long-term growth, underscoring the government's role in pursuing structural change. In addition, a rice-supply emergency in 1972–73 prompted further intervention in agricultural production and marketing, which accentuated the state's importance in managing sectoral problems. The country faced a critical rice shortage resulting from poor weather and serious missteps by the state logistics agency, Bulog. Rice scarcities had been a major factor in the popular restiveness under Sukarno, and the new government created Bulog in 1967 to stabilize agricultural prices and supplies. The rice crisis contributed to a new round of inflation and sparked violent student demonstrations that unsettled the regime. The senior leadership, already concerned with food security, made concerted efforts to regulate the rice market and foster self-sufficiency in this staple crop.

If these developments hinted at a redirection in economic policy, the change was manifest with the onset of the oil boom. The burgeoning petroleum sector produced a revenue windfall that altered the structure of the economy and the priorities of policymakers. Oil and gas output grew rapidly as the government resolved long-standing organizational

36. R. William Liddle, "The Relative Autonomy of the Third World Politician: Soeharto and Indonesian Economic Development in Comparative Perspective," *International Studies Quarterly* 35, no. 4 (1991); Glassburner, "Political Economy and the Soeharto Regime," 31–35. For a structural class analysis of these tendencies, see Richard Robison, *Indonesia: The Rise of Capital* (Sydney: Allen and Unwin, 1986), 132–37.

problems and rationalized relations with the foreign firms that dominated production. The volume of exports increased by 52 percent
between 1971 and 1974, while the price of Indonesian crude jumped by
300 percent in 1974 as a result of OPEC increases. Oil and gas activities
quickly became the driving component of economic growth. By 1974 the
hydrocarbon sector contributed 22 percent of GDP (nearly doubling its
share from the preceding year), 70 percent of export earnings, and 55 percent of government revenues.[37] The boom accentuated nationalist proclivities in managing the economy, as expanding resources furnished the
wherewithal to pursue an ambitious agenda of state-led development.
The shift in outlook was especially salient in trade policy, public enterprise, and industrial strategy.

Although the government relaxed many restrictions on imports and
exports during the stabilization period, new forms of protection were
introduced in the early 1970s. The government faced growing dissent over
foreign domination of the economy, most dramatically in the Malari riots
of early 1974, along with protectionist claims from domestic business
interests. Such pressures encouraged measures to insulate domestic producers and subsidize non-Chinese, or indigenous (*pribumi*) entrepreneurs.
The government maintained relatively high tariff levels, imposed an array
of quantitative import restrictions, and created trade monopolies for key
commodities and products. In addition, the regime announced measures
to favor *pribumi* access to employment, credit, and ownership. These policies were explained in terms of the need to stabilize markets, protect local
production, and promote indigenous welfare, though they also provided
copious economic rents to associates and allies of the regime.

In the early years of the New Order, the government took steps to
divest some state holdings and to improve the financial performance of
public enterprises. Many foreign-owned firms nationalized under Sukarno
were turned back to private ownership, while authorities sought to put
state companies on a commercial footing, especially by limiting their
access to public credit. Denationalization was important for signaling the
private sector (especially foreign investors), but it actually had little effect
on the dimensions of the public economy. The petroleum windfall essentially reversed efforts to rationalize the state sector.[38] The new resources
induced a rapid expansion of public investment, and government firms

37. Woo, Glassburner, and Nasution, *Macroeconomic Policies,* 55.
38. A. D. Habir, "State Enterprise: Reform and Policy Issues," in Hal Hill and Terence
Hull, eds., *Indonesia Assessment, 1990* (Canberra: Australian National University, 1990), 95.

accounted for a growing proportion of equity and output, especially in industry and infrastructure. Financial discipline slackened as the public sector grew.

The 1975 debacle surrounding Pertamina, the state petroleum corporation, called attention to the problems of disciplining a rapidly expanding state apparatus. The crisis also underscored the challenges of preserving credibility in a volatile fiscal situation. At the heart of the Pertamina crisis was a confrontation between nationalist interests based in the state enterprise sector and the technocrats centered in the national planning agency Bappenas. The incident dramatized important shifts in political equilibrium wrought by the oil boom.[39] The events of the crisis can be recounted briefly: In February and March 1975, the state petroleum corporation Pertamina defaulted on two sizable short-term loans to foreign banks. This set in motion a frantic effort by the Indonesian government, foreign donors, and creditors to reschedule the corporation's debts and avoid a balance of payments crisis. Inquiries soon uncovered a staggering $10.5 billion in loans, including $1.5 billion in short-term borrowing that had been undertaken by Pertamina management, largely without the knowledge or sanction of the main financial authorities. The total volume of debt exceeded the government's entire budget. The ensuing bailout depleted the country's external reserves by two-thirds and absorbed an estimated 80 percent of official foreign borrowing over the following year, as the country's foreign debt burden approximately doubled.[40]

Under the direction of General Ibnu Sutowo, Pertamina had become, in the early years of the oil boom, the embodiment of nationalist aspirations. As head of the military-controlled corporation Permina since 1957, Sutowo had gained a reputation as an aggressive state entrepreneur. Soeharto named Sutowo president-director of the giant Pertamina (a merger of three state oil firms) in 1968. From there, the general consolidated his control of the oil sector and fortified his position within the regime.[41] Pertamina's production-sharing agreements with major foreign producers contributed to a revival of the industry, which had deteriorated badly during Sukarno's rule. Bolstered by political leverage and new revenues, Sutowo pursued an ambitious program of expansion and diversification. Pertamina was involved in all dimensions of the petroleum industry,

39. Robison, *Indonesia,* 153–54; Liddle, "Relative Autonomy," 421.
40. For a detailed background, see Peter McCawley, "Some Consequences of the Pertamina Crisis in Indonesia," *Journal of Southeast Asian Studies* 9, no. 1 (1978): 1–27.
41. Bruce Glassburner, "In the Wake of General Ibnu: Crisis in the Indonesian Oil Industry," *Asian Survey* 16, no. 12 (1976): 1100.

including exploration, production, refining, marketing, and transport. The company established numerous subsidiaries and joint ventures in areas as far-flung as liquefied natural gas (LNG), steel production, shipping, tanker charters, oil services, insurance, air services, telecommunications, rice production, frozen foods, and tourism.

Pertamina's headlong growth sharpened the regime's internal tensions over approaches to development. The economic technocrats favored fiscal restraint, market incentives, and foreign involvement in the economy. Portions of the bureaucracy and the officer corps, prominently represented by Sutowo, advocated a more assertive state role in guiding industrialization, protecting domestic producers, and encouraging *pribumi* interests.[42] In the early 1970s Pertamina was an empire unto itself. Its vast resources allowed the management to create a virtually independent development program, as the conglomerate became a huge source of off-budget spending and autonomous borrowing from abroad. Pertamina's sprawling empire also fostered a prodigious web of patronage that enhanced Sutowo's political position and expanded the regime's support base.[43]

The economic advisers attempted to bring the firm under control, including participation in a joint managing board, but chief executives ignored or evaded their oversight.[44] Soeharto valued effective leadership, and Ibnu Sutowo's rise was often attributed to his ability to "get things done." The general's control of patronage also afforded him substantial political weight. Despite public expressions of concern about corruption and financial excess, Sutowo relied upon his political influence, as well as the support of foreign oil firms and banks involved with Pertamina, to avoid accountability. Pertamina's activities created a dual track in economic strategy, as the orthodox macroeconomic program was paralleled by a growing statist agenda, integrally linked to clientelist politics.[45]

By shifting influence back to the technocrats, the Pertamina crisis encouraged greater coherence in economic management and a further redirection of policy. Soeharto temporarily rebuffed the nationalists by supporting the economists in their efforts to resolve the financial emer-

---

42. Variously referred to as the "technicians," "engineers," or "entrepreneurs," the term refers to those officials favoring a strong government role in the economy, especially through aggressive efforts to develop high technology industries and other activities fostering backward and forward linkages. These figures were often allied with others seeking limits on foreign involvement and government support of national firms and *pribumi* interests. See Bresnan, *Managing Indonesia,* 260; Liddle, "Relative Autonomy," 416–17.

43. McCawley, "Some Consequences of the Pertamina Crisis," 2–7.

44. McCawley, "Some Consequences of the Pertamina Crisis," 10–11.

45. Robison, *Indonesia,* 154–55; Damien Kingsbury, *The Politics of Indonesia* (Melbourne: Oxford University Press, 1998), 80.

gency. Sutowo's authority was rescinded within months, and he was quietly removed the following year. A large bailout package negotiated with private creditors and major donors allowed the government to reschedule Pertamina's loans, while authorities sought to regain control of public finance and state enterprises. Government firms were required to obtain sanction from the Ministry of Finance for all borrowing and were prohibited from taking any short-term credit. After a broad review of public sector spending, several major projects were modified, rescheduled, or curtailed. This made the public sector more accountable to the executive, as firms and managers had reduced latitude.

These events reinforced norms of performance within the state sector. The Pertamina fiasco conveyed the lesson that unrestrained rent seeking and profligacy were unsustainable. This did not result in widespread probity, much less rigorous standards of efficiency. Patronage and corruption flourished in the following years, enabled by the development of large capital projects and the proliferation of government contracts. But these tendencies were tempered by a greater sense of caution in the expansion of public investments, as well as by admonitions from senior leaders to produce results (mainly in terms of production) and to observe limits in the diversion of resources. At a critical moment, the Pertamina affair reined in the excesses of a burgeoning state. This element of central discipline substantially influenced the subsequent course of development.

The arc of Pertamina's rise and fall also highlighted the preoccupation with credibility among senior members of the economic bureaucracy. The technocrats used a variety of supervisory mechanisms and commitment devices in their attempts to control Pertamina's activities and in subsequent efforts to contain the fallout from the crisis. In 1970, a government commission found evidence of corruption in the petroleum conglomerate, providing an impetus for additional supervision. Under Law No. 8 of 1971, key members of the economic team were included in the governing board. As Sutowo and his allies resisted oversight, the technocrats enlisted foreign sources of control. In 1972 the minister of finance concluded a standby agreement with the IMF, despite the Fund's stance that an agreement was unnecessary because of Indonesia's strong macroeconomic program.[46] By leveraging the influence of the IMF, the economic advisers were able to impose domestic controls on borrowing by state enterprises. When Pertamina disregarded the rules, the United States suspended bilateral aid. The Indonesian government then entered into a new IMF standby agreement that specifically limited medium- and long-term borrowing by

46. Woo, Glassburner, and Nasution, *Macroeconomic Policies,* 63.

Pertamina. At this point, company managers simply turned to short-term financing, which proved to be the enterprise's undoing. A sudden increase in foreign interest rates in 1974 undermined Pertamina's debt position, leading quickly to default.

In the bailout that followed, the technocrats relied heavily on engagement with international donors, banks, and the multilateral institutions. The central forum was the IGGI meeting in 1976, in which major donors agreed to provide some $3.4 billion in immediate financial assistance and longer-term project support. The donors' gathering was preceded by a large loan from U.S. and commercial banks to shore up foreign reserves, as well as negotiations with major donors on restructuring the finance of major capital projects.[47] Thus, support from commercial markets and donors helped to signal confidence as Indonesian negotiators went into the IGGI discussions. Coordinating policy with international institutions and markets carried the political risk of inciting domestic resentment, which had been powerfully demonstrated in the 1974 antiforeign violence. The senior economic team, however, concluded that external sources of restraint would strengthen their hand in seeking macroeconomic stability.

Managing the Dutch Disease

The resource windfall produced common symptoms of the Dutch disease. The rapid influx of external revenues increased the money supply, which spurred inflation and caused the exchange rate to appreciate. The prices of nontradables (e.g., construction, real estate, and services) increased relative to tradables (e.g., export agriculture and manufactures), resulting in a shift of resources away from productive activities toward trade and the service sector. The Dutch disease embodies a cluster of economic changes. Most resource-exporting economies experience a contraction of traditional exports and manufacturing, which narrows the revenue base. The declining ability to generate revenues apart from the resource sector renders the economy more sensitive to price shifts in the dominant export. Imports also surge as the exchange rate appreciates and foreign goods become cheaper. Much of the import bill is spent on consumption goods, which further discourages local production and places negative pressure on the balance of payments. When oil and gas receipts are high, these structural problems are less apparent. When revenues recede, as inevitably happens, the economy is vulnerable to a wrenching contraction. The

47. Bresnan, *Managing Indonesia,* 188–89.

volatility of economic growth is among the most prominent consequences of the resource syndrome.[48]

As a major oil exporting country, Indonesia in the 1970s was hardly remarkable in exhibiting the adverse effects of the resource boom. What was remarkable, however, was the response of economic policymakers to some of the major distortions incurred by the windfall. Members of the senior economic team became increasingly concerned about Indonesia's eroding competitiveness, especially in export agriculture, which was a key to absorbing labor and reducing rural poverty.[49] The fallout from the Pertamina crisis also heightened concern with managing foreign debt, suggesting the need for a reliable basis of generating foreign exchange. These concerns led policymakers to devalue the rupiah by 50 percent in November 1978.

The 1978 devaluation, a singular action unmatched by other OPEC producers, was largely justified by economic theory rather than compelling data of the moment. The rupiah, pegged at 415 to the dollar since 1971, had become overvalued. Estimates at the time found that Indonesia's competitiveness in nonoil exports had significantly eroded against most other countries, especially its neighbors in East and Southeast Asia. In the years immediately preceding the devaluation, however, nonoil export receipts were strong, and output was rising.[50] The economists focused instead on evidence of declining terms of trade for nonoil commodities and the diminishing returns for local producers. Corrective action was motivated by the prospect that worsening incentives would erode commodity exports and manufacturing. Discussion of the issue at the time also raised prospects of slumping oil revenues and depletion of the hydrocarbon sector, creating a further impetus to bolster other sources of earnings.[51]

The devaluation illustrated the continued influence of the Berkeley group, as well as the conflicting political incentives surrounding economic policy. The driving motive for devaluation was technocratic concern with the structure of the economy and the preservation of a broad revenue

48. Michael Ross, "The Political Economy of the Resource Curse," *World Politics* 51, no. 2 (1999); Terry Lynn Karl, *The Paradox of Plenty: Oil Booms and Petro-States* (Berkeley: University of California Press, 1997), 46–54.

49. Mari Pangestu and Amar Bhattacharya, *Indonesia: Development Transformation and Public Policy* (Washington, DC: World Bank, 1993), 15; H. W. Arndt, "The Oil Bonanza and Poverty," in Arndt, ed., *Indonesian Economy,* 67.

50. Howard Dick, "Survey of Recent Developments," *Bulletin of Indonesian Economic Studies* 15, no. 1 (1979): 2–3.

51. Dick, "Survey of Recent Developments," 4; Woo, Glassburner, and Nasution, *Macroeconomic Policies,* 85.

base.[52] A strong political rationale backed up this orthodox stance, as those most adversely impacted by overvaluation included agricultural producers and (nonextractive) resource exporters, many of whom were on the outer islands. The argument for directing benefits to the rural areas and regional groups fit in with the regime's general goals of poverty reduction and equity, while addressing a potentially troublesome source of popular restiveness.

Leaders were also under pressure from import-competing interests and small- to medium-scale manufacturers seeking state protection, as well as urban consumers concerned about inflation. This led to some contradictory policies. In the wake of devaluation the government introduced a complicated array of price controls, subsidies, and trade regulations that to some degree undermined the goal of promoting nonoil exports.[53] The incentives from the currency adjustment nonetheless fostered an expansion of commodity production until the second major oil price shock. These additional nonoil revenues, along with the conservative borrowing induced by the Pertamina affair, significantly improved Indonesia's debt position and helped to cushion the economy from the worst effects of a downturn in petroleum markets.

The Second Windfall

Beginning in 1979 Indonesia experienced another massive windfall from oil and natural gas, as the Iranian revolution and the Iran-Iraq War disrupted supplies, sending international prices soaring. The average price for Indonesian crude doubled to about $28 per barrel by 1980, increasing to $35 the following year.[54] Indonesia's total exports of oil and LNG jumped from about $9 billion in 1979 to nearly $14 billion in 1981. Energy exports grew from 53 percent of government revenue in 1978–79 to 62 percent by 1981–82, while oil and gas revenues exceeded 70 percent of export proceeds.[55]

The revenue surge was initially treated with caution, since the economists were concerned about inflation, and a cumbersome administration

52. An account from one of the key members of the economic team is provided by Radius Prawiro, *Indonesia's Struggle for Economic Development: Pragmatism in Action* (Kuala Lumpur: Oxford University Press, 1998), 114–17.

53. Dick, "Survey of Recent Developments," 5–7; see also Anne Booth and Amina Tyabji, "Survey of Recent Developments," *Bulletin of Indonesian Economic Studies* 15, no. 2 (1979): 1–44.

54. These figures are the annual average price, as estimated by the U.S. Energy Information Administration in the *Annual Energy Review 2000.* http://www.eia.doe.gov/emeu/aer/pdf/pages/sec11_13.pdf.

55. Hill, *Indonesian Economy,* 46; Robison, *Indonesia,* 376; Bresnan, *Managing Indonesia,* 190.

had difficulty absorbing the new inflows.[56] By the end of 1979 external reserves had grown, and several ministries and regional governments significantly underspent their budgeted funds. The technocrats lost much of their influence as budget constraints and balance of payments problems faded from view. The tsunami of revenues sidelined concerns for efficiency in favor of ambitious plans for economic expansion and structural change. Soon enough, the windfall fueled a new round of spending and state sector expansion. A large component was directed to subsidies, especially on fuel, rice, and fertilizer.[57] The growth of the development budget afforded an opportunity for governing elites to advance goals of state-led industrialization and import-substitution.

Nationalist interests again took the initiative, putting forward a program of sectoral development that was largely outside the sway of the Bappenas economists. A leading figure was the minister of research and technology, Dr. B. J. Habibie, an energetic advocate of technological development and large-scale industry, and the embodiment of the entrepreneurial state. In this, he was substantially joined by the minister of industry, who emphasized the import-substitution goals of the Third Development Plan and pressed for large state investments in industrial projects.[58] Fortified by the second windfall, state planners pushed ahead with the expansion of the steel and LNG complexes, along with projects in petrochemicals, refining, electricity generation, aluminum, mining, telecommunications, fertilizer, pulp and paper, and cement. In all, more than $19 billion was slated for these schemes.[59] The construction of a modern industrial infrastructure fit in with the larger objectives of promoting an integrated, independent national economy. This called for limiting the influence of foreign capital, protecting domestic production, and encouraging indigenous business.[60] Policies for licensing, contracting, credit, and procurement were nominally intended to favor small and medium firms and to foster *pribumi* enterprise. Investment restrictions limited the extent of foreign involvement, while high tariffs and nontariff barriers were intended to insulate import-substitution activities.

56. Ross Garnaut, "Survey of Recent Developments," *Bulletin of Indonesian Economic Studies* 15, no. 3 (1979): 2–3; Jeffrey Winters, *Power in Motion: Capital Mobility and the Indonesian State* (Ithaca: Cornell University Press, 1996), 129.

57. Bresnan, *Managing Indonesia,* 211.

58. Bresnan, *Managing Indonesia,* 214–15. See also Thee Kian Wie, "Reflections on Indonesia's Emerging Industrial Nationalism," Working Paper No. 41 (Brisbane: Murdoch University Asia Research Centre, 1994).

59. Robison, *Indonesia,* 181.

60. Robison, *Indonesia,* 147.

The growth of state largesse spurred patronage and rent distribution. Although the New Order had evidently consolidated power by the late 1970s, the regime was buffeted by dissent from many quarters. In addition to the Malari disturbances of 1974, which targeted foreign and Chinese interests, protests and petitions were launched by middle-class intellectuals, Muslim politicians, students, and senior military officers. Their grievances included corruption, foreign domination of the economy, the suppression of religious values, politicization within the military, and the lack of political pluralism. The revenue windfall allowed Soeharto to assuage some of these pressures and to shore up his inner circle.

Surging oil revenues funded popular subsidies, a hike in public sector salaries, increases in the defense budget, enhanced funding for military-controlled business ventures and state enterprises, and additional state patronage.[61] With initial support from the senior economic team, the State Secretariat, or Sekneg, established the Government Procurement Team with broad authority for procurement, tendering, and project implementation. This new unit was intended to rationalize capital spending, improve the efficiency of projects, support *pribumi* enterprise, and limit the degree of "leakage" or rent distribution through the contracting process. In fact, the State Secretariat served as a central conduit for channeling resources to senior military officers, ethnic Chinese associates, the president's family, and other elite allies of the regime.[62] In true patrimonial fashion, such largesse was also used to discipline elites, as several participants in the protests associated with the 1980 Petition of Fifty lost access to contracts and credit.[63]

At the apex of the oil boom, the opposing currents of ideology and economic policy were in sharp contention. The forces of nationalism, populism, and patrimonial distribution had freer rein, but they were arrayed against groups that emphasized macroeconomic stability and restraint of the state. A strategy of state-led development was politically feasible as long as export revenues were abundant, though it hampered private capital formation. By the end of the 1970s the pattern of incentives discouraged foreign and domestic business, and credibility among market actors was at its lowest ebb since the New Order had come to power. This was reflected in the foreign and domestic investment approvals tracked by BKPM, which declined in value by about three-quarters between 1973 and

---

61. Liddle, "Relative Autonomy," 420–21.

62. Winters, *Power in Motion,* 128–35.

63. D. L. Bevan, Paul Collier, and J. W. Gunning, *The Political Economy of Poverty, Equity, and Growth in Nigeria and Indonesia, 1950–86* (Oxford: Oxford University Press for the World Bank, 1999), 262.

1976 and remained at less than half the 1973 level throughout the rest of the windfall period. Considering only foreign business, the decline was even steeper, as realized investment fell from about $500 million in 1975 to under $100 million in 1981.[64] The problems of the business environment were paralleled by the mediocre performance of the state sector. The bureaucracy and public enterprises were overextended, inefficient, and substantially corrupt.

These circumstances would seem to preclude sustained growth and structural change, yet there were mitigating factors (apart from strong export performance) that staved off pure predation and economic decay. Soeharto and other senior leaders were committed to such fundamentals as growth, low inflation, and rural development. Even while revenues crested and the statist drive had greatest momentum, the technocrats were able to exert countervailing influence with the president and induce a degree of prudence in macroeconomic management. For instance, the domestic fuel subsidy was a crucial popular measure, yet concerns about its budgetary impact prompted the government to implement two politically risky fuel price hikes in 1979 and 1980. The regime's sectoral priorities, while more problematic, were not entirely counterproductive. Although state enterprises produced at an enormously high cost, the investment in intermediate and capital goods and agro-allied industries increased output and deepened the structure of the economy.[65] Furthermore, leaders sought to contain inefficiencies in the state sector through such measures as replacing customs and tax administrators and attempting to rationalize procurement and contract implementation.

The subsidies for rice and fertilizer highlighted another distinctive aspect of the New Order's priorities, the emphasis on agricultural development. During the years of the resource boom, perhaps a quarter of development spending went to agricultural development and fertilizer subsidies, in addition to substantial expenditures on rural infrastructure.[66] The continuing attention to agricultural output and rural incomes was a major departure from the structural biases common to oil exporting countries.[67] These priorities were largely peculiar to Indonesia. For a leadership concerned about rural radicalism and discontent in the outer islands, agricultural development provided major distributional benefits. Self-

64. Winters, *Power in Motion,* 117.
65. Hill, *Indonesian Economy,* 157–58.
66. Bresnan, *Managing Indonesia,* 191.
67. C. Peter Timmer, *Dutch Disease and Agriculture in Indonesia: The Policy Approach,* Development Discussion Paper No. 490 (Cambridge: Harvard Institute for International Development, 1994).

sufficiency in rice was another central goal in view of the crises under Sukarno and the shortages just prior to the oil boom. The promotion of nonoil exports, which generally expanded during the windfall period, was also seen as an antidote to a possible balance of payments crisis in the event of sagging energy exports.

Shocks and Adjustment in the 1980s

The global recession that had bypassed Indonesia during the second windfall now alighted. Several factors, beginning with a drop in export income, converged in this downturn. Traditional exports began to flag in 1980 as the exchange rate appreciated (eroding the incentives of the previous devaluation) and world demand subsided. In the oil and gas sector, revenues peaked in 1981 and then declined as production and prices dropped in response to international recession. Rising interest rates and shifts in the value of the major currencies also sent Indonesia's debt service soaring. Foreign debt payments nearly tripled between 1980–81 and 1983–84. Since the revenue squeeze was not offset by a reduction in imports or public spending, the current account went massively into deficit.[68] After six years during which growth averaged 7.5 percent, the economy contracted by 0.3 percent in 1982 and grew only 3.3 percent the following year.[69]

The government's response to the new crisis displayed much the same ambivalence and political contention as the management of the windfall. Market-oriented stabilization measures were accompanied by an intensification of administrative controls and public interventions. In some respects, Indonesia's downturn was less acute than other debtor countries', which may have contributed to the diffident response. Compared to Mexico and Brazil, its debt position was relatively manageable, and its export base was broader than most other oil producers, which lessened some of the impact of a slack oil market.[70] By 1983, however, the eco-

68. E. Thorbecke, "Macroeconomic Disequilibrium and the Structural Adjustment Program," in Erik Thorbecke et al., eds., *Adjustment and Equity in Indonesia* (Paris: Centre of World Food Studies, OECD Development Centre, 1992), 42–43.

69. Pangestu and Bhattacharya, *Development Transformation,* 7–9.

70. At onset of the 1982 debt crisis, Mexico had a debt-to-export ratio of 139 percent, nearly a third of its debt was short-term, and the average interest rate for long-term obligations was 21 percent. Indonesia, by contrast, had a debt-to-export ratio of only 39 percent, about 18 percent in short-term obligations, and an average interest rate of 16 percent. See Wing Thye Woo and Anwar Nasution, "The Conduct of Economic Policies in Indonesia and Its Impact on External Debt," in Jeffrey D. Sachs, ed., *Developing Country Debt and the World Economy* (Chicago: University of Chicago Press for NBER, 1989), 114.

nomic picture was sufficiently grave that corrective action was unavoidable. Early initiatives included a further devaluation of the rupiah, the elimination of food subsidies, cuts in fuel subsidies (prompting a 60 percent increase in the domestic fuel price), and a sweeping effort to reschedule or curtail forty-eight large capital projects, including many of the core ventures advanced by the economic nationalists. Even defense spending came under the budget-paring knife.

The onset of crisis once again enhanced the role of the technocrats and the multilateral financial institutions, who focused on orthodox stabilization measures. In addition to budget cutting and new export incentives, the government sought to reform the tax regime, including a simplified system of assessment, better enforcement, and the introduction of a value-added tax (VAT). The financial system, which was dominated by a handful of government banks, was significantly liberalized by deregulating interest rates, removing credit ceilings, and curtailing the use of targeted credit. Monetary policy was also carefully managed to avoid problems of inflation and capital flight. All these measures fit in with a strategy of demand management, revenue enhancement, and market reform.[71]

In other areas of economic policy, however, the government favored an administrative approach to managing resource constraints. This was especially evident in trade, where a battery of new restrictions and regulations were imposed. Nearly 1,800 items were placed under import licenses or quotas, and more than 250 import items were banned outright. Many quotas were allotted to a small number of licensees, which provided extraordinary rents to the favored traders. The import restrictions were linked to a countertrade scheme through which foreign firms holding government contracts were required to offset their imports with purchases of Indonesian nonoil exports. Countertrade did little to improve the trade balance while substantially penalizing the economy through price manipulation by countertrade partners.[72] Trade policy exemplified the divisions within the regime. Even as segments of the government experimented with barter and foreign exchange rationing, the Finance Ministry pursued devaluations and tariff reductions.[73] A particularly daring intervention by Soeharto was the virtual suspension of the Customs Service in 1985, as inspections and collections were delegated to a Swiss firm, the Société Générale de Surveillance (SGS). The recourse to external sources of

71. Thorbecke, "Macroeconomic Disequilibrium," 43.
72. Woo, Glassburner, and Nasution, *Macroeconomic Policies,* 113.
73. Woo, Glassburner, and Nasution, *Macroeconomic Policies,* 113.

restraint reflected a desire by elements of the regime to assert control over state institutions and to enhance the credibility of reform commitments.[74]

A further reduction in state resources swung policy toward liberalization and a market-led strategy. During 1986 the oil price plummeted from $28 to less than $12 before rebounding to $18.[75] The year's revenues for oil and gas were about $5 billion, or about a third of receipts in 1981. Energy exports dropped from 62 percent of government revenues to 30 percent, and development expenditures fell by a fifth.[76] The current account deficit escalated, as did the ratio of debt service to exports. Despite conservative budgeting, a major deficit loomed for 1986–87, threatening one of the regime's economic axioms. The slide in the petroleum sector created an urgent need to find new sources of government revenue and foreign exchange. Declining export earnings and rising debt service also compelled political leaders to reconfigure the scope of patronage and withdraw from an agenda of state-led development.[77] Changing markets and fiscal realities prompted a shift from short-term stabilization to a broader adjustment of the economy. The strategic change entailed a renewed emphasis on private investment and production in the nonoil sectors of the economy.[78]

As the predicament deepened, the government introduced a series of reforms. In May, trade restrictions were substantially loosened with the aim of promoting exports. Producers of exports were allowed to import many of their own inputs with duties reduced or eliminated. Debate was sharpening over the "high cost economy," a code for the welter of regulations, administrative bottlenecks, and corrupt payments faced by businesses, especially those with a large trade component.[79] The supply response to the trade incentives was disappointing, however, and in Sep-

---

74. M. Hadi Soesastro, "The Political Economy of Deregulation in Indonesia," *Asian Survey* 29, no. 9: 860. It is noteworthy that the SGS was engaged by the Nigerian government in 1979 to perform preshipment inspections, although without significant internal customs reform.

75. Richard Robison, "Authoritarian States, Capital-Owning Classes, and the Politics of Newly-Industrializing Countries: The Case of Indonesia," *World Politics* 41, no. 1 (1988): 66; Economist Intelligence Unit, *Indonesia Country Profile, 1988–89* (London: Economist Intelligence Unit, 1988), 39.

76. Hill, *Indonesian Economy*, 46–47; World Bank, *Indonesia: Stability, Growth, and Equity in Repelita VI* (Washington, DC: World Bank, 1994), Statistical Annex, table 5.4.

77. Pangestu and Bhattacharya, *Development Transformation*, 8–10.

78. Winters, *Power in Motion*, 155–57.

79. Soesastro, "Politicial Economy," 854; Ali Wardhana, "Economic Reform in Indonesia: The Transition from Resource Dependence to Industrial Competitiveness," in Henry S. Rowen, ed., *Behind East Asian Growth: The Political and Social Foundations of Prosperity* (London: Routledge, 1998), 129.

tember, with little consultation or advance notice the government announced a further 45 percent devaluation of the rupiah. This initiative was motivated by the deteriorating terms of trade for both oil and nonoil products and an increasingly poor prognosis for the balance of payments.[80] When the crisis had emerged in 1982, Indonesia was able to turn to foreign aid and loans to stem some of the trade and budget gaps, but there was growing awareness that a reliance on external finance would worsen balance of payments problems and diminish the country's standing in global capital markets. In view of the fact that there was no current indication of overvaluation, the 1986 measure was a preemptive effort to stave off further deterioration in the budget and external finances. Devaluation approached the problem through a market lens, using changes in relative prices to generate higher export earnings and broaden the tax base.

On the heels of devaluation, more extensive liberalization of trade and investment was enacted. The number of items under quota or import license was reduced and regulations on exports were relaxed. The regime also sought to revitalize incentives for foreign investors by lowering the barriers to entry, facilitating joint ventures, and strengthening investment guarantees.[81] One important dimension of investment liberalization was the decision to discourage the distinction between *pribumi* and non-*pribumi* enterprise in favor of references to "economically weak groups," which would include small-scale capital as well as indigenous entrepreneurs. This allowed a broader range of firms to utilize incentives and state credit. Trade reform still left many large, profitable monopolies in the hands of the regime's inner circle, ethnic Chinese and members of the ruling family.[82]

The technocrats were accompanied by voices from the universities, the media, and the private sector clamoring for a better investment environment.[83] This meant fewer overt regulations or restrictions, fewer hidden costs, and a reduction in favoritism and monopoly. A decisive step in this direction came with the October 1988 package (*Pakto*) and associated measures that constituted the "big bang" in Indonesia's liberalization.

80. Anne Booth, "Survey of Recent Developments," *Bulletin of Indonesian Economic Studies* 22, no. 3 (1986): 1.

81. Wardhana, "Economic Reform," 131; Winters, *Power in Motion,* 156.

82. Winters, *Power in Motion,* 184–90.

83. Soesastro, "Political Economy," 859; R. William Liddle, "The Politics of Shared Growth: Some Indonesian Cases," *Comparative Politics* 19, no. 2 (1987): 143–44; MacIntyre, "Politics and the Reorientation of Economic Policy in Indonesia," in Andrew J. MacIntyre and Kanishka Jayasuriya, eds., *The Dynamics of Economic Policy Reform in South-east Asia and the South-west Pacific* (Singapore: Oxford University Press, 1992), 147–49.

These policies encompassed trade, investment, finance, and sectoral reform. Many of the major import licenses—including a number of the lucrative trade monopolies—were removed, and tariffs were subsequently reduced. Investment was opened further, and restrictions on agriculture, industry, and shipping were scaled back.

The centerpiece of the package, however, was banking and finance. The reforms ended the dominance of the state financial institutions by opening the banking sector to private entry, permitting more extensive foreign participation, allowing banks to expand their branches and activities, widening the scope of authorized foreign exchange banks, and withdrawing the state banks' virtual monopoly on deposits from state enterprises.[84] The bank reforms were paralleled by other measures to deepen capital markets. Longer-term monetary instruments were permitted, and a secondary market was opened. The stock market was substantially liberalized by easing requirements for listing equities, rescinding practices that distorted prices, and allowing a wider array of trading and brokerage activities. In addition, regulations on insurance, venture capital, and nonbank finance were loosened.[85]

While the policies of the early 1980s focused mainly on shoring up the short-term budget and balance of payments, the later reforms aimed at restoring incentives, expanding production, increasing competition, and bolstering confidence among market actors. These policy changes created a fundamental shift in economic strategy and the structure of the economy. Capital flight was stanched, investment approvals increased, nonoil exports expanded, and manufacturing output grew vigorously. The reforms helped to restore macroeconomic stability and jump-start growth, eliciting strong responses from investors and producers.

The oil downturn displayed notable paradoxes. Indonesia faced the greatest challenges to economic growth and stability since the 1960s, although unlike that earlier period, the problems of the 1980s stemmed largely from exogenous shocks. Despite these formidable difficulties, however, the country recorded impressive economic achievements. Although growth dipped badly in 1982–83 and 1986–87, the economy grew at an average rate of more than 6 percent from 1981 through 1990, exceeding 7 percent in several years. Inflation averaged 8.6 percent, substantially lower than the boom years.[86] Foreign debt grew at an alarming rate but

84. Djisman S. Simandjuntak, "Survey of Recent Developments," *Bulletin of Indonesian Economic Studies* 25, no. 1 (1989): 21–23; Hill, *Indonesian Economy,* 36.

85. Woo, Glassburner, and Nasution, *Macroeconomic Policies,* 105.

86. World Bank, *World Development Indicators,* http://devdata.worldbank.org/dataon line/.

remained manageable. Indonesia was not at risk of default, and the government was able to preserve many essential components of development spending, especially infrastructure investments. In 1984, owing to good weather and favorable policies, Indonesia became self-sufficient in rice production, and agricultural exports continued to expand in volume throughout the decade. Furthermore, a surge of investment in manufacturing during the latter half of the decade substantially diversified the economy. By the early 1990s, manufacturing exports replaced oil and gas as the largest component of export income. Indonesia had ceased becoming an oil economy but was now an export economy with oil.

How was the regime able to manage the turbulence of the 1980s and put the economy on a better footing? One part of the explanation must take into consideration the advantages carried over from the windfall era. Prior decisions regarding fiscal control, rationalization of the state sector, debt management, devaluation, and export diversification fostered a relatively strong position as recession descended, affording greater leverage to policymakers.[87] The continued influence of the technocrats, and their ability at crucial moments to gain Soeharto's backing for decisive measures, was also a major factor. The regime responded rapidly to significant changes in revenues or external prices—often within a matter of weeks, usually no more than a few months. This was facilitated, of course, by good relations between the government, donors, and the multilateral financial institutions, which enabled the flow of external resources in support of stabilization and adjustment measures. One essential benefit was the ability to sustain much of the development budget without veering toward deficits or depleting reserves. Moreover, cooperation with external actors was integral to sustaining credibility with market participants. On the heels of devaluation, the open capital account gave rise to bouts of capital flight, but the government was able to reverse the exodus through the use of monetary policy rather than capital controls, which served to enhance confidence in commitments to macroeconomic stability.[88] Finally, Indonesia was in a fortunate neighborhood when the government embarked on reform. Foreign direct investment from Japan, which surged after 1986, was instrumental in Indonesia's postreform growth.[89] The incentives proffered by the Indonesian government also accelerated a shift

87. Wardhana, "Economic Reform," 140; Soesastro, "Political Economy."

88. Woo, Glassburner, and Nasution, *Macroeconomic Policies,* 106.

89. Thee Kian Wie, "Japanese Direct Investment in Indonesian Manufacturing," *Bulletin of Indonesian Economic Studies* 20, no. 2: 90–106; see also Alasdair Bowie and Daniel Unger, *The Politics of Open Economies: Indonesia, Malaysia, the Philippines, and Thailand* (Cambridge: Cambridge University Press, 1997), 61.

of low-wage, labor-intensive manufacturing from Hong Kong, South Korea, Singapore, and other regional exporters to Indonesia.[90]

From Oil Boom to Investment Boom

Indonesia's trajectory of policy reform converged fortuitously with changes in the international economy. The Iraqi invasion of Kuwait and the ensuing Gulf War helped to boost oil and gas prices, increasing export receipts by more than 25 percent in 1990–91. Unlike previous revenue surges, however, this episode did not induce a shift in strategy or a new round of domestic spending. Much of the transitory windfall was devoted to paying down foreign debt and developing infrastructure, while liberalization continued to guide the policy agenda.[91] Far more important over the longer term, the country's turn toward greater integration with the world economy coincided with the boom in private global capital flows, manifest in both direct and portfolio investment. Indonesia's accommodating investment climate increased its attraction as an emerging market during a buoyant phase of financial globalization and mobile corporate capital. Approvals of direct foreign investment by the national agency BKPM jumped from $9 billion in 1990 to $40 billion by 1995.[92] Portfolio investment surged, from $275 million as late as 1992 to $4.1 *billion* only two years later.[93] In addition, the expansion of global and intraregional trade furnished an outlet for Indonesia's export push, as nonoil exports grew by about 20 percent on average between 1985 and 1994.[94] Fueled by new capital and favorable market conditions, Indonesia entered a new phase of economic expansion and diversification.

There are several noteworthy aspects of Indonesia's strong economic performance in the wake of adjustment. First, growth was exceptionally

---

90. Thee Kian Wie, "The Investment Surge from Asia's NICs into Indonesia," in Hal Hill and Terry Hull, eds., *Indonesia Assessment, 1990* (Canberra: Research School of Pacific Studies, Australian National University, 1990), 66–79.

91. Donald K. Emmerson, "Indonesia in 1990: A Foreshadow Play," *Asian Survey* 31, no. 2 (1991): 186; see also Anwar Nasution, "Survey of Recent Developments," *Bulletin of Indonesian Economic Studies* 27, no. 2 (1991): 3–43.

92. Investment approvals are typically far in excess of realized investments. Figures on actual DFI show an increase in "realized" investment from $1.1 billion in 1991 to $5.7 billion in 1993. See Thee, "Japanese Direct Investment," 90, 92; and the Indonesian Investment Coordinating Board (BKPM), *Trend of Investment Realization, 1990–2005,* http://www .bkpm.go.id/en/figure.php?mode=baca&t=Facts%20and%20Figures.

93. Alexander Irwan, *Financial Flows and the Environmental Strategy in Indonesia in the 1990s* (Washington DC: World Resources Institute, 1997), 5; World Bank, *World Development Indicators:* http://devdata.worldbank.org/dataonline/.

94. Wardhana, "Economic Reform," 130.

high, averaging 8.1 percent from 1989 to 1996, and in excess of 9 percent during selected years.[95] Building upon the expansion of preceding decades, this new round of investment-driven growth was even more impressive than that achieved during the stabilization period, which arose from a narrower base. Second, the pattern of growth was quite diverse. Although Jakarta and a few other centers were particularly dynamic, there was a distribution of investment and production both geographically and among sectors. Large-scale ventures and foreign investment were important to many capital- and technology-intensive activities, but there was also a considerable stratum of small- and medium-scale local firms in manufacturing, agricultural processing, and services.[96] Manufacturing included production for both export and the domestic market, as investors moved into textiles, footwear, food processing, plywood, consumer electronics, furniture, and a host of other items. The composition of nonoil exports shifted away from primary products, as manufactures assumed a much greater share. In agriculture, rice production expanded as well as other food crops such as maize and cassava. There was growth in the major export crops—rubber, tea, coffee, cocoa, and palm oil—along with lesser items such as coconuts, tobacco, cloves, and other spices. Many were cultivated in the outer islands as well as Java, and except for tea and palm oil, the majority of output was from smallholders rather than large estates.[97] The rapid expansion of service industries such as banking, finance, transport, communications, and tourism also had broad employment effects. Third, the economic expansion of the early 1990s had a relatively positive distributional impact. Absolute poverty diminished substantially, not just in income terms but also in dimensions such as literacy, education, infant survival, and life expectancy.[98] Measures of income equality do not suggest a highly skewed distribution for this high-growth phase in Indonesia. Furthermore, the dispersion of investment and growth meant that there was some perception of benefits beyond Java and the urban concentrations.

The robust performance of the early 1990s, however, could not obscure deep-seated problems in the New Order's economic model. The

95. World Bank, *World Development Indicators,* http://devdata.worldbank.org/dataon line/.

96. Hal Hill, *Indonesia's Industrial Transformation* (Singapore: Institute of Southeast Asian Studies, 1997).

97. Hill, *Indonesian Economy,* 125.

98. Anne Booth, "Poverty and Inequality in the Soeharto Era: An Assessment," *Bulletin of Indonesian Economic Studies* 36, no. 1 (2000): 73–104; Thorbecke, "Macroeconomic Disequilibrium," 52–54.

technocrats, policy economists, and segments of the foreign donor and business communities expressed concern over inefficiencies in the structure of the economy and continuing impediments in the policy regime.[99] Apart from differences among policy elites, the regime's broader social coalition was increasingly tenuous. Voices among the domestic media, Muslim groups, students, academics, and the business class took up questions of equity and social justice. Much attention focused on imbalances in the pattern of growth, the murky institutional setting, and perennial issues of clientelism and corruption. Even as the economy flourished, a chorus of social protest and criticism raised questions about the foundations of growth and the regime's political future.[100]

Foreign capital provided an important focal point. Reforms in trade, investment, and finance attracted a wave of direct investment from Japan, the East Asian newly industrializing countries, the United States, and Europe, extending well beyond the energy sector to manufacturing, mining, construction, estate agriculture, banking, and tourism.[101] The resurgence of external involvement in the economy evoked long-standing anxieties that foreign ventures would crowd out local entrepreneurs and undermine import-competing activities. Domestic business groups, who were increasingly heterogeneous and independent, sought protection and support through industry associations, the media, and back-channel solicitation of political leaders.[102] Within the cabinet, nationalists worried that foreign capital would erode domestic initiatives in high-technology and basic industries. In addition, relations with external donors were complicated by increasing concerns over human rights and other domestic policies. In 1992 the regime responded to Dutch criticisms over its repressive policies in East Timor by dissolving the IGGI (which had been coordinated by the Netherlands) and replacing it with the Consultative Group on Indonesia (CGI), facilitated by the World Bank. This did not signal a rupture with multilateral institutions or other donor governments, though it did indicate the degree to which domestic political problems intruded upon the country's international reputation.

The controversial role of domestic business conglomerates was another central issue. Most of these large, diversified corporations were

99. Andrew MacIntyre, "Power, Prosperity, and Patrimonialism: Business and Government in Indonesia," in Andrew MacIntyre, ed., *Business and Government in Industrializing Asia* (Ithaca: Cornell University Press, 1994), 255–58; Hal Hill, "Survey of Recent Developments," *Bulletin of Indonesian Economic Studies* 28, no. 2 (1992): 22–24.

100. Schwarz, *Nation in Waiting,* 295–97.

101. Thee, "Japanese Direct Investment," and Thee, "Investment Surge."

102. Andrew J. MacIntyre, *Business and Politics in Indonesia* (Sydney: Allen and Unwin, 1990).

fairly young, and economic liberalization permitted them to rapidly expand the scale and scope of their operations. The majority were owned or controlled by ethnic Chinese entrepreneurs who had close relations with the regime. They enjoyed numerous advantages including trade monopolies, government contracts and credit, and preferred status as foreign partners in joint ventures.[103] The conspicuous growth of the conglomerates sharpened invidious distinctions between *pribumi* and non-*pribumi* interests. Ethnic resentment was bound up with concerns over monopoly and the collusive nature of state-business relations. These issues extended to Soeharto's family, whose business interests proliferated in the late 1980s and early 1990s. Soeharto's wife, several of his six children, and other relatives were variously involved in car manufacturing, telecommunications, roads and transportation, tourism, importing, and many other lucrative areas. Critics of the regime quipped that Soeharto's commitment to the development of *pribumi* enterprise started (and largely ended) at home.[104]

The patrimonial foundations of Indonesian capitalism posed the greatest liabilities for continued development. The web of relationships between the president, his family, senior military officers, ethnic Chinese magnates, and other allies and retainers foreclosed competition, aggravated social tension, and spurred political dissent.[105] The regime's continuing policy reforms stayed well clear of the crucial trade monopolies held by the president's relatives and prominent Chinese associates, and they did little to curtail the preferential dispensation of government contracts or special access to credit. Collusion and favoritism were intimately bound up with endemic corruption in the public sector and much of the business community. This was broadly resented on the grounds of ethics and inequality, and was criticized by economists who viewed it as a hindrance to economic dynamism and a liability for the country's reputation. Furthermore, Soeharto's personal position as gatekeeper and manager of the system was increasingly problematic. As strong economic performance continued into the mid-1990s, questions of economic management grew less urgent and the technocrats consequently lost much of their leverage within the regime. The sprawling business interests of the president's family and key associates such as Bob Hasan and Liem Sioe Liong appeared

103. Schwarz, *Nation in Waiting,* chap. 5; Bresnan, *Managing Indonesia,* 255–57.

104. Schwarz, *Nation in Waiting,* 147.

105. See, for instance, Sofyan Wanandi, "The Post Soeharto Business Environment," and Jamie Mackie, "Tackling the 'Chinese Problem,'" both in Geoff Forrester, ed., *Post-Soeharto Indonesia: Renewal or Chaos?* (Bathurst: Crawford House, 1999); and Ahmad D. Habir, "Conglomerates: All in the Family?" in Donald K. Emmerson, ed., *Indonesia beyond Suharto: Polity, Economy, Society, Transition* (Armonk: M. E. Sharpe, 1999), 168–202.

to command a greater share of Soeharto's attention. In addition, the question of political succession loomed larger. The 1992 elections delivered a reduced majority (of 68 percent) to the ruling Golkar party, yet the structures of corporatist control appeared stable and Soeharto was diffident about contemplating a change of leadership. The concentration of political and economic power in a strong executive raised the specter of economic disruption, should a succession crisis arise from Soeharto's departure.[106]

Structural and institutional problems also persisted. Financial services flourished in the wake of liberalization, but the precipitous growth of banks and capital markets created a realm of poorly supervised economic activity that posed a hazard to economic stability.[107] Many of the new banks, established under the umbrella of the conglomerates, carried out large volumes of intrafirm transactions, largely in disregard of regulatory strictures. The banking industry was feebly supervised, and banks often relied upon their political connections to avoid the scrutiny of regulators. A number of high-profile episodes of mismanagement and scandal afflicting major banks in the early 1990s prompted efforts to strengthen prudential guidelines, but the web of influence undermined effective oversight. While the banking bubble was sustained by economic growth and burgeoning capital markets, the insubstantial foundations of many institutions and the opaque practices throughout the industry threatened a major dislocation in the financial system.

Symptoms of the "high-cost economy" remained troublesome, despite the continuing liberalization of trade and investment. Excessive regulation, bureaucratic and legal hindrances, corruption, and inflated input costs from trade monopolies and public enterprises created a difficult environment for the development of manufacturing and some nonoil exports. The size and scope of the state sector was another factor limiting competitiveness. More than two hundred government-owned enterprises accounted for nearly a third of GDP by the mid-1980s. State-owned firms were inefficient, while numerous monopolies on trade and production created price rigidities and limited entry in many areas of the economy. As early as 1986, the president announced intentions to privatize major public ventures, but little progress followed. Even as reform proceeded in other dimensions of economic policy, state-sponsored industrial and technological development was championed by minister for research and tech-

106. R. William Liddle, "Indonesia's Threefold Crisis," *Journal of Democracy* 3, no. 4 (1992): 60–74.
107. David C. Cole and Betty F. Slade, "Why Has Indonesia's Financial Crisis Been So Bad?" *Bulletin of Indonesian Economic Studies* 34, no. 2 (1998): 65.

nology Habibie, who pursued a national aircraft project along with other costly ventures. Far from rationalizing the public sector, ten leading projects were given special status and placed under Habibie's direct control. These enterprises made substantial claims on public finances and substantially influenced the direction of industrial policy.

Regional disparities created additional tensions. The regime made efforts to disperse central resources during the petroleum boom, and some observers have credited the New Order with a sound record of regional redistribution.[108] The structural adjustment measures of the 1980s, furthermore, boosted cash crop production and commodity exports in many parts of the archipelago. Nonetheless, groups in some of the outer islands looked askance at the perceived developmental advantages of Java and the capital. The resulting political contention focused on calls for greater balance in government spending and revenue sharing, though there were more forceful challenges to the control of Jakarta. In addition to nationalist demands from East Timor, which had been occupied by Indonesia in 1975, the regime faced pressures for autonomy or independence from the resource-rich areas of Aceh and Riau (in Sumatra), East Kalimantan, and Irian Jaya. As distributional concerns and centrifugal demands attained growing salience, questions arose regarding stability in economically important areas of the country.

The decade of reform following the nadir of oil prices displayed striking contradictions. From 1986 through 1996 the economy was reinvigorated and substantially restructured. Rapid growth was restored, production and revenues diversified from the energy sector, and Indonesia was more broadly integrated into the global economy. An active, heterogeneous private sector emerged, and the country advanced in export and capital markets. The regime could draw upon an earlier record of stability and prudent macroeconomic management in fostering credible commitments for investors and producers. Indonesia's reputation was enhanced by its regional position, and, as the 1990s wore on, by growing exuberance over the world's emerging markets, of which the country was a select member. The political problems and structural flaws in the economy were overlooked or discounted by many investors.

Yet observers and analysts noted chronic problems in the nation's political economy. A vigorous reform impulse gave way by the mid-1990s to policy drift, as the regime largely exhausted the possibilities of macroeconomic policy change and temporized on key changes in sectoral policy

108. Hill, *Indonesian Economy*, 215; Mari Pangestu and Iwan Jaya Azis, "Survey of Recent Developments," *Bulletin of Indonesian Economic Studies* 30, no. 2 (1994): 38–39.

and institutional performance. State enterprises were largely untouched, and there were few initiatives in critical areas of legal and administrative reform. The influence of the Berkeley mafia waned, as nationalist, protectionist, and patrimonial interests contested the terrain of economic policy. The interests of Soeharto's inner circle consistently trumped efforts to expand competition and open crucial areas of the economy. Corporate activities and capital markets were opaque, rife with political collusion, and predicated on questionable practices. Indonesia's economy, increasingly driven by trade and global capital flows, reflected acute tensions between the domestic structure of patrimonial capitalism and the exigencies of external transparency. In the heady days of 1996, rising investment and vigorous growth prompted optimistic economic projections, and there were few premonitions of the speed and depth of the impending economic ruin.[109]

109. Hal Hill, *The Indonesian Economy: Crisis, Causes, Consequences, and Lessons* (Singapore: ISEAS, Singapore, 1998), 5.

CHAPTER 5

Nigeria

Division, Distribution, and Decline

Nigeria's policy regime and the country's evolution within the global economy differed substantially from those of Indonesia. Nigerian elites responded to different incentives, exacerbating the weaknesses of the rentier economy and avoiding needed adjustments in response to exogenous shocks. With the arrival of the initial petroleum windfall, Nigerian leaders pursued a set of policies that intensified the macroeconomic distortions embodied in the Dutch disease and consequently increased the concentration of the economy around petroleum rents. The oil bust of 1981 was aggravated by mismanagement and malfeasance under the civilian Second Republic, while the military government that seized power in 1984 flirted unsuccessfully with homegrown austerity measures, as economic performance continued to decline.

Not until 1986 did the new regime of General Babangida engage foreign creditors and commit to a formal adjustment package. The reform initiative, however, succumbed to inconsistent policies and uneven implementation. Nigeria's Structural Adjustment Program yielded little domestic supply response in the nonoil sectors of the economy, and it had scant effect in alleviating the country's growing isolation in international markets. The rapid deterioration of economic management was compounded by the repercussions of a political succession crisis in 1993, culminating with yet another coup. The country's already dismal image worsened under the pall of predatory rule. Nigeria's global isolation deepened under international sanctions. Policy failures, administrative decay, and political crisis instigated a downward economic spiral. To shed light on the background to these crises, I now turn to the historical perspective on Nigerian development.

Colonialism and Nationalism

Nigeria's colonial boundaries incorporated numerous political entities, social and cultural groups, and economic domains. Prior to the arrival of

Europeans, this territory was home to sprawling empires, numerous centralized states, and a multiplicity of smaller, segmentary lineage societies. In the early nineteenth century, the jihad of Usman dan Fodio encompassed much of the northern domain, sweeping south and east from the Sokoto Caliphate to hold sway over the Hausa states, numerous communities in the savanna and northern forest belts, and portions of other large societies such as the Yoruba. To the northeast of the emirates lay the historical empire of Kanem-Bornu. The Tiv, a segmentary society, limned the Muslim areas to the southeast. The coastal and forest regions west of the Niger River were home to several Yoruba and Edo states, while the areas to the east included small states and several decentralized societies, of which the Igbo were the largest.

European involvement in Nigeria began in the late fifteenth century when the Portuguese established commercial and military outposts. The southern areas of the country became a major locus of the transatlantic slave trade. Britain projected its influence in the early eighteenth century and began formal colonization in 1861 with the establishment of the coastal Colony of Lagos, followed in 1900 by the Protectorates of Southern and Northern Nigeria. These were amalgamated in 1914 into a single territory, although the British maintained separate administrative systems throughout the colonial era. In Northern Nigeria, the colonial administration was guided by Lord Lugard's doctrine of indirect rule, which conferred substantial autonomy to the emirs and insulated many Muslim legal and religious institutions from colonial influence. The administration of the south was more intrusive in many respects. Politically, most indigenous authority was undermined by the imposition of British authorities and the appointment of "warrant chiefs" as local proxies. Culturally, the open door to missionary activities had profound effects on religion and education. Economically, production and trade were transformed by the concentration of commerce, investment, and colonial enterprise in Lagos and other coastal centers, and by the spread of export agriculture.

In 1939 the colonial government established three regions that were ethnically and economically distinct.[1] The predominantly Muslim Northern Region encompassed the Hausa-Fulani emirates and the northeastern Kanuri areas, as well as Nupe, Kabe, Gwari, and Tiv populations. The Western Region, where the Yoruba were in the majority, also contained Edo, Ijaw, Urhobo, and Igbo minorities, in a comparatively plural religious setting. In the Eastern Region, which was overwhelmingly Christian,

---

1. James S. Coleman, *Nigeria: Background to Nationalism* (Berkeley: University of California Press, 1958), 46–49.

the Igbo were the largest group, alongside substantial minorities including the Efik, Ibibio, Ijaw, Isekiri, and Ogonis. Lagos, the capital, was a predominantly Yoruba city in the southwestern corner of the country. Together, the three largest ethnolinguistic groups made up two-thirds of Nigeria's people, a pattern that would have important effects on political competition and the course of development.

Cultural and linguistic differences among the regions were overlaid by varying economic activities. Export production of cocoa and palm oil predominated in the forest zones of the Western Region, palm produce was prevalent in the geographically similar Eastern Region, and groundnuts and cotton were crucial to the semiarid Northern Region. Solid minerals, including limestone, tin, and iron ore, were broadly though unevenly distributed.[2] Import trade, wholesale distribution, and manufacturing were dominated by a few large European trading firms and Levantine interests. Under colonial rule, the development of manufacturing was comparatively limited and geographically concentrated. Lagos was the industrial and commercial center, with secondary concentrations in some eastern cities and in Kano and Kaduna in the north. Manufacturing activity was largely confined to labor-intensive, light consumer goods for local consumption. As to infrastructure, basic road and communications networks were heavily concentrated in the southern zones, while a limited rail network linked the Lagos port to export centers up-country. Regional disparities in manufacturing and infrastructure were mirrored by inequalities in human capital, as formal education and modern commercial and administrative skills were far more prevalent among the southern peoples than those of the north.

British rule formed a classic open economy based upon the export of agricultural commodities and solid minerals and the importation of foreign manufactures, with state revenues derived mainly from the taxation of trade.[3] Notwithstanding Britain's reputation as a guardian of economic liberalism, the colonial administration intervened substantially in the economy. Government authorities established numerous public enterprises in infrastructure, production, and commerce, while officials regulated external trade and the commerce in major commodities. For the most part local producers were drawn toward cash crop production by market inducements rather than the types of levies or edicts that were

2. Petroleum was discovered in 1956, though not commercially developed in significant amounts until the early 1970s. See Scott R. Pearson, *Petroleum and the Nigerian Economy* (Stanford: Stanford University Press, 1969), 15–18.

3. The model is discussed in Peter Kilby, *Industrialization in an Open Economy: Nigeria, 1945–1966* (Cambridge: Cambridge University Press, 1969).

commonly used in many other African colonies.[4] The bulk of export production came from smallholders, and there was limited investment in plantation agriculture. Government-controlled commodity boards, created on the eve of World War II, generated large revenues by maintaining a large spread between the local producer price and the border price of major agricultural exports. The effective level of taxation was as high as 50 percent for crops such as cocoa, and the commodity boards amassed large surpluses for regional treasuries in the postwar years.[5]

During the late colonial period, a federal system of government was built upon the regional structure. In 1946 Governor Richards set in place a constitution giving significant political autonomy to the regional governments, including separate advisory assemblies. Successive reforms under governors MacPherson (1951) and Lyttleton (1954) expanded the administrative and legislative powers of the regions, introduced elections for the regional and national legislatures, and conferred a significant fiscal authority to regional governments, including the right to retain a substantial portion of locally derived revenues. During this period, the rapid growth of anticolonial nationalism led to a negotiated settlement between Nigerian nationalists and the British government, culminating with elections in 1959 and independence in 1960. As representative political institutions took shape, the regions supported geographically based parties with distinct ethnic character. Each region was controlled by a hegemonic political party, creating separate ethnoregional domains by the time of independence. The Eastern Region was controlled by the Igbo-dominated National Council of Nigeria and the Cameroons (NCNC, later renamed the National Convention of Nigerian Citizens), the Western Region by the Yoruba-based Action Group (AG), and the Northern Region by the Northern People's Congress (NPC), based among the Hausa-Fulani elites. Each of these parties played a two-level political game, securing their regional position against local minorities and other challengers while also seeking to advance their position at the federal level. Nationally, political competition was a basic three-way struggle among leading ethnoregional parties, although smaller groups attained increasing political leverage over time.

The transition from colonial rule resulted in northern dominance of the first postindependence government. The 1957 constitutional settlement allotted representation in parliament on the basis of regional popu-

4. Gerald K. Helleiner, *Peasant Agriculture, Government, and Economic Growth in Nigeria* (Homewood, IL: Richard D. Irwin, 1966).
5. Helleiner, *Peasant Agriculture,* 248.

lation and stipulated that the party with a plurality in the national legislature could form the federal government.[6] An earlier colonial census (1952–53) indicated that the Northern Region held 53 percent of the total population, and the NPC's regional dominance ensured an electoral plurality in the National Assembly. Sir Abubaker Tafawa Balewa, deputy leader of the NPC, became prime minister in the new federal government, while Sir Ahmadu Bello, the Sardauna of Sokoto, maintained his pivotal role as party leader and Northern Regional premier. The NPC sustained its electoral strength in the 1959 transitional elections, and the British governor invited Tafawa Balewa to form the independent government, consolidating the political power of the northern elites. With control of the federal executive and a secure regional base, the northern party was able to maintain control of the political center through selective alliances with rival southern parties, combined with efforts to undermine or divide opponents.

The First Republic: Patronage, Competition, and Political Crisis

The newly independent government followed a pragmatic economic strategy built upon the central features of the open economy. Foreign revenues derived mainly from export agriculture and solid minerals, although petroleum, which had been discovered in the late 1950s, grew steadily in importance.[7] Federal and regional governments sought to develop their rudimentary manufacturing base by promoting basic import-competing industries. Nigerian political elites were not ideologically hostile to foreign investment, external trade, or private enterprise, though they favored a substantial role for government as a vehicle of development. State initiative was often rationalized as a catalyst of private sector growth, and public spending concentrated on infrastructure and social services with the intention of facilitating market activity. The developmentalist approach of the late colonial period was carried over by the postcolonial governments, who variously sheltered, subsidized, and created strategic enterprises at both federal and regional levels. Economic nationalism and myriad pressures for patronage also induced a more assertive state role, including expanded state employment and public investment, increased protection for many domestic enterprises and sectors, and policies ostensibly aimed at domestic redistribution. The first National Development Plan for 1962

---

6. Richard Sklar provides an extensive analysis of party dynamics during this period in *Nigerian Political Parties* (Princeton: Princeton University Press, 1963).

7. Pearson, *Petroleum and the Nigerian Economy,* 34.

through 1968 outlined an eclectic strategy calling for an expansion of the government's institutional machinery and planning capacities, the development of infrastructure and some large-scale public industries, an articulation of legal and financial incentives to foreign business, and the provision of assistance to local private enterprise.[8] The plan embodied a haphazard set of priorities and targets, which provided vague policy direction. Moreover this "national" plan (in fact, a federal plan accompanied by three separate regional blueprints) highlighted the relative weakness of federal authorities.[9] Economic management was hampered by the division of powers and the fractious dynamics of the federal system. The regional authorities exercised a great deal of control over key policies and locally derived revenues, leaving the government in Lagos with limited sway over resources or institutions.

The diverse ideological profiles of the regional governments belied considerable similarities in economic management. The Northern People's Congress was relatively conservative, while the eastern NCNC had social-democratic orientations, and the southwest Action Group took an assertive populist stance. Despite such outward differences each of the regions effectively became a distinct clientelist system fed by the revenues from commodity exports and disbursed through public enterprises and financial institutions.[10] The regional authorities channeled the resources from the commodity boards to politically controlled development corporations and loan schemes. Prominent banks in each region became virtual adjuncts to the ruling political parties, serving as repositories for export proceeds and party finances. Party elites consolidated their position through the dispensation of jobs, capital, and licenses to allies and clients.[11] Regional governments created publicly owned ventures in light importing-substituting manufactures and assumed control of several failing private businesses. Government firms provided employment and dispensed patronage to contractors, suppliers, and distributors. Political criteria dictated the allocation of subsidies and protection for local private business. An indigenous entrepreneurial class concentrated in retail trade, construction, transport, small-scale manufacturing, agricultural process-

8. D. Olu Ajakaiye, "Impact of Policy on Public Enterprise Performance in Nigeria," *Nigerian Journal of Economic and Social Studies* 26, no. 3 (1984): 376–77.

9. Edwin Dean, *Plan Implementation in Nigeria, 1962–1966* (Ibadan: Oxford University Press, 1972), 30.

10. Richard Sklar and C. S.Whitaker Jr., "Nigeria," in James S. Coleman and Carl G. Rosberg Jr., eds., *Political Parties and National Integration in Tropical Africa* (Berkeley and Los Angeles: University of California Press, 1964).

11. Sayre P. Schatz, "Pirate Capitalism and the Inert Economic of Nigeria," *Journal of Modern African Studies* 22, no. 1 (1984): 45–58.

ing, and services began to emerge under the tutelage of the regional authorities. These nascent class groups were politically allied to the dominant sectional parties and depended upon the state for their continued viability.

The institutions of parliamentary rule bequeathed to the First Republic were at cross-purposes with the structures of federalism, a contradiction that ultimately proved fatal to the new democracy. The stresses of competition among communal groups and sectional parties could not effectively be contained by the emergent political system.[12] Through the ruling NPC, Hausa-Fulani elites secured dominance of the federal government, prompting fears of political exclusion among other communal groups. The northern party entered into expedient alliances with eastern and midwestern politicians as a way of dividing southern loyalties and diffusing opposition. Federal authorities subdivided the Western Region to weaken the AG's political base and judicially harassed Chief Obafemi Awolowo, the party's leader and regional premier who was a key political rival. Such maneuvers sharply exacerbated political tensions. An intercommunal bargain was clearly necessary for national stability in Nigeria's heterogeneous society, but the prospects for such a compact rapidly diminished as communal politics grew increasingly acrimonious.

Economic performance was increasingly undermined by political contention and fragmentation. A weak central government, mounting political uncertainty, and the dissipation of resources among competing patronage networks were detrimental to the economy. The federal government, hampered by constitutional restrictions and political resistance from the regions, had limited authority to establish a binding national framework of rules or to channel public resources effectively. Contentious politics in the parliament and the cabinet hampered effective long-term planning and fiscal discipline. In addition, divisions among regional blocks posed fundamental dilemmas for planning, investment, and growth. The ruling party in each region held a virtual monopoly of local patronage and electoral control. While securing power in their own bailiwick, sectional elites also sought to reduce the power of rivals by encroaching on other regions and encouraging political divisions among competitors. In the Northern Region, the NPC government pursued a "northernization" policy intended to strengthen local administration and entrepreneurship, often at

12. Larry Diamond, "Nigeria: The Uncivic Society and the Descent into Praetorianism," in Larry Diamond, Juan J. Linz, and Seymour Martin Lipset, eds., *Politics in Developing Countries,* 2d ed. (Boulder: Lynne Rienner, 1996). A detailed history of politics in the First Republic is found in Larry Diamond, *Class, Ethnicity, and Democracy in Nigeria: The Failure of the First Republic* (Syracuse: Syracuse University Press, 1988).

the expense of "nonindigenes" residing in the north. In their federal capacities, NPC leaders located a number of capital projects and public ventures
in the north, leading opposition parties to charge a regional bias in public
investment and resource allocations. The southern parties lacked a com-
manding position in the federal government, but they adopted similar
strategies of regional hegemony and federal contestation.

This structure of competition resulted in a set of mutual vetoes on policy, resource control, and the consolidation of property rights. No single
group or coalition could effectively dominate the national political and
economic system, as each segment faced challenges from multiple contenders. Within the regions, ruling parties held sway through the mobilization of communal loyalties and the control of patronage. Each of these
ethnoregional segments was concerned to check the power and opportunities of competitors so as to prevent the formation of an elite property base
that could translate into rival political power. At the national level leaders
sought to maintain political control by dividing and balancing key rivals,
which entailed piecemeal bargaining, selective inducements, and occasional coercion. Political strategies of ad hoc redistribution impeded a
compact organized around production and growth. Moreover, the disposition of property rights did not emerge from an encompassing legal order
but was largely a process of political bargaining with segmented parties
and regional elites who would provisionally guarantee the assets of particular clients within their sphere of control.

In the early years of the First Republic, a series of conflicts over political formulas and alliances led to political breakdown. The controversy
over the 1962–63 national census intensified struggles over power,
resources, and identity. Initial census returns showed large population
increases in the south, which would have effaced the northern majority
and potentially ended the parliamentary plurality of the NPC. The central
(northern-controlled) government challenged the results and pushed
through a highly controversial recount that restored the north's population advantage.[13] The final tabulation registered an improbably large
increase in the national population, suggesting that all regions had vigorously inflated the tally. Elements of the eastern NCNC were so angered by
the census controversy that they withdrew from their coalition with the
northern NPC. The 1964 federal elections aggravated strains throughout
the system when a growing tide of violence, intimidation, and polling malpractices provoked an electoral boycott among disgruntled southern

---

13. Rotimi T. Suberu, *Federalism and Ethnic Conflict in Nigeria* (Washington, DC: United
States Institute of Peace Press, 2001).

opposition parties. The growing use of gerrymandering, electoral fraud, and violence eroded the stability and legitimacy of the regime. The NPC, claiming a landslide in the Northern regional polls, bolstered their dominance over the federal government. Mass violence erupted in the southwest and other areas, leading politicians to call on the military to sustain order. The government's evident weakness amid rising ethnic and regional tensions eventually prompted a military coup in January 1966.

The fissures within the Nigerian federation reached a crisis at this point. The violent coup resulted in the deaths of the prime minister, the northern regional premier and Chief Akintola, premier of the newly formed Mid-West Region. The new regime, led by Major General Aguiyi Ironsi and dominated by Igbo officers, transformed Nigeria from a federation into a unitary state, while declaring an intention to return to civilian rule.[14] The ethnic composition of the junta and the ruthlessness of the coup intensified communal tensions, and in July 1966 a group of northern and middle-belt elements in the military staged a countercoup, killing General Ironsi and purging Igbos from the government and military ranks. Army chief of staff Lt. Colonel Yakubu Gowon, a Christian from the middle belt, assumed leadership of the new regime. Gowon reestablished the federal system while attempting to diffuse the monolithic ethnic blocs through political decentralization. His government subdivided the four regions into twelve states, prepared to revise the constitution, and repeated a commitment to restore democracy. The second coup, however, aggravated the already seething resentments among Nigeria's ethnic communities. Pogroms erupted against Igbo enclaves in the north after the first coup, and a new spate of violence prompted a mass exodus of Igbo civilians and military personnel to their eastern regional heartland. In May 1967, Lt. Colonel Emeka Ojukwu led Igbo officers and political leaders in repudiating the authority of Lagos and declaring the secession of the Biafran Republic. Thus began a civil war lasting until January 1970, in which more than a million lives were lost through combat and famine.

The War Economy: Sovereignty and Statism

Among other challenges, the civil war created unprecedented demands on economic management. Prior to secession the government of the Eastern Region had appropriated all locally derived revenues (including those from the burgeoning oil sector, located in the east) and seized control of

---

14. This period is detailed by Robin Luckham, *The Nigerian Military: A Sociological Analysis of Authority and Revolt, 1960–67* (Cambridge: Cambridge University Press, 1971).

major public enterprises located in the region.[15] Petroleum activities were curtailed throughout much of 1967 and 1968, which, along with the loss of the region's commerce in cash and food crops and its share of industrial output, accounted for as much as a quarter of the nation's total.[16] Foreign investment and aid dropped precipitously. While prosecuting the war, federal authorities sought to maintain domestic production, conserve scarce foreign exchange, curtail domestic consumption, and create new sources of public revenue to supplant losses from the foreign sector. These goals were substantially accomplished through a rigorous regime of taxation, fiscal reform, and administrative controls on foreign exchange, trade, and investment. Despite the war's destruction, the conclusion of the conflict left the country with a resilient economy. Manufacturing production and foreign investment rebounded considerably by 1969, though agricultural performance was less buoyant. Most significantly, the government was able to finance a costly and protracted military campaign mainly through internal resources. External public debt increased by scarcely 10 percent during the war.[17] Nigerian leaders drew lessons from the crisis management of the wartime economy, emphasizing the importance of technocratic oversight and national mobilization in realizing the nation's developmental potential.[18]

Gowon placed bureaucrats and former politicians in key policy roles.[19] The executive devolved strategic policy responsibilities to a coterie of senior civil servants who became known as the "super" permanent secretaries, more commonly super permsecs.[20] The super permsecs occupied key positions in the Ministries of Finance, Economic Development, Petroleum, Defense, Industry, and Trade, and they became de facto powers

15. S. K. Panter-Brick, "From Military Coup to Civil War, January 1966 to May 1967," in S. K. Panter-Brick, ed., *Nigerian Politics and Military Rule: Prelude to the Civil War* (London: Athlone, 1970), 48–49.

16. Wouter Tims, *Nigeria: Prospects for Long-Term Development* (Washington, DC: World Bank, 1974), 24.

17. Tims, *Nigeria,* 24.

18. This was reflected in the Second National Development Plan: "A developing country in the context of twentieth century Africa and of changing world technology is really in a state of permanent crisis hardly distinguishable in its essence from war-time mobilization." Federal Republic of Nigeria, *Second National Development Plan, 1970–74* (Lagos: Federal Government Printer, 1970), 31.

19. This relationship is elaborated by Henry Bienen, *Armies and Parties in Africa* (New York: Holmes and Meier, 1978). On the role of technocrats see also Thomas J. Biersteker, *Multinationals, the State, and Control of the Nigerian Economy* (Princeton: Princeton University Press, 1987), 72.

20. They included Allison Ayida of the Ministry of Economic Development, Ahmed Joda at the Ministry of Information, Philip Asiodu of the Ministry of Industries (and later Petroleum) and Ime Ebong of the Ministry of Finance.

behind the throne in matters of economic policy.[21] This small group embodied a technocratic clique who steered the country through a dramatic shift in economic strategy and policy.

The super permsecs played a leading role at the Ibadan Conference on Reconstruction and Development hosted in 1969 by the Nigerian Institute of Social and Economic Research and the Ministry of Economic Development.[22] Convened as the end of the war was in sight, the conference laid out a blueprint for the postwar economic regime and elaborated the foundations of the Second National Development Plan for 1970 through 1974. Drawing lessons from the war, the new framework represented a significant departure from the economic policies of the 1960s. Planners acknowledged postwar resource constraints and the demands of reconstruction; they were invigorated by the growing power of the federal government and their presumed abilities to guide national development. Central authority was greatly enhanced by the federal victory, as well as by Gowon's division of the regions into states and changes in revenue allocation that shifted resources to the federal account. Economic bureaucrats were inspired by the possibilities of centralized economic management and emboldened by their growing influence within the regime. Alison Ayida summed up the technocratic attitude, stressing that "the executive, made up of Ministers, planners, administrators, and other public officials . . . are in a position to determine and maintain the objectives and targets of development policy."[23]

The new direction in economic policy also reflected disappointment with earlier approaches to development.[24] Government planners were critical of an "open-door" strategy of growth, citing declining terms of trade for Nigeria's agricultural exports, shortfalls in anticipated foreign capital, and the discouraging performance of indigenous business.[25] Political and

21. See, for example, Peter Koehn, "The Role of Public Administrators in Public Policy Making: Practice and Prospects in Nigeria," *Public Administration and Development* 3 (1983): 1–26; and A. A. Ayida, *Reflections on Nigerian Development* (Lagos: Heinemann, 1987), 252.

22. The proceedings of the conference were published in A. A. Ayida and H. M. Onitiri, eds., *Reconstruction and Development in Nigeria* (Ibadan: Oxford University Press, 1971).

23. Ayida and Onitiri, *Reconstruction and Development*, 7.

24. The notion of the Nigerian state as economic catalyst was prevalent among Nigerian scholars and planners during the 1960s. See, for example, O. Teriba, "Development Strategy, Investment Decision, and Expenditure Patterns of a Public Development Institution: The Case of Western Nigeria Development Corporation, 1949–62," *Nigerian Journal of Economic and Social Studies* 8, no. 2 (1966): 241; and O. Aboyade, "Nigerian Public Enterprises as an Organizational Dilemma," *Public Enterprise in Nigeria* (Ibadan: Nigerian Economic Society, 1973), 34.

25. Sayre Schatz has emphasized the disappointing performance of indigenous entrepreneurs as a factor contributing to the reassessment of development strategy; see Schatz, *Niger-*

economic elites increasingly emphasized the need to assert sovereignty over the national economy. General Gowon's postwar policy of national reconciliation, encapsulated in his avowal of "no victor, no vanquished," helped to restore national morale in the aftermath of the devastating conflict. The government reiterated its promise of restoring civilian rule, although a transition agenda was slow to emerge. The regime outlined a six-year program of constitutional and administrative reform, anticorruption efforts, reorganization of the armed forces, the revival of party organization, and transitional elections. The political program was accompanied by plans for economic reconstruction and an ambitious five-year development scheme.

The Early Windfall Years, 1970–75

The rapid growth of petroleum revenues encouraged this postwar agenda. As hostilities receded, foreign firms resumed oil exploration and production activities in the southeast. Petroleum output accelerated rapidly, doubling to a million barrels per day during 1970 and surpassing two million barrels per day in 1973. Nigeria joined the Organization of Petroleum Exporting Countries (OPEC) in 1971, the same year the state oil company, the Nigerian National Oil Corporation, was established. The OPEC-inspired price hikes of 1973–74 caused a threefold rise in export revenues within a year. Changes in Nigeria's tax and royalty policies further increased the government's take as prices rose. Petroleum receipts increased from ₦1.9 billion in 1973 to ₦5.4 billion a year later, increasing to 30 percent of GDP, 80 percent of government revenue, and 95 percent of total exports. Very quickly, state planners saw boundless horizons. Public expenditure was originally slated for ₦3 billion under the Second National Development Plan for 1970 through 1975 but rose sharply as the plan was revised and extended to reflect the new resources. Spending under the succeeding five-year plan reached ₦42 billion—a tenfold increase in spending within half a decade.

Oil rents accrued directly to the federal government, which encouraged the centralizing tendencies of the military regime. Concerns over revenue generation were quickly supplanted by struggles over distribution as the newly bountiful state was beset with pressures for spending and

---

ian Capitalism (Berkeley: University of California Press, 1977), 238. Adeoye A. Akinsanya offers a broader discussion of the disillusionment with "open door" policies in "State Strategies toward Nigerian and Foreign Business," in I. William Zartman, ed., *The Political Economy of Nigeria* (New York: Praeger, 1983), 158–61.

largesse.[26] The windfall era was marked by a decisive shift of economic strategy toward nationalism and *étatisme.* Rising income prompted a rapid expansion of government activities, spearheaded by the growth of the bureaucracy and the state enterprise sector. Nationalist goals gained momentum among the senior bureaucracy, military, and political elites. Some wartime restrictions on trade and currency were relaxed, but high rates of protection and economic regulation produced a relatively closed trade and investment regime. Nigeria's fixed currency soon became overvalued, reflecting the relative price changes emanating from the revenue surge. Overvaluation provided subsidies to consumers and importers (especially domestic producers who relied on imported inputs), thus furnishing a politically expedient avenue of redistribution for elites and popular sectors. In consequence, there were virtually no political incentives to adjust the exchange regime. The government also maintained high duties and extensive regulation of trade and foreign exchange. The rationale for these policies was to nurture local production and conserve scarce resources, but such measures were also encouraged by the ancillary benefits of generating bureaucratic rents and creating levers of patronage.

In the period following the civil war, expansive goals of industrialization supplanted the more modest aims of import substitution, creating a large role for state investment and ownership. State-owned enterprises (SOEs) grew precipitously in both number and variety. The existing commodity boards, public utilities, development finance institutions, and regional enterprises were joined by new industrial ventures, agricultural development schemes and irrigation authorities, federally owned or federally controlled banks, joint ventures with foreign firms in various manufacturing and financial activities, expanded public services, and dozens of enterprises created by the newly established state governments. The haphazard expansion of public ownership and control produced an unmistakable shift in the scope and influence of the public sector, as SOEs came to dominate several markets and to serve as a locus for politically inspired distribution. Federal officials, state military governors, and senior bureaucrats used their leverage over resources to bolster political control and address pressures from key constituencies while creating personal outlets of accumulation.

In addition to expanding the state sector, leaders sought to promote local investment and production by transferring ownership in the private

26. These factors are analyzed by Tom Forrest in *Politics and Economic Development in Nigeria,* 2d ed. (Boulder: Westview, 1995), 133–36.

economy. A program of Africanizing foreign-owned assets was launched with the Nigerian Enterprises Promotion Decree (commonly known as the Indigenization Decree) of 1972, which set out guidelines for investment and stipulated the transfer of equity from foreign owners to domestic private hands. The decree categorized enterprises into two schedules and specified the levels of non-Nigerian ownership to be permitted in each area. Most small- to medium-scale ventures in services and light manufacturing were reserved exclusively for Nigerians, while larger capital- and technology-intensive activities were open to foreign control, with Nigerian participation. For activities such as banking and insurance, some foreign participation was permissible but Nigerian equity control was mandated. The Nigerian Enterprises Promotion Board, created to implement the program, supervised the process of share transfers and monitored changes in ownership. Those most affected by the initial phase of the indigenization program were the Lebanese community, a long-standing immigrant group with a leading position in small-scale manufacturing, distribution, import-export activities, and some services. Most were compelled to sell off their enterprises or to cede equity to Nigerian investors. Many foreign investors, however, retained de facto control of their enterprises through the widespread practice of fronting through fictitious Nigerian owners, who received formal title (and generous stipends) but exercised no real authority. Among Nigerians, the massive share transfers from indigenization created a windfall, especially for those in the southwest with close access to equity markets. Entrepreneurs throughout the country found profitable opportunities in fronting for expatriate proprietors and diversifying their own portfolios.[27]

A growing class of local entrepreneurs relied on political machination, illicit transactions, corruption, and a range of "directly unproductive, profit-seeking activities" that largely precluded capital formation.[28] New domains of rent seeking were created by state investments, contracts, trade and currency controls, and indigenization transfers. Entrepreneurs secured rents by colluding with public officials and exploiting many

27. Biersteker, *Multinationals, the State, and Control of the Nigerian Economy,* provides a fuller discussion of rent seeking under the indigenization program.

28. Sayre Schatz has applied the term *pirate capitalism;* see Schatz, "Pirate Capitalism and the Inert Economy of Nigeria," *Journal of Modern African Studies* 22, no. 1 (1984): 45–57. The concept of DUP (directly unproductive, profit-seeking activities) is Jagdish Bhagwati's, providing an elaboration of Anne Krueger's notion of rent seeking that incorporates additional forms of arbitrage and speculation. See Jagdish N. Bhagwati, "Directly Unproductive, Profit-Seeking (DUP) Activities," *Journal of Political Economy* 90 (1982): 988–1002, and Anne O. Krueger, "The Political Economy of the Rent-Seeking Society," *American Economic Review* 64, no. 3 (1974): 291–303.

opportunities for arbitrage or fraud. Government procurement and projects offered copious rake-offs for state officials and private contractors. Most public projects were drastically inflated by these costly side payments, and jockeying for spoils frequently hampered the implementation of important programs.

Private manufacturing and agriculture relied extensively on subsidies and nonmarket premiums, and real productive capacity expanded only modestly. Merchants and speculators often created manufacturing ventures as shells for attracting state loans, securing import licenses, and expediting the profitable resale of price-stabilized commodities. Retired military officers and northern businessmen took up commercial farming in growing numbers, largely to secure consignments of subsidized fertilizer and other inputs.[29] External trade also afforded many outlets for securing rents. Speculators gravitated toward import-export activities, which afforded easy access to foreign exchange, quick turnover, and high liquidity. Once an import license or procurement order was inveigled from officials, the proceeds could be inflated by under- or over-invoicing, skirting customs, or simply absconding with funds. Customs fraud and smuggling reached prodigious levels.[30] The collusion among military officers, politicians, bureaucrats, and business cronies gave rise to a convergence of interests around the emerging rentier state and politically regulated markets.

The oil boom produced other social and economic problems. The overheated economy fostered inflation, a problem aggravated by the government's regular creation of money to finance recurring deficits. Rural residents flocked to the cities, pushed by unfavorable agricultural conditions and pulled by labor demand and the allure of urban amenities. Volatile urbanization fed crime and social violence, which attained troubling new dimensions in the 1970s. These problems also reflected widening social inequalities, as the mass of peasants and the urban poor perceived a growing chasm with the nouveau riche political elite and their cronies. This was exacerbated by heightened corruption, inextricably associated in the popular mind with the oil boom.[31]

The problem of corruption was obviously not new in Nigeria, having

29. Michael Watts, "Agriculture and Oil-Based Accumulation: Stagnation or Transformation?" in Michael Watts, ed., *State, Oil, and Agriculture in Nigeria* (Berkeley: Institute of International Studies, 1987), 80.

30. See, for example, Toyin Falola and Julius Ihonvbere, *The Rise and Fall of Nigeria's Second Republic, 1979–84* (London: Zed Books, 1985), 105–9.

31. Karin Barber, "Popular Reactions to the Petro-Naira," *Journal of Modern African Studies* 20, no. 3 (1982): 436–37.

long been recognized and extensively documented by several official commissions of inquiry.[32] The windfall era was distinguished by pervasive,
massive, and unabashed malfeasance throughout the public and private
sectors. The 1975 "cement armada" was a defining event: during the rev-
enue-fueled construction boom, officials from the Ministry of Defense and
their cronies procured some sixteen million tons of cement, far in excess of
actual demand or port capacity. Nigeria's main seaport was clogged for
weeks with hundreds of vessels which languished in Lagos harbor as bulk
cement hardened in their hulls.[33] A commission of inquiry detailed the
scandal, which symbolized for many Nigerians the grand new scale of corruption in the ballooning oil economy. Many government contracts never
progressed beyond the exchange of kickbacks and "mobilization fees," the
official disbursements that were issued when implementation began. Once
the fees were paid, projects were often abandoned, and the empty shells of
incomplete buildings and useless factories can be observed to the present
day.

During this period of headlong growth, there were few mechanisms in
place to monitor public spending or to gauge the performance of public
institutions. The already weak fiscal and administrative discipline evident
under preceding regimes dissipated amid the flood of new resources. The
lack of accountability provided broad license for misconduct, while a competitive rush for influence and spoils encouraged malfeasance. Elites saw
the windfall as an opportunity for personal benefit as well as the entrenchment of power, while public clamor for largesse intensified political pressures for access to resources.

The growth of corruption was substantially influenced by the contentious distributional politics of the boom era. Ethnic, regional, and religious antipathies were spurred by group perceptions of inequality and
competition over public patronage. The revenue windfall shifted the
incentives and strategies of Nigeria's military rulers in addressing these

32. See, for example, the reports of the Foster-Sutton Commission, in the *Report of the
Tribunal Appointed to Inquire into Allegations Reflecting on the Official Conduct of the Pre-
mier of, and Certain Persons Holding Ministerial and Other Public Offices in the Eastern
Region of Nigeria,* Cmnd. 51 (London: HMSO, 1957), the *Report of the Coker Commission of
Inquiry into the Affairs of Certain Statutory Corporations in Western Nigeria* (Lagos: Ministry
of Information, 1962), vols. 1–4, and the *Comments of the Federal Military Government on the
Report of the Tribunal of Inquiry into the Affairs of the Electricity Corporation of Nigeria for
the Period 1st January, 1961 to 31st December, 1965* (Lagos: Federal Ministry of Information, 1968).

33. The cement scandal is discussed by Gavin Williams and Terisa Turner, "Nigeria," in
John Dunn, ed., *West African States: Failure and Promise* (Cambridge: Cambridge University Press, 1978), 156. See also Forrest, *Politics and Economic Development in Nigeria,* 57–58.

tensions. Gowon and other senior officials, concerned with the security challenges of competitive communalism, focused substantially on the need to consolidate national stability. As he maneuvered within fragmented political-military elites and confronted the distributional demands of popular sectors, Gowon adopted parallel strategies of institutional change and informal patronage. The regime sought administrative and fiscal changes to accommodate or restructure key constituencies, while elites used piecemeal bargaining to mollify competing interests.

Distributional strategies played out through statutory, discretionary, and informal dimensions. In the first instance, the government shifted statutory allocations through state creation and revenue distribution. The subdivision of four regions into twelve states ostensibly reduced sectional dominance, as the Yoruba, Igbo, and Hausa-Fulani were divided among several states, and communally dominated parties were dissolved. States offered administrative and political recognition for a wider array of groups, including several aggrieved minorities. While state creation appeared to decentralize governance and broaden representation, however, fiscal realities actually concentrated the central powers of military authorities. Unlike the former regions, the states had negligible independent revenue and were heavily reliant on transfers from the federal government. The petroleum boom magnified these central resources exponentially, such that the federal authorities became the fiscal lifeline of the subordinate tiers of the federation. Further, the military state governors had few constraints from central rulers on their authority or fiscal discretion, and most established personal fiefdoms under their patronage. The advent of a rentier state under military rule reinforced fiscal and political centralization, offsetting efforts to map out a more dispersed federal system.

The corollary to state creation was the reform of revenue allocation. Methods for generating and distributing revenue were repeatedly amended in the postcolonial era. For several years after independence the principle of derivation prevailed, under which regional or state governments retained a large proportion of the revenues raised from local economic activity, including export commodities. With the advent of oil production (based in the restive southeastern states), the derivation principle was sidelined by the federation account, which became the central repository for all export revenues. In line with changes suggested by the 1970 Dina Commission, proceeds from the petroleum sector were appropriated by central authorities who then dispersed resources from the federation account to the states according to a complex formula that weighted population, relative need, equity, land area, and derivation. These criteria were in continual flux after independence, as a succession of public commissions and ad hoc reforms frequently revised the criteria for sharing central revenues.[34] Furthermore, a lack of budgetary transparency and political accountability meant that federal authorities had wide latitude in making actual disbursals and allotting resources. During the windfall years, the net effect of the changes in revenue distribution was to consolidate the fiscal authority of the central government and broaden its discretion.

Another major channel of state largesse was the enormous discretionary spending afforded by the petroleum revenue windfall. The so-called Udoji awards were a prominent example. At the beginning of 1975 the government abruptly bestowed a large increase in civil service compensation, calculated retroactively to the previous year. The immense wage hike was an official response to the 1974 report of the Public Service Review Commission under the chairmanship of Chief Jerome Udoji, which recommended sweeping reform of the public service including merit-based recruitment, incentives for performance, managerial innovation, and better remuneration. The bonus was largely unaccompanied by other steps to restructure the public sector, and it amounted to little more than a windfall of petroleum rents for state employees. This created a surge in the money supply and public consumption, which further accelerated inflation and aggravated fiscal imbalances. The awards also prompted competitive demands from professionals and other private sector workers for equivalent increases.

Further outlets for rents and patronage were created by the proliferation of state-owned enterprises and large capital projects, the expansion of contracts and procurement, and the establishment of manifold subsidies for fuel, services, and basic commodities. State-owned enterprises proliferated from about 250 enterprises in 1970 to more than 800 within the decade. Public ventures at both the federal and state levels extended to virtually every area of the economy.[35] A spate of capital projects in infrastructure and industry were rushed into the pipeline by bureaucrats anxious to secure influence and discretionary funds. These ventures created enormous opportunities for employment, contracts, and other ancillary

34. See Rotimi Suberu, *Federalism and Ethnic Conflict in Nigeria* (Washington, DC: United States Institute of Peace Press, 2001), G. D. Olowononi, "Revenue Allocation and the Economics of Federalism," in Kunle Amuwo, Adigun Agbaje, Rotimi Suberu, and Georges Herault, eds., *Federalism and Political Restructuring in Nigeria* (Ibadan: Spectrum Books, 1998), 247–60, and Akpan H. Ekpo, "Fiscal Federalism: Nigeria's Post-Independence Experience, 1960–90," *World Development* 22, no. 8 (1994): 1129–46.

35. These are detailed in Peter Lewis, "State, Economy, and Privatization in Nigeria," in John Waterbury and Ezra Suleiman, eds., *The Political Economy of Public Sector Reform and Privatization* (Boulder: Westview, 1990).

benefits, giving rise to intense competition to seize spoils. The dramatically expanding scope of politically mediated distribution allowed public officials to direct new resources to influential groups. Plans on steel production, for instance, were repeatedly shelved and resumed as key interests contended over the location of the projects and the control of implementation. Sectional lobbying resulted in plans for an unwieldy iron and steel complex with operations in several states throughout the country. Political rationales trumped economic design, and the steel program became a vortex of squandered resources.

Several policies channeled resources to the private sector. A second round of indigenization in 1977 enabled private entrepreneurs to move into terrain previously controlled by foreign and immigrant capital, as a third schedule of enterprises was added and many transnational firms relinquished some equity to domestic owners. The second Indigenization Decree was no more successful than the first in transferring real managerial or entrepreneurial control to Nigerian hands, although it did further disperse the acquisition of shares among local groups (especially in the southwest) and state governments (especially in the north). Notwithstanding these share transfers the state continued to dominate ISI activities, the financial sector, and public goods. Development finance institutions dramatically expanded their capital base and the range of their operations, while federal authorities acquired majority ownership in the nation's leading commercial banks. The government also conferred diverse subsidies to popular sectors through the growth of public education and health programs, inexpensive electricity and telephone services, price-controlled fuels, and public transportation. These provisions were typically uneven, sporadic, and of poor quality, but they were perceived by the public as part of an expanding domain of state-supported entitlements that bolstered the political reach of military elites and their civilian allies.

In addition, political leaders fostered or tolerated an array of practices that afforded channels of informal distribution. The maelstrom of corruption, fraud, and mismanagement that emerged in the windfall years was not simply an artifact of rapid growth or administrative disarray. Elites utilized these conditions to construct or solidify networks, along with the impulse to advance personal accumulation. The general absence of fiscal oversight and bureaucratic accountability encouraged public officials to regard their offices as personal sinecures for extracting state resources. State elites and allied social groups colluded in diverse ways. Military and civilian segments of the regime variously established patronage arrangements, as did senior civil servants, state enterprise managers, clusters surrounding the petroleum, electricity, and telecommunications sectors, and

myriad communal networks. Richard Joseph has emphasized the importance of ethnicity as an ordering feature of informal distribution, since
clientelism in different sectors and institutions was often constructed along
communal lines.

These relationships were fluid and diffuse. While central authorities
could be seen to act as gatekeepers in mediating the flow of public
resources, elites did not exert the political control or administrative discipline to construct stable patronage structures or channels of distribution.
Distributional politics were contentious, dispersed, and unregulated, with
few boundaries on the appropriation of state resources. Political leaders
adapted to loose structures of patronage and corruption as part of their
calculus of rule, though this failed to encourage either political stability or
capital formation. On the political side, fragmented elites and diffuse competition for resources undermined regimes and the social pacts they sought
to construct. Economically, the imperative of distributional politics and
the failure to establish consistent rules for regulating markets and allocating patronage led to the dissipation of central resources, with consequences for economic performance. In the near term, surging revenues,
investment, and external finance temporarily obscured these costs for
Nigerian rulers.

General Gowon's early political capital was exhausted in the face of
political shortcomings and economic problems. In addition to mounting
concerns over corruption and economic mismanagement, the regime temporized over the long-promised democratic transition. In October 1974
Gowon announced that the transition program would be extended
indefinitely. He promised to move forward on constitutional reform, the
creation of new states, and turnover among the increasingly controversial
governors but made no headway in the following months. Intensifying factionalism among the nation's elites, reflecting both regional and functional
divisions, undermined the regime's support base. Shortly after the war an
influential group of senior civil servants within the regime, most of whom
were from the south, floated the idea of a "national movement" that would
continue the military-technocratic alliance (perhaps under the guise of a
single-party state) to continue an agenda of development and national
integration. They were naturally opposed by civilian politicians from various regions who sought a return to power and the increasingly attractive
potential of patronage in the windfall economy. A northern segment of
intellectuals and notables were concerned that southern influence was
becoming entrenched in Gowon's regime, and they worked through their
networks in the armed forces to resist the planned civilian transfer. Much
of the military also sought continued domination in a petro-state, and a

decade of rule aggravated internal division and political rivalries.[36] In July 1975 Gowon was overthrown in a bloodless coup while traveling abroad. Brigadier Murtala Mohammed, a northern Muslim and a key figure in the July 1966 revolt, became head of state.

Statism and Declining Institutional Capacity, 1975–79

Murtala invigorated the nation with his reformist zeal and assertive nationalism.[37] He pledged an end to the policy drift and corruption that afflicted the preceding regime and recommitted the military to expeditiously hand over government to civilians. He took steps to weed out inefficiency and misconduct within the state apparatus and drew upon the grand aims of the Third Plan (1975–80) to project a new phase of expansive state capitalism. His regime also made tentative efforts toward corporatist arrangements with labor. The 1975 coup, however, was symptomatic of widening problems of factionalism and ambition within the military, and Murtala was assassinated in a failed coup attempt just nine months after taking power. He was succeeded by his second in command, General Olusegun Obasanjo, who continued the regime's central policies and orientations. The Murtala-Obasanjo period is commonly regarded as a single regime.

The 1975 coup had substantial support among northern elites and intelligentsia who sought the return of executive control to their region. The new regime clearly shifted influence away from the southern and middle-belt elements that were prominent in Gowon's administration, though the Murtala-Obasanjo government did not rule in an overtly sectional manner. Like his predecessor, Murtala sought collegial arrangements within the governing circle and did not accumulate personal power. His regime, however, made changes in organization and personnel that strengthened executive authority and bolstered the supremacy of the military. The new leaders summarily dismissed Gowon's military governors along with the super permsecs, a substantial tier of the upper bureaucracy, and a number of state enterprise managers and boards. This began a wider purge that eventually ousted more than 10,000 civil servants. Murtala restructured the executive decision-making apparatus in ways that reduced the influence and autonomy of the military governors while also asserting military precedence over the mainly civilian cabinet. A new

---

36. Billy Dudley, *An Introduction to Nigerian Government and Politics* (Bloomington: University of Indiana Press, 1982), 97–100.

37. Williams and Turner, "Nigeria," 171.

Council of States, composed of the governors, occupied a middle tier
between the Supreme Military Council and the cabinet-level Federal Executive Council. Senior bureaucrats were restricted from participation in
upper-level policy deliberations unless invited by the military.[38] Policy
leverage shifted to the military-run cabinet department, initially headed by
Obasanjo.

Notwithstanding their nationalist orientations and reformist pronouncements, the Murtala-Obasanjo regime lacked a strong ideological
focus. These leaders did not clearly outline a model of state capitalism, nor
did they articulate a populist agenda, although they adopted policies generally linked to these strategies. The government made tentative efforts to
organize labor along corporatist lines, but this did not extend to a broader
strategy of corporatist regimentation of interest groups. Ideology aside,
the government launched the most assertive phase of state-led development in Nigeria's postcolonial experience. State investment and ownership
were expanded across a broad range of sectors and activities. The Third
Plan ultimately reached ₦42 billion in expenditures, fourteen times the size
of the preceding plan. The plan document outlined a program in which
public expenditures would furnish the bulk of resources, and government
activities would provide an engine of growth. In the manufacturing sector,
this period saw the development of public capital projects and foreign joint
ventures in cement, automobile assembly, machine tools, pulp and paper,
iron and steel, sugar refining, fertilizer, and petrochemicals. These projects
absorbed vast resources, serving as central vehicles of distributional politics
through dispersed industrial location, employment, and ancillary benefits.
Alongside manufacturing investments, the government sank large sums
into infrastructure and services. Electricity, telecommunications, roads, air
and rail transport, and shipping were all large items of expenditure in the
1970s, leading to substantial growth in utilities and transport networks.
The government also created large federal ventures in cargo, airports, river
transport, and the supply of basic commodities.

An increasingly nationalist direction was seen in the organization of
the petroleum sector. In 1977 the NNOC was combined with elements of
the Ministry of Petroleum to form the Nigerian National Petroleum Corporation (NNPC), with jurisdiction over exploration, production, monitoring, refining, and distribution. The NNPC increased its equity in most
foreign joint ventures to 60 percent, while gaining wider authority over
upstream and downstream petroleum operations. The federal government also stepped up efforts to increase refinery capacity and to introduce

---

38. Dudley, *An Introduction to Nigerian Government and Politics,* 101.

allied industries such as petrochemicals and fertilizer in proximity to the refineries.

Agricultural policy in the 1970s focused on heavy capital investments, subsidies of major inputs, and government control of commodity markets. The earliest large-scale rural projects were located in the northern states, and along with a few industrial ventures and the expansion of infrastructure, they implied a nominal redistribution of resources to that historically neglected region. With World Bank funding and technical assistance, the federal and state governments established integrated Agricultural Development Projects (ADPs) that sought to deliver packages of inputs, infrastructure, credit, and extension services to smallholders (up to 80,000 families in each catchment area) cultivating food crops. By the late 1970s, under pressure to expand the program, the government established four more ADPs in the middle belt and outlined plans to include all states over the next decade. The federal government also created three expansive River Basin Development Authorities (RBDAs) in the north with the intention of promoting the production of wheat, rice, and tomatoes as food crops through the expansion of arable land and the establishment of large state production programs. By the end of the Third Plan, thirteen RBDAs were planned throughout the country. In addition, large subsidies were extended for fertilizer and other inputs, while the government furnished modest credit facilities through the federally owned Nigerian Agricultural Bank (NAB). In the market domain, the regional Marketing Boards for export crops were replaced by seven federal Commodity Boards that set prices and standards for leading cash and food crops.

State authorities also expanded their efforts to promote indigenous business. The Adeosun Commission, set up to review the implementation of indigenization programs, issued a report highly critical of lax compliance by firms and the undue concentration of beneficiaries in Lagos and other southern states. The government consequently took over 120 companies that were judged to be out of compliance with the program, and issued a second indigenization decree in 1977 that introduced a third schedule of enterprises and expanded the coverage of each schedule. More than a thousand enterprises were eventually affected by the program.[39] Most of the larger, capital-intensive and more technologically sophisticated ventures were allowed majority foreign ownership, while several prominent foreign-owned companies in manufacturing and distribution

39. Eghosa Osaghae, *Crippled Giant: Nigeria since Independence* (Bloomington: Indiana University Press, 1998), 101–2; Biersteker, *Multinationals, the State, and Control of the Nigerian Economy,* 200.

were conveniently exempted from the more stringent regulations.[40] The second phase of indigenization unquestionably expanded domestic equity holdings, including significant shares of multinational enterprises. Not all of these shares went to private hands, as several state governments and holding companies, especially in the north, acquired shares on behalf of their residents. Foreign firms generally did not lose managerial or financial control, yet the government's increasingly assertive stance toward share transfers raised concerns within the private sector about nationalization and induced several large foreign investors to withdraw from the market.

An expansion of financial outlets accompanied the transfer of equity. The Nigerian Industrial Development Bank and the more recently established Nigerian Bank for Commerce and Industry were the federal government's premier development finance institutions. The NIDB had a history of support for joint ventures and investment by foreign firms, while the NBCI, created under Gowon, focused on domestically owned enterprise and was an important source of finance for the acquisition of shares under the indigenization program. The resources of these institutions were dwarfed by the major commercial banks, whose foreign equity was diminished from 60 percent to 40 percent as the federal government took a greater share.

Yet even as leaders increased the responsibilities and prerogatives of the state, they diminished the capabilities of public institutions to perform key functions. The discrepancy between responsibility and capacity was exacerbated during the windfall years. Although Murtala's concerns about excessive influence and possible self-aggrandizement among the super permanent secretaries had validity, the regime simply ousted a seasoned policy cohort without installing effective replacements. The ensuing civil service purges led to further depletion of experienced personnel throughout the state apparatus. In the wake of Murtala's housecleaning, the cabinet and senior echelons of the bureaucracy were staffed by an assortment of former politicians, military officers, and career civil servants, reflecting little institutional cohesion or expertise. Moreover, as the public sector continued to expand through the early 1980s, meritocratic criteria eroded and organizational discipline weakened. Economic management and institutional performance declined accordingly.

The unraveling of economic oversight was evident in 1978, as fiscal constraints and balance of payments problems converged in a sharp economic decline. World oil prices were temporarily depressed by changes in global energy markets, and Nigeria's policies toward foreign oil compa-

---

40. Forrest, *Politics and Economic Development in Nigeria,* 155–56.

nies had not induced sufficient exploration or production, causing output to flag along with prices. Although official projections suggested a drop of as much as 40 percent in petroleum revenues, the government failed to adequately rein in expenditures.[41] The cumulative demands of a growing bureaucracy, new states, proliferating capital projects, large public enterprise deficits, and chronic pressures for discretionary outlays all sustained the momentum of spending, yielding an unprecedented fiscal deficit for 1978. The drive for government expenditure was matched by the growing appetite for imports, as popular consumption and public capital projects created accelerating demand for foreign goods. The slump in foreign exchange receipts created a widening deficit in the current account, met partly through the rapid depletion of reserves. In addition, the government borrowed $1.7 billion from international financial markets, its largest foray into global borrowing, decisively expanding the nation's external debt.[42]

The regime's response to these macroeconomic imbalances was at once impulsive, ineffectual, and counterproductive. A severe "austerity" budget sheared expenditures on large capital projects, services such as education, and other recurrent costs. Monetary restraint limited inflation but also suppressed borrowing and domestic investment. Trade and currency restrictions were tightened in an effort to stem imports and conserve foreign exchange. These measures coincided with the broader investment restrictions accompanying the indigenization program. The net effect was to aggravate recession while further insulating the economy from international markets. Gross domestic product dropped by about 7 percent in 1978, as the welter of regulations on foreign exchange, trade, and investment served to further dampen foreign interest.

These problems were mirrored by pervasive microeconomic problems. An overvalued exchange rate, unpredictable regulations, import compression, and scarce capital all served to discourage investment in manufacturing and export agriculture. At the same time, arbitrage between official and parallel markets, and the ready ability to skirt administrative restrictions, served to encourage speculation, smuggling, and capital flight. Moreover, the government's failure to realize a large volume of investment in ostensibly productive activities proved a major constraint on growth and structural change. A broad roster of industrial and agricultural projects was hampered by poor planning, erratic funding, bureaucratic

---

41. Forrest, *Politics and Economic Development,* 145.
42. Anthony Kirk-Greene and Douglas Rimmer, *Nigeria since 1970: A Political and Economic Outline* (London: Hodder and Stoughton, 1981), 138.

inefficiency, and pervasive corruption. Major initiatives in steel, mining, petrochemicals, pulp and paper, machine tools, automobiles, sugar processing, and other activities foundered amid political infighting over rents. Several were completed late, at excessive cost, and operated at a fraction of planned capacity. Others, including the massive venture in iron and steel, never came to fruition. Similar problems plagued many of the Agricultural Development Projects and nearly all of the River Basin Development Authorities. Efforts to expand infrastructure—notably in telecommunications and electric power—produced enormous fiscal losses, erratic coverage, and deteriorating service. The government sought to subcontract the Airways and the Railway Corporation to foreign managers, but this failed to arrest a downward slope in these services.[43] In the financial sector, the expansion of development finance institutions and the nationalization of major commercial banks served mainly to restrict access to credit while expanding the scope of politically induced allocations.

During the oil boom, policymakers were virtually indifferent to questions of policy credibility or international competitiveness. Economic windfall, and the political structure of the regime, influenced the setting for choice. Elites were in the throes of a windfall-induced mania through the early 1980s, and they regarded flagging oil receipts to be transitory. Optimistic market forecasts about petroleum revenues and the easy availability of credit from global money markets created a soft budget constraint in which fiscal reckoning could be delayed or averted by external resource flows. The large volume of foreign income spurred growth and obscured serious deficiencies in local investment, market structure, and enterprise performance. Periodic surges in petroleum receipts and a reasonably consistent trend in direct foreign investment reinforced domestic perceptions that Nigeria held a favorable position in international markets. In consequence, there was little sense of urgency in advancing policies to enhance the country's competitive position. In fact the obverse was true, and policymakers bargained hard to secure increased rents and promote nationalist goals.

Political factors were equally important. The changes within the executive branch created a more diffuse structure of decision making. In contrast to their predecessors, Murtala and Obasanjo charted more collegial and consultative approaches to rule. In the wake of the civil service purges there was no influential technocratic cohort, and many central policies

---

43. In 1978 the Dutch airline KLM was brought in to improve operations in Nigeria Airways, while India Railways were engaged to revive the moribund Nigeria Railway Corporation. Both contracts were short-lived and effected only temporary improvements.

were referred to ad hoc consultative groups formed by the regime.[44] This enhanced central policy direction in areas where the regime had strong prior commitments (notably the political transition), while aggravating factionalism and rent-seeking pressures in many areas of economic policy. Economic concerns were generally subsidiary to the regime's central political goals, especially the desire for a timely extrication from military rule. There was strong pressure to appease distributional demands from elites as a means of buying social peace and acquiescence in political reform.

The political transition formed the centerpiece of the Murtala-Obasanjo program. In 1975 the regime appointed a Constitutional Drafting Committee to outline a new charter for the political system. As the committee completed its work a Constituent Assembly composed of elected and appointed members was convened to debate and ratify the document, providing a measure of public legitimacy to the military-run exercise. The 1979 constitution marked a clear departure from previous constitutional design. The Westminsterian model was discarded and an American-style presidential system with a bicameral legislature was adopted. The revised federal system featured nineteen states (a further seven having been introduced by Murtala in 1976) and established a formal third tier of local government below the state level. There was an effort to explicitly address distributional concerns through the principle of "federal character," which required ethnic and regional balance in government hiring and appointments. The constitution affirmed the foundations of a mixed economy, emphasizing the federal government's authority to control leading activities and enterprises.

In the wake of constitutional reform the military approved the reemergence of political parties. Five parties contested the 1979 elections, reflecting a clear lineage from the groupings of the earlier civilian regime. The Unity Party of Nigeria (UPN) was headed by Obafemi Awolowo and drew support from the same southwestern Yoruba constituency that had been the foundation for the Action Group. In the southeast the Nigeria People's Party (NPP) quickly established a strong base among the predominantly Igbo states, reflecting the popularity of leader Nnamdi Azikiwe, the former head of the NCNC. The National Party of Nigeria (NPN) presented a distinctive profile. Centered on a group of northern notables who had been associated with the Northern Peoples Congress, the party did not feature a strong central personality. Their presidential candidate, Shehu Shagari, was a former cabinet minister with a modest

44. Ladipo Adamolekun, *Politics and Administration in Nigeria* (London: Hutchinson, 1986), 126.

reputation. Building upon a large base of northern Hausa-Fulani voters, the NPN was the most successful of the new parties in creating a genuine national profile and reaching out to constituencies in other parts of the country. The leadership constructed a diverse, ethnically plural political machine sustained through the dispersal of patronage. Within the northern states the NPN was challenged by the People's Redemption Party (PRP), whose radical populist message was carried by Mallam Aminu Kano, previously the leader of the Northern Elements Progressive Union. Another party with a base in the northeast, the Great Nigerian People's Party (GNPP), was led by Waziri Ibrahim, who broke away from the NPP. While espousing nominal differences in their platforms, the parties were essentially organized around personalities, elite networks, and communal appeals rather than ideology or programs.

The Tipping Point: The Second Republic
and Distributional Politics

The 1979 elections inaugurated the Second Republic under a cloud of controversy. The NPN secured a narrow plurality at all levels, with slightly more than a third of the seats in both houses of the National Assembly, governorships in seven of the nineteen states, and a third of the presidential vote. The two main parties in opposition, the UPN and NPP, together held two-fifths of the legislative seats and 46 percent of the presidential votes. Challengers contested the presidential poll, arguing that the NPN's Shehu Shagari had failed to secure the necessary distribution of votes among different states in the federation as required by the constitution. An expedient ruling by the Supreme Court affirmed that the election met the threshold (25 percent of the vote in two-thirds of the states), but this initial dispute set the stage for the bitter struggles over political control that were to characterize the regime throughout its tenure.

The return of civilian rule transferred control of the state to a fragmented political class divided by region, ethnicity, religion, faction, and economic interest. As noted earlier, the core of the political parties consisted of seasoned politicians from the First Republic, many of whom also served as civilian officials under military rule. These elites had strong ethnic and regional solidarities, leading the parties to revive aspects of the three-way sectional competition that had suffused the previous civilian regime. Southern constituencies resented the domination of the state by the "northern" NPN, while northern elites were concerned to preserve their uncertain hold on power. Overtures by the NPN toward an alliance with the eastern-centered NPP proved unworkable, which reinforced regional antipathies. In addition, revised federal institutions and the presidential system encouraged more heterogeneous political alliances, giving minority groups increased leverage in coalition building and distributional contention. Religious strains overlapped with ethnic concerns. Civilian competition animated a host of communal tensions, and elites became increasingly polarized over the course of the civilian regime.

Veteran politicians were joined by political aspirants drawn from the private sector, retired military officers, and the professions. The oil boom fostered a large new stratum of entrepreneurs and business elites who were substantially involved in trade, real estate, construction, and speculative activities but had comparatively limited commitments in manufacturing and other productive ventures. As both allies and clients to the political class, business figures supplied political finance and collaborated in business ventures, while soliciting government contracts, import licenses, regulatory favors, and other considerations. Moreover, the widespread business activities of politicians and civil servants blurred the distinction between government and private interests. There were few evident differences between business elites and political leaders over the direction of economic policy or the conditions for investment. Accumulation was structured around the collusive relations between business and state elites.

Multiple sets of distributional pressures shaped the new political system. Party organizations and individual politicians had pressing needs for resources to contest elections and bolster their support networks. They sought discretion over jobs, contracts, finance, and new projects to placate constituents and build patronage structures. The return of civilian rule also intensified popular demands on leaders for a wide array of benefits. Organized labor, students, business groups, professionals, ethnic and regional interests, and local advocates pressured the new political elite for preferential policies, subsidies, and spending on social programs, development, and perquisites. Politicians, state employees, and private sector cronies endeavored to build their own property bases. The rentier state was central to these distributional struggles, as contending groups and segments focused on access to public largesse. Controlling political office, or obtaining special entrée to the state, was regarded as a necessary vehicle for securing resources and market opportunities.[45] The premium on winning and holding political power imparted special intensity and ruthless-

45. See Richard Joseph, *Democracy and Prebendal Politics in Nigeria: The Rise and Fall of the Second Republic* (Cambridge: Cambridge University Press, 1987), and Larry Diamond, "Class Formation in the Swollen African State," *Journal of Modern African Studies* 25, no. 4 (1987): 567–96.

ness to the competition for offices and spoils.[46] A diffuse coalition of public officials, private sector figures, and popular interests converged around the patronage and rents flowing from the state-dominated economy.

The proliferation of access points within the state encouraged fragmentation and expansion of patronage. The term *prebendalism,* taken from Weber's discussion of various forms of patrimonial rule, has been applied to this scenario.[47] In the prebendal system, state officials treat their positions as personal sinecures, and politicians appropriate public resources for personal and communal gain. This is contrasted with a more cohesive patronage system or political "machine" in which distributional politics serve longer-term strategies of political dominance and organization building. Prebendalism is distinguished by its diffuse character and by the precedence of short-term distributional pressures to sustain political compliance. These factors undermine the formation of stable institutions and work against long-term political and economic strategies. Resources are largely dissipated in current consumption since political actors cannot channel surplus for investment. These political factors were apparent in economic policy and performance during the civilian republic.

Economic management under the Shagari administration was haphazard at best. The presidency did not provide strong oversight or programmatic guidance. Policies were improvised among a circle of presidential advisers, officials in peak economic ministries, and the Central Bank, with little formal coordination or lines of authority. The ruling NPN, an assemblage of notables and ethnic networks loosely organized around the allocation of patronage, was lacking in cohesive leadership or organizational discipline. Technocratic figures within the party were essentially sidelined during the transition process, and patrimonial elements quickly gained ascendance in the administration. President Shagari, a retiring personality with limited stature in the party hierarchy, deferred to political chieftains. The party's legislators and governors were frequently autonomous of the national leadership. Opposition parties also controlled the majority in the assembly and most of the state governments, further weakening control of the federal center and creating a wide domain of patronage structures beyond the reach of the presidency and the ruling party. The absence of cohesion at the center, compounded by dissension throughout the federal system, made it virtually impossible to sustain macroeconomic discipline or to build stable market institutions. Indeed, the political

46. Claude Ake, "How Politics Underdevelops Africa," in Adebayo Adedeji and P. Bugemba, eds., *The Challenges of African Economic Recovery and Development* (London: Frank Cass, 1989), 316–29.

47. Joseph, *Democracy and Prebendal Politics in Nigeria,* 56–57.

strategies of the NPN and its chief competitors created powerful disincentives to fiscal discipline or institution building.

The Second Republic spanned the apex of the petroleum boom. A second oil windfall in 1979 arose from surging international prices (following the Iranian revolution) and rising Nigerian output. Petroleum revenues increased from $9.5 billion in 1978 to $25 billion in 1980. Federal revenues totaled ₦12 billion in 1980, more than double the budget of two years earlier. The balance of payments showed a large surplus with international reserves growing to $10.3 billion.[48] The influx of resources prompted a new rash of spending and consumption. The pro-market pronouncements of the NPN manifesto bore little relation to the strategy of the party in power, as the Shagari government advanced an agenda of state-led growth and programs of populist redistribution in line with the preceding military regimes.[49] Large capital programs in manufacturing, infrastructure, and agriculture moved forward. Massive projects such as the Ajaokuta steel complex and the new Federal Capital in Abuja were accelerated. The administration expanded subsidies on staple commodities, utilities, and transportation. Federal resources devoted to education, health, and housing increased dramatically, as did spending on police and justice, as the civilians attempted to shift responsibility for domestic security away from the armed forces.[50] The flood of federal spending was matched by the states, whose budgets were swelled by federal transfers, loans, and liberal guarantees for external borrowing. The spree in the early years of the Second Republic was barely monitored or disciplined by central authorities. The atmosphere of the new windfall removed any residual budgetary prudence. The relative autonomy exercised by state governments, legislators, party factions, public enterprises, and elements of the civil service multiplied the outlets for dissipation, through direct spending and pervasive corruption.

The patterns of economic management followed a consistent political logic that flowed from the institutions and elite coalitions of the civilian regime. A polarized, competitive political class sought to channel patronage and rents to particular constituencies while buying general popular acquiescence through the expansion of public services and social programs. In addition to allocations through fiscal policy, the administration furnished largesse through trade policy, finance, and regulatory discretion.

48. World Bank, *Nigeria Structural Adjustment Program: Policies, Implementation, and Impact* (Washington, DC: World Bank, 1994).

49. See Ladun Anise, "Political Parties and Election Manifestoes," in Oyeleye Oyediran, ed., *The Nigerian 1979 Elections* (London and Basingstoke: Macmillan, 1981).

50. Osaghae, *Crippled Giant,* 132–33.

Most of the austerity measures imposed under Obasanjo were relaxed, including a substantial liberalization of imports. The increasingly overvalued exchange rate provided an implicit subsidy on foreign currency and supported an import binge. From 1979 to 1980 imports grew by 24 percent, while their composition shifted away from the capital and intermediate goods that serve as inputs to production. In 1977, consumer goods constituted 29 percent of imports, and by 1980 they claimed 40 percent. Bank lending also expanded with the major government-controlled commercial banks disbursing copious loans to well-connected borrowers under scant oversight. These measures not only allowed for targeted favors to cronies but furnished general benefits through cheap consumer goods and economic stimulus.

Omnipresent corruption had been an increasingly prominent factor in economic mismanagement under the preceding military regimes, but in the Second Republic it became the driving force in the declining fortunes of the economy and the basic viability of civilian rule. Corrupt practices compromised the formulation of policies, the performance of public agencies, and the oversight of authorities. The diversion of funds was closely linked to capital flight, fiscal indiscipline, and chronic institutional disarray. The extravagant sums appropriated by officials and cronies were essentially a dead loss to the economy since corrupt gains were typically spirited abroad rather than invested locally. One credible estimate places capital flight during the Second Republic in excess of $14 billion.[51] Any attempt to measure corruption can only be approximate, though the Nigerian press and public commissions reported considerable malfeasance, and occasional samples of these sources document hundreds of millions of dollars in illicit gains.[52] A single presidential adviser, Umaru Dikko, was widely reputed to have become a billionaire during his control of the special Task Force on Rice, which distributed licenses for importation. The constant parade of reports about official corruption and the conspicuous consumption displayed by the politicians served to erode the domestic legitimacy of the Second Republic as it further tarnished the country's international reputation.

51. Forrest, *Politics and Economic Development in Nigeria,* 171. Another estimate puts total capital flight at $63 billion from 1970 through 1996. See James K. Boyce and Leonce Ndikumana, "Is Africa a Net Creditor? New Estimates of Capital Flight from Severely Indebted Sub-Saharan African Countries, 1970–1996," Working Paper No. 5, University of Massachusetts, Department of Economics (2000), 41.

52. Larry Diamond, "The Political Economy of Corruption in Nigeria," paper presented at the 27th annual conference of the African Studies Association, Los Angeles, 1984; and Falola and Inhonvbere, *The Rise and Fall of Nigeria's Second Republic,* 108–9.

These trends produced a sustained economic crisis beginning in 1981. International oil prices began to flag, and more stringent OPEC quotas reduced Nigerian exports, causing a large drop in income. Petroleum revenues declined to $12 billion by 1982, less than half the figure of two years earlier. After cresting in 1980, government revenues fell by 40 percent in 1981 and dipped another 18 percent in 1983.[53] The resource constraints were clearly recognized, yet political forces sustained the velocity of government spending and imports. Shagari's administration had neither the inclination nor the capacity to control expenditure or to impose restraint on party elements and various tiers of the federation.[54] The impending 1983 elections accelerated demands for political finance and increased the urgency among political elites in the scramble for rents. In the face of plummeting revenues, federal expenditures climbed in 1981, diminished only modestly the following year, and rose again in the 1983 election year, when the budget deficit topped 11 percent of GDP.

The government was slow to react to the new fiscal realities. After introducing a profligate budget for 1982, leaders belatedly followed with a set of improvised austerity measures. Officials revived various restrictions on imports and attempted better enforcement of the trade regime in an effort to stem violations.[55] These new administrative controls were widely skirted and simply created new opportunities for rents. Export receipts diminished by 60 percent between 1980 and 1983, but high spending on imports continued, and the current account moved sharply into deficit. In the absence of a coherent policy response, leaders coped by running down foreign reserves, building up arrears on trade and fiscal commitments (including public sector salaries), and incurring large volumes of domestic and external debt. From 1981 forward Nigeria borrowed heavily from official and private lenders, and long-term foreign debt more than tripled—from $4 billion to $13.5 billion—in the course of the civilian regime. To this must be added a large stock of short-term debt that accumulated rapidly in the latter years of civilian rule. In addition, the federal government drew on the domestic banking system, and credit to government increasingly crowded out private sector credit.

The worsening balance of payments situation induced the Shagari administration to approach the International Monetary Fund in 1982 to facilitate bridge finance and debt rescheduling. Talks with the Fund

53. Central Bank of Nigeria, *Perspectives on Economic Policy Reform in Nigeria* (Lagos: Central Bank of Nigeria, 1993), 36.
54. Osaghae, *Crippled Giant,* 158.
55. The government required import preinspection by the Swiss company Société Générale de Surveillance (SGS).

quickly stalemated, however, over the central features of a stabilization program: devaluation of the naira, trade liberalization, and removal of the subsidy on domestic petroleum products. Policymakers were unwilling to contemplate these reforms on the eve of elections, and talks with the multilateral institutions soon broke off. The impasse with creditors compounded the negative international effects of a restrictive trade and investment regime. Taken along with the mercurial shifts in macroeconomic policy and regulation arising from an unstable rentier system, Nigeria's position in global markets continued to erode.

The elections of 1983 provoked the collapse of the Second Republic. Campaigns and polling were surrounded by political rancor, violence, and fraud. The governing NPN sought to consolidate its position as a dominant party by making inroads into opposition precincts, mainly through inducement and fraud. Opposition groups contested NPN hegemony by mobilizing their own communal bases and patronage networks. The major parties fielded youth auxiliaries that fomented intimidation and violence. The Federal Electoral Commission (FEDECO) lacked resources and autonomy, allowing for widespread irregularities and misconduct. While the NPN generally prevailed in efforts to rig elections at the federal level, opposition parties commonly interfered with polls in states or localities under their control. The media played an important role in exposing malpractices, though partisanship and inflammatory reporting exacerbated tensions and intensified public disaffection.

The elections fostered a political business cycle that put the economy into a tailspin. Spending accelerated as petroleum revenues reached their lowest point in five years. Consumer subsidies, high public sector payrolls, and government-owned companies bloated the budget. The NPN used such agencies as the Nigerian National Supply Company (NNSC) and the Rice Task Force to flood the market with cheap commodities in time for the elections. State governments similarly increased their spending, counting on federal government loans and guarantees for fiscal cover. Parties and candidates at all levels sought to bolster their war chests, placing additional demands on public resources and enlisting support from clients in the private sector. Uncertain incumbents sought to grab what they could in the twilight of the administration, leading to increasingly flagrant and grand levels of corruption. The audacity of such misconduct was displayed in a series of fires in public buildings intended to destroy evidence of illegal activities. The headquarters of the national telecommunications company (the tallest building in Lagos) was gutted by such a blaze. The Defense Ministry and the power company had similar incidents. The outright destruction of state property was emblematic of a general deterioration of public institutions. Major services including electricity and public sanitation virtually collapsed in major cities, while functions such as transport, communications, education, health, and general administration eroded rapidly.

The elections nullified whatever legitimacy remained for the civilian regime. The ruling NPN swept the polls with solid majorities in both houses of the assembly, twelve state governorships, and 47 percent of the presidential vote—exceeding the combined total for the leading opposition parties, the UPN and the NPP. While the NPN undoubtedly benefited from a sizable bandwagon effect as constituencies gravitated toward the party as a recognized fount of patronage, the scope of the electoral victory was clearly driven by massive vote-buying, fraud, and intimidation. As before, these malpractices were not the sole provenance of the NPN, but the party's control of the federal machinery and regional networks allowed for much more extensive manipulation than their challengers. The election provoked widespread indignation and political violence, especially in the restive southwestern states where the ruling party encroached on the UPN heartland. Shehu Shagari was inaugurated for a second term amid promises of improved economic governance, but the elections underscored the pervasive impediments to reform. The regime did not survive the New Year.

Buhari's Interregnum: Correctives and Drift

The Second Republic was deposed on the last evening of 1983 in a largely peaceful coup d'état that installed Major-General Muhammadu Buhari, a Muslim from Katsina, as head of state. The revolt was initially welcomed by much of the Nigerian public, for whom the civilians had forgone any semblance of credibility. In their early months General Buhari and his chief of staff, Major-General Tunde Idiagbon, took a number of dramatic steps to curtail political corruption and impose accountability on the civilian political class. Dozens of politicians were arrested and investigated, and a number of prominent officeholders, including several state governors and many legislators, received lengthy prison terms for financial misconduct. The military government also attempted to restore a measure of social order and civility to an unruly public arena. A "War Against Indiscipline" (WAI) employed slogans, civic education, and military-style regimentation to promote such virtues as queuing, anticorruption, and public sanitation.

The new military leadership offered little innovation in economic policy. Although buffeted by a structural crisis as the oil boom subsided, the regime avoided any basic reevaluation of the prevailing *dirigiste* approach, relying instead on stopgap measures of fiscal retrenchment, martial discipline, and public sloganeering. Buhari did not bring in a dynamic economic team but simply revived Murtala and Obasanjo's decision-making structure, along with their ad hoc policy approach. Confronting virtual bankruptcy and a steep downward economic slide, Buhari's central response was stringent fiscal austerity and tightened administrative controls. Public spending was cut by 27 percent in 1984 and remained virtually flat the following year, the regime's last in power. Reductions were achieved by curtailing disbursements for large projects, reducing government payrolls, and trimming subsidies on health, education, and consumer commodities. Spending on major capital projects, including steel and the new capital, was temporarily frozen. The regime undertook a purge of more than 15,000 federal civil servants and public enterprise employees. The states followed suit, presiding over retrenchments three times as large as the federal cuts. Federal authorities introduced user fees in the health sector and floated potential increases in university fees, which were militantly resisted by students. The scope and level of consumer subsidies were reduced, and the allocation of commodities through the NNSC was narrowed to public employees.

The enormous shortfall in the balance of payments (totaling $5.8 billion for 1983) reflected a trade deficit arising from the civilians' import binge and heightened obligations from the accumulating foreign debt. Seeking to restore the country's international financial standing, the regime aimed at righting the trade balance and channeling scarce foreign exchange to debt service. The government attempted to compress imports mainly through administrative controls including wider import bans, restrictions on import licenses, and better screening of license allocations. These measures, in tandem with broader anticorruption efforts, may have reduced fraud in the trade regime but largely failed to reallocate imports toward productive purposes. There was a widespread perception that the regime's northern cronies benefited disproportionately from licenses and other commercial outlets.[56]

Buhari's resistance to more basic macroeconomic and institutional reform hindered recovery. The compression of imports, along with reductions in public spending, aggravated economic decline, while stringent monetary policies and perennially weak incentives dampened private

56. On the Buhari stabilization regime, see Adebayo Olukoshi and Tajudeen Abdulraheem, "Nigeria: Crisis Management under the Buhari Regime," *Review of African Political Economy* 12, no. 34 (1985): 96–97.

investment. Manufacturing suffered an especially sharp decline, as the index of manufacturing production dropped by 37 percent from 1981 to 1984, and manufacturing activities contracted to their lowest percentage of GDP since the late 1970s. Solid mineral production and export agriculture remained chronically depressed, although available evidence suggests that domestic food production was resilient.

The greatest impediment to stabilization was the mounting external debt, which by 1984 had reached $18 billion, amounting to 160 percent of exports.[57] The government sought to meet its servicing commitments while looking for ways to reschedule with bilateral and commercial creditors. Buhari's government resumed talks with the IMF only to bog down once again over the government's refusal to consider key policy changes such as devaluation, trade liberalization, and a reduction of fuel subsidies. The government was equally diffident about privatization and financial liberalization. In the absence of an IMF standby agreement and an open door to rescheduling, Nigeria sought without success to open back-channel discussions with bilateral creditors in the Paris Club. They also experimented with barter arrangements through countertrade deals with Brazil, France, Romania, Austria, and others in an effort to circumvent foreign exchange constraints. The countertrade initiative did not significantly alleviate trade bottlenecks, and critics alleged that Nigeria was fleeced by trading partners

The enthusiasm that had greeted Buhari's intervention quickly palled as repression and economic drift worsened. The regime promulgated a series of sweeping security decrees and gave the internal security agencies broad latitude. They persecuted dissidents including labor and professional groups, and took a heavy-handed stance toward the media. Many Nigerians believed the regime to have a strong sectional bias, departing from their military predecessors. Southerners perceived a northern cast to Buhari's political appointments, his regime's dispersal of economic benefits such as import licenses, and the insistence on preserving enterprises and projects that benefited the northern states. In addition, there appeared to be disparities in the treatment of former Second Republic officials, as many former opposition politicians were prosecuted while senior NPN leaders were spared. Moreover, throughout their tenure Buhari and Idiagbon remained silent about the possibility of another civilian transition. Public disaffection quickly set in, and there were many expressions of relief when the regime fell to another military intervention.

57. Central Bank of Nigeria, *Perspectives on Economic Policy Reform,* 19.

Babangida: Approaching Reform

Major-General Ibrahim Babangida, a Muslim from Niger State, ousted Buhari and Idiagbon in a largely peaceful coup on August 27, 1985. Babangida was no stranger to such intrigues, having been involved in coups and military politics for more than a decade. The new leader promised dramatic changes in both policy and style, pledging to arrest the economy's downward slide, unfetter the political arena, and implement democratic reform. Babangida declared an economic state of emergency and opened a nationwide "IMF debate" on the nation's economic future.[58] Meanwhile, the new leadership quietly pursued discussions with the World Bank as Babangida became convinced of the need to work with the Bretton Woods institutions. Public debate revealed widespread opposition to IMF policies, and Babangida used political legerdemain to advance a reform agenda. Citing popular opinion, the president repudiated the IMF in a December speech and announced that Nigeria would not accept conditional finance. Within a month, however, he unveiled a Structural Adjustment Program (SAP), a "homegrown" package featuring budgetary restraint, exchange rate reform, trade liberalization, a reduction of subsidies, increased agricultural prices, financial liberalization, and partial privatization. Although presented under a nationalist mantle, the SAP was a conventional adjustment program negotiated principally with World Bank officials. Formally launched in July 1986, the SAP set the stage for a November standby agreement with the IMF that included standard conditionalities and monitoring. Holding to its promise to "reject the IMF loan," the government did not draw on the available IMF funds, although the World Bank quietly supplied adjunct financing. Most important, the Fund's endorsement facilitated debt negotiations and opened the door to new lending from the Bank and bilateral donors.[59]

Concurrent with his announcement of the adjustment package Babangida also inaugurated the Political Bureau to frame the details of the transition to democracy, promised for 1990. The members of the bureau, appointed by the executive, were mandated to canvass popular views on political reform, to discuss the principles and structures of the

---

58. Thomas Biersteker and Peter Lewis, "The Rise and Fall of Structural Adjustment in Nigeria," in Larry Diamond, Anthony Kirk-Greene, and Oyeleye Oyediran, eds., *Transition without End: Nigerian Politics and Civil Society under Babangida* (Boulder: Lynne Rienner, 1997), 307.

59. The background to the SAP is covered by Thomas M. Callaghy, "Lost between State and Market: The Politics of Economic Adjustment in Ghana, Zambia, and Nigeria," in Joan Nelson, ed., *Economic Crisis and Policy Choice* (Princeton: Princeton University Press, 1990), 305–7.

new civilian regime, and to make recommendations to the regime the following year. At the outset, Babangida linked economic adjustment to political liberalization and regularly sought to offset the contentious politics surrounding these two programs by manipulating the pace, timing, and content of reforms.

The SAP heralded a course of stabilization that continued for much of Babangida's tenure in office, despite notable lapses. The policies connected with the adjustment program, lasting well beyond the sunset of the initial package in 1988, altered basic tenets of Nigeria's prevailing economic strategy. The regime amended policies affecting trade, exchange rates, public enterprises, agricultural incentives, state employment, and subsidies. The import licensing system was abolished, and tariffs were substantially reduced, although selective import bans remained. The government instituted a dual exchange rate system, shifting most nongovernment transactions to a Second-Tier Foreign Exchange Market (SFEM), an auction-based window. The Central Bank's SFEM auctions, beginning in September 1986, quickly produced a two-thirds devaluation of the naira.[60] Agricultural producer prices were decontrolled, and the commodity boards were dissolved, which rapidly boosted export activity. The government also divested eighteen agricultural parastatals and closed the public company that imported consumer commodities. Staff reductions were implemented in other public firms and agencies. Subsidies for fuel and fertilizer were reduced substantially though not eliminated outright.

The IMF agreement permitted negotiations to move forward on the country's $20 billion external debt. An initial round of rescheduling was concluded in 1987 with the Paris and London Clubs that reduced the nominal debt-service ratio from 72 to 31 percent.[61] A steep decline in global oil prices during 1986 produced large shortfalls in government finance and the balance of payments, plunging the economy into recession. Nonetheless, productive sectors benefited from buoyant agricultural prices and better access to foreign exchange. Output of traditional export crops such as cocoa, palm produce, and cotton grew rapidly, and manufacturing witnessed a significant though short-lived revival, reversing several years of decline.[62] Economic growth resumed, and the balance of payments improved substantially.

60. Prior to devaluation, the naira had dropped incrementally, from about $1.50 = ₦1 in the early 1980s, to nearly par with the dollar on the eve of the SFEM. After initiation of the auction, the naira was valued at about ₦3.5 = $1. See the World Bank, *Nigeria's Structural Adjustment Program: Policies, Implementation, and Impact* (Washington, DC: World Bank, 1994), 10.

61. World Bank, *Nigeria's Structural Adjustment Program,* 90.

62. Economic restructuring during the early years of the SAP is detailed by Paul Lubeck, "Restructuring Nigeria's Urban-Industrial Sector within the West African Region: The

The SAP also produced widespread popular hardship. Retrenchment and declining real wages cut across swaths of the public and private sectors. Public resentment focused on the new adjustment policies, even though many economic problems were inherited from preceding regimes or arose from exogenous revenue shocks. In mid-1987, while the regime was framing its democratic transition program, students, traders, and organized labor launched a series of anti-SAP protests. The tumultuous demonstrations underscored the depth of public resentment and prompted a tactical retreat from the stabilization program. In January 1988 the president announced a "reflationary" budget that featured compensatory measures such as increases in wages and public spending, a cap on interest rates, and a promise to sustain the petroleum subsidy. The multilateral institutions responded by withholding endorsement of Nigeria's economic performance, and the IMF declined a new standby facility when the existing agreement lapsed in early 1988.

Wavering on Reform, 1988–90

Popular pressure and crosscurrents within the regime gave rise to inconsistent economic policies. While preserving core elements of the adjustment program, leaders selectively circumvented policies and steadily relaxed macroeconomic discipline.[63] The exchange rate was unified under the market-based auction system in 1987, but officials manipulated the auctions in an effort to stabilize the naira. Seeking to arrest the depreciation of the naira, the Central Bank selectively restricted participation in weekly bidding and allowed price collusion among key financial institutions. Regardless of these interventions, the naira continued to weaken against major currencies. Trade policy was also contradictory. The government rationalized tariffs and provided new export incentives even as they extended import bans on such items as wheat and barley. Officials pushed through two increases on domestic fuel prices that significantly reduced subsidy levels, but relented on further adjustments in the face of political unrest.[64] Confronted with accelerating inflation, there was an effort to radically contract the money supply by withdrawing the deposits of public agencies and corporations from the banking system, a move with only temporary effect.

Interplay of Crisis, Linkages, and Popular Resistance," *International Journal of Urban and Regional Research* 16, no. 1 (1992): 6–23.

63. Biersteker and Lewis, "Rise and Fall of Structural Adjustment in Nigeria," 313–20.

64. A two-tiered pricing structure was introduced in 1989 as a means of phasing in a price increase on fuels.

The regime moved forward with other reforms. A decree on public sector reform was released in 1988, and a specialized agency, the Technical Committee on Privatization and Commercialization (TCPC), was created to supervise the sale and restructuring of state enterprises. Several small and medium-sized enterprises were sold or liquidated, and a new wave of retrenchment eliminated several thousand workers from major public firms. Financial liberalization was also introduced. Entry requirements for the financial services industry were relaxed at the end of 1986, and restrictions on interest rates were subsequently lifted. Along with exchange rate reforms, these policies encouraged the creation of new private banks and finance companies.[65]

The multilateral institutions responded favorably to these policy changes, and a new IMF facility was extended in 1989, although once again the government deferred to political sensitivities by refusing to avail themselves of IMF resources. The Fund's endorsement renewed access to finance from other donors and permitted further rescheduling of the external debt that now exceeded $30 billion. The government also created a debt-swap program through which foreign creditors were invited to accept domestic equity. The program was slow to take off. Indicative of Nigeria's tenuous international credibility, few creditors were interested in acquiring stakes in the domestic economy.

Despite uneven performance on key macroeconomic targets, the growth of the economy accelerated. From 1988 through 1990 the GDP grew at an average rate of 6.5 percent, and for the first time in several years there was positive growth per capita in both agriculture and manufacturing.[66] These favorable indicators were offset by adverse trends. The debt-service ratio remained well above a fifth of export income, unemployment rose sharply, and inflation surged above 50 percent. The government's "reflationary" policies of 1988 fostered monetary growth that aggravated inflation. Public restiveness erupted again in mid-1989 with a spate of "SAP riots" in several universities and urban commercial districts, resulting in numerous deaths. The government responded violently to the riots but followed with a new compensatory package of job creation, health and transport subsidies, and accelerated food production.

The SAP riots highlighted the political dilemmas of reform arising from elite fragmentation and distributional pressures on the state. Babangida's initial seizure of power was symptomatic of growing faction-

---

65. See Peter M. Lewis, "Economic Statism, Private Capital, and the Dilemmas of Accumulation in Nigeria," *World Development* 22, no. 3 (1994): 445.

66. Central Bank of Nigeria, *Perspectives on Economic Policy Reforms,* 8.

alism within the military, and he was mindful of an uncertain support base within the armed forces. Having weathered an apparent coup attempt within four months of taking power, he could not count upon institutional backing for either his political or economic programs. Babangida's initial commitment to orthodox reforms brought him into contention with members of the ruling council, civilian elites, and popular sectors that relied upon the patronage associated with the windfall economy. Economic adjustment was therefore inaugurated by a narrow circle of leaders in the absence of a supporting constituency.[67] A combination of deft politics and coercion allowed Babangida to sustain these policies for several years before political considerations eroded reform.

The politics of structural adjustment has been characterized in the image of a two-level game, as state leaders must simultaneously negotiate the foreign and domestic arenas.[68] Faced with the cross-cutting demands of external creditors and internal constituencies, policymakers face tensions among the long-term imperatives of economic restructuring and more immediate distributional pressures from politically salient groups. Babangida negotiated the reform process through a combination of political manipulation, popular sidepayments, dispensation for key elite groups, expansion of the parallel economy, and overt repression. He soon earned the sobriquet "Maradona" (after the famous Argentine soccer player) for his alacrity in selling programs, balancing different interests, and disarming potential opponents. The general employed rhetorical skill and personal charm to convince the nation of his reformist intent.[69] While these talents eventually wore thin, Babangida demonstrated guile at critical moments including the crisis-filled months of 1993. He frequently altered the schedule of the democratic transition program, reorganized the political parties, and created new states, all of which served as diversionary tactics to sustain public expectations. By offsetting political reform with shifts in economic policy, the leadership gained leeway in balancing these tenuous programs.

67. This pattern of reform is emphasized by John Waterbury, "The Political Management of Economic Adjustment and Reform," in Joan Nelson, ed., *Fragile Coalitions: The Politics of Adjustment* (New Brunswick: Transaction Books for the Overseas Development Council, 1989). See also Jeffrey Herbst, "The Structural Adjustment of Politics in Africa," *World Development* 18, no. 7 (1990).

68. See Robert D. Putnam, "Diplomacy and Domestic Politics: The Logic of Two-Level Games," *International Organization* 42, no. 3 (1988); Howard Lehman, *Indebted Development* (New York: St. Martin's Press, 1993); and David F. Gordon, "Debt, Conditionality, and Reform: The International Relations of Economic Policy Restructuring in Sub-Saharan Africa," in Thomas M. Callaghy and John Ravenhill, eds., *Hemmed In: Responses to Africa's Economic Decline* (New York: Columbia University Press, 1993), 108.

69. Diamond, "Nigeria: The Uncivic Society," 443–44.

The regime implemented a string of high-profile measures to compensate popular sectors as means of assuaging popular opposition to adjustment. These included the 1988 budget and the package of employment and social subsidies in the wake of the 1989 riots. The government also created a Directorate for Food, Roads, and Rural Infrastructure (DFRRI) to provide special assistance to the rural areas, a network of People's Banks and Community Banks to extend credit to small-scale and local borrowers, and the Better Life for Rural Women Program, sponsored by the first lady, intended to promote rural crafts production and small-scale enterprise. These initiatives were poorly funded, erratic, and permeated with corruption, yielding new rents for elites but meager results for the supposed beneficiaries.[70] In addition, officials belatedly allowed moderate wage increases for the public and private sectors and delayed removing the fuel subsidy.

These carrots were accompanied by sticks. The regime employed repressive tactics against trade unions, students, academic staff, and intellectual critics of the SAP.[71] Officials seized an opportunity to weaken the peak labor confederation, the Nigeria Labour Congress (NLC), when factional struggles disrupted the organization in 1988. The regime summarily replaced the incumbent leaders with an appointed administrator and then supervised elections that installed a more compliant leadership. Student organizations were especially militant, and leaders sought to curb protests by closing universities, arresting students, and unleashing police violence against campus protests. The senior-level Academic Staff Union was suspended, and officials admonished other professional organizations protesting the adjustment program.[72] When activists tried to organize meetings in 1989 and 1990 to discuss alternatives to the SAP, the government banned the gatherings. Public discourse was further hampered by military decrees allowing broad powers of detention and oversight of the press.

Structural adjustment and the underlying fiscal crisis reduced traditional outlets for state patronage. Government contracts diminished, as did the rents from import licenses and subsidized commodities and largesse from state enterprises. In the course of economic restructuring,

70. See Julius O. Ihonvbere, "Economic Crisis, Structural Adjustment, and Social Crisis in Nigeria," *World Development* 21, no. 1 (1993): 146.

71. On the popular sectors, see Attahiru Jega, "Professional Associations and Structural Adjustment," in Adebayo Olukoski, ed., *The Politics of Structural Adjustment in Nigeria* (London: James Currey, 1993), and Yusuf Bangura and Bjorn Beckman, "African Workers and Structural Adjustment: A Nigerian Case Study," in Olukoshi, *Politics of Structural Adjustment.*

72. Jega, "Professional Associations," 106–7.

however, state officials were able to exercise substantial control over emerging markets, and these new sources of rents offered a degree of respite for economic elites.[73] For instance, speculators responded quickly to the liberalization of cocoa markets since the cash crop was an easy medium for obtaining foreign exchange. Speculative pressures on cocoa (as a proxy for naira) became so intense that the local price of cocoa briefly rose above the world price, delivering premiums to well-placed operators who could amass hard currency.[74] The privatization program also created a wide circle of beneficiaries as well-connected insiders took advantage of equity sales and the divestiture of physical assets.

Financial services became the center of a new bonanza. The opening of bank licenses in 1986 invited a torrent of entrants to the industry. The number of commercial and merchant banks tripled to 120 firms within four years.[75] Several hundred unlicensed finance and mortgage companies were also created, often with links to the new banks. Many flocked to this burgeoning sector from activities in manufacturing, trade, and the professions, as well as the civil service and a large concentration of retired military officers. Entrepreneurs were first attracted by the margins from dealing in foreign exchange and financing the purchase of hard currency. The deregulation of interest rates also fostered arbitrage in money markets. Political connections heavily influenced the licensing and regulation of the new financial institutions. The growing financial services sector offered alternatives to the diminishing arena of rent seeking in trade, enabling the regime to steer new opportunities to allies and cronies.[76]

An expanding realm of parallel markets and illegal activities also shaped the post-SAP economy. Smuggling of petroleum and other merchandise, drug trafficking, money laundering, and commercial fraud were leading endeavors. Petroleum smuggling was undertaken by top military officers and civilian cronies. Senior officials arranged lifting contracts for their own companies, or else they simply chartered tankers and covertly filled them at terminals of the national petroleum company. The revenues siphoned in this fashioned can only be guessed but possibly reached billions of dollars. In addition, the continued domestic subsidy on refined fuels, along with currency differentials, created an enormous gap in fuel

73. Lewis, "Economic Statism," 445.

74. Abdul Raufu Mustapha, "Structural Adjustment and Agrarian Change in Nigeria," in Olukoshi, *Politics of Structural Adjustment,* 121–22. See also Julian Ozanne, "Dealers Play for High Stakes," *Financial Times,* March 12, 1991.

75. M. O. Ojo, "A Review and Appraisal of Nigeria's Experience with Financial Sector Reform," Central Bank of Nigeria, Research Department Occasional Paper No. 8 (1993), 10.

76. Tony Hawkins, "Why the Cap Did Not Fit," *Financial Times,* March 16, 1992.

prices with the CFA states. A lively covert trade in Nigerian fuels, accounting for about 10 percent of domestic consumption, flowed to regional neighbors.[77] More broadly, the devaluation of the naira cheapened Nigerian manufactures relative to the surrounding Francophone countries, where the CFA remained overvalued. The disparity encouraged a large unrecorded export trade from Nigeria to neighbors in the subregion.

Other illicit activities flourished. Nigeria in the 1980s became a major transshipment point for South Asian heroin and cocaine from Latin America. Many of the proceeds were laundered through the domestic banking system. Narcotics trafficking was tolerated and possibly abetted by senior officials. An extensive web of international commercial fraud also emanated from Nigeria in the late 1980s. The 419 schemes, named for the local criminal code on fraud, took a variety of guises from propositions for money laundering to seemingly legitimate business solicitations. Remarkably, these activities netted several hundred million dollars annually. The 419 operations flourished under government indifference or collusion.

In short, liberalization contracted traditional sources of rents and patronage while opening new areas of speculation, arbitrage, and parallel activities, nearly all of which were mediated by political authorities. While the SAP was able to achieve macroeconomic stabilization, policy change did not elicit a sustained supply response in productive activities that could alter the structure of the oil-dependent economy. Facing high prices for foreign exchange, insecure property rights, and unstable markets, manufacturers and agricultural producers had diffident reactions to adjustment policies. While price reforms produced an expansion of agricultural exports, production was hampered by high input costs, poor infrastructure, price volatility, and a dearth of supporting institutions, and the growth of output slowed. Similarly, the manufacturing sector was invigorated by the availability of hard currency and the export incentives created by devaluation. A few areas, notably textiles, experienced a surge of output. The incentive structure was tenuous, however, as manufacturers confronted poor infrastructure, expensive inputs, scarce and expensive credit, and an erratic regulatory and policy setting. The uneven performance of the "real" economy contrasted with the vitality of rent-driven activities in finance and other nontradable areas.

Babangida's initial embrace of orthodox reform was prompted by a genuine intent to restructure the economy and revitalize performance. Pre-

77. World Bank, *Nigeria's Structural Adjustment Program,* 57.

vailing fiscal constraints, if nothing else, were sufficient to induce Babangida to cooperate with the Bretton Woods institutions and to seek accommodation with international creditors. Babangida's early policy pronouncements and his senior economic appointments demonstrated a broader concern with restructuring the rentier economy and providing new incentives for capital formation. With the introduction of the SAP, his regime challenged basic features of *dirigiste* strategy and repealed many protectionist trade and investment policies. Finance Minister Kalu I. Kalu, a former World Bank official, along with a handful of senior appointees and civil servants, were consistent in advocating reform and seeking effective implementation of the regime's policy changes. Yet technocratic figures within the regime were few in number and politically isolated. Babangida did not delegate policy authority to capable agencies or departments within government, and he furnished only sporadic political cover for reform elements. Ultimately, the impetus for reform rested upon Babangida's personal commitment, his discretion, and his political adroitness. A social coalition did not gather among elites or popular sectors in support of the regime's agenda. Elements of the traditional rentier coalition sought to preserve the status quo or to gain particular dispensations from reforms. The armed forces were fragmented, increasingly venal, and suffused with political rivalries. There was no broader institutional foundation for economic change within the public service. As the regime's incentives shifted, the reform agenda quickly unraveled. Babangida accumulated personal power and moved toward more a predatory form of rule.

From Reform to Decline, 1990–93

Two pivotal developments in 1990—a failed coup and a new revenue windfall—marked a watershed in the direction of the regime. In April, Babangida narrowly averted a coup d'état led by a group of junior officers from the delta region with the backing of a local businessman. The abortive revolt was a dangerous expression of communal tension (as the mutineers threatened to "excise" the northern states from the federation) and a violent symptom of factionalism within the military.[78] In the wake of the coup attempt, dozens of military personnel were executed and hundreds were questioned or detained. The president also accelerated the relocation of the capital from Lagos to Abuja, which was deemed more

---

78. See Julius O. Ihonvbere, "A Critical Evaluation of the 1990 Failed Coup in Nigeria," *Journal of Modern African Studies* 29, no. 4 (1991): 601–26.

secure.[79] Babangida retreated from democratic reform, introducing new conditions and institutional changes that deferred the handover of power. Corruption and rentier activities grew more urgent as the president and his ruling circle sought to amass resources as a hedge against insecurity.[80] The regime stepped up patronage in order to bolster support. These impulses were propelled by a large infusion of revenues in the wake of the Iraqi invasion of Kuwait.

The disruption of world markets during the Gulf crisis pushed oil prices from $16 per barrel in August to more than $33 in October, before they settled back to $17 by the following January. Nigeria garnered a revenue windfall of about $5 billion from the price shock, which leaders seized as a reprieve from fiscal constraints. The regime increased its outlays and expanded the money supply. Babangida also removed a large proportion of state spending from the official budget, which increased his personal discretion and further reduced transparency. Massive sums were diverted to so-called dedicated accounts earmarked for special projects such as the federal capital, the recently started Liberian peacekeeping mission, and various projects such as the steel complex and an aluminum smelter. According to the most authoritative estimate, $12.4 billion was sidetracked to off-budget accounts from 1988 through 1994, an amount equal to about a fifth of total petroleum revenues for the period.[81] By 1992 extrabudgetary spending equaled nearly two-thirds of total expenditures, amounting to 17 percent of GDP.[82] The special accounts were completely opaque and the funds were never accounted for.

The miniboom rekindled the pathologies of the Dutch disease. The momentum of spending quickly outstripped the transient increase in revenues, fostering ever-larger deficits in the budget and the balance of payments. The windfall was also fully monetized, thus fueling imports, consumption, and inflation. The budget deficit grew to 10 percent of GDP in 1992, financed mainly by advances from the Central Bank.[83] In 1992 credit to the public sector grew by 110 percent, the money supply expanded by 71 percent, and inflation again topped 50 percent.[84] High domestic inflation, monetary expansion, and rising imports eroded the value of the naira,

79. Osaghae, *Crippled Giant,* 248.

80. This accentuated tendencies noted by Ihonvbere, "A Critical Evaluation of the Failed 1990 Coup," 611–13. See also Forrest, *Politics and Economic Development,* 246.

81. The findings of the 1994 Okigbo panel of inquiry were not officially released for a decade. See "Okigbo Report Indicts IBB, Two Others," *Punch* (Lagos), May 16, 2005.

82. World Bank, *Nigeria's Structural Adjustment Program,* 23.

83. Central Bank of Nigeria, *Economic Policy Reforms,* 36.

84. World Bank, *Nigeria's Structural Adjustment Program,* 36. Central Bank of Nigeria, *Annual Report and Statement of Accounts, 1994* (Lagos: Central Bank of Nigeria, 1995), 1.

which declined by an additional 65 percent against the dollar. The government continued its contradictory approach to exchange rate policy. The Central Bank liberalized the exchange system but attempted to shore up the naira by injecting foreign exchange into the auction market.[85] This was unsustainable, and the currency continued to depreciate. Confronted with erosion of the naira, the government targeted a rate of ₦22 = $1 as a benchmark, and soon revived the dual exchange rate. Inflation also created severe fiscal and trade distortions. Official prices on fuel, fertilizer, and power were not adjusted upward, and the implicit subsidies aggravated the deficit. As domestic prices on fuel and fertilizer dipped further below neighboring markets, smuggling accelerated, and shortages within Nigeria worsened. Fuel scarcity increased transport fares and interrupted public services such as electricity and waste disposal.

Increasing macroeconomic turbulence pushed the financial system toward insolvency. The rapidly growing banking and financial services industries were tenuously regulated, and weaknesses in the system set the stage for a financial crisis. Many firms were heavily leveraged, inadequately capitalized, and exposed in volatile interbank money markets. A series of high-profile failures undermined confidence in the financial system, leading quickly to a series of defaults and growing evidence of insolvency. Problems in the financial sector grew steadily, and by the end of Babangida's tenure a third of the nation's banks were distressed.[86]

Mismanagement of the economy gradually fostered a breach with creditors and donors. In February 1991 the government signed its third standby agreement with the IMF and negotiated a large new debt restructuring package. A deal with the London Club of private creditors allowed the government to buy back $3.4 billion in commercial debt at a discount on the secondary market, in addition to exchanging $2 billion for collateralized par bonds and canceling $1.2 billion in promissory notes.[87] The Paris Club also rescheduled $3.2 billion in bilateral debt. Nigeria's total debt stock diminished by nearly a fifth—from $33.5 billion in 1991 to $28.8 billion the following year. However, profligate spending and the government's delinquency on debt service once again built up external obligations.[88] When the standby arrangement expired in April 1992, nego-

85. T. J. Ntekop, "The Foreign Exchange Market in Nigeria," *Bullion* (Lagos) 16, no. 3 (1992): 30.

86. Agusto and Co., *1993/94 Banking Industry Survey* (Lagos: Agusto and Co., 1994), 1.

87. Tony Hawkins, "An Urgent Need of Debt Relief," *Financial Times,* March 16, 1992.

88. While defaulting on obligations to bilateral creditors, the government serviced its debt to the World Bank and its obligations to holders of par bonds. Officials within the finance ministry and the Central Bank distinguished between "lenders of last resort" and other creditors.

tiations with the Bretton Woods institutions remained dormant. As macroeconomic performance deteriorated and arrears built up on external debt, it was evident that a new IMF facility could not be considered. The collapse of accord with the Fund also hampered relations with the World Bank and precluded any further rescheduling with the creditor groups. By this time the regime had virtually abandoned the pretense of economic oversight, leading to policy drift, institutional decline, and flourishing corruption. According to some estimates discrepancies in the nation's petroleum accounts totaled $5.2 billion in 1991 and 1992, and the World Bank privately excoriated the government for a "lack of transparency" in its finances.[89] With the passing of the miniboom, oil revenues modestly declined, and the GDP recorded lackluster growth of 3.6 percent, less than half the rate of two years earlier and barely positive in per capita terms.[90] Manufacturing output slumped by 4.8 percent, and indices of production declined for important crops such as cocoa, rubber, rice, and maize. The worsening debt predicament created a huge jump in the balance of payments deficit, as external reserves slipped to their lowest level in five years.

The tenuous political transition was a growing source of uncertainty. Toward the end of 1992 Babangida extended the democratization schedule for a third time, announcing June presidential elections in advance of an August 1993 handover. Pending the transition, the military would ostensibly delegate major responsibilities to a civilian Transitional Council headed by a well-known corporate executive, Chief Ernest Shonekan. In fact the council lacked independent legal standing and failed to operate as a shadow cabinet in either political or economic affairs. The military and the bureaucracy retained control over decision making, but the new layer of civilian governance and the pending change of regime aggravated incoherence within the state. As political change drew near, government officials were inclined to delay key policy changes or reverse earlier reforms in order to mollify important interest groups. The central bank restored an auction system for foreign exchange in a further bid to slow depreciation of the naira, and the official rate fell increasingly out of line with values on the parallel market. The civilian Transitional Council proposed removing the fuel subsidy, but military leaders overruled the civilians by asserting that fuel prices would not change until after the transition. Efforts to reform state enterprises fell dormant, and there was little

89. The World Bank report is discussed by Michael Holman in "'Inconsistencies' in State Funds," *Financial Times,* March 16, 1992; the figures on petroleum accounts are taken from that report and subsequent personal interviews with Nigerian sources, Lagos, January 1993.

90. Central Bank of Nigeria, *Annual Report and Statement of Accounts, 1992* (Lagos: Central Bank of Nigeria, 1993), 70.

progress in divesting publicly owned firms or restructuring their operations.

A protracted crisis surrounding the political transition plunged the country into political turmoil and economic paralysis.[91] Presidential elections were conducted on June 12 in an orderly fashion and apparently produced a victory for Chief M. K. O. Abiola, a prominent Yoruba Muslim business magnate. However, the results were immediately sequestered, and Babangida, alleging irregularities, declared the poll invalid. In the weeks that followed the annulment, the president came under intense pressure to cede power at the appointed deadline. Babangida hastily abdicated on August 27 and relegated authority to a caretaker Interim National Government headed by Chief Shonekan. This maneuver did little to quell popular indignation over the invalidation of the elections, and the transfer of authority to civilians in the absence of a clear transitional framework left the new government without direction or legitimacy.

The transition crisis was marked by civil violence and intensifying ethnic and regional tensions, creating widespread trepidation about a political breakdown.[92] The economy slowed as workers demonstrated, fearful depositors staged a run on the banks, manufacturers and traders searched in vain for capital, and the business community was transfixed by the political impasse. Shonekan attempted to restore public confidence by announcing a date for new elections and releasing political detainees. The government also resumed talks with the IMF, focusing on the sticking point of the domestic fuel subsidy. This issue proved fatal to the caretaker council. In November the administration announced a sevenfold increase in the fuel price, whereupon the Nigeria Labour Congress staged a general strike. Major General Sani Abacha, the former chief of staff whom Babangida had appointed as defense minister in the interim government, forced Shonekan's resignation within three days. Having already sidelined most Babangida loyalists from the military and the security forces, Abacha proceeded to consolidate his personal power. He abruptly ended speculation about the political transition by revoking the existing democratization program and dissolving the tiers of elected civilian government.

Abacha: Predation and Decline

By appearances, Abacha's regime had many of the same features as that of his predecessor. Echoing Babangida, the new ruler promised an eventual

91. See Peter M. Lewis, "Endgame in Nigeria? The Politics of a Failed Democratic Transition," *African Affairs* 93, no. 372 (1994): 323–40; and Osaghae, *Crippled Giant,* 281.
92. Diamond, "Nigeria: The Uncivic Society," 459.

handover to democracy and went through the motions of creating the central features of a transition program. In substance, Abacha quickly moved toward a more predatory form of rule, characterized by the centralization and personalization of power, increasing repression, economic malfeasance, and the degeneration of public institutions. The economy was ravaged by erratic policies, mismanagement, and unvarnished plunder by Abacha and his inner circle.[93] The ruler's domestic support coalition narrowed to a skeletal base, and Nigeria became increasingly isolated in global markets. Many of these trends originated at least a decade earlier and were evident during the final years of Babangida's rule. Abacha, however, clearly accelerated the downward spiral of poor governance and economic failure.

Upon seizing power, Abacha unveiled a cabinet predominantly composed of civilians, including several veteran politicians, technocrats, and prominent figures from the recently aborted transition. In the domain of economic policy, there were substantial pressures to abandon the orthodox approach charted by Babangida. An important segment of the cabinet argued for a return to populist economic programs. There was strong public sentiment for a revaluation of the naira, while manufacturers lobbied for protectionist measures. Abacha had reappointed Dr. Kalu I. Kalu, an initial architect of the SAP, as finance minister, largely as a gesture to placate the donors. Kalu was quickly sidelined, however, and the resulting 1994 budget dismantled the SAP in favor of a *dirigiste* and nationalist program. The new package revived administrative controls on finance, trade, and foreign exchange. The exchange rate was fixed at 22 naira to the dollar (diverging widely from the parallel market rate of about 50), and all foreign exchange was to be allocated directly by the CBN. The parallel foreign exchange market was officially proscribed. Interest rates were fixed, tariffs were increased, and import bans extended. A value-added tax (VAT) was introduced to increase domestic revenue. The regime preserved major fiscal commitments to industrial projects, the federal capital, and regional peacekeeping, most of which remained outside the budget.

Nigeria's 1994 policy reversal was notable, even in a region with a fitful record of adjustment. Many leaders in Africa wavered on orthodox policies and obfuscated implementation of key reforms, but relatively few abandoned these programs altogether.[94] Abacha's new budget was an

93. Margaret Levi discusses a "despoiling" dictatorship, recalling Pareto's definition of spoliation as personal gain at the expense of general welfare. In Levi's analysis, this represents a corrosive form of resource extraction by rulers. See Margaret Levi, *Of Rule and Revenue* (Berkeley: University of California Press, 1988), 3n.

94. Nicolas Van de Walle, "Economic Reform in a Democratizing Africa," *Comparative Politics* 32, no. 1 (1999): 21–41.

egregious failure. The revival of currency controls eliminated incentives for exports and choked off foreign exchange for legitimate producers, while stoking the black market and encouraging rent seeking. Well-connected elites who secured a coveted allocation of foreign exchange made a killing on the arbitrage between the official and posted rates. Speculation and macroeconomic instability drove the naira to ₦120 = $1 on the parallel market before it stabilized at ₦82 = $1. Although interest rates were officially capped at 21 percent, actual rates ran much higher owing to surcharges, special fees, and other furtive practices within the banking industry. The cost of capital and the scarcity of hard currency severely hampered productive activities. Manufacturing output declined by 5 percent, and capacity utilization dropped to a nadir of 27 percent. The value of cocoa exports was half that of 1988. Overall, nonoil exports plummeted to $244 million, little more than half their value two years earlier. The current account was deeply in deficit, and external reserves diminished to only $211 million in the third quarter of 1994. Gross domestic product registered no growth for the year.[95]

The abysmal results of the 1994 budget compelled Abacha's government to return to a semblance of orthodoxy. Much of the cabinet was reassigned or replaced, including Finance Minister Kalu, who ironically had been an opponent of the failed package. The succeeding budget returned to stabilization goals of fiscal discipline and low inflation, accompanied by a somewhat more open trade and exchange regime. The government resumed a market-based window for foreign exchange, although the dual exchange rate was maintained. The indigenization regulations were substantially relaxed, tariffs were reduced, and some import restrictions were rescinded. A major hike in fuel prices was implemented by late 1994. Officials vacillated on privatization, as they initially precluded further sales and attempted to reassert state control of the four largest commercial banks. In a subsequent policy statement, Finance Minister Anthony Ani implied sweeping prospects for divestiture, including upstream oil assets and major public utilities. Little action was taken on such promises.

The regime contrived outward improvements in the macroeconomic picture. On the fiscal side, the Finance Ministry created a "balanced" budget by withholding disbursements for capital projects and delaying payment of some salaries. The government also curtailed much of its debt service and accumulated a large backlog of external commitments. By 1997 arrears on external debt exceeded $15 billion, and even the national petroleum corporation fell into delinquency of $1 billion on its joint venture

95. World Bank, *World Development Indicators.*

commitments as officials withheld critical funding for the oil industry. On the monetary side, the central bank suppressed growth of the money supply by squeezing liquidity from the banking system and building up foreign reserves. These gambits briefly produced some favorable indicators: by 1997 the fiscal deficit gave way to apparent surplus; the balance of payments moved from enormous shortfalls to a small positive balance; in official measures, inflation declined from 73 percent to 9 percent; the market value of the naira stabilized (at the low level of about 82 to the dollar); and foreign reserves topped $4 billion.[96] Economic growth increased to 3.3 percent by 1996. The statistics, however, were largely concocted of smoke and mirrors. Temporary improvements in oil prices and output furnished the only factor for growth in an otherwise stagnant economy. The budgetary "balance" was secured at the expense of essential spending on infrastructure, maintenance, and other public disbursements, while severe contraction of the money supply depleted investment and undermined nonoil production. This picture was aggravated by prodigious capital flight and disinvestment by foreign firms, prompted by continued political instability, strike activity, and deteriorating infrastructure. In the midst of a supposedly favorable macroeconomic picture, gross fixed capital formation dropped by 26 percent from 1994 to 1996, and the index of manufacturing diminished steadily throughout Abacha's rule, yielding a net decline of 8 percent. When the price of oil plummeted again in 1998, the GDP posted a decline of 1 percent.

Underlying the policy contradictions and deficiencies of economic management, the massive diversion of public resources by Abacha and his inner circle dissipated government capabilities. Abacha constructed a predatory structure centered on his family, a small group of retainers, and a narrow circle of civilian cronies. Relying on a few key military and intelligence officials, he otherwise sought to insulate his ruling circle from the mainstream armed forces. He also worked through a handful of notables and business figures, including well-placed Lebanese middlemen, in seeking to monopolize major business opportunities and to exploit parallel markets. The general reputedly took large covert holdings in the aluminum smelter, construction activities in Abuja, and other major capital projects. Nigerian peacekeeping activities in Liberia and Sierra Leone were conducted off-budget, and government statements of their peace-

---

96. World Bank, *Nigeria Structural Adjustment Program.* These figures are all open to question, especially in the area of inflation. A credible unofficial estimate is that inflation ran 150 percent in 1994, and subsided to double-digit levels after 1995. See Peter M. Lewis and H. Stein, "Shifting Fortunes: The Political Economy of Financial Liberalization in Nigeria," *World Development* 25, no. 1 (1997): 5–22.

keeping costs were well above UN estimates of these expenses. When the fuel distribution system collapsed in 1997, mainly from lack of maintenance in the country's four refineries, regime insiders cornered the lucrative market in imported petroleum products, using Lebanese intermediaries to secure contracts and organize international shipments. Abacha was widely believed to have stakes in the financial sector as a silent partner in important banks and nonbank institutions. Meanwhile his regime detained hundreds of bankers under the antifraud Failed Banks Decree, purportedly to clean up the crisis-ridden financial sector. A clear political motive could be also discerned in the regime's attempt to confiscate assets and undermine economic influence among the Yoruba, who dominated the banking industry and were strongly aligned with Chief Abiola and the dissident movement.[97] In addition to monopolizing government largesse and expanding the domain of patrimonial control, Abacha skimmed billions of dollars in oil revenues to sequestered accounts and special purposes, including an estimated $1.4 billion in cash collected by his national security adviser, Ismaila Gwarzo, from the Central Bank to be delivered to the ruler and his eldest son Mohammed. The magnitude of embezzlement and off-budget sequestration possibly reached a fifth of oil earnings, or a quarter of the budget, in the latter years of the regime.[98]

Institutional degradation was a natural consequence of personal rule. Abacha intentionally weakened central institutions of the state, while allowing malfeasance and neglect to erode other functions. The ruler undermined the military, ostensibly the core of his support base, in order to defuse challenges to his dominance. Alleging coup attempts on two occasions, the regime conducted major arrests among the officer corps and purged or reshuffled dozens of others. Political ambition and pervasive corruption further weakened organizational coherence within the armed forces. Staff reductions, eroding compensation levels, organizational tinkering, and insufficient funding took a heavy toll on the civil service and major public enterprises. Public services including electricity, rail, and air transport deteriorated. The domestic fuel system broke down when all the country's refineries collapsed, creating the spectacle of endless queues at filling stations in a major OPEC producer country. Many of these public sector failures, including the fuel crisis, could be attributed to the outright plunder of funds by senior officials. Agencies for the regulation of banking and financial services were inadequately funded and frequently undercut

97. William Reno, *Warlord Politics and African States* (Boulder: Lynne Rienner, 1998), 202.

98. Jibrin Ibrahim, *Democratic Transition in Anglophone West Africa* (Dakar: CODESRIA, 2003), 28.

by intervention from the executive. The health and education sectors were incapacitated by austerity measures and the political harassment against medical professionals, teachers, senior academics, and students. The influence of the judiciary was substantially weakened by military decrees, while the regime appointed pliant judges and induced others to serve its purposes. At every turn, important functions of economic governance degenerated markedly.

Nigeria's international isolation was both a cause and a consequence of the deteriorating conditions of governance. The regime's contradictory policies and adversarial stance toward key foreign firms deterred external investment. Abacha's reputation for massive corruption, and the unfathomable operating environment for business, created further impediments. As repression and human rights abuses mounted under the dictatorship, international sanctions by major donors and trading partners sequestered the Nigerian economy from most global linkages. The United States reacted to the initial nullification of elections and Abacha's draconian response to opposition. When the regime summarily executed Ken Saro-Wiwa and eight other Ogoni activists in November 1995, Nigeria was suspended from the Commonwealth, as the United States, Britain, and other major powers extended sanctions on travel, trade, aid, and military assistance. These measures, as well as the government's delinquency in debt service, nearly suspended relations with the World Bank and other donors. Nigeria was virtually shut out of major capital markets, trade networks, and aid opportunities. Institutional decline and economic stagnation were deeply entwined.

CHAPTER 6

Comparing Economic Performance

In the preceding analysis, I have drawn the linkages between institutional choice, policy selection, economic performance, and structural change, which affect the path of development over time. The empirical record of comparative economic performance in Indonesia and Nigeria helps to clarify and underscore these factors. In this chapter I assess relative performance in growth, income, the structure of the economy, patterns of investment, trends in savings and consumption, management of the external sector, the composition of trade, relative equity, and key indicators of social well-being. The distinctions between Indonesia and Nigeria are as instructive as they are striking.

Output and Income

A useful starting point is the comparative trend in economic growth, which offers a vivid contrast. As seen in table 1, Indonesia's gross domestic product (GDP) between 1965 and 2004 expanded by 5.9 percent on average, a rate nearly double that of Nigeria's. If we leave aside the worst years of Indonesia's financial crisis, growth rates stand at 6.9 percent and 3.5 percent, respectively. This underscores the large disparity in economic performance.

As is clear from the periodization in table 1, Indonesia surpassed

TABLE 1. Average GDP Growth

	Indonesia	Nigeria
1965–70	5.4	5.5
1971–80	7.9	4.9
1981–90	6.4	1.3
1991–96	7.8	2.8
1991–2000	4.4	2.7
2001–4	4.6	4.7
1965–2004	*5.9*	*3.5*

Source: World Bank, *World Development Indicators.*

Nigeria's performance in nearly all periods including the oil boom, the years of declining oil markets and adjustment efforts, and the turbulent 1990s. Average growth in the two countries was virtually identical from 1965 through 1970, the decisive period of crisis and stabilization in Indonesia, and of instability and civil war in Nigeria. Both economies grew slowly in the mid-1960s and then accelerated in postcrisis recoveries. The years 1971 through 1980 were shaped by the petroleum windfall and the accompanying volatility in energy markets. Indonesia managed these fluctuations and sustained an average growth rate of nearly 8 percent, while Nigeria was beleaguered by price shocks and registered a bit less than 5 percent average growth.

Beginning in 1981, international prices and demand slackened for OPEC production, depressing revenues, imports, and growth among members of the cartel. While Indonesia experienced several years of slowdown, the government's adjustment efforts fostered recovery and the economy grew by 6.4 percent on average from 1981 through 1990. Nigeria's initial crisis was steeper and more sustained than that of Indonesia, with growth *declining* by an average of 5.9 percent from 1981 through 1984, before stabilization efforts began to yield improvement. Nigeria concluded the decade with an average growth rate of 1.3 percent.

The first half of the 1990s saw a period of steady high growth for Indonesia and a new round of doldrums in Nigeria. From 1991 through 1996, Indonesia's GDP expanded by 7.8 percent on average. When we include the crisis years of 1997–98, and the weakness of the ensuing recovery, Indonesia's growth declined to 4.4 percent for the decade. By contrast, Nigerian growth averaged only 2.7 percent through the end of the decade. This anemic performance is clearly contrasted with Indonesia's fluctuations among robust growth and distress.

Figure 1 illustrates widely differing patterns of economic growth. Indonesia's long periods of high growth were punctuated by episodic downturns arising mainly from exogenous shocks, usually followed by quick recovery. Nigeria also experienced fluctuations triggered by external events, though such episodes were sharper, more frequent, and more sustained, reflecting that country's economic rigidity and a lesser propensity of government to adjust.

Naturally, disparities in long-term growth produced a widening gap in the relative size of the two economies (fig. 2). In 1965 the gross domestic product of these countries was comparable, though Nigeria's economy was somewhat larger. However, by the 1970s the magnitude of the Indonesian economy already exceeded that of Nigeria. The divergence accelerated dramatically in the 1990s, when Indonesia entered a new phase of

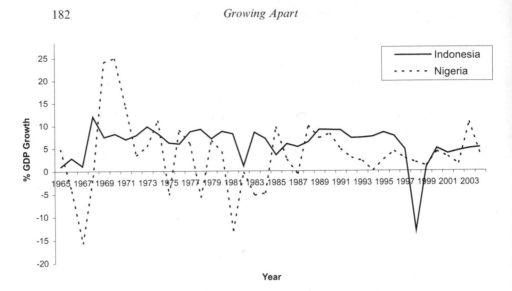

Fig. 1. GDP growth, 1965–2004. (Data from World Bank, *World Development Indicators.*)

high growth, while Nigeria had a sustained decline. By 1995, the ratio of the two economies was about 5:1 in Indonesia's favor, although the Indonesian population was just double that of Nigeria. The gap between the two economies diminished only slightly in the wake of the Indonesian economic crisis and Nigeria's most recent oil windfall.

Variations in growth have produced substantial differences in per capita income. As seen in table 2, there is increasing disparity in growth rates, resulting in a shift in the relative position of the two economies over time. Indonesia's per capita income declined during the first few years of the 1960s, but then recorded strong and consistent growth for nearly three decades. Average incomes expanded by at least 5 percent throughout the oil boom and the 1980s. Over a thirty-five year span after 1965, per capita income grew at an average rate of 4.1 percent. In real terms, this reflected a fourfold increase in income.

Notwithstanding political instability and civil conflict, Nigeria's first decade of independence reflected a higher rate of income expansion than Indonesia's. In 1965, the baseline year, Nigeria's per capita income exceeded that of Indonesia, a gap that widened in the early 1970s with the end of the Nigerian civil war and the impact of the initial oil windfall. Thereafter, trends altered decisively as Indonesia grew steadily while Nigerians lost ground.

The growth of Nigeria's per capita income was volatile during the oil

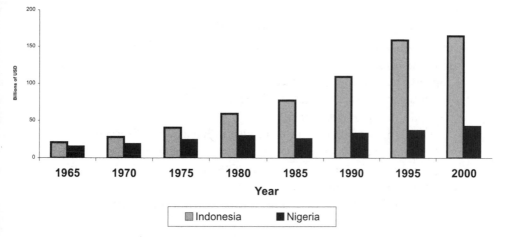

Fig. 2. GDP at market prices (constant 2000 USD). (Data from World Bank, *World Development Indicators.*)

TABLE 2. Income per Capita

	Indonesia	Nigeria
Real GDP per capita (constant 1996 USD)		
1965	903	1,064
1975	1,425	1,058
1985	2,285	1,030
1995	3,642	926
2000	3,637	713
Growth of GDP per capita (%)		
1961–70	1.9	2.6
1971–80	5.4	2.1
1981–90	4.5	−1.5
1991–2000	2.9	0.0
1965–2000	*4.1*	*0.7*
Growth of population (annual %)		
1965	2.2	2.7
1975	2.4	2.9
1985	1.8	3.0
1995	1.4	3.0
2000	1.3	2.4

Note: Real GDP per capita: Laspeyres index (USD, constant 1996 prices) calculated from Penn World Tables. Other figures calculated from World Bank, *World Development Indicators.*

boom, averaging less than 3 percent for the 1970s. After 1980, there was significant erosion in incomes, declining by an average of –1.33 percent over fifteen years. By 1995, Nigerian real per capita income had slipped by about 10 percent since the mid-1960s and by 2000, average income had dropped by a third from the level of 1975. An extraordinary gap was evident in the mid-1990s as Indonesia's per capita income was more than two and a half times that of Nigeria.

Trends in income growth were also influenced by divergent rates of population expansion. The growth of population, shown in table 2, slowed considerably in Indonesia from the 1970s through the 1990s, largely in response to population programs undertaken by government. In Nigeria, where no serious effort was made to stem population growth, the rate of increase was much more rapid.

Structure of the Economy

The two economies also reflect different degrees and types of structural change. The expansion of petroleum production transformed the agrarian foundations of both economies. Thereafter, diversification varied dramatically, as Indonesia achieved industrial growth and expanded nontraditional exports, while Nigeria developed a highly concentrated, insecure mineral export economy.

Table 3 shows the changing sectoral composition of GDP. The impact of extractive industries is evident in both economies. The rise of Indonesia's oil and gas sector was followed by a process of industrialization. From the late 1960s through the late 1970s, the Indonesian mining sector (the leading component in industry) more than doubled its proportion of national output, principally at the expense of agriculture. Manufacturing increased its contribution to GDP during the oil boom and gained ground more rapidly in the 1980s, as mining saw a relative decrease. Agriculture continued to diminish in proportion, although at a slower rate.

Nigeria differs in important respects. Extractive industry also dominated the economy by the late 1970s, though without fostering a decisive shift toward manufacturing or broader economic diversification. During the boom years, oil extraction more than tripled as a share of national output, contributing nearly half of GDP by 1980. Agriculture declined substantially as a share of value added. The manufacturing sector, however, did not achieve a takeoff. Starting from a low base, manufacturing nearly doubled as a proportion of Nigerian GDP during the oil boom, though it failed to reach 10 percent of total output. Beginning in the early 1980s, a process of deindustrialization can be seen in the declining proportion of

TABLE 3. Structure of the Economy, 1965–2000

Sectoral Distribution of Value Added (% GDP)	Indonesia			Nigeria		
	Agriculture	Manufacturing	Industry	Agriculture	Manufacturing	Industry
1965	56	8	13	55	5	12
1975	30	10	33	32	5	29
1985	23	16	36	37	9	29
1995	17	24	42	32	5	47
2000	17	25	46	29	4	44

Source: World Bank, World Development Indicators.

manufacturing and the correspondingly large role of the mining sector. By 2000, manufacturing comprised a smaller proportion of Nigerian output than three decades earlier. Furthermore, agriculture actually increased as a share òf GDP during the 1980s, reflecting some revival of export activities but also the relative stagnation of manufacturing and urban services.

The differential growth of sectors shapes the course of structural change. In both cases, resource extractive activities showed uneven performance as a consequence of both exogenous factors and internal economic structure. After 1980, the slump in global energy markets significantly reduced the value of exports. However, the impact of changing income streams from oil and gas was affected by the comparative development of the energy sector. Indonesia diversified into downstream energy operations, notably liquefied natural gas (LNG) production for export. Nigeria, which flared associated natural gas and did not develop downstream production, relied entirely on exports of crude petroleum. As a result, international market fluctuations in the energy sector affected Nigeria more adversely.

Most telling, however, is the performance of other productive sectors, beginning with agriculture. As seen in table 4, Indonesia's agricultural sector reflected moderate growth in the 1970s and 1980s. Agricultural output per capita was consistently positive, and contrary to expectations arising from the Dutch disease model, agriculture was robust during the oil boom years. Nigeria reflected incremental growth in agricultural production, though never large enough to achieve increases in output per capita.

Indonesia sustained expansion in manufacturing from the 1970s through the late 1990s, with especially strong performance after 1985. Nigeria grew very rapidly during the 1960s and achieved strong manufac-

TABLE 4. Sectoral Growth, 1961–2000

Average Sectoral Growth (%)	Indonesia	Nigeria
Agriculture		
1961–70	2.9	1.8
1971–80	4.5	0.5
1981–90	3.7	2.3
1991–2000	2.0	3.3
Manufacturing		
1961–70	4.7	14.9
1971–80	14.1	11.5
1981–90	12.4	3.1
1991–2000	5.6	1.5

Source: World Bank, *World Development Indicators.*

turing growth during the period of high oil earnings. In the 1980s, when export revenues declined and debt mounted, the resulting foreign exchange shortages and import compression sharply curtailed manufacturing activities, reducing growth to a crawl.

In sum, Indonesia achieved substantial transformation toward industrial expansion and more diversified activities in the real sectors of the economy. Nigeria, by contrast, persisted as an oil monoculture. This is further illustrated by focusing on the position of the resource sector in the two countries, shown in table 5.

Petroleum production grew rapidly after 1970, nearly doubling in volume for each country over the course of the decade. Although the energy sector became central to both economies, the degree of dominance was greater and more lasting in Nigeria. After the 1973 price rise, oil quickly exceeded 90 percent of Nigeria's export values and three-fourths of government revenue. Thereafter, the energy sector comprised more than 95 percent of exports and contributed at least 75 percent of public revenue.

In Indonesia, energy exports increased from slightly less than half of total exports in the early 1970s to at least 75 percent at the end of the decade. Exports of oil and gas yielded more than a quarter of government

TABLE 5.   Petroleum Sector, 1965–Present

	Crude Oil Production: Average Barrels/Day (millions)		% of Total Exports		% of Government Revenues	
	Indonesia	Nigeria	Indonesia	Nigeria	Indonesia	Nigeria
1965	0.5	0.3	36	26	—	7
1970	0.9	1.1	40	58	28	26
1975	1.3	1.8	75	93	56	81
1980	1.6	2.1	—	96	69	81
1985	1.2	1.5	68	97	66	75
1990	1.3	1.7	43	97	34	79
1995	1.3	1.8	22	—	—	—
2000	1.3	1.3	24	—	—	—
MR	1.1	2.2	22	96	25	76

Source: Data on crude oil production from 2003 OPEC *Annual Statistical Bulletin.* Data on percentage of total exports: for Indonesia, Central Bureau of Statistics; for Nigeria, Pearson 1969, Forrest 1995, and (for 2003) U.S. Department of Energy, Energy Information Administration, *Nigeria Country Analysis Briefs.* Data on percentage of government revenues: for Indonesia, Woo, Glassburner, and Nasution 1993; for Nigeria, Pearson 1970, Forrest 1995.

Note: MR (most recent) figures are 2003 estimates. The figures for total exports and percentage of government revenues for Indonesia and Nigeria are from Economist Intelligence Unit, *Indonesia Country Report* (2004) and *Nigeria Country Report* (2004) and World Bank, *Global Development Finance 2004.* The figures on percentage of government revenues for Indonesia are for 1970–71, 1975–76, 1980–81, 1984–85, 1990–91.

— = no data.

revenues at the beginning of the boom and grew to over two-thirds of revenue by 1980. In the course of the next decade, however, the relative
importance of the energy sector diminished significantly. By the early
1990s, oil and gas production accounted for 43 percent of exports and a
slightly smaller share of public revenues. As seen in table 6, Indonesia's
exports of manufactured goods expanded rapidly in the 1980s, increasing
from a tenth of export revenues at mid-decade to half of exports by the
mid-1990s. The continued prevalence of energy exports is clearly evident
for Nigeria.

Further, the composition of the energy sector differed among the two
countries, as Indonesia exploited natural gas supplies, brought LNG production onstream in the 1970s, and subsequently introduced additional
downstream operations. By 1995, 40 percent of Indonesia's energy exports
were provided by crude oil, another 35 percent derived from LNG, and the
balance came from oil condensate or other refined products.[1] In Nigeria,
virtually all energy exports derived from crude petroleum. When a new
LNG facility commenced operation in 1999, Nigeria began to export a
proportion of its enormous natural gas reserves. Prior to that time, nearly
all gas associated with oil extraction was flared or reinjected.

TABLE 6.   **Composition of Exports, 1965–2000 (% share of merchandise exports)**

	Indonesia			Nigeria		
	Fuel Minerals and Metals	Other Primary Products	Manufactures	Fuel Minerals and Metals	Other Primary Products	Manufactures
1960	33	67	0	8	89	3
1965	43	53	4	32	65	2
1970	44	54	1	62	36	1
1975	75	—	1	93	—	0
1980	76	22	1	95	4	1
1985	75	14	11	96	3	0
1990	48	16	34	97	2	0
1996	26	—	51	96	—	1
2000	25	—	57	99	—	1

Source: World Bank, *World Development Report* (various) and *World Development Indicators.*
Note: — = no data.

1. U.S. Embassy, Jakarta, *Petroleum Report Indonesia 2000,* Appendix 7,
http://www.usembassyjakarta.org/econ/petro-toc.html.

Investment, Savings, and Consumption

The comparative economic performance of Indonesia and Nigeria has been associated with different patterns of investment, linked to variations in savings and consumption. Table 7 provides a summary of the relevant trends, showing consistently high savings and investment in Indonesia, alongside uneven performance in Nigeria. Nigerian regimes have sustained high levels of politically driven consumption, which has crowded out productive investment and done little to build capital stock.

During the 1970s savings and investment were relatively high in both countries, spurred by windfall revenues and strong growth. Average investment rates were nearly identical over the course of the decade, though Indonesia exceeded the rate of savings in Nigeria. Over the following two decades, however, a marked disparity is evident as Indonesia sustained high rates of investment and savings while Nigeria's ebbed substantially.

Despite significant pressures on the balance of payments and periodic slumps in growth, Indonesia maintained a rate of capital formation in the 1980s averaging more than 29 percent of GDP. Investment grew further over the next several years, averaging 30 percent in the early 1990s and then slowing with the onset of the economic crisis, yielding an average rate of 27 percent for the entire decade.

Nigeria achieved a sound rate of investment during the petroleum boom, averaging nearly 23 percent of GDP. With the decline of oil prices and the rise of debt, however, investment and savings contracted rapidly, as vividly illustrated in figure 3. During the mid-1980s, investment rates diminished to single digits, yielding an average for the decade of just 15.8 percent—a bit more than half the rate in Indonesia during this period. Nigeria reflected a modest recovery during the 1990s but lagged significantly on a comparative basis.

TABLE 7. Investment and Savings, 1970–2000

	Indonesia	Nigeria
Gross capital formation (% GDP)		
1970–80	21.6	22.7
1981–90	29.2	15.8
1991–2000	26.7	20.1
Gross domestic savings (% GDP)		
1970–80	26.2	23.5
1981–90	31.0	17.3
1991–2000	29.5	24.4

Source: World Bank, World Development Indicators.

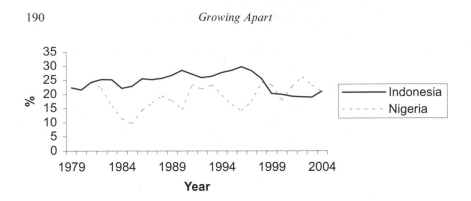

Fig. 3. Gross fixed capital formation (% of GDP). (Data from World Bank, *World Development Indicators.*)

Moreover, the composition of investment, shown in table 8, differed substantially in the two economies. Private investment in Indonesia grew steadily as a proportion of GDP from the 1970s through the 1990s, eventually surpassing the magnitude of public sector investment. Private investment increased proportionally by a third over those two decades, while the relative share of public investment diminished from half that of the private sector to little more than a third.

Three contrasting patterns stand out for Nigeria. First, the share of public investment continued to increase substantially from the mid-1970s onward, averaging more than 10 percent of GDP throughout the 1980s and 1990s. Second, private investment nearly collapsed in the 1980s, diminishing to little more than 5 percent of GDP and reviving only modestly in the following decade. Third, the relative shares of public and private investment shifted from about 1:2 in the 1970s to the inverse, 2:1 in the next decade, and approximately 1:1 by the 1990s. The conclusion is

TABLE 8.　Public and Private Investment (% GDP)

	Indonesia	Nigeria
Public investment		
1970–80	7.3	6.8
1981–90	9.7	10.5
1991–MR[a]	7.8	10.4
Private investment		
1970–80	14.5	15.9
1981–90	17.9	5.3
1991–MR[a]	20.9	11.7

Source: Pfeffermann, Kisunko, and Sumlinski 1999.
[a]MR (most recent): 1998 for Indonesia, 1994 for Nigeria.

that Nigeria's scant investment has been substantially furnished by government, while private activity has dwindled.

As implied by the difference in savings rates, consumption in Nigeria was substantially higher than in Indonesia. From the 1970s forward, as seen in table 9, total consumption in Nigeria (government and private) varied from about three-fourths of GDP to more than 80 percent. Furthermore, the comparatively high rate of government consumption grew in the course of the period.

Indonesia's consumption rates were consistently below those of Nigeria during these three decades. The trend in government consumption also varied, with expansion from the mid-1970s through the mid-1980s, and then attenuation to less than 10 percent of GDP from 1987 onward.

The External Sector

Here we consider central features of the external economic picture: the evolution of debt, exchange rate policies, and patterns of trade and investment. The comparison reinforces earlier observations about variations in macroeconomic management and the different position of these countries in the international economy. Generally speaking, Indonesia reflected a sustainable debt position, an increasingly strong investment profile, realistic exchange rates, and a diversified pattern of trade. Nigeria's debt obligations were increasingly untenable, while investment has been erratic at best. Authorities largely failed to maintain realistic exchange rates or to diversify trade. Indonesia has been more extensively integrated into global markets, reflecting higher levels and a broader range of investment and trade.

The management of foreign debt, essential to the balance of pay-

TABLE 9. **Government and Household Consumption, 1970–2000 (average % GDP)**

	Indonesia	Nigeria
Government consumption		
1970–80	9.2	11.4
1981–90	10.2	14.2
1991–2000	7.5	13.7
Private consumption		
1970–80	64.7	65.2
1981–90	59.7	68.5
1991–2000	62.5	62.0

Source: World Bank, *World Development Indicators.*

ments, is a crucial factor in macroeconomic performance. Although both countries had episodes of imprudent borrowing and financial distress, Indonesia reveals better overall management of foreign obligations for much of the period under consideration. Table 10 and figure 4 outline the main features of external debt. Overall borrowing by public and private sectors was greater in Indonesia, as might be expected from the size and growth of the economy. The Pertamina crisis and the spate of controversial industrial projects remind us that such borrowing was neither carefully managed nor efficiently utilized. Yet until 1997, Indonesia carried a manageable debt load and met external obligations without recourse to the IMF or donor rescheduling. As seen in table 10, Indonesia reflected a comparatively lower ratio of debt to GDP during much of the 1980s and early 1990s.

A further contrast can be found in the composition of debt. Short-term borrowing is often a signal of impending distress, since these loans carry higher interest rates and shorter maturities, and they often elude regulation by government supervisors. Indonesia's short-term borrowing (fig. 4) was comparatively lower than that of Nigeria through much of the 1980s and 1990s, showing a significant rise in the years leading up to the financial crisis.

Nigeria initially had a lower debt stock in both absolute and proportional terms. By the late 1970s, however, external obligations began to accumulate, and short-term commitments grew precipitously with the onset of distress. Nigeria was a prominent African casualty of the 1982 debt crisis, giving rise to repeated IMF programs (in 1987, 1989, 1991, and again in 2000) with associated Paris Club rescheduling. In spite of regular restructuring of debt, Nigeria accumulated sizable arrears on foreign payments throughout the 1990s.

TABLE 10.   External Debt, 1970–2000

	Indonesia		Nigeria	
	% GDP	Billions of Current USD	% GDP	Billions of Current USD
1970	47	27.6	7	0.8
1975	36	11.5	6	1.7
1980	27	20.9	14	8.9
1985	42	36.7	66	18.6
1990	61	69.9	117	33.4
1995	62	124.4	121	34.1
2000	88	144.4	75	31.4

Source: World Bank, *World Development Indicators.*

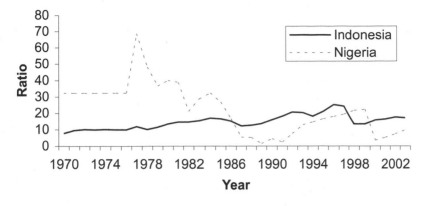

Fig. 4. Short-term debt/total debt. (Data from World Bank, *World Development Indicators.*)

   The management of foreign exchange provides one of the strongest points of contrast between the two countries. Figure 5 summarizes the trends. Indonesia experienced a modest period of overvaluation during the height of the oil boom, but the 1978 devaluation brought the rate back into alignment, and exchange rates have generally remained at realistic levels. The Nigerian currency was already overvalued at the onset of the petroleum windfall and reflected a steady appreciation over the next fifteen years. The spread between the parallel market and the official rate reached more than 4:1 before corrective measures were taken in the middle of the 1980s. Beginning in 1986, devaluation brought Nigeria's exchange rate into alignment for several years, but a new round of revenue windfalls and policy-induced distortions caused significant overvaluation in the 1990s.
   Exchange rate management is integrally linked to the performance of trade. Having previously noted the composition of exports, I return to other dimensions of trade and investment. Both Indonesia and Nigeria rely on trade as a major proportion of income, demand, and inputs to production. Their comparative reliance on trade, however, has varied over time, reflecting changing economic structures and positioning in global markets.
   Figure 6 shows the position of trade as a proportion of GDP. In 1965, trade accounted for about a tenth of Indonesia's domestic economy. The ratio declined significantly during the early 1960s as policy distortions worsened, production foundered, and the country was isolated in international markets. The global marginality of the Indonesian economy was soon arrested by stabilization policies, and the commodity boom of the

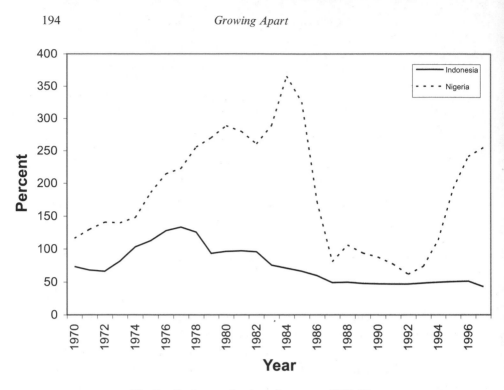

Fig. 5. Real overvaluation of currency, 1970–97.

1970s dramatically increased the salience of trade. Manufactured goods supplanted energy exports in the 1980s, and trade accounted for around half of Indonesia's GDP throughout the period in question.

Nigeria's trade reflects an adverse trajectory. During the period considered here, Nigeria began with a predominantly agricultural export economy in which trade accounted for about a quarter of GDP. Exports grew rapidly during the period of the oil windfall, doubling the proportion of trade to about half of GDP. The really extraordinary change occurred from the late 1980s onward, as deindustrialization became more acute and the economy slowed. For most of the 1990s, petroleum exports equaled more than 70 percent of Nigeria's recorded output, as productivity dwindled in areas of the economy outside the oil enclave.

The geographic distribution of trade is an equally important sign of diversification and economic flexibility. Table 11 displays global patterns of imports and exports for both countries. This clearly illustrates the importance of Indonesia's regional position, as more than two-thirds of exports in the early 1990s went to Asian states (including more than a third to Japan), and over half of the country's imports came from regional

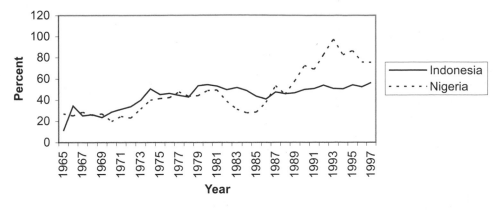

Fig. 6. Total trade (as % of GDP). (Data from World Bank, *World Development Indicators.*)

economies. Nigeria's trade is overwhelmingly concentrated in Europe and North America, with merely 10 percent of recorded exports going to Africa and 5 percent of imports deriving from the region by the year 2000.

As with trade, patterns of investment reflect a divergence of growth and diversification. Figure 7 depicts the trend of foreign direct investment (FDI) in both countries. Levels of FDI were roughly comparable from the 1970s through the late 1980s, while external investment in Nigeria periodically exceeded that for Indonesia. Direct investment in Indonesia, however, escalated dramatically after the mid-1980s. In the decade leading up to the financial crisis, foreign direct investment in Indonesia significantly outstripped investment in Nigeria. Overseas investment became increas-

TABLE 11.   Geographic Distribution of Trade (% of total trade)

	Destination of Exports			Origins of Imports		
	1970	1990	2000	1970	1990	2000
Indonesia						
Europe	15	12	14	22	21	13
United States and Canada	13	14	14	18	13	12
Japan	41	43	23	25	29	16
Developing Economies: Asia	24	25	38	21	25	38
Nigeria						
Europe	74	37	25	63	61	44
United States and Canada	14	55	46	15	9	9
Developing Economies: Africa	1	7	10	1	1	5

Source: United Nations Conference on Trade and Development, *Handbook of Statistics.* Europe is defined as European Union 25 for 2000.

Note: Coverage is not comprehensive; columns do not total 100 percent.

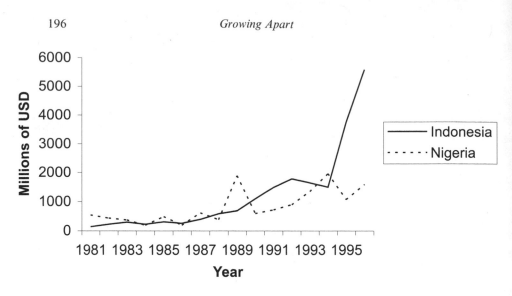

Fig. 7.   Foreign direct investment. (Data from World Bank, *World Development Indicators.*)

ingly diverse, as companies moved into a variety of productive activities in
manufacturing, agriculture, solid minerals, services, and energy. Investments in Nigeria, however, have continued to focus on the energy sector,
where changing production opportunities and erratic funding from the
Nigerian state have affected the levels of activity over time.

The story of portfolio investment (table 12) is more straightforward.
In the early 1990s, Indonesia emerged as a significant global market,
attracting a considerable volume of portfolio investment that averaged
about $4 billion annually from 1992 through 1996. Nigeria, with an
increasingly marginal global position, was simply absent from bond and
equity markets.

In a concluding observation on the external sector, the geographic origin of investment provides a further illustration of regional position and

TABLE 12.   Portfolio Investment (millions of USD)

	Indonesia		Nigeria	
	Bonds	Equity	Bonds	Equity
1990	26	312	0	0
1995	2,248	4,873	0	0
2000[a]	−2,050	−1,021	0	0
MR[a]	600	1,131	−452	0

Source: Aryeetey and Nissanke 1999.
[a]World Bank, *World Development Indicators* for 2000 and MR (most
recent): 2003 for Indonesia, 2002 for Nigeria.

neighborhood effects. Table 13 shows the leading sources of foreign investment in Indonesia, indicating the importance of capital from the regional neighborhood. Among the ten leading countries, six are in the Asia-Pacific region, accounting for nearly 70 percent of approved investment. Japan heads the list (with 24 percent of total investment), while the United Kingdom is the only non-Asian state to appear in the top five. While comparable figures are not available for Nigeria, it is well known that American, British, French, Dutch, and Italian capital dominate the oil and gas sector, where the preponderance of investment is directed. Investment in Nigeria from sub-Saharan Africa has traditionally been negligible, although there has been recent involvement by South Africa firms in such areas as telecommunications.

Poverty, Equity, and Social Provisions

I turn finally to questions of poverty, distribution, and the provision of social services. On these issues especially, the comparison is encumbered by data problems. We simply lack sound empirical information in some areas (for instance, unemployment and education in Nigeria), while in other cases the data are subject to controversy (as for poverty figures in Indonesia).[2] Bearing such problems in mind, we may still venture conclusions about the relative performance of these countries at improving the living standards for their people. It is clear that the Indonesian government, over a period of three decades, made steady and significant progress in reducing absolute poverty and furnishing basic services to a large por-

TABLE 13.   Foreign Investment in Indonesia, by Origin: Cumulative Approved Nonoil Investment, 1967–99 (billions of USD)

Japan	36.2
United Kingdom	21.2
Singapore	19.2
Taiwan	16.1
Hong Kong	14.5
United States	10.5
South Korea	9.4
Australia	9.4
Germany	8.3
Netherlands	6.2

Source: Indonesian Investment Coordinating Board (BKPM).

2. See, for example, Hal Hill, *The Indonesian Economy since 1966* (Cambridge: Cambridge University Press, 1996), 195.

tion of the population. Furthermore, growth proceeded in a context of relatively balanced distribution, in spite of the evident disparities rooted in clientelist politics and uneven regional development. Nigeria achieved strides in improving incomes and services during the period of the oil windfall, but the 1980s and 1990s saw a degeneration of income, deepening poverty, and a serious deterioration of social services, all against a backdrop of widening inequalities.

Estimates of poverty and income inequality are complicated by the existence of diverse sources, but it is possible to draw meaningful comparisons. The summary data are shown in table 14. Indonesia displayed a reduction of poverty from the 1960s onward. The incidence of poverty in 1970 was estimated at 60 percent.[3] Poverty diminished to 40 percent by the middle 1970s, and somewhat more than a quarter of the population in the early 1980s. On the eve of the economic crisis, reliable estimates placed the poverty rate at less than 15 percent.[4]

TABLE 14.   Incidence of Poverty (% of population below poverty line)

	Indonesia	Nigeria
1976	40.1	—
1978	33.3	—
1980	28.6	28.1
1981	26.9	—
1984	21.6	—
1985	—	46.3
1987	17.4	—
1990	15.1	—
1992	—	42.7
1993	13.5	—
1996	17.5	65.6
1999	23.4	70.6
2002	18.2	—
2003	17.4	70.2
2004	16.7	—

Source: Hill 1996; Bureau of Public Statistics, Indonesia, "Official Poverty Measurement in Indonesia"; Akanji 2000.

Note: Poverty measures reflect the percentage of people at or below the nationally defined poverty line for each country. — = no data.

3. Mari Pangestu and Amar Bhattacharya, *Indonesia: Development Transformation and Public Policy* (Washington, DC: World Bank, 1993), 3.

4. This is measured as the percentage of total population living below the national income poverty line. See Hill, *Indonesian Economy,* 193–94, and Anne Booth, "Poverty and Inequality in the Soeharto Era: An Assessment," *Bulletin of Indonesian Economic Studies* 36, no. 1 (2000), 78.

Nigeria has experienced an expansion of poverty since the 1960s, revealing an uneven trend. Poverty apparently diminished during the boom period of the 1970s, and then rose sharply during the economic slump of the 1980s. The proportion of Nigerians living below the poverty line soared from about 28 percent in 1980 to 46 percent by mid-decade. The poverty rate then seems to stabilize somewhat during the period of adjustment (registering about 43 percent in 1992) before expanding again to a stunning 66 percent by 1996. Estimates at the end of the decade place the poverty rate over 70 percent.[5]

The differences in poverty are mirrored by variations in equity, depicted in figure 8 and table 15. While evidence is fragmentary, Indonesia apparently begins with a more equitable income profile than Nigeria, and it maintains relative equity over the period of comparison. By the middle of the 1990s, Indonesia's Gini index (a composite measure of income inequality) is measured at .36, slightly lower than two decades earlier, and relatively low from an international perspective. In the wake of the economic crisis, the Gini index appears to decline further. Table 15 displays household data with shares of income accruing to different segments of the population.[6] While this does not firmly substantiate the trends in the Gini index, it does reflect a distribution more equitable than that of Nigeria.

Nigeria displays a concave trend of income distribution, similar to the trend in poverty. Through the mid-1980s, Nigeria's income distribution

TABLE 15.   Distribution of Income (% share)

	Indonesia		Nigeria	
	Lowest 20%	Highest 20%	Lowest 20%	Highest 20%
1976	6.6	49.4	—	—
1987	8.8	41.3	—	—
1990	8.7	42.3	—	—
1992	—	—	5.1	49.0
1993	8.7	40.7	4.0	49.3
1995	8.4	43.1	—	—
MR[a]	8.4	43.3	4.4	55.7

Source: World Bank, *World Development Indicators.*
Note: — = no data.
[a]MR (most recent): 2002 for Indonesia, 1997 for Nigeria.

5. These are estimates based upon household consumption. See O. O. Akanji, "Incidence of Poverty and Economic Growth in Nigeria," presented at the IAOS conference "Statistics, Development and Human Rights," Montreux, Switzerland, September 4–8, 2000, 8.

6. Hill, *Indonesian Economy,* 194. See also United Nations University, World Institute for Development Economics Research (WIDER), *World Income Inequality Database,* V2.0a, 2005, http://www.wider.unu.edu/wiid/wiid.htm.

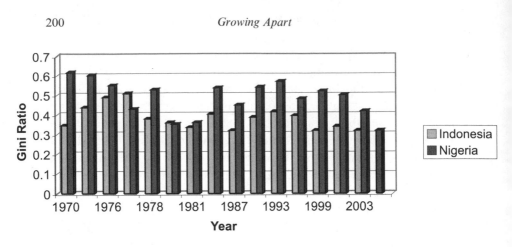

Fig. 8. Gini Index for Indonesia and Nigeria. (Data from United Nations University/World Institute for Development Economics Research [WIDER], *World Income Inequality Database;* Bureau of Public Statistics, Indonesia.)

appears to converge with Indonesia toward a more equitable profile, with a Gini index of .36 in 1981. Thereafter, income differentials evidently grow wider, as a Gini index of .54 is reported for 1984, an index of .57 for 1993, and an index of .52 is recorded in 1999, all reflecting a high degree of inequality. These figures—also substantiated by data on income shares among the population—indicate that Nigeria ended the 1990s with a very inequitable income profile, showing little progress since the eve of the oil boom.

In spite of data problems, the available information gives rise to some inferences. First, Indonesia achieved comparatively broad-based economic growth from the early 1970s through the mid-1990s. Sustained economic expansion was associated with a large reduction in poverty and the persistence of comparatively good income distribution. This recognizes the substantial poverty that remained and the wide variations in regional and sectoral development. The political and social tensions emerging from the inequities of the New Order were an inherent liability of that growth model. Nonetheless, Indonesia registers genuine contrasts with the growth and equity performance of Nigeria.

Second, Nigeria's fragile gains in poverty reduction and improved distribution—by-products of the petroleum windfall—were reversed by an extended period of economic malaise and poor governance. As growth declined, more Nigerians sank into poverty, and the distribution of income became much more unequal. The effects of autocracy and predation by narrowing elites are evident in the path of economic change from the 1980s onward.

A selected view of other social indicators underscores the main features of comparison. Indonesia's educational endowments, measured in terms of school enrollments (table 16) and general literacy (table 17), considerably exceeded those of Nigeria in the 1960s. Nigeria made rapid progress in raising enrollments and literacy during the 1970s, and indeed, some indicators converged with Indonesia by the early 1980s. A few years later, Nigeria apparently lost ground as school enrollments declined. By the middle of the 1990s, Indonesia registered a greater proportion of non-primary enrollments and substantially higher overall literacy levels than those of Nigeria.

These trends are echoed in the state of public health (table 18). Indonesia's advances in reducing infant and child mortality have been much greater and more sustained. While Nigeria apparently reduced infant mortality at a rapid pace in the 1970s, thereafter progress slowed significantly. Indonesia reduced infant mortality by 74 percent between

TABLE 16.   School Enrollment (% gross enrollment)

	Primary		Secondary		Tertiary	
	Indonesia	Nigeria	Indonesia	Nigeria	Indonesia	Nigeria
1965	72	32	12	5	1	0
1970	80	44	16	5	3	1
1975	86	50	20	8	2	1
1980	107	109	29	18	4	3
1985	117	104	41	34	7	4
1990	115	91	44	25	9	4
1995	113	—	52	—	11	4
2000	110	98	57	36	15	8

Source: New York University Development Research Institute, Global Development Network Growth Database. Secondary and tertiary enrollment for Nigeria: World Bank, *World Development Indicators.*

Note: — = no data.

TABLE 17.   Illiteracy Rate (% of people aged 15 and above)

	Indonesia	Nigeria
1970	44	80
1975	37	74
1980	31	67
1985	25	59
1990	21	51
1995	16	44
2000	13	36

Source: World Bank, *World Development Indicators,* and Globalis.

TABLE 18. Public Health

	Infant Mortality Rate (per 1,000 live births)		Life Expectancy at Birth, total (years)		Mortality Rate, under Age 5 (per 1,000 live births)	
	Indonesia	Nigeria	Indonesia	Nigeria	Indonesia	Nigeria
1960	—	—	42	40	216	204
1970	118	139	48	43	172	201
1980	90	99	55	46	128	196
1990	60	85	62	50	83	136
2003	31	98	67	45	41	198

Source: World Bank, *World Development Indicators;* and World Resources Institute, *World Resources 1994–95.*

Note: — = no data.

1970 and 2003, showing a rate two-thirds lower than that of Nigeria. In the area of child mortality, the comparison is even more striking. Nigeria's rate of mortality for children under five has risen substantially since the early 1990s, reversing the improvements of preceding years. Overall, Nigeria has made little perceptible progress in the decades since independence, in marked contrast to Indonesia, which has seen an 80 percent reduction in child deaths.

The data are suggestive rather than definitive. In addition to questions of validity and comparability, the figures are specified at the national level, which of course veils important intranational variations by gender, region, and urban-rural residence. The available information nonetheless traces a clear and consistent distinction in economic outcomes over three decades, showing Indonesia's surpassing performance in growth, structural change, poverty reduction, and social provisions. The comparison further highlights the magnitude and pace of Nigeria's economic decline in the 1980s and the country's continuing stagnation in the succeeding decade.

CHAPTER 7

After the Fall

The Dynamics of Attempted
Reform in Indonesia

The diverging paths of Indonesia and Nigeria abruptly changed course on the eve of the millennium. In the throes of the Asian financial crisis, Soeharto's regime collapsed in May 1998, and with it the growth coalition forged by the New Order over a period of decades. Political reforms led to a fledgling democratic regime the following year, against a backdrop of economic decline, social turmoil, and institutional disarray. Almost simultaneously, Nigeria experienced momentous political change. The fortuitous death of military dictator Sani Abacha, just three weeks after Soeharto's departure, marked the end of more than a decade of predatory authoritarian rule. Reform elements within the military engineered a transition to civilian rule within a year. Nigeria's weak institutions, stagnant economy, and turbulent social divisions provided the central challenges for the newly elected leaders in 1999.

There are strong parallels in the ensuing course of events. In each instance, political reform was carried out by insiders from the old regime, and incumbents substantially dictated the path of transition. In consequence, the succeeding governments have grappled with deficits of popular legitimacy, the inherited disarray of the state apparatus, and the myriad challenges of crafting workable democratic institutions. In both cases, economic triggers were instrumental in the collapse of support coalitions for the old regime, and economic revitalization has been a pressing challenge for leaders in the new government. Notwithstanding efforts at reform, lagging economic performance has continued to undermine legitimacy and stability in both countries. Among many endemic problems, corruption on a grand scale poses obstacles to economic and political restructuring. Moreover, political liberalization has been accompanied by explosive social violence as ethnic, religious, regional, and class tensions have erupted into open conflict. The depth and character of these multiple crises are remarkably similar in both cases.

The apparent convergence of Indonesia and Nigeria after decades of disparate performance prompts several questions. What accounts for the sudden collapse of Soeharto's New Order? Are similar factors evident in the demise of the Abacha regime and the subsequent path of reform in Nigeria? How will democratization affect the political economy of these states? What are the political requisites for economic restructuring and improved governance in these countries and in comparable states undergoing political reform?

As I have elaborated in earlier chapters, the institutional conditions in neopatrimonial regimes generally impede capital formation and undermine economic growth. High levels of discretion by rulers, a narrow concentration of resources (most acute in rentier states), and the arbitrary functioning of institutions create high propensities for forfeiture of private assets and therefore hamper private investment. A central issue, consequently, is whether political liberalization and democratic reform can open the way to needed institutional change: can democratic governments improve the management of state resources, make credible commitments to producer groups, and craft new coalitions for growth?[1]

There are sound reasons to infer that political reform can lead to improvements in economic governance. The advent of constitutional rule, elected government, and a formal opposition, along with the assertion of countervailing institutions such as the legislature and the judiciary, create new pressures for the accountability of leaders. Further, a plural arena of civic association and an independent media can broaden public demands regarding transparency and government performance.[2] In light of the central categories of analysis treated here, democratization has the potential to improve leadership selection, to increase constraints on the discretion of rulers, and to open political space for new reform coalitions.

It is evident, however, from two decades of global reform, that the "virtuous circle" of political and economic liberalization is rarely evident.[3] More commonly, political liberalization gives rise to new problems of eco-

---

1. Richard Sandbrook and J. Oelbaum, "Reforming Dysfunctional Institutions through Democratization: Reflections on Ghana," *Journal of Modern African Studies* 35, no. 4 (1997): 607.

2. Stephan Haggard and Robert Kaufman, *The Political Economy of Democratic Transitions* (Princeton: Princeton University Press, 1995), 151.

3. Leslie Elliot Armijo, Thomas Biersteker, and Abraham Lowenthal, "The Problems of Simultaneous Transitions," in Larry Diamond and Marc Plattner, eds., *Economic Reform and Democracy* (Baltimore: Johns Hopkins University Press, 1995); Joel S. Hellman, "Winners Take All: The Politics of Partial Reform in Postcommunist Transitions," *World Politics* 50, no. 2 (1998): 203–34; and Peter Lewis, "A Virtuous Circle? Democratization and Economic Reform in Africa," in Calvin Jillson and James Hollifield, eds., *Pathways to Democracy* (London: Routledge, 2000).

nomic change even as old liabilities are foreclosed. Competitive politics increases access points for policy lobbying and expands the range and number of veto players in the political system, which can foster stalemate and obstruct essential reforms.[4] The new political arena also multiplies pressures for patronage among politicians, state elites, and their constituencies, while institutional turbulence affords new outlets for corruption. In addition, market reforms create avenues for collusion and political capture, as elites seek to shape the reform process for particular advantage and to steer rents to selected groups or individuals.[5] Political liberalization and economic change are therefore contingent processes of institutional design and contention among salient interests.

An analysis of the full range of transitional challenges in the two countries is beyond the scope of these chapters. The focus here is on the process of political and institutional reform and the effects on economic performance. The following two chapters provide a summary account of major developments in each country since the late 1990s. Each narrative emphasizes a set of crucial issues: the causes for the collapse of authoritarian rule; the introduction of new political institutions; the central challenges of economic reform; and the context of distributional politics in the new democratic regime. A concluding section summarizes the key themes arising from the cases and furnishes propositions about the political conditions of economic restructuring in the two states.

Cracks in the Edifice

In many respects, Indonesia in the mid-1990s appeared to be a fortunate outlier among low-income developing countries as well as resource-exporting economies.[6] The New Order regime had achieved better macroeconomic management than other petroleum-rich states, and the country's economic structure had broadened substantially beyond the hydrocarbon enclave. Economic reforms and a resurgent investment boom at the beginning of the decade spurred major growth in the manufacturing sector, accompanied by advances in agriculture. Manufactured exports in fact eclipsed oil and gas as a source of foreign exchange, and the resource component of state revenues was declining. The chief economic indicators were positive, and the country's balance of payments situation was sound.

---

4. Andrew J. MacIntyre, *The Power of Institutions: Political Architecture and Governance* (Ithaca: Cornell University Press, 2003), 39–40.

5. This is elaborated by Joel Hellman, "Winners Take All."

6. Hal Hill, *The Indonesian Economy in Crisis: Causes, Consequences, and Lessons* (Singapore: ISEAS, Singapore, 1998), 5.

A strong sign of investor confidence was the large inflow of portfolio investment, reaching $6 billion by 1996, and the growing volume of domestic and foreign investment approvals by the government investment agency, mainly in nonoil activities.

There were, nonetheless, significant doubts about political and economic stability over the longer term. Soeharto's regime was structured around the ruler's personal control and a high degree of discretion, forming an unstable admixture of bureaucratic and patrimonial elements. This system of neopatrimonial rule was antithetical to the development of institutions required for sustained growth, as discussed earlier. The liabilities in the precarious institutional machinery of the New Order were increasingly evident. Over the course of his rule, Soeharto skillfully improvised a set of relationships and institutional guarantees to engender investment and growth. The regime's economic success formed the basis of the implicit social compact that maintained the system. An authoritarian corporatist structure, based upon the military and the ruling party, Golkar, stabilized the political system. By the 1990s, however, there were growing signs of institutional weakness and dissatisfaction among major elements of the regime's coalition. Robust economic growth and increasing repression, though temporarily effective in quelling challenges to the regime, could not obscure the deeper stresses in the system.[7]

Features of the political regime fostered misgivings about the extended economic picture. Soeharto had frequently reconciled clientelist pressures with technocratic direction toward a developmental agenda, yet his balancing act was increasingly strained.[8] Technocrats, economists, and business analysts commonly decried the bottlenecks of the "high-cost economy," a coded term that encompassed corruption, nepotism, and collusive behavior as well as bureaucratic hurdles and weak institutions.[9] A cluster of prominent interests created basic obstacles to further liberalization and competitiveness. Leading cronies of the regime exercised prodigious economic power and personal influence, while the business interests of Soeharto's own family constituted a growing set of claims. Sino-Indonesians, prominent among the regime's inner circle, had amassed

7. Adam Schwarz, *A Nation in Waiting: Indonesia's Search for Stability,* 2d ed. (Boulder: Westview, 2000), 311, 319.

8. Hilton Root, *Small Countries, Big Lessons: Governance and the Rise of East Asia* (Oxford: Oxford University Press, 1996).

9. Radius Prawiro, *Indonesia's Struggle for Economic Development: Pragmatism in Action* (Kuala Lumpur: Oxford University Press, 1998), 269, and Ali Wardhana, "Economic Reform in Indonesia: The Transition from Resource Dependence to Industrial Competitiveness," in Henry S. Rowen, ed., *Behind East Asian Growth: The Political and Social Foundations of Prosperity* (London: Routledge, 1998), 129.

extensive holdings in several dozen large conglomerates. Contemporary estimates placed Sino-Indonesian control of large-scale corporate assets as high as 60 percent, and the collusive relations between this group and the regime provoked tensions with *pribumi* (indigenous) business interests and popular sectors.[10] The president's wife and six children, moreover, had extended their own business activities into manufacturing, trade, infrastructure, banking, hotels, and tourism, among their prominent holdings. As the ruler increasingly focused on these interests, the technocrats found their influence was significantly diminished. The strong performance of the economy also encouraged complacency and abated Soeharto's attention to needed policy and institutional reforms. Foreign investment and encouraging levels of growth obscured many of the weaknesses in the institutional environment and the structure of markets.

Leadership stability was also a growing concern. As is typical in neopatrimonial regimes, the person of the ruler was a wild card in the course of events. Soeharto was advancing in age, and after his wife died in April 1996, there was much speculation about whether he would stand for a seventh presidential term.[11] There was keen awareness that Soeharto's personal authority was the linchpin of the political economy, as the ruler had long sustained the fragile coalitions and institutional contrivances that fostered economic success. Economic performance would obviously deteriorate if he unstintingly favored the patrimonial demands of his inner circle; if he left the stage altogether, prospects were even more uncertain.

Two dilemmas came to the fore, the first institutional, the second distributional. A growing discrepancy was evident between the requirements of global market institutions and the idiosyncratic arrangements of the New Order.[12] Liberalization measures in the 1980s and 1990s significantly reduced the economy's insulation from global forces, especially in capital markets, banking, and an expanding array of exports. Yet Indonesia possessed weak formal institutions, and the economy was dominated by a set of informal arrangements that were increasingly at odds with the requisites of globalization.[13] An opaque domestic financial system, closely held corporate governance within the family-owned conglomerates, and weak

10. Kwik Kian Gie and B. N. Marbun, eds., *Konglomerat Indonesia* (Jakarta: Pustaka Sinar Harapan, 1993).

11. R. William Liddle and Rizal Mallarangeng, "Indonesia in 1996: Pressures from Above and Below," *Asia Survey* 37, no. 2 (1997), 167–68.

12. Prawiro, *Indonesia's Struggle for Economic Development,* 317–18.

13. Root, *Small Countries, Big Lessons,* 108–9; Richard Borsuk, "Markets: The Limits of Reform," in Donald Emmerson, ed., *Indonesia beyond Suharto: Polity, Economy, Society, Transition* (Armonk: M. E. Sharpe, 1999), 139–40.

government regulatory capabilities gave rise to widespread vulnerabilities in the private sector. These were aggravated by growing foreign investment and financial integration. While political management could temporarily negotiate this tension, these flaws rendered the economy vulnerable to adverse shocks. The rapid withdrawal of confidence spurred by the Asian financial crisis was a direct outcome of these institutional weaknesses.[14]

The second issue emanated from the growing distributional pressures on the regime. Rapid growth in Indonesia had unquestionably expanded the private sector, greatly increased the middle class, and substantially reduced poverty. Yet the unequal distribution of assets and power aggravated deep tensions over economic hegemony.[15] The New Order was a highly centralized political-economic system. Continuing the patterns inherited from Dutch colonial rule and the Sukarno regime, Soeharto moved even further to concentrate power in Jakarta, enlisting the territorial organization of the military as an adjunct of state control.[16] With the advent of large resource revenues in the 1970s and 1980s, the regime consolidated its fiscal control. Resources were mainly located in the outer islands, but the rents from oil and gas, as well as other exports such as gold and timber, went directly to the center. The oil boom expanded the web of patrimonial relationships with ethnic Chinese elites, family members, and other cronies, further concentrating assets and social power.

Strong macroeconomic performance could not efface the widening array of distributional tensions, which lined up along three axes. The first was resentment toward the wealth and collusive relations among the ruling family and their orbiting cronies. *Pribumi* business interests resented the regime's favoritism toward the ethnic Chinese; middle-class Indonesians also took umbrage at the dominance of the conglomerates and the flagrant wealth of the ruling family; and Muslim leaders were increasingly affronted by the corruption and nepotism of the center.[17]

The second major dimension arose from discord among the outer

---

14. Stephan Haggard, *The Political Economy of the Asian Financial Crisis* (Washington, DC: Institute for International Economics, 2000), 44–45, and Schwarz, *Nation in Waiting,* 315.

15. Schwarz, *Nation in Waiting,* 129–32.

16. Though fiercely anticommunist, the New Order ironically employed a Leninist structure in this respect. The military's political role was formalized in the doctrine of *dwifungsi* or dual function, in which the armed forces had an institutionalized place in government. The territorial organization created a set of institutions parallel to the state, which defined military control down to the village level. See Harold Crouch, *The Army and Politics in Indonesia* (Ithaca: Cornell University Press, 1978), 345.

17. Schwarz, *Nation in Waiting,* 329.

islands. East Timor pressed forcefully for independence after more than two decades of Indonesian occupation. The resource-rich areas of Aceh (in northern Sumatra, the site of major gas deposits) and Irian Jaya (a gold mining region) harbored strong popular sentiments for fiscal and political autonomy, accentuated by growing secessionist movements.[18] Other areas also sought greater attention and resources from the center.

The third dimension of distributional pressure arose from major popular sectors. The large Islamic organizations encompassed many rural dwellers aggrieved over land and local governance. Urban workers agitated for better incomes, services, and trade union rights. These resentments were aggravated by the narrowing scope of the regime's coalition. Though Soeharto sought to placate the Muslim community and manage various factions within the military, power and influence increasingly centered on the ruler's inner circle.[19]

Signs of political opposition gathered even as the economy prospered. An array of Muslims, secular nationalists, trade unionists, and groups in the outer islands were openly in contention with the regime.[20] A pivotal event was the rioting in Jakarta that erupted in July 1996, when the government staged a raid on the headquarters of the Democratic Party (PDI) to oust defiant supporters of Megawati Soekarnoputri. Megawati, the daughter of Indonesia's first president, struggled to maintain her leadership of the PDI, one of two officially approved opposition parties, which she had headed since 1993. The regime, increasingly concerned about her political independence, attempted internal maneuvers to remove her before turning eventually to force. Though authorities rapidly quelled the unrest, Megawati attained a higher profile among antiregime dissidents. The July disturbances were also marked by attacks on ethnic Chinese-owned businesses, which shook investor confidence and added to pressures for political reform.

Crisis and Collapse

These myriad strains on the system came to a head with the challenges of leadership succession and the disruptions of the Asian financial contagion.

18. Michael Malley, "Regions: Centralization and Resistance," in Donald Emmerson, ed., *Indonesia beyond Suharto: Polity, Economy, Society, Transition* (Armonk: M. E. Sharpe, 1999), 101.

19. Robert W. Hefner, *Civil Islam: Muslims and Democratization in Indonesia* (Princeton: Princeton University Press, 2000), 163–65. See also R. William Liddle, "Regime: The New Order," in Emmerson, *Indonesia beyond Suharto.*

20. Schwarz, *Nation in Waiting,* 269–70.

The New Order embodied contradictions that could only temporarily be kept in check by tough leadership. Some form of political dislocation was to be expected as Soeharto's power waned. The ruler's unwillingness to deal with essential issues of distribution and institutional continuity created systemic vulnerabilities that would be exacerbated when he left the scene. While the 1998 crisis was not preordained, the exogenous financial shocks brought on regime change sooner, more rapidly, and in more disruptive circumstances than would have been the case under stable economic conditions.[21]

Indonesia's experience stands in marked contrast to that of Malaysia, where government policies earlier sought to assuage distributional pressures through the New Economic Policy. Prime Minister Mahathir Mohamad also focused more clearly on problems of succession and managed his own departure after weathering the Asian financial crisis.[22] Indonesia's passage from neopatrimonial rule, by contrast, came through a rupture with the old regime that left in its wake institutional and social collapse, prolonging the effects of economic crises. There is a notable contrast between the two Southeast Asian nations in institutional stability and economic performance.

The dramatic events surrounding the downfall of Soeharto have been extensively reported, and a brief review can highlight the main dynamics. In July 1997, on the heels of the collapse of the Thai baht, capital outflows from Indonesia prompted a sharp decline in the value of the rupiah. After a brief attempt to defend the currency, the government allowed a float, whereupon the rupiah plummeted. Another brief period of stopgap austerity measures was pursued, including the postponement of major capital projects and limits on external borrowing.These interim efforts proved ineffectual, leading to a standby agreement with the IMF in October that totaled $43 billion in multilateral and bilateral assistance. Apart from standard requirements for low inflation and fiscal and monetary restraint, the Fund specified a package of systemic reforms to deal with distressed banks, inefficiency in the public sector, corporate insolvency, and endemic corruption. These initial measures were further elaborated in subsequent letters of intent in January and April 1998. Departing from its traditional focus on macroeconomic stabilization, the Fund called for extensive sectoral and institutional changes that targeted the avenues of patronage favored by the regime.

---

21. Haggard, *Political Economy of the Asian Financial Crisis,* 114–16, and Hill, *Indonesian Economy in Crisis,* 9–10.

22. Haggard, *Political Economy of the Asian Financial Crisis,* 107.

The multilateral package appeared to reduce Soeharto's discretion, especially as reform measures challenged the interests of key cronies and the first family. The IMF pressed for the immediate closure of sixteen banks, including several owned by family members and close associates. There were also stipulations for budgetary discipline and far-reaching institutional change, with a quarterly cycle to review progress on reform. The Fund's program created nationalist resentments, and the stringent external policy package fueled speculation about the president's slipping authority. Soeharto vacillated over reform and sought to protect members of his inner circle from the most severe consequences of the new policies, though he had limited policy options or leeway for disbursing patrimonial resources.[23] His inconsistent approach to reform and contentious relations with the Bretton Woods institutions substantially undermined the government's domestic and international credibility. The reputation for prudent macroeconomic policies and political stability cultivated over decades virtually evaporated in a matter of months.

The speed and scope of the extensive IMF reform program, however necessary, nonetheless strained the capabilities of the distressed Indonesian state.[24] Indeed, a central paradox of reform was embodied in the weak institutions and limited capacities of these states to impose regulatory discipline on their unwieldy banking and corporate sectors. In addition, the Fund's insistence on the familiar tools of stabilization, including budgetary austerity and tight money, aggravated the economic distress provoked by the financial crisis and imposed heavy costs on the regime's domestic social coalition. Here as elsewhere during the crisis, the IMF's focus on macroeconomic discipline was paradoxical for a country with a strong record of prudent economic policy.[25] Moreover, the far-reaching injunctions for structural reform were insupportable within the context of a personalized, clientelist regime.

Cross-pressured by economic necessity and political imperatives, Soeharto pursued erratic, stop-go cycles of policy change and reversal. This was evident in the attempts to grapple with the foundering banking system. While acceding to core conditionalities of the IMF program, Soeharto also

23. Hadi Soesastro and M. Basri, "Survey of Recent Developments," *Bulletin of Indonesian Economic Studies* 34, no. 1 (1998): 20.

24. The "orthodox paradox" of state capacity and neoliberal reform has been noted by Miles Kahler, "Orthodoxy and Its Alternatives: Explaining Approaches to Stabilization and Adjustment," in Joan Nelson, ed., *Economic Crisis and Policy Choice* (Princeton: Princeton University Press, 1990), 55.

25. Hill, *Indonesian Economy in Crisis,* 51–52. Criticisms of the IMF's role in Asia by the international economist Jeffrey Sachs are summarized by Soesastro and Basri, "Survey of Recent Developments," 17.

sought to shield the interests of cronies and family members, backtracking on policies and weakening regulatory institutions. In the decade prior to the crisis, the scope of Indonesia's financial services ballooned, from an industry initially dominated by 7 state-owned banks to about 240 institutions, many of which were privately owned by principals in the major conglomerates.[26] Most of the new institutions were highly leveraged, and prudential regulations were commonly flouted as the banks provided finance to allied companies within the large business groups.[27] Immediately after the October IMF agreement the government was compelled to close 16 banks, along with the cancellation of major capital projects. Shuttering the banks, however, provoked a crisis of confidence that quickly led to distress throughout the financial system. Plummeting currency values, rising interest rates, and a shortage of credit pushed much of the private sector into formal bankruptcy. By January 1998 the vast majority of the companies listed in the stock exchange were technically insolvent.

Soeharto confronted two core issues: the first was the rapidly mounting distress in the financial and corporate sectors, which threatened economic collapse; the second, probably more urgent for the regime, were the protests from family members and prominent cronies over precipitous actions that threatened their assets and privileges. Leaders backed off from aggressive restructuring and alleviated much of the immediate pressure on the financial system. Several of the bank closures were retracted, and fifteen large capital projects were reinstated without fanfare. More important, Bank Indonesia provided emergency loans and subsequently extended blanket liquidity credits, with the rationale of preventing systemic breakdown in the banking industry. The government credits, however, were not allocated by any clear criteria, and this indiscriminate largesse posed enormous problems of moral hazard, in effect giving the conglomerates a blank check.[28] Distressed companies had an indefinite lifeline in the form of government guarantees to their principal bank. This created, in essence, an officially subsidized run on the banks, fostering a massive buildup of government debt and accelerating capital flight.

Soeharto was erratic in his approach to the Bretton Woods institutions, continually vacillating on major elements of reform.[29] The presi-

26. Judith Bird, "Indonesia in 1998: The Pot Boils Over," *Asian Survey* 39, no. 1 (1999), 173.

27. George Fane and Ross H. McLeod, "Banking Collapse and Restructuring in Indonesia, 1997–2001," *Cato Journal* 22, no. 2 (2002): 277–95.

28. Ross McLeod, "Dealing with Bank System Failure: Indonesia, 1997–2003," *World Development* 40, no. 1 (2004): 107.

29. Bird, "Indonesia in 1998," 27–28.

dent's January budget ignored major IMF targets, notably the requirement for fiscal restraint. This prompted a free fall of the rupiah, panic buying of major commodities, and a downgrade of Indonesia's financial instruments to junk-bond status by the international rating services. Within two weeks, however, Soeharto again acceded to the Fund, signing a second letter of intent and announcing further curtailment of the contentious capital projects.[30] The agreement also called for an end to initiatives such as the "national car" venture (promoted and owned by the president's son) and aircraft manufacturing (championed by B. J. Habibie, the minister of research and technology and a close associate of the president), along with the termination of trade monopolies for cloves, timber products, and other key commodities controlled by family members or prominent cronies.

Equivocation toward the donors further undermined confidence among the domestic business community and global markets. The president's apparent obeisance to international financial institutions stirred domestic resentment and aggravated tensions with members of the ruling circle. At the same time, many in the private sector and technocratic circles felt that Soeharto was prevaricating on essential reforms in order to shield the cronies and family interests.[31] A rising tide of public commentary called for a change of leadership. Meanwhile, arrangements proceeded apace to renew Soeharto's tenure for a seventh presidential term. The president's candidacy was formalized by the ruling party, Golkar, in January, and the heavily managed electoral system insured his reelection. Only a week after concluding the second IMF memorandum in January 1998, Soeharto announced that B. J. Habibie would be his vice presidential candidate. This was a red flag to international markets in view of Habibie's nationalist stance and his longtime prominence in Soeharto's inner circle. The president's choice was widely viewed as a rebuke to the Washington institutions.[32]

Soeharto also flirted with the introduction of a currency board to stabilize the rupiah, a further sign of distance from the multilateral banks. Following the January IMF memorandum, the rupiah continued its descent to a nadir of Rp17,000 = $1. The crash attracted Soeharto to the

30. A notorious photograph from the signing of the second standby agreement, widely circulated in the media, showed IMF Director Michel Camdessus standing over Soeharto with arms folded, as the Indonesian leader bowed to sign the papers. Indonesians saw the body language as highly symbolic.

31. Schwarz, *Nation in Waiting,* 341.

32. Schwarz, *Nation in Waiting,* 343. See also Colin Johnson, "Survey of Recent Developments," *Bulletin of Indonesian Economic Studies* 34, no. 2 (1998): 5.

idea of a currency board to manage foreign exchange, modeled on existing institutions in Hong Kong and Argentina.[33] For several weeks he consulted regularly with Johns Hopkins economist Steven Hanke, an advocate of the currency board system. This drew sharp criticism from the Bretton Woods institutions and the U.S. government. Along with an earlier announcement of a moratorium on debt repayments, the government appeared to be steering away from orthodox economic policies. The IMF deferred payment of the next tranche of the standby facility.

Soeharto was handily reelected in March by the People's Consultative Assembly (MPR), with Habibie as vice president. He promptly unveiled a cabinet featuring his daughter Tutut, one of the leading ethnic Chinese cronies, Bob Hasan, and a host of others known to favor nationalist policies and crony interests. The entrenchment of leading nationalist and patrimonial elements at the highest echelons of the regime sent a powerful signal to domestic and international audiences of the regime's intentions regarding economic reform.[34]

Although the elections appeared to hand Soeharto victory in the political battle, the foundering economy created massive social dislocation and eliminated the vestiges of legitimacy that remained for the regime. The ruler's political inflexibility and the accelerating economic collapse soon instigated a rupture in the New Order's frail coalition.[35] The government's inconsistent economic policies aggravated the crises in the financial and corporate sectors, deepening qualms among much of the business community. The military, while offering guarded support for the president, was internally divided along religious, factional, and personal lines, and increasingly concerned for their own corporate integrity. The middle class, buffeted by retrenchment in the banking and manufacturing sectors, was increasingly ambivalent toward the regime. Organized labor was resentful over job losses and the government's heavy-handed political manipulation of the labor movement. The ethnic Chinese community was increasingly insecure in light of economic volatility and the rising incidence of ethnic violence. Major Islamic groups squared off in different camps as Amien Rais, leader of Muhammadiyah, the largest Muslim mass organization, went into open opposition against Soeharto. The Muslim organizations could credibly claim to speak for large segments of the rural population, which had been involved in struggles over land rights and local govern-

33. Soesastro and Basri, "Survey of Recent Developments," 50.

34. Richard Borsuk, "Markets: The Limits of Reform," in Emmerson, *Indonesia beyond Suharto,* 142.

35. Margot Cohen, "To the Barricades," *Far Eastern Economic Review* (May 14, 1998): 21–24.

ment. These tensions were accompanied by continued restiveness in the outer islands, including pressures for independence from East Timor and secessionist challenges in Aceh and Irian Jaya.

The crisis came to a head when student groups took to the streets.[36] Demonstrations in major cities were punctuated by riots and further attacks on ethnic Chinese communities. Seeking to arrest the downward spiral in the economy, Soeharto attempted to get the reform program back on track, signing a third IMF agreement in April. The agreement promised to accelerate efforts on bank restructuring, bankruptcy, corporate restructuring, and privatization. By this time, however, the government lacked credibility, and the public generally viewed the Fund as a contributor to the crisis.[37] Within a month the government lifted fuel subsidies, provoking rioting and a new round of student protests. When six student demonstrators were killed by security forces in Jakarta, the unrest sharply escalated, culminating in several days of widespread mayhem in Jakarta. Rioters sacked the Chinese district and committed grievous ethnic violence. Students virtually occupied the parliament compound. Fissures were evident in the military, as special forces controlled by Soeharto's son-in-law provoked violence and vowed to defend the regime, while the more reserved army commander, Wiranto, gradually acknowledged the inevitability of political change. The marines installed around the parliament building showed considerable sympathy for the students.

The senior echelons of the regime soon broke ranks. As leaders of the ruling Golkar party called for Soeharto to resign, prestigious Muslim leaders stepped forward to negotiate an exit, and military commanders quietly suggested a political resolution to the crisis. Soeharto attempted to dissemble for a few days, promising new elections within two years and suggesting a caretaker "reform committee" to prepare for political change. These efforts to placate the opposition proved futile, however, and on May 21 Soeharto resigned without fanfare, handing the government to Vice President Habibie.[38]

In the Wake of the New Order

Soeharto left in his wake a deep economic crisis that threatened to erase years of growth and poverty reduction. Leading institutions, including the military, the ruling party, central regulatory agencies, the judiciary, and

36. Schwarz, *Nation in Waiting*, chap. 11.
37. "Indonesia Shudders," *Economist*, May 19, 1998, 39.
38. Johnson, "Survey of Recent Developments," 9.

the civil service, were in disarray. With the ruler's departure, the architecture of the New Order crumbled, leaving a set of governing structures riddled with corruption, short of capacity, and lacking in purpose. Many commentators referred to the situation as one of wholesale institutional collapse, so great was the sense of sudden disintegration. The economic crash prompted a breakdown of the authoritarian regime, and the resulting crisis of governance further eroded the foundations of the economy.

B. J. Habibie inherited power without legitimacy or a clear apparatus of rule.[39] Seeking to assuage opposition pressures, the new president rapidly opened the political domain to greater participation and pluralism. Popular dissent nonetheless continued as students and elements of civil society pressed for a rapid transition to democracy and called for accountability by elements of the old regime. The Golkar leadership attempted to refashion the party in a reform profile, and Habibie soon made clear his intention to contest elections set for the following year. Political party activity was restored, and by the time of the elections forty-eight parties entered the political arena. Golkar faced assertive opposition from the Democratic Party of Struggle (PDI-P), the secular nationalist group headed by Megawati Soekarnoputri, who had emerged as the leading opposition figure. Amien Rais also came forward as a major presidential contender as leader of the PAN, trading on his pivotal role in the opposition during the final months of the old regime and his extensive Muslim base among the Muhammadiyah. Another Muslim leader, Abdurrahman Wahid (Gus Dur), leader of the Nahdlatul Ulama, Indonesia's major "traditionalist" Muslim organization, entered the contest under the banner of the PKB. He could claim a large following in the villages and towns of East Java.[40] Other lesser parties emerged around several ideological poles, including clusters of Muslim or Islamist parties, and populist or Sukarnoist associations. On economic matters there was a substantial convergence of views. In spite of their diverse interests and philosophies, the parties were generally distrustful of the Bretton Woods institutions, and they commonly favored nationalist and populist programs to alleviate economic hardship.

The economy continued its descent, aggravated by political instability

---

39. David Bourchier, "Habibie's Interregnum: *Reformasi,* Elections, Regionalism, and the Struggle for Power," in Chris Manning and Peter van Diermen, eds., *Indonesia in Transition: Social Aspects of Reformasi and Crisis* (Singapore: Institute of Southeast Asian Studies, 2000), 15.

40. Marcus Mietzner, "From Soeharto to Habibie: The Indonesian Armed Forces and Political Islam during the Transition," in Geoff Forrester, ed., *Post-Soeharto Indonesia: Renewal or Chaos* (Bathurst: Crawford House, 1999); Hefner, *Civil Islam,* chap. 7.

and contentious relations with the donors. In 1998 alone the GDP declined by 13.2 percent (representing a drop of fully 18 percent over the previous year's modest growth).[41] More than 90 percent of the firms listed on the Jakarta stock exchange were technically insolvent, and the banking system was deeply in distress. Bank Indonesia and the newly established Indonesian Bank Restructuring Agency (IBRA) struggled to gain a handhold on the enormous crisis in the financial and corporate sectors. Capital flight among domestic and foreign business was considerable. Many of the assets and much of the expertise among the ethnic Chinese community had fled, with uncertain prospects of return. Habibie reshuffled his cabinet, brought back some of the senior technocrats who had been marginalized by Soeharto, and sought to improve relations with the Bretton Woods institutions. The IMF responded by relaxing important conditions and furnishing additional resources, and the World Bank stepped in with supplementary finance and compensatory packages to alleviate the mass privation arising from the crisis. Despite his inconsistent pronouncements on the economy, Habibie largely accommodated the central orthodox package of the donors. He also took tentative steps to investigate the holdings of the first family and leading cronies.[42]

Habibie was preoccupied with his own ruling position and the question of how to amend the political system. The regime scheduled new elections that allowed for open competition, though it preserved the system of indirect election of the president by the People's Consultative Assembly, consisting of the elected parliament and additional appointed members. The formal political position of the military within the electoral process and the legislature was reduced, though not eliminated. Habibie also introduced two broad decentralization laws (Nos. 22 and 25 of 1999), which signaled a departure from the highly concentrated ruling structures of the preceding forty years, and created the groundwork for subsequent institutional reform.[43]

Economic management grew increasingly unsteady as the elections approached. A major scandal erupted in August with the revelation that Bank Bali, on a flimsy pretext, had transferred some $80 million to a front company controlled by the treasurer for the ruling Golkar party.[44] The stain of corruption soon embroiled senior officials in Bank Indonesia, the

41. See the Economist Intelligence Unit, *Indonesia Country Report, 3d Quarter 1999* (London: Economist Intelligence Unit, 1999), 5.

42. Johnson, "Survey of Recent Developments," 10.

43. Anne Booth, "Survey of Recent Developments," *Bulletin of Indonesian Economic Studies* 35, no. 3 (1999): 27–30.

44. Booth, "Survey of Recent Developments," 5.

Finance Ministry, and IBRA, casting a shadow on these critical institutions. The multilateral development banks expressed strong concerns, and the currency dipped as markets reacted to the deepening scandal. The emerging crisis in East Timor further weakened international confidence in the government and the investment climate. Oversight of the economy unraveled, as key officials fought personal allegations or quit the government altogether.[45] There was a general recognition that the deep systemic problems in the economy could not be addressed without a significant change in leadership and the composition of government.

Regime Change and the Deficit of Governance

The unexpected outcome of the 1999 elections altered the salient forces in Indonesian politics. Despite an assertive bid for the presidency, Habibie was eliminated in the last moments of contestation. On the eve of the election, the MPR voted to reject the incumbent's customary "accountability" speech marking the end of each presidential term. The de facto withdrawal of confidence by the MPR caused Habibie to withdraw, throwing the contest open to opposition forces on the eve of the presidential vote.[46] Megawati Soekarnoputri had the highest profile among opposition candidates and was widely believed to hold a popular advantage. Her party, the PDI-P, achieved a plurality in the parliamentary polling but was far short of the majority needed to guarantee the presidency. In the last-minute caucusing within the MPR, Abdurrahman Wahid, leader of the Islamic NU and the PKB party, was able to gather a coalition among "modernist" Muslim factions, elements of Golkar, and even some segments of Megawati's party. Wahid gained the presidency, and, in a palliative move, Megawati was invited to assume the vice presidency.[47] Indonesia achieved a regime change that brought forward new political elements, though without displacing incumbent elites. The political transition gave rise to an inchoate arena of shifting elite coalitions and contentious popular interests.

Wahid entered the presidency amid high expectations, promising a new era of civility, respect for fundamental rights, transparency in government, and responsible economic management. He had a reputation for moderation and a degree of political alacrity. His contentious relations

45. Booth, "Survey of Recent Developments," 33.

46. Marcus Mietzner, "The 1999 General Session: Wahid, Megawati, and the Fight for the Presidency," in Manning and van Diermen, *Indonesia in Transition,* 46.

47. R. William Liddle, "Indonesia in 1999: Democracy Restored," *Asian Survey* 40, no. 1 (2000): 38.

with the New Order regime in its final years made him relatively acceptable to *reformasi* elements, in sharp contrast to Habibie.[48] These initial advantages, however, soon dissipated in the face of Wahid's ineffectual leadership and the new government's failure to address critical challenges in national affairs. Wahid proved to be a capricious executive, given to contradictory statements and unpredictable shifts of position, erratically responding to different interests and factions, frequently traveling overseas while domestic problems festered, and burdened by chronic health problems.

The lack of effective delegation by the executive only served to accentuate these liabilities. The new cabinet contained multiple parties and interests, reflecting the compromises underlying Wahid's tenuous electoral coalition.[49] The PDI-P gained key economic appointments, including the coordinating minister for the economy and the minister of investment and state enterprises, while other posts (including finance, planning, trade, and industry) were dispersed among different parties. In addition, the president assembled a number of auxiliary policy groups and advisory panels, which lacked formal standing and institutional linkages. This created a nebulous set of actors in the policy arena, consulted by the executive on a sporadic basis. Despite regular meetings of the various bodies, channels for assessing and determining policy were not clarified, and the process remained subject to the whims and idiosyncrasies of the president.[50]

Political and institutional weaknesses compounded these problems. The New Order, despite its parliamentary mantle, was presidential and hierarchical: Soeharto, in concert with the military, created and captured the institutional components of the system. The political transition introduced competitive elections and raised the standing of the parliamentary system. The regular parliament, the DPR, emerged as a significant counterweight to the executive, and the larger MPR, which met annually, quickly asserted its prerogative to affirm or rescind confidence in the president. This attenuated decades of unchallenged executive power and opened the door to a more independent and assertive role for parliamentary institutions.[51] The members of these bodies were quick to grasp their opportunities, forcing the executive to contend with new sources of deliberation, criticism, and obstruction. The contentious mood was a defining

48. See Mietzner, "1999 General Session," and Hefner, *Civil Islam,* chap. 7.
49. Mietzner, "1999 General Session," 56, and Liddle, "Indonesia in 1999," 38–39.
50. Confidential interview, Jakarta, June 2000; George Fane, "Survey of Recent Developments," *Bulletin Indonesian Economic Studies* 36, no. 1 (2000): 20; Ross McLeod, "Survey of Recent Developments," *Bulletin of Indonesian Economic Studies* 36, no. 2 (2000): 9.
51. McLeod, "Survey of Recent Developments," 11–12.

feature of posttransition politics, and the motives of the politicians varied from political agendas to self-dealing.

Parliamentary institutions were themselves fragmented among several important parties and factions. In the parliamentary vote of June 1999, approximately 34 percent went to the PDI-P (Megawati's party), 22 percent to the former ruling party Golkar, 13 percent to Wahid's PKB, 11 percent for the Development Party (PPP), and 7 percent to the PAN, Amien Rais's party. Within the DPR, 38 seats were allocated to the military, and in the larger MPR, 200 government appointees (drawn from the regions and various "mass" organizations) joined the parliamentarians.[52] The fragmentation of parties and interests gave rise to a contentious political space. The electoral deal that brought Wahid to office began to fray almost immediately, as the constituent parties and interests jockeyed for political position and the distribution of spoils. With no assurances of parliamentary support, the president continually had to bargain among the elements of a rapidly dissipating coalition.

The new government signaled a pragmatic approach to the economy, as early statements expressed a desire to pursue market-oriented policies, to engage with the global economy, and to enhance the troubled relations with the multilateral financial institutions. The coordinating minister for the economy, Kwik Kian Gie, was a prominent economist with a reputation as a critic of the corruption and crony relations of the old regime. He was joined by a colleague from the PDI-P, Laksamana Sukardi, who as minister for investment and privatization promised assertive steps toward liberalization and reform of the state sector. President Wahid's initial conciliatory statements toward the international financial community, and his condemnation of endemic corruption and opaque dealings, provided some encouragement that the new government was committed to change.[53]

Yet the senior economic team was hardly unified, and the president himself faced divergent pressures from his party and traditional constituency. The finance minister was drawn from the PAN, Amien Rais's party, in partial recompense for the political debts. The Muslim constituencies embodied in the five Islamic axis parties generally favored nationalist and populist policies, and were largely opposed to the orthodox package proffered by the multilateral institutions. Such views were prevalent among Wahid's own eastern Javanese base. In addition, the disparate elements of the cabinet and the parliament struggled over the con-

---

52. Liddle, "Indonesia in 1999," 33–34.
53. Djisman S. Simanjuntak, "The Indonesian Economy in 1999: Another Year of Delayed Reform," in Manning and Van Diermen, *Indonesia in Transition,* 74–75.

tours of central reforms in an effort to capture the nominal benefits and hidden gains from the economic recovery effort. The massive resources encompassed in rehabilitating the financial and corporate sectors, and renovating markets, attracted party elites, beleaguered cronies, arriviste politicians, and their allies, in a many-sided struggle over rents.

The government's approach to the economy was consequently ambivalent, inconsistent, and ineffective in addressing the structural problems inherited from the previous regime and the financial crisis. The template for economic policy was set out chiefly by the IMF in a new Letter of Intent (LOI) in January 2000, linked to agreements for further assistance from the World Bank, the United States, and other bilateral donors. The agreement prescribed macroeconomic, sectoral, and institutional reforms, many of which were reflected in the government's new budget. The letter contained familiar injunctions for fiscal and monetary restraint, low inflation, and trade liberalization but also called for accelerated efforts to resolve corporate debt, restructure insolvent banks, and substantially divest state ownership of inefficient public enterprises.[54] Anticorruption efforts featured prominently in the LOI, which provided for improved audit procedures and special investigative bodies, as well as the budget, which included an increase in public sector compensation. The government also highlighted such measures as poverty alleviation, improved tax administration, and fiscal devolution as part of a broader initiative to implement the 1999 decentralization laws.

Crucial commitments, however, were not followed through, as economic governance fell into policy drift and institutional disarray. First, the government's economic team and peak institutions were in turmoil. Minister Kwik, affiliated with Megawati's party, was not effective in his coordination role among the various ministries and departments, and was soon replaced by a figure considered more politically loyal to the president. Minister Laksamana was also ousted without notice, causing great resentment among the PDI-P, a vital coalition partner.[55] More important, the fragmented circle of advisory units surrounding the presidency, though replete with strong economic talent (including most of Soeharto's most prominent technocrats), were stymied in providing authoritative guidance.

54. International Monetary Fund, *Letter of Intent,* and Government of Indonesia and Bank Indonesia, *Memorandum of Economic and Financial Policies Medium-Term Strategy and Policies for 1999/2000 and 2000,* January 20, 2000, http://www.imf.org/external/np/loi/2000/idn/01/index.htm. See also George Fane, "Survey of Recent Developments," *Bulletin of Indonesian Economic Studies* 36, no. 1 (2000): 21.

55. R. William Liddle, "Indonesia in 2000: A Shaky Start for Democracy," *Asian Survey* 41, no. 1 (2001): 209.

Disorganization at the pinnacle of government made sustained policy direction virtually impossible.

Second, the central institutions charged with executing the economic program were hobbled by organizational weakness and political intervention. Bank Indonesia formally attained new autonomy under the democratic regime, but President Wahid quickly fell out with the BI governor, reportedly over the latter's refusal to make expedient appointments to state-controlled banks.[56] When the governor could not be induced to resign, he was arrested on a pretext of involvement with the Bank Bali scandal. The government also instigated a shake-up at the bank restructuring agency IBRA, which slowed the already halting progress of asset sales and bank consolidation. Here too, many observers saw a heavy political hand, as IBRA's jurisdiction included the assets and companies of well-connected individuals, and the vast resources at stake were a potent lure for the political parties. Laksamana's ouster bore the same stamp and hampered potential movement on privatization, an important policy area substantially dormant under preceding governments. A further cabinet reshuffle replaced a number of ministers (including finance) from outside Wahid's party with those closer to him politically.[57] The other key institutional spheres crucial to economic governance, notably the civil service and the judiciary, were disordered, overextended, and suffused by corruption.

Third, parliamentary independence became a substantial impediment as well as a crucial source of accountability.[58] The parliament resisted subsidy reductions and price deregulation, hampered asset sales and debt resolution by IBRA, and criticized privatization and corporate restructuring initiatives. Slow progress on constitutional change and other key legislation further impeded the reform process. The mixed motives among parliamentarians bear emphasis. Some of the contention with the executive reflected the populist orientations of politicians in opposition to IMF orthodoxy. In other instances, partisanship trumped policy concerns, and those outside Wahid's narrowing support base opposed the president as a matter of course. Often enough, parliamentarians had private interests in particular decisions or policies that swayed their approach.

---

56. McLeod, "Survey of Recent Developments," 6.

57. Eric D. Ramstetter, "Survey of Recent Developments," *Bulletin of Indonesian Economic Studies* 36, no. 3 (2000): 5.

58. Ross McLeod, "After Soeharto: Prospects for Reform and Recovery in Indonesia," Departmental Working Papers (RSPAS, Australian National University, 2003), 17–18, http://rspas.anu.edu.au/economics/publish/papers/wp2003/wp-econ-2003-10.pdf.

The combative legislature did seek to hold the government to account and placed growing pressure on a president that many came to view as flighty and incompetent. Two corruption scandals compounded the mounting resentment toward Wahid, resulting in parliamentary demands for greater accountability. It came to light that about $4 million was improperly diverted from the state logistics agency, Bulog, at the behest of the president, and another $2 million was received as a "contribution" from the Sultan of Brunei and channeled through an NU charity. The appearance of misappropriating funds further damaged confidence in the executive, and the July MPR session compelled Wahid to make concilia-tory gestures including heightened powers for Vice President Megawati.[59]

The corruption scandals and the government's evident reluctance to take on powerful entrenched interests (aside from the Soeharto family) raised concerns about the corrosive effects of "KKN" (corruption, crony-ism, and nepotism). Wahid apparently sought to protect the assets of four of the largest conglomerates from being dismantled, including those of Liem Sioe Liong, Soeharto's closest crony. The DPR was also lenient in its investigation of illicit government loans to the conglomerate Texmaco, as legislators argued that the bailout was justified by the company's impor-tance to the national economy.[60] These signs of favoritism and impropri-ety fueled broader perceptions of rampant corruption and collusive rela-tions among political and economic elites. The growing disillusionment over reform did little to improve a subdued investment climate.

Additional factors hampering economic activity were the increasing sense of political instability and an unraveling security situation. The com-munal pressures evident during the last years of Soeharto's reign had burst into violent discord, which spread and intensified throughout the archipel-ago. New violence in Aceh and West Papua (Irian Jaya) underscored the challenge of separatist pressures. Sectarian violence erupted among Mus-lim and Christian communities in Ambon, Sulawesi, and the Moluccas, and Madurese and Dayak ethnic conflicts took a bloody toll. Periodic anti-Chinese violence also occurred in Jakarta and in other parts of Java. Much of the discord did not directly impact areas of economic impor-tance, though the general sense of insecurity negatively influenced investor perceptions.

59. Michael Malley, "Indonesia in 2001: Restoring Stability in Jakarta," *Asian Survey* 42, no. 1 (2002): 125, and McLeod, "Survey of Recent Developments," 6–7.
60. McLeod, "Survey of Recent Developments," 12.

Inertia and Performance

The calamitous economic scenario of 1998 was followed by hesitant and uneven signs of recovery. Economic growth registered near zero in 1999, rebounded to nearly 5 percent the following year, and then slowed to about 3 percent in 2001. Inflation was brought down considerably from its peak during the crisis, but remained in the range of 10 to 14 percent. This partly reflected obdurate fiscal problems and monetary growth, an outcome of the rising costs of the crisis, political pressures on spending, and weak management at the center. The rupiah, after recovering more than 60 percent of its value from the 1998 low, resumed a slow downward slide and remained volatile. The poverty rate, which had doubled in the course of the crisis, remained discouragingly high, with about 20 percent of the population below the official poverty line.[61] The lingering economic malaise was aggravated by a weak investment response, which was clearly linked to the institutional deficits and political dilemmas of the new regime.

Much of the recovery in overall growth could be attributed to consumption, which fell only modestly at the height of the crisis and then recovered quickly. Consumption among both households and businesses was bolstered by the drawdown of existing assets, expenditure switching from imports to domestic goods, and (for firms) the utilization of installed capacity. Asset holders, both foreign and domestic, held off new investments.[62] After bottoming out in 1998 at the depth of the crisis, investment by domestic and foreign firms resumed erratically. Although trends in direct and portfolio investment fluctuated considerably, the magnitude of investment remained well below precrisis levels.[63] On the eve of the crisis in 1996, the annual volume of private capital going to Indonesia had reached $11 billion; the next four years saw a net private outflow of some $32 billion only partially offset by huge official inflows of $20 billion.[64] The scope and duration of Indonesia's investment drought was especially severe.[65]

Fluctuations in investment and performance were neither uniform nor

---

61. Fane, "Survey of Recent Developments," 31.

62. McLeod, "Survey of Recent Developments," 16; Booth, "Survey of Recent Developments," 24–25.

63. Andrew MacIntyre and B. P. Resosudarmo, "Survey of Recent Developments," *Bulletin of Indonesian Economic Studies* 39, no. 2 (2003): 147; Mari Pangestu and Miranda S. Goeltom, "Survey of Recent Developments," *Bulletin of Indonesian Economic Studies* 37, no. 2 (2001): 148.

64. Fane, "Survey of Recent Developments," 18.

65. Eric D. Ramstetter, "Survey of Recent Developments," *Bulletin of Indonesian Economic Studies* 36, no. 3 (2000): 34–36.

consistent. One prominent economist remarked on the "disconnect" between the discouraging profile of macroeconomic indicators, and the more resilient economic conditions for many households and enterprises.[66] The crisis had varying effects across the economy. Finance, construction, and the large corporate sector reflected the greatest impact. Manufacturing activities, which had plummeted in the crisis, made a sporadic recovery. Paper, chemicals, minerals, and transport equipment rebounded briskly, while food, textiles, footwear, wood products, and iron and steel were sluggish at best.[67] The devaluation of the rupiah furnished benefits for exporters of resources and agriculture. Many small-scale enterprises were also resilient, as they were less dependent on bank finance or imports, and mainly served domestic markets. The lagging pace of investment suppressed growth, but existing infrastructure and physical plant furnished the basis for renewed output, as export demand gradually revived.

Institutional factors were prominent among the impediments to an investment-led recovery in Indonesia. First, the morass in the banking sector played havoc with public finances, strangled flows of domestic credit, and cast a broader shadow on the credibility of the government's efforts to restructure the postcrisis economy. The cost of the financial bailout had ballooned to more than $60 billion, approaching half of GDP. Both IBRA and BI showed major deficits of capacity and autonomy in trying to recapitalize the banking system and dispose of assets. The Bank Restructuring Agency trailed its own timetable (and was well behind the comparable programs of other crisis-affected Asian states) in seeking to resolve the distress of the leading banks. Many of the resolution exercises claimed by IBRA and the central bank were questioned by experts as to their adequacy, transparency, and effectiveness. Substantial assets appeared to have been shuffled among state-managed accounts rather than transferred to private buyers, and in several instances the former owners of insolvent banks apparently maintained their interest even after they were supposedly divested.[68]

Corporate restructuring was integrally related to the banking crisis, as many of the prominent banks were part of the leading business groups, and their portfolios included substantial intergroup lending, in violation of legal restrictions. The resolution of corporate debts was entangled in a

66. Mohammed Sadli, cited by Liddle, "Indonesia in 2000," 218.

67. Ramstetter, "Survey of Recent Developments," 25–27; McLeod, "Survey of Recent Developments," 15.

68. Howard Dick, "Survey of Recent Developments," *Bulletin of Indonesian Economic Studies* 37, no. 1 (2001): 23.

skein of technical and political problems.[69] Given the opaque dealings of the major conglomerates and their close ties with authorities, the task of identifying corporate debts and assets, properly valuing liabilities and collateral, and imposing settlements on stakeholders was a formidable challenge. The problems of regulatory capacity have been noted. In addition, many of the prominent cronies of the old regime retained their political leverage. The besieged governor of BI had been close to Soeharto's inner circle, and, under further pressure from President Wahid, the independence of the central bank was widely challenged. Further, the parliament frequently questioned or blocked settlements concluded by BI and IBRA. In addition, the peak agencies in charge of corporate and financial restructuring had limited reach in enforcing agreements with debtors. The weak, corrupt court system provided little assistance in supporting the authority of regulators.

The disarray afflicting the financial, corporate, and legal systems, along with turbulence in government and the economic bureaucracy, presented a discouraging picture to asset holders. The unsound credibility of policy and institutions seriously hampered the response of investors, even as the immediate crisis abated.[70] While a diversified structure of production offered sources of resilience, the economy suffered central deficits of investment and capital formation. Despite a significant recovery of many productive activities and a revival of exports, including a major increase in oil and gas receipts, economic growth did not exceed 5 percent, and there were no signs of a return to the high-growth trajectory that preceded the crisis. Reacting to policy drift and the intractable problems of restructuring key sectors and institutions, the multilateral financial institutions curtailed support. In December 2000 the IMF suspended disbursements to Indonesia, and two months later the World Bank cut its annual lending program by two-thirds.[71]

Political and economic travails led to the removal of Abdurrahman Wahid. Cumulative frustrations over weak leadership, institutional failure, economic stagnation, rising insecurity, pervasive corruption, political collusion, and poor accountability prompted the parliamentary bodies to take more forceful action against the president. Parliamentarians were particularly dissatisfied with Wahid's response to the Bulog and Brunei scandals, his apparent interventions on behalf of conglomerates and

69. R. William Liddle, "Indonesia in 2000," 217; Fane, "Survey of Recent Developments," 37–41.

70. Hill, *Indonesian Economy in Crisis,* 89, and McLeod, "Survey of Recent Developments," 16.

71. Dick, "Survey of Recent Developments," 10.

selected magnates, and his failure to effectively devolve power to Megawati, despite formal promises to the MPR. The parliament censured the president twice over the corruption scandals, followed by a full session of the MPR in July, which voted to remove Wahid and replace him with the vice president, Megawati Soekarnoputri.[72] Wahid tried unsuccessfully to preempt impeachment by attempting to dissolve the assembly and appointing a new head of police. Ultimately, however, the courts, the military, and the parties supported the assembly's action, and Megawati ascended to the presidency.

A New Start?

President Megawati faced widespread skepticism regarding her abilities to improve the political system and the economy. Detractors pointed to a style that was aloof and disengaged, and some questioned her basic competence to govern. Further, her party held a relatively weak plurality in parliament, requiring effective bargaining and coalition building in order to push through effective policies.[73] The new president's credentials as an opposition leader no longer afforded much political capital, and the PDI-P did not have a strong profile in support of change, notwithstanding the reform elements within the party.

The new president stepped into an extraordinarily difficult situation. On the economic side, recovery efforts were clearly flagging, as reflected by slow growth, anemic investment, the sprawling, unresolved crises in the banking and corporate sectors, enfeebled state institutions, massive public debt, and chilly relations with creditors and donors.[74] The growing leverage of parliamentary institutions and their increasing polarization from the executive posed further obstacles to effective government action.

Only months prior to the ouster of President Wahid, the government presided over a momentous administrative change, as the central provisions of the 1999 decentralization laws were put into effect. The big bang of decentralization devolved resources, authority, and personnel from Jakarta to the regions, districts, and municipalities, causing enormous dislocation in the structure of government.[75] The many uncertainties in the system of rule were compounded by separatist agitation and seemingly epidemic violence across the nation. After September 2001, the govern-

72. Malley, "Indonesia in 2001," 125–26.
73. Michael Malley, "Indonesia in 2002: The Rising Cost of Inaction," *Asian Survey* 43, no. 1 (2003): 136.
74. Pangestu and Goeltom, "Survey of Recent Developments," 141.
75. Dick, "Survey of Recent Developments," 31.

ment was also absorbed by security challenges arising from radical Islamist groups and antiterrorist efforts, alongside the continuing regional and communal conflicts.

Megawati sought to rationalize economic management and tackle some of the institutional problems that languished under Wahid, replacing the economic team, tightening the process of consultation and policy formation, and changing leadership in peak agencies such as BI and IBRA.[76] Her key economic appointments indicated a return of technocratic influence over macroeconomic policy. Dorodjatun Kuntjoro-Jakti, a respected economist from the University of Indonesia, was called from a post as U.S. ambassador to serve as coordinating minister for the economy. Other prime economic appointments, including finance, brought in capable figures. Lakasama Sukardi was restored to Investment and State Enterprise, and his ministry attained control over the troubled IBRA. Kwik Kian Gie returned to head the state planning agency Bappenas. Senior advisers from the Berkeley mafia gained renewed access, and talented younger technocrats had important roles. The unwieldy assemblage of informal policy groups was rationalized, and the policy process improved.

The government also sought to normalize relations with donors. A new IMF Letter of Intent was concluded a month after Megawati's accession, followed by supplementary commitments from the World Bank and other donors in the Consultative Group on Indonesia (CGI). The IMF agreement allowed greater headway with creditors, as well as a general increase in market confidence. The successful political transition and signals from the multilateral institutions boosted domestic assessments of the economy.[77] Still, important controversies remained. The detailed prescriptions in the IMF program, encompassing the banking and corporate sectors, the legal domain, institutional issues, and fiscal devolution, signaled a new and unwelcome degree of external micromanagement of the reform process. This prompted growing debate about Indonesia's relations with the Fund, particularly as the end of the recovery program drew into view.

The new president's attentions were quickly drawn to the rising separatist challenges in Aceh and in West Papua (Irian Jaya), two leading resource-producing regions. Megawati visited both areas and the government extended new autonomy arrangements for each region, with a more palliative effect in West Papua than in Aceh.[78] Conciliatory political ges-

76. R. Y. Siregar, "Survey of Recent Developments," *Bulletin of Indonesian Economic Studies* 37, no. 3 (2001): 278.

77. Siregar, "Survey of Recent Developments," 282.

78. Malley, "Indonesia in 2002," 140.

tures, however, were backed by a stronger stance toward separatist militants, and Megawati backed a vigorous new military campaign in Aceh. Continuing religious violence in the Moluccas was another central concern. In the wake of the September 11 attacks, officials were more forceful in confronting the Laskar Jihad movement, and the Islamic militants were induced to withdraw from the islands. Meanwhile, high-profile bombings in Bali in October 2002 and the Jakarta Marriott hotel a year later raised the specter of domestic terrorism and served to aggravate fears over the security situation.

The decentralization process had important implications for managing the distributional pressures underlying much of the regional and communal restiveness. By allowing greater leeway in areas of policy, revenue, and administration, the reforms could potentially enhance the market potential of Indonesia's far-flung regions and localities. However, a market-enhancing devolution was far from assured, as the reforms posed considerable hazards. Fiscal and administrative disarray threatened to further disrupt an already fragile economy. Among the most immediate concerns were the allocation of funding and personnel and the delivery of statutory resources. In addition, the dispersal of authority quickly gave rise to regulatory confusion, as the various subnational units imposed new taxes and commercial requirements. A welter of confusing restrictions and levies among (or within) islands posed additional barriers to commerce and investment, and new outlets for rent seeking and corruption. Observers raised concerns that devolution would help to consolidate the power of local patrons and strongmen, particularly if regional authorities colluded with local business interests or territorial commanders of the cash-strapped military. There was also some apprehension that decentralization could accentuate regional inequalities over the longer term, arising from disparities in resources, geography, and governance.

Despite its limited political capacities, the new government sought to address important areas of institutional reform. In addition to shifting personnel at IBRA and placing the agency under Laksamana's ministry, the president appointed a new governor and deputy governor for Bank Indonesia, both of whom were well regarded as capable and independent professionals. In addition, an amended law governing BI autonomy, after wending its way through the legislative process for several years, was finally approved at the end of 2003. Among other provisions, the amendment clarified BI's role as lender of last resort and delineated an oversight body for the central bank. Laws on state finance were also approved. Privatization efforts moved ahead after a long period of inactivity with the floating of shares in PT Telkom and Indosat.[79] The efforts to resolve some of the critical deficiencies in peak regulatory agencies were important for advancing the structural dimension of the postcrisis reforms. In the political domain, the MPR moved deliberately if slowly in approving constitutional amendments that would more fully democratize the regime, approving an independent electoral commission, a fully elected MPR to replace the admixture of elected and appointed delegates, a further reduction in the political representation of the military, and provision for the direct election of the president in 2004, replacing the process of indirect selection by the assembly for the first time in decades.[80]

The Limits of Reform

Efforts at reform were significantly advanced by the devolution of policy authority and the development of core capacities in economic administration. The improvements were most evident in macroeconomic management. Tight monetary policy and more effective fiscal management reduced inflation, diminished the budget deficit, stabilized the currency, and generally improved the balance of payments. Economic growth accelerated modestly, from 3.8 percent in Wahid's final year to 4.3 percent in 2002 and 5.1 percent in 2004. Improved growth was aided by rising oil and gas revenues and strong markets for other selected exports including textiles, garments, and solid minerals. Indonesia continued to draw on the Extended Fund Facility under IMF supervision until December 2003, when the Fund concluded its final review and Indonesia moved to a staff-monitored policy regime, with no further borrowing from the Fund. The departure from a formal IMF program with its attendant conditionalities was broadly popular. The acceptance of external monitoring of policy performance was seen within government as a necessary compromise for signaling credibility and sustaining the confidence of international markets.[81]

Although macroeconomic performance improved markedly from the quagmire of preceding governments, the new administration made less effective headway in the institutional arena. More rapid implementation was evident in bank restructuring, debt resolution, privatization, and decentralization. By February 2004, IBRA wound up its operations, claiming a high rate of debt resolution and successful reorganization of the

79. A. S. Alisjahbana and Chris Manning, "Survey of Recent Developments," *Bulletin of Indonesian Economic Studies* 38, no. 3 (2002): 277.

80. Alisjahbana and Manning, "Survey of Recent Developments," 278.

81. Lloyd R. Kenward, "Survey of Recent Developments," *Bulletin of Indonesian Economic Studies* 40, no 1 (2004): 10.

banking system. The agency had recovered less than a third of the nominal value of the debts under its jurisdiction, though this recovery rate could be viewed as acceptable within the context of Indonesia's difficult legal and financial environment.[82] The IMF noted IBRA's accelerated achievements under the new government and offered a modestly favorable evaluation of its performance. The Jakarta Initiative Task Force (JITF), the corporate debt restructuring body, also completed its operations, noting nearly a hundred cases of debt workouts totaling more than $20 billion in value.

While manifesting more vigor, however, these units were less effective in restructuring important domains of the economy. Even as they concluded their operations, scandals in the banking industry and the corporate sector continued apace. The most problematic elements in the financial sector were the large state banks, which, despite waves of consolidation and recapitalization, continued to show signs of financial vulnerability, opaque practices, and crony relations. Fraud and asset stripping were also evident in some of the smaller private banks.[83] Similarly, the debt resolution practices of both IBRA and JITF evidently left assets in the hands of the original owners who had originally dissipated their firms.[84] The stock market showed wide fluctuations, and there were recurring indications of market insecurity. While nominal targets of financial and corporate reform were attained, successive administrations were unsuccessful at reestablishing deeper economic confidence. Essential problems of information asymmetry and political collusion undermined trust in these markets and deterred investors from committing assets.

The chronic institutional deficits of the new regime were underscored by the prevalence of corruption throughout public life and the private economy. An incessant stream of public revelations highlighted self-dealing in parliament, the parties, the central government, regulatory agencies, banks, major companies, resource-based industries, local governments, and the judiciary. Both domestic and international audiences shared the perception that corruption was endemic, massive, and unrestrained. These views were confirmed by local polls and by Indonesia's poor rankings in Transparency International's Corruption Perceptions Index. The dimensions of malfeasance were suggested in September 2001, when government auditors reported the misuse of approximately $1.1 billion in the previous eighteen months.[85]

82. Kenward, "Survey of Recent Developments," 30.
83. Stephen V. Marks, "Survey of Recent Developments," *Bulletin of Indonesian Economic Studies* 40, no. 2 (2004): 164.
84. Kenward, "Survey of Recent Developments," 30.
85. Siregar, "Survey of Recent Developments," 297.

More important, the changing patterns of corruption and rent distribution had a crucial influence on the economic climate. Under the New Order, corruption and rent seeking were pervasive in scope and astronomical in scale, yet these practices were also regimented by the ruler and core elites. Clientelist relations were managed from the center, and the ruler linked favors and privileges to implicit expectations of performance.[86] In consequence, Soeharto was able to mitigate some of the growth-suppressing effects of corruption. In the posttransition environment, a situation of unregulated corruption and competitive clientelism quickly emerged. Institutional turbulence, a fragmented party system, the entry of new political actors, and the state's discretionary control of vast financial and corporate assets all converged in competitive rivalries over resources. Political factions and business elites contended over the capture of key agencies and policies. The diffuse competition over rents and resources embroiled parliamentarians, party leaders, regulators, senior officials, civil servants, local administrators, the military, and disparate business interests. In the absence of coordination by elements of government or the political parties, these struggles increased uncertainty and dissipated resources. The roiling domain of corruption and clientelism reduced trust and undermined entrepreneurial networks, whether based on ethnicity or political relationships. More generally, the new context of competitive rent distribution suppressed investment and encouraged capital flight. Corruption and rent seeking became a greater hindrance to growth.

In sum, the shifting institutional terrain created pervasive dilemmas of credibility in the wake of the Soeharto dictatorship. At the formal level, these weaknesses played out as problems of design and capacity in peak institutions of economic oversight, an unreliable judiciary, an overextended public administration, and murky corporate governance. At the informal level, the new regime disrupted the clientelist relations that had stabilized economic affairs under authoritarian rule, while political competition and social unrest gave rise to widespread market uncertainty. In the absence of an effective rule of law or commitment mechanisms by government, asset holders responded with risk-averse strategies and avoided investments in fixed assets. The chronic deficiencies of investment prevented Indonesia's recovery to a high-growth trajectory, regardless of macroeconomic stabilization and peripheral reforms.

86. Andrew MacIntyre, "Funny Money: Fiscal Policy, Rent-Seeking, and Economic Performance in Indonesia," in Mushtaq H. Khan and K. S. Jomo, eds., *Rents, Rent-Seeking, and Economic Development: Theory and Evidence in Asia* (Cambridge: Cambridge University Press, 2000): 249, and McLeod, "After Soeharto: Prospects for Reform and Recovery in Indonesia," 4–5.

Discouraging policy performance and political realignment sullied the political prospects for President Megawati Soekarnoputri.[87] In the 2004 elections, new reform parties and a revitalized Golkar appeared as leading challengers to the incumbent and her PDI-P base. The elections yielded a decisive second-round victory for Susilo Bambang Yudhoyono, a former military commander and intermittent minister for security affairs under both Wahid and Megawati. The attraction of voters to Yudhoyono, a military figure with a reform profile, evoked comparisons with earlier experiences in the Philippines, where Corazon Aquino, an incumbent president with strong opposition credentials but a middling record in office, had been replaced by Gen. Fidel Ramos. The voters' flight to authority in the wake of disappointing civilian performance raised questions about the character of leadership under democratic rule, and the requisite conditions for a revitalization of institutions and economic governance.

Coalitions: Managed and Competitive

With the collapse of the New Order, Indonesia has moved rapidly from a system based upon circumscribed elites and managed social coalitions to a system with plural elites and competitive social coalitions.[88] This does not suggest that Indonesia's political process has become broadly inclusive. A narrow stratum of elites, including elements associated with the previous regime, continues to dominate party and governmental affairs. Nonetheless, access to power has become more diverse and less clearly bounded. Popular constituencies have greater space for mobilization and further outlets for political participation. As new interests, factions, and personalities emerge in the embryonic democratic system, the social foundations of the regime are becoming less regimented and more volatile than was the case under authoritarian corporatist rule. Along with greater access, however, the new political landscape is also more fragmented and contentious. A wider array of groups and interests has a place in the political arena, yet pluralism is nested within weak institutions and tenuous alliances. Institutional uncertainty and political insecurity increase polarization among groups, aggravate competitive tensions, and hamper cooperation over key policies and institutional change.

Fragmented political parties and competitive elites constitute a central arena of the new political system. Golkar, the former ruling party, has suf-

---

87. Direct presidential elections were adopted in 2004, after a hiatus of nearly five decades.
88. Marcus Mietzner, "From Soeharto to Habibie," 87, and MacIntyre, *Power of Institutions,* 148.

fered a decline in fortunes but has repositioned itself to pursue competitive electoral politics. The other central poles in the system are the secular nationalists, chiefly the PDI-P and Susilo's new Democratic Party, and the Muslim central axis parties, including PAN, PKB, and more ideological Islamists. In the absence of a dominant party, shifting coalitions of minority parties have formed to compete over institutions, state resources, and political spoils.[89] The fragmentation of the party system has resulted in a factionalized legislature and a cabinet dispersed among party-based political appointments. This fractious structure slowed major legislation and crucial institutional changes—notably in areas of constitutional reform, debt restructuring, and distress resolution in the banking system.

While the political weight of the military has been significantly diminished, the TNI retains a salient position. The armed forces leadership has nominally accepted the need to retreat from the military's "dual role" and to pursue reforms toward professionalization, yet many officers are concerned to protect the corporate position of the military as well as their own economic interests. The territorial organization of the military has remained intact, creating a presence for the armed forces down to the localities. It is estimated that less than a third of the military's expenses are covered by the formal budget, giving rise to a large domain of private enterprises controlled by the territorial commands.[90] These include both legitimate and clearly illicit operations. Further, the security problems and weak governance evident during the first administrations have spurred public sentiments for strong leadership: two of the three leading presidential candidates in 2004 had a military background. The armed forces remain a potential veto player on important policy and institutional reforms.

The shifting social base of the regime, at both elite and mass levels, affects the political space for economic policy. The alliance between state elites and producer groups has largely dissipated in the post-Soeharto era. While the former cronies associated with the New Order have less overt influence, economically powerful elites continue to maneuver for influence over policy and political access, requiring the cultivation of new relationships with politicians, parties, and key state officials. The ethnic Chinese community generally finds itself in a political and economic limbo. The interests of traditional economic insiders are no longer guaranteed with the certainty that obtained under authoritarian rule.

89. See R. William Liddle, "Regime: The New Order," 67–68, and Schwarz, *Nation in Waiting,* chap. 12.

90. John Bresnan, *Managing Indonesia: The Modern Political Economy* (New York: Columbia University Press, 1993), 155; Malley, "Indonesia in 2002," 142.

Another important change in the current political arena is the increased domain for popular sectors (notably urban workers and the Muslim constituency) to press their concerns through open political channels. The growing realm of nongovernmental organizations, popular groupings, and the independent media, broadly encompassed under the rubric of "civil society," is a factor of rising importance. The associations engaged in advocacy and mobilization place new pressures and demands on government, and they have an important influence in shaping the public sphere. Civil society is a major source of pressure for accountability, improved governance, reduced corruption, and a stronger rule of law.

This new configuration presents a central dilemma of coordination. The proliferation of actors and entry points to the political process has produced a fragmentation of interests and a greater array of veto players. Andrew MacIntyre has captured the dynamic well in his discussion of institutional structure and developmental outcomes.[91] The dispersion of groups and influence in the post-Soeharto era fosters extreme dispersion of authority, reflecting a diametric movement away from the extreme concentration of authority under Soeharto. This dispersion has debilitated the political system and hampered institutional change, compounding the dilemmas of reform.

Distribution and Social Conflict

In the context of more open, competitive politics, distributional struggles have intensified among regional, ethnic, religious, and class groupings. The financial crisis aggravated pressures among the downwardly mobile middle classes, workers, and the urban poor, merging with long-standing tensions among the outer islands and numerous communal groups. The new political system allows for a wider arena of mobilization in a setting where alliances and institutions are in flux. The resulting uncertainty has sharpened communal identities, increased militancy among many groups, and frequently aggravated a security dilemma that induces polarization and conflict. The most salient conflicts in the post-Soeharto era flow directly from the nature of the state and the dominant coalition under the New Order. The old regime's collusion with ethnic Chinese entrepreneurs fed pervasive tensions between the indigenous majority and the Sino-Indonesian community, resulting in considerable violence and economic dislocation.

Resource-based conflicts have proliferated in the outer islands, partic-

91. See MacIntyre, *Power of Institutions.*

ularly Aceh and West Papua, where separatist pressures currently drive conflict with the central government.[92] The collapse of the old regime diminished the perceived authority of Jakarta and opened prospects for a renegotiation of the relations between the center and the periphery. This emboldened secessionist forces in resource-rich areas of the archipelago, which have intensified their bid for independence. In an effort to address some of the political sources of conflict, the government has opened the way toward administrative and fiscal decentralization. However, the failure to resolve critical issues regarding financial autonomy and property rights in resource-producing areas, along with the often draconian responses of security forces in seeking to quell resistance, have precluded resolution of these conflicts. Another source of conflict stems from land and migration issues, often an outcome of the *transmigrasi* (resettlement) policies of the New Order in their efforts to reduce population pressures in Java. Religious and ethnic violence in Maluku and West Kalimantan are major instances where demographic change has instigated communal tension.

The extreme fiscal and bureaucratic centralization of previous regimes has been an important structural factor in the multiple conflicts erupting in postreform Indonesia. Habibie spurred decentralization by establishing the legal groundwork for administrative devolution and changes in government financial systems. Since the big bang of 2001, new authorities have struggled with issues of subnational financing, capacity, and institutional design. Decentralization raises concerns that local power centers will emerge to capture resources.[93] Beyond the important questions of capacity and authority, the crucial issue of fiscal structure and local property rights are critical to distributional contention. Dispersion from the center is essential to ameliorating the centrifugal pressures on the state.

Indonesia's Challenge

The New Order dictatorship steered Indonesia away from some of the most common liabilities of rentier states and clientelist politics, and in so doing changed the structure of production and ownership in the economy. Yet Soeharto's neopatrimonial rule undermined the creation of strong for-

92. Michael Ross, "Resources and Rebellion in Aceh, Indonesia," in Paul Collier and Nicholas Sambanis, eds., *Understanding Civil War: Evidence and Analysis,* vol. 2, *Europe, Central Asia, and Other Regions* (Washington, DC: World Bank, 2005).

93. George Fane, "Change and Continuity in Indonesia's New Fiscal Decentralisation Arrangements," *Bulletin of Indonesian Economic Studies* 39, no. 2 (2003): 159–76; Syaikhu Usman, "Indonesia's Decentralization Policy," SMERU Working Paper, September 2001, http://ideas.repec.org/p/eab/govern/123.html.

mal institutions that would outlast his tenure. With the collapse of the old regime, institutional weakness, structural problems of resource dependence, and distributional rivalries have shaped the context of democratic reform. The political system has moved from rigidity, centralization, and hierarchically managed coalitions to fluidity, dispersion, and fragmented coalitions. A history of sound macroeconomic management and integration into global markets furnishes advantages in confronting reform, yet the turbulent political environment and the structure of incentives arising from distributional contention create important obstacles to change.

CHAPTER 8

Predatory Rule, Transition, and Malaise in Nigeria

Nigeria's political and economic conditions in the late 1990s differed substantially from those of Indonesia. In marked contrast to Indonesia's decades of growth and economic diversification, Nigeria developed an oil monoculture in which virtually all foreign exchange, and the preponderance of government revenues, were derived from crude oil exports.[1] In consequence, the political economy was overwhelmingly concentrated on the distribution of rents from the central state. Debt pressures and plummeting oil prices induced military rulers to experiment with structural reforms in the late 1980s, though General Ibrahim Babangida pursued erratic policies, and his adjustment program collapsed after 1990. General Sani Abacha, drawing upon the practices of his predecessor, created a predatory regime based upon the personal accumulation of power, wholesale plunder of public revenues, and monopolization of outlets for seizing rents.

General Abacha's surprising death in June 1998 capped nearly a decade of declining governance and economic performance. Under the rule of Babangida and Abacha, power was increasingly concentrated by the head of state and a small inner circle, in contrast to more collegial governing structures under preceding military regimes. The personalization of authority fostered a degeneration of institutions. Although the Nigerian state had long-standing institutional deficits, the 1990s saw a period of accelerated decline in structures of rule and the provision of public goods.[2] These rulers purposely weakened central state institutions including the peak agencies of economic management, crucial regulatory agencies, the judiciary, the civil service, local governments, and the military itself. Fiscal

---

1. Michael Watts, "Agriculture and Oil-Based Accumulation: Stagnation or Transfomation?" in Michael Watts, ed., *State, Oil, and Agriculture in Nigeria* (Berkeley: Institute of International Studies, 1987), 64–66; Peter Lewis, "Economic Statism, Private Capital, and the Dilemmas of Accumulation in Nigeria," *World Development* 22, no. 3 (1994): 443.

2. Eghosa E. Osaghae, *Crippled Giant: Nigeria since Independence* (Bloomington: Indiana University Press, 1998), 312.

shortfalls and calculated neglect led to a deterioration of education and health services, along with key elements of infrastructure including electricity, telecommunications, and domestic fuel supply. While promising democratic reform, both leaders prolonged their transition schedules and methodically undermined the institutions of civilian rule including elections, political parties, and constitutional provisions. The state was hollowed out by the lack of resources and the accumulation of personal power by autocratic rulers.[3]

Economic governance steadily deteriorated during this period.[4] Babangida's early focus on arresting the decline of the economy fostered cooperation with the multilateral financial institutions, which encouraged efforts toward orthodox economic reform.[5] After a few years of tentative stabilization, however, fiscal and monetary management became increasingly capricious, and the policy regime broke down. Institutional reforms including privatization and banking liberalization were politicized and captured by clientelist pressures.[6] Babangida did not install a capable economic team, and he weakened the Ministry of Finance and the Central Bank. He intensified the plunder of the treasury, shifting huge categories of expenditure off-budget and diverting resources to service his core support network. Abacha exacerbated these problems. His economic policies veered between populist programs and a cautious return to some elements of stabilization. Off-budget spending and outright embezzlement reached unprecedented proportions, siphoning as much as a fifth of oil revenues to the regime's discretionary purposes in some years.[7] Policy inconsistency, stupendous corruption, and collapsing institutions virtually choked off nonoil investment and rendered Nigeria a pariah in most global markets.

The resulting economic stagnation affected patronage structures and rent distribution. As economic prospects diminished in the real economy, there was an increasing premium on rent-based income arising from government contracts, licenses, arbitrage on controlled prices, and other politically regulated gains.[8] Babangida sought a fairly broad distribution of

3. William Reno, *Warlord Politics and African States* (Boulder: Lynne Rienner, 1999).

4. Peter Lewis, "From Prebendalism to Predation: The Political Economy of Decline in Nigeria," *Journal of Modern African Studies* 34, no. 1 (1996): 91–94.

5. Thomas Callaghy, "Lost between State and Market: The Politics of Economic Adjustment in Ghana, Zambia, and Nigeria," in Joan Nelson, ed., *Economic Crisis and Policy Choice* (Princeton: Princeton University Press, 1990), 305–7.

6. Peter Lewis and Howard Stein, "Shifting Fortunes: The Political Economy of Financial Liberalization in Nigeria," *World Development* 25, no. 1 (1997): 5–22.

7. Tom Forrest, *Politics and Economic Development in Nigeria,* 2d ed. (Boulder: Westview, 1995), 246–47.

8. Lewis, "Economic Statism," 444–45.

rents to build his support coalition and maintain stability. Abacha, however, confined the scope of patronage and sought to monopolize a large domain of rent distribution. In addition to increasing state repression, Abacha was concerned to limit autonomous economic power among groups opposed to his regime, notably the Yorubas who dominated the banking industry.[9] The malfeasance of the center led to a rapid deterioration of essential public goods. By the mid-1990s the regime siphoned funds needed to sustain petroleum production activities, causing the country's refining and fuel distribution systems to collapse. The ruler and a handful of cronies reaped windfall rents through "emergency" importation and distribution of fuel. Abacha further appropriated the returns on major government projects and directly embezzled a substantial portion of the oil income (estimates run as high as $6 billion over a four-year period) while also denying rents to elites outside the ruling circle.[10]

Distributional tensions intensified throughout this period. Both military regimes were dominated by northern Muslims (as was the preceding regime of General Buhari), which alienated southern groups including the Yoruba, the Igbo, the minorities of the Middle Belt, and the Niger Delta, who felt excluded from political influence and patronage. The annulment of the 1993 elections, in which a Yoruba was the putative winner, aggravated these resentments.[11] Moreover, the concentration of authority and discretionary control over resources accentuated the stresses in Nigeria's federal system. Most groups complained that the formal provisions of federalism were ignored or undermined by authorities in the center. The dearth of revenues apart from oil rents meant that states and local governments were entirely dependent upon Abuja for the distribution of largesse.[12] Many communities, notably those of the Niger Delta, believed that income distribution was highly skewed to their disadvantage. The opaque financial administration of these regimes aggravated suspicions that central authorities were commandeering resources that should legally be allocated to subnational governments and southern regions. These dis-

---

9. Reno, *Warlord Politics,* 202–4.

10. "As U.S. Probes $6 Billion Loot," *P. M. News* (Lagos), November 8, 1999.

11. Bola A. Akinterinwa, "The 1993 Presidential Election Imbroglio," in Larry Diamond, Anthony Kirk-Greene, and Oyeleye Oyediran, eds., *Transition without End: Nigerian Politics and Civil Society under Babangida* (Boulder: Lynne Rienner, 1997), 275–76.

12. See, for instance, O. B. C. Nwolise, "How the Military Ruined Nigeria's Federalism," in Ebere Onwudiwe and Rotimi Suberu, eds., *Nigerian Federalism in Crisis* (Ibadan: Programme on Ethnic and Federal Studies, 2005), 120; and Cyril I. Obi, "The Impact of Oil on Nigeria's Revenue Allocation System: Problems and Prospects for National Reconstruction," in Kunle Amuwo, Adigun Agbaje, Rotimi Suberu, and Georges Herault, eds., *Federalism and Political Restructuring in Nigeria* (Ibadan: Spectrum Books and IFRA, 1998), 268.

tributional concerns were naturally exacerbated by the course of economic stagnation and widening poverty. Military rulers periodically created new states and local governments as a means of symbolically addressing distributional pressures—a practice that also had the convenient liability of slowing the schedule of political reform.[13] The contentious boundaries of the new administrative units gave rise to additional polarization and conflict, especially in the oil-producing Niger Delta.

The Collapse of Predatory Rule

General Abacha's autocracy proved to be unsustainable. His support base shrank to a small circle of security personnel, advisers, and business fixers, and his government was increasingly isolated by international sanctions. He polarized and alienated much of the armed forces and grew estranged from the northern elites who would normally furnish his reservoir of support. Southern ethnic groups bitterly opposed his regime, while much of the business class was aggrieved by the depths of mismanagement and the global marginality of the economy. Abacha's descent into personal predatory rule was untenable amid Nigeria's plural elites, widespread clientelist networks, distributional pressures, and powerful demands for patronage. The general sought to consolidate political control by preparing a stage-managed political transition that would afford him a veneer of civilian legitimacy. While vigorously suppressing dissent, he laid groundwork for the creation of a civilian facade for his regime. This included a supervised exercise of constitutional reform, the certification of several officially screened political parties, and restricted elections for the legislature and local government, which served as prelude to an intended presidential poll in 1998. As the election approached, the five legal political parties announced their selection of General Abacha as the sole presidential nominee "by acclamation," relegating the election to a mere formality.[14]

The general's plans for a "self-succession" in civilian garb spurred widespread apprehension that Nigeria was careening toward civil conflict and political collapse.[15] The political machinations ended abruptly when Abacha died (officially of a heart attack) in June 1998. The ruler's sudden demise at this moment of impending crisis was believed by many to be the

13. Dan Agbese and Etim Anim, "The State Elections of 1991," in *Transition without End,* ed. Diamond et al., 222–23.

14. Peter Lewis, Barnett Rubin, and Pearl T. Robinson, *Stabilizing Nigeria: Sanctions, Incentives, and Support for Civil Society* (New York: Council on Foreign Relations and Century Foundation, 1998).

15. Lewis, Rubin, and Robinson, *Stabilizing Nigeria,* 4–7.

work of conspirators within the military establishment.[16] Regardless of the cause of his death, reform elements within the Supreme Military Council (the central ruling committee) seized the opportunity to appoint Abdul-salami Abubakar, the Chief of Defense Staff, to replace Abacha. Abubakar had a reputation as a quiet, nonpolitical officer, who was well positioned to oversee the political extrication of the military. Within days of taking office, he opened the political arena by releasing several high-profile detainees and relaxing restrictions on the media and civic organizations. Abubakar entered into dialogue with political elites and activists, and sought to normalize ties with the United States, Great Britain, and the Commonwealth. There were also broad hints about the imminent release of Chief Abiola, who had been interned for several years. Despite these initial signals, many Nigerians were skeptical of the military's intentions, and critics cautioned against another prolonged transition that would serve as window dressing for further predation. Popular suspicions deepened when Chief Abiola died in custody during a meeting with visiting U.S. diplomats, only a month after Abacha's death.

General Abubakar and the ruling military council soon jettisoned Abacha's transition program, scrapped the official political parties, and annulled the previously engineered elections. Many senior officers accepted the need for reform, having wearied of the factionalism and politicization within the armed forces. Their tentative consensus on the need to withdraw from politics, however, was offset by concerns to protect their organizational and economic interests. In the absence of strong political parties or civic opposition, incumbent elites could largely control the reform process. Abubakar's regime dictated the timing, pace, and content of the democratization program. Indeed, the prospect of political transition encouraged many officers to decamp to the civilian political class, where they formed an influential component of the leading parties. The regime's transition agenda called for a process of party registration, elections, and constitutional revision prior to the inauguration of the new civilian regime in May 1999. As the transition moved forward, the regime also furnished copious rents and sidepayments, as the officer class anticipated the loss of power and senior leaders sought to avoid restiveness within the military. Senior officers secured oil production blocks worth tens of millions of dollars, valuable land parcels, public properties, and other benefits.[17] In the months leading to the handover of power, the

16. Tim Weiner, "U.S. Aides Say Nigeria Leader Might Have Been Poisoned," *New York Times,* July 10, 1998, section A, 4.

17. "Generals in Jitters," *Tempo* (Lagos), June 19, 1999.

regime rapidly depleted the country's foreign reserves, which plummeted from $7.1 billion to an estimated $4 billion in the first quarter of 1999, despite modestly increasing revenues. At the same time, leaders sought to stabilize the economy during the brief transition period. Economic management, however, essentially reflected a holding operation rather than initiative toward reform.

Democratic Beginnings, Military Legacies

When political party activity was revived in 1998, three associations were certified under the official provisions requiring parties to demonstrate broad geographic support. The largest of these, the People's Democratic Party (PDP), was a multiethnic collection of veteran politicians joined by an influx of political newcomers, including a cohort of retired military officers. Many of the party's founders were associated with the so-called Group of 34, a cluster of civilian notables who had dissented in the final stages of Abacha's fraudulent transition.[18] The PDP's leading elements had prominent roles under the abortive Babangida transition and the earlier Second Republic. The party chose as its presidential candidate Olusegun Obasanjo, the former military ruler who had relinquished power to civilians two decades earlier. Approaching the elections with strong electoral machinery and considerable resources, the PDP quickly established dominance over its contenders. The All People's Party (APP) was not substantially different in its elite origins or social composition, but the party had inroads in many areas of the far north and included a number of prominent politicians and notables closely associated with Abacha's transition effort. The Alliance for Democracy (AD), on the other hand, was chiefly composed of politicians and activists who had supported Chief M. K. O. Abiola, including many leaders of the antimilitary opposition during the Abacha years. The AD had a strong sectional base in the southwestern Yoruba states, though relatively thin support elsewhere. Nonetheless, electoral authorities certified the party in an effort to avoid marginalizing the politically strategic southwestern region.[19] The disparate origins of the APP and the AD did not prevent the two parties from entering into an electoral coalition behind AD candidate Olu Falae, a former finance minister.

18. Adewale Maja-Pearce, *From Khaki to Agbada* (Lagos: Civil Liberties Organization, 1999), 79.

19. The elements of the transition are discussed by Peter Lewis, "An End to the Permanent Transition?" in Larry Diamond and Marc Plattner, eds., *Democratization in Africa* (Baltimore: Johns Hopkins University Press, 1999).

Abubakar's regime prepared a hasty schedule of political party certification, voter registration, campaigns, and sequential elections for local, state, and national offices. With a little over five months to prepare for elections, the Independent National Electoral Commission (INEC) was considerably overextended. The elections themselves were marred by general administrative confusion and substantial evidence of fraud.[20] International and domestic observers raised significant questions about the integrity of the polls in several regions, though these flaws were generally tolerated by much of the Nigerian public, who sought a rapid end to military rule. The PDP's Olusegun Obasanjo won the presidency with a substantial electoral margin over Falae, and the PDP captured solid majorities in the legislature and state governments.

In the interregnum between February elections and the May 29 transfer of power, the military regime convened a committee to review the transitional constitution, the contents of which were largely unknown to Nigerians. After the constitutional conference sponsored by Abacha had issued its recommendations in 1995, the regime had shrouded the draft in secrecy as rumors circulated about ad hoc changes inserted by the dictator. Following the 1999 elections, details of the constitution filtered out in piecemeal fashion, but politicians and government officials were largely ignorant of the central institutions and laws that would govern the new civilian republic. Abubakar promulgated the constitution just one week before the inauguration of the elected government. This authoritarian legacy of constitutional change provided the new regime with tenuous foundations, as the civilian politicians were unfamiliar with the basic mechanisms of government and ambivalent about the legitimacy of their fundamental charter.[21]

Obasanjo's electoral victory evoked mixed reactions. Critics of military rule regarded him as a member of the traditional elite whose candidacy was accepted, if not engineered, by the military establishment and allied ruling segments. From this perspective, little positive change could be expected from the new regime. Although Obasanjo is Yoruba, many among his own ethnic community initially regarded him as a factotum of the northern interests who purportedly dominated the armed forces and the majority party. Supporters, on the other hand, noted the retired general's long career as a public citizen, including his advocacy of better gov-

---

20. See *Observing the 1998–99 Nigeria Elections: Final Report* (Atlanta and Washington, DC: Carter Center and the National Democratic Institute, 1999), 29–30.

21. See, for instance, Otive Igbuzor, *A Critique of the 1999 Constitution Making and Review Process in Nigeria,* CFCR Monograph Series No 1. (Abuja: Citizens' Forum for Constitutional Reform, 2002).

ernance in Africa, and his support for anticorruption efforts through the international nongovernmental group Transparency International. As one of the most prominent political detainees held by General Abacha, Obasanjo had legitimate democratic credentials among foreign observers who had worked with him in government and civic life.

The Politics of Attempted Reform

President Obasanjo signaled intentions for reform in the early months of the civilian regime. The new president expressed a need for change and took measures to assert his political independence, which mitigated concerns that he was simply a creature of the armed forces or political bosses. He soon won the allegiance of the Yoruba constituency that had been skeptical toward his candidacy under the PDP. Among his earliest initiatives, Obasanjo purged the military of more than ninety "political" officers who had been associated with previous coups and military regimes, and showed resolve in seeking to consolidate civilian authority over the armed forces.[22] Efforts to professionalize the military were bolstered by external assistance in training and the revision of institutional doctrine.

On the economic front, the president acknowledged the economic shambles inherited from preceding military regimes, noting the degeneration of infrastructure, the corrosive effects of endemic corruption, and the oppressive toll of widespread poverty. The new administration promised economic revitalization and needed improvements in governance. Targeting corruption as a leading source of poor economic performance, the president unveiled policies to address this chronic blight. Most of the oil production blocks and land grants handed around in the final months of Abubakar's regime were rescinded. The government suspended major government contracts, initiated a review of contracting procedures, and promised a comprehensive overhaul of procurement practices. The presidency forwarded a draft anticorruption law to the National Assembly, which among other measures called for the establishment of an independent anticorruption commission.[23] In addition, the government pledged to

22. Remi Oyo, "President Obasanjo Cleans Up the Military," Inter-Press Service, June 13, 1999. See also Bronwen Manby, "Principal Human Rights Challenges," in Robert Rotberg, ed., *Crafting the New Nigeria: Confronting the Challenges* (Boulder: Lynne Rienner, 2004), 185.

23. Norimitsu Onishi, "Nigeria Leader Amazes Many with Strong Anti-Graft Drive," *New York Times,* November 23, 1999, section A, 1. See also Emmanuel O. Ojo, "The Military and Political Transition," in Adigun Agbaje, Larry Diamond, and Ebere Onwudiwe, eds., *Nigeria's Struggle for Democracy and Good Governance* (Ibadan: Ibadan University Press, 2004), 78.

follow sound macroeconomic policies and took steps to reopen discussions with the multilateral financial institutions, which had largely fallen dormant during Abacha's rule. Leaders publicly called for a major reduction in the country's oppressive foreign debt, estimated at $30 billion. Many Nigerians anticipated that favorable international reactions to the new regime would produce a dramatic "democracy dividend" in the form of foreign investment, trade, and possible cancellation of external debt by major donors.

The incoming leadership also sought to address some of the nation's pressing distributional conflicts. The new constitution provided for a substantial increase (from 3 to 13 percent) in the proportion of oil revenues accruing to the states of the Niger Delta.[24] Further, a new publicly administered Niger Delta Development Commission (NDDC) was inaugurated to furnish resources and programs for the acute developmental needs of the southern oil-producing communities. Replacing earlier agencies for the Niger Delta that had been plagued by corruption and inefficiency, the government pledged that the NDDC would operate with transparency and accountability. In addition to the contention in the Niger Delta, other regional partisans voiced dissent over provisions of the 1999 constitution, particularly in the areas of revenue allocation and administrative devolution. Critics demanded the implementation of "true federalism" to reduce the dominance of the center and allow for greater political and fiscal autonomy among states and localities.[25]

Although the first months of Obasanjo's civilian administration promised change, enthusiasm soon dissipated along with the momentum for reform. Political lassitude stalled major initiatives as the government proved increasingly ineffective in addressing such pressing issues as the economy, rising communal conflict, and constitutional reform. There were numerous obstacles to change. President Obasanjo was unable to assert a clear agenda or to gather a durable coalition behind his leadership. The president, along with his finance minister, Adamu Ciroma, represented an earlier generation of leaders who had presided over the state expansion of the oil boom. There were no prominent reformers among the economic team and little constituency for economic liberalization within the government. Although the new leaders worked pragmatically with the multilateral financial institutions, they were clearly ambivalent about orthodox

24. V. Adefemi Isumonah, "Southern Minorities, Hegemonic Politics, and Revenue Allocation in Nigeria," in Onwudiwe and Suberu, *Nigerian Federalism in Crisis,* 173.

25. Kola Olufemi, "The Quest for 'True Federalism' and Political Restructuring: Issues, Prospects, and Constraints," in Onwudiwe and Suberu, *Nigerian Federalism in Crisis.*

economic policies and provided little impetus toward a program of economic restructuring.

Personality also played a role. The president was viewed by many as arrogant and distracted, which hampered his ability to communicate with political opponents (or even many ostensible allies) and rendered him distant from the public. He was not averse to heavy-handed tactics that skirted the boundaries of ethics and law, leading to accusations that he harbored authoritarian approaches to rule, regardless of his electoral imprimatur. Having been recruited by a coterie of party elites, the president initially lacked an independent support base or strong footing within his own party.[26] His cabinet and staff presented a motley assemblage of political operatives, veteran politicians, arrivistes, and younger technocrats, most with their own agendas. Overall, much of the executive branch reflected the maneuvering and factionalism of the PDP as a party, which blunted the effectiveness of senior leadership.

The worsening impasse between the presidency and the new legislature created a central source of inertia. The national assembly, emerging from a weak party system and fluid patronage networks, proved more independent and contentious than previous cohorts in Nigeria. Unconstrained by organizational discipline, legislators pressed the limits of their power and prerogatives, seeking control over fiscal affairs and legislative agendas as well as their own rules and perquisites.[27] The legislature was wracked by political divisions and scandals, which led to the ouster of the first speaker of the House and two Senate presidents. Though Obasanjo sought to exploit these weaknesses to press his own agenda, legislators vigorously resisted executive pressure or legislation by fiat. Contention between the legislature and the executive hampered progress on essential public issues, notably passage of the budget, the anticorruption bill, electoral legislation, privatization measures, and laws affecting the Niger Delta. The rancor in the assembly became so widespread that Obasanjo eventually faced an unsuccessful campaign for impeachment, launched by a caucus from his own party. After gaining concessions in private negotiations with the president, his opponents relented a few months before the second elections.

The executive also confronted a great deal of turbulence and opposi-

---

26. See, for instance, "Obasanjo as a Politician," *This Day* (Lagos), October 28, 2001; and "PDP: A House Divided Against Itself," *This Day* (Lagos), March 22, 2002.

27. Sufuyan Ojeifo, "Clerk Indicts Senate on N650m Contracts," *Vanguard* (Lagos), July 25, 2000.

tion among the states. In sharp contrast to the centralized control of state administrators under military regimes, the new civilian governors were fractious and independent.[28] Several governors emerged as local strongmen by gaining influence over vigilante groups, electoral machines, patronage networks, or party factions within their states. A number of state leaders openly challenged the power and legal authority of the central government. In the Muslim-majority northern states, a dozen governors (many from the opposition All People's Party) introduced comprehensive codes of Shari'a law that extended to the criminal sphere and largely displaced the authority of civil law. Several northern governors enforced the new measures through the formation of *hisbah* (religious vigilantes) answerable to the state house. Governors in the Niger Delta, while agitating for a greater share of central revenues, bolstered their local power by allying with ethnic militias and seeking to build independent patronage networks. Some of these leaders became embroiled in local communal conflicts, and more than one was linked in the media to oil smuggling and arms trafficking. Obasanjo also had protracted feuds with governors in the east and the middle belt, as well as public tensions with the Lagos State governor from the opposition Alliance for Democracy. Several areas, including Delta, Rivers, Anambra, and Plateau, descended into lawlessness, prompting direct intervention from federal authorities.

Division within the government was accompanied by resurgent pressures from civil society. Political liberalization reopened the arena of popular mobilization and activism. The trade union movement, invigorated by increased autonomy and independent leadership under democratic rule, contended with the government over key economic issues, especially the question of oil subsidies and fuel pricing. The administration's deliberations over fuel price reform met with a string of general strikes and protests, hampering the reduction of subsidies urged by donors. The proliferation of ethnic associations and vigilante groups aggravated communal tensions and pressed the government to address distributional concerns. The northern movement for the expansion of Shari'a law increased the political salience of Islamist organizations and regional advocacy groups while raising further issues of constitutional design and communal power-sharing. Interest associations and advocates of civic reform called for government attention to problems of education, health, gender equity, corruption, law and order, and legal reform. The organized private sector was also vocal though not unified in its aims. Some business groups advo-

---

28. Olu Ojewale, "Battle of the Elephants," *Newswatch* (Lagos), March 5, 2001.

cated broad liberalization and institutional reform, while others lobbied for special protection and the preservation of government support.[29]

Macroeconomic Management: Policy Adrift

The administration's pronouncements on economic reform soon descended into a political quagmire. The executive failed to articulate an economic program in the first term and addressed economic affairs in piecemeal fashion. There was slow and uneven movement across the domains of economic management. The government showed weak fiscal oversight and little initiative for institutional change. Economic priorities outlined in official statements were largely disregarded, and the budget was shaped by factional bargaining and patronage pressures. A prominent example was the new national soccer stadium in Abuja, initially estimated at $450 million, an amount greater than the annual budget provisions for health and education.[30] The government also retained a number of moribund capital projects while failing to revive critical infrastructure including the oil refineries and the decrepit electricity network. While civilians avoided the large off-budget outlays favored by previous military rulers, the new leaders did not make visible improvements in the transparency of financial flows. Federal allocations were not clearly specified or tracked, and fiscal affairs within the states were largely opaque. Further, the executive and the legislature were at loggerheads over outlays and the distribution of patronage, which repeatedly blocked passage of the annual budget, normally the guiding framework for near-term economic policies. In the absence of an approved budget, fiscal operations and programs were adrift.[31]

The absence of fiscal control hampered negotiations with donors and creditors. The new government quickly entered into policy dialogue with the World Bank and resumed borrowing after a hiatus of several years. They also began extended discussions with the IMF, resulting in a Letter of Intent in August 2000, the first accord with the Fund in nearly a

29. Jon Kraus, "Capital, Power, and Business Associations in the African Political Economy: A Tale of Two Countries, Ghana and Nigeria," *Journal of Modern African Studies* 40, no. 3 (2002): 395–436; and the Nigerian Economic Summit Group, *Economic Action Agenda 2002* (Lagos: Nigerian Economic Summit Group, 2002).

30. Patrick Andrew, "World Bank Flays Cost of Abuja Stadium," *Daily Trust* (Abuja), December 13, 2001.

31. See, for instance, Maureen Chigbo, "Obasanjo: Democracy Sans Dividend," *Newswatch* (Lagos), January 8, 2001; and Chijuma Ogbu, "Dangers of Another Delayed Budget," *Post Express* (Lagos), November 6, 2000.

decade.[32] The new IMF agreement provided for standard improvements in macroeconomic policy as well as progress on privatization, the liberalization of key economic activities, and institutional reform. Bowing to domestic political sensitivities, the government was circumspect about the IMF accord and refused to borrow the standby funds available through the program. More important, however, the agreement opened the door to discussions with the Paris Club on debt restructuring and possible cancellation, which formed a central goal of the new leadership. Improved relations with the multilateral financial institutions eased interactions with the bilateral donors, which thawed after the chill of the Abacha years.

Fiscal indiscipline was a central obstacle to economic restructuring. Government outlays were inflated by a variety of projects and political sidepayments. The legislature was a further source of expansionary pressures, as lawmakers sought to increase spending in their constituencies along with their own institutional perquisites. The executive and the ruling party had another set of fiscal prerogatives, while the peak institutions of economic management—the Central Bank and the Finance Ministry—exercised little discipline over allotments or spending. In consequence, the government repeatedly missed key fiscal targets and other macroeconomic goals, and the Fund soon deemed Nigeria to be out of compliance with the Letter of Intent. The accord lapsed quietly in 2002, and Fund officials came to an understanding with senior Nigerian leaders to suspend discussions until after the 2003 elections.[33] A new accord was politically impossible during the campaign season, and the political business cycle made a stabilization program unworkable. The attempts at rapprochement with the Bretton Woods institutions did little to enhance the country's dismal international credibility.

Privatization and Liberalization: Contested Terrain

A number of areas were critical to economic revival and restructuring. Major infrastructure including fuel supply, transportation, power, and communications operated at levels far below national demand, and some were in a virtual state of collapse. Moreover, nonoil production showed meager levels of investment and productivity, broadly hampering economic expansion. The banking and financial services industries were in

---

32. "Nigeria Letter of Intent and Memorandum on Economic and Financial Policies of the Federal Government for 2000" (Washington, DC: International Monetary Fund, July 20, 2000), http://www.imf.org/external/np/loi/2000/nga/01/index.htm.

33. The strains are reflected in the statement by the Fund's Gary Moser, "The IMF and Nigeria, an Enduring Relationship," *This Day* (Lagos), April 15, 2002.

turmoil, largely a result of the inconclusive shakeout in the wake of a banking crisis in the mid-1990s.[34] A further rationalization of vulnerable banks in the early months of the civilian regime failed to restore solvency and confidence, leaving authorities to continue rearguard efforts to discipline errant financial institutions. Chronic instability in the financial sector was aggravated by macroeconomic volatility, pervasive corruption, fraud, and money laundering. Much of the banking industry retreated to foreign exchange dealings and other fee-based services, which did little to expand credit or to deepen financial markets.

The central policy responses involved a combination of privatization, selective liberalization, and regulatory change. By the end of the oil boom in the early 1980s, Nigeria had the largest state sector in sub-Saharan Africa. Hundreds of public enterprises performed poorly and generated high costs. General Babangida outlined an extensive privatization agenda under the auspices of the Structural Adjustment Program, as noted in chapter 5. The government created an agency for privatization and state enterprise reform, and officials claimed that some eighty-eight enterprises were eventually divested under Phase I of the reform program. This considerably overstated the actual transfer of assets. Many of the nominal divestitures were simply liquidated with no accounting; others were divested to investment funds owned by state governments; and a few of the enterprises were discovered, upon examination, not to exist at all.[35] A number of firms released a proportion of equity without relinquishing controlling interest or managerial authority to private owners. Most significantly, the initial privatization exercise did not affect any of the leading state investments in energy, infrastructure, or large-scale manufacturing, which comprised the bulk of the government's portfolio. The first round of divestiture reshuffled the margins of the public sector. Moreover, there was limited transparency in the process, and considerable opportunity for collusion and insider gains.[36]

Privatization efforts largely fell dormant in the 1990s apart from a handful of government-owned banks and insurance companies. Abacha's finance minister briefly floated the possibility of divesting downstream petroleum operations (notably refineries), and perhaps even upstream assets, though the offer was generally dismissed as an effort to placate the international community. Though the military regime did not act on its

34. Lewis and Stein, "Shifting Fortunes."

35. Peter M. Lewis, "The Political Economy of Public Enterprises in Nigeria," PhD dissertation, Princeton University, 1992.

36. Thomas Biersteker and Peter Lewis, "The Rise and Fall of Structural Adjustment in Nigeria," in Diamond et al., *Transition without End,* 324.

pronouncements, officials broadened the policy discussion to include all major assets under government ownership. The Obasanjo administration took steps toward a second round of privatization and state sector reform. Early in the civilian regime, Vice President Atiku Abubaker was appointed as chair of a new policy group, the National Council on Privatization, which included participants from government, the private sector, and organized labor. The Bureau for Public Enterprise (BPE), the administrative body of the council, was reinvigorated with a broad mandate to carry out divestiture and enterprise reform. The BPE prepared initiatives for the privatization of most of the core public ventures including refineries, gas, petrochemicals, power, telecommunications, ports, airways, railways, banking, hotels, steel, fertilizer, pulp and paper, and other manufacturing activities.[37]

Divestiture nonetheless proceeded slowly because of technical and political obstacles. State enterprises were highly leveraged, garnered low returns, and typically lacked valid records of their assets or accounts. The BPE, seeking to place many of the larger offers with external buyers, faced enormous difficulties in assessing and documenting assets with sufficient transparency to succeed in international markets. The country's poor reputation limited investor response. Deficiencies of information in equities markets and the corporate and banking sectors aggravated these problems. Further, there was considerable political resistance to the privatization process. Enterprise managers and supervising ministries often responded to privatization initiatives with passive noncompliance and sometimes direct obstruction. Organized labor formed another major base of opposition. Trade unions sought to maintain public sector employment and defended an active state role in the economy.[38] The stance of the unions resonated with a broader nationalist constituency that resisted the idea of privatization, especially to foreign owners. Segments of the political class, the business community, and much of the general public were highly skeptical about selling off the state sector. The National Assembly was an important source of resistance as well. Some politicians sought accountability and pressed leaders to ensure a transparent process of implementation. A more significant source of opposition, however, came from elites who attempted to capture rents from the divestiture program,

37. The activities of the Bureau for Public Enterprise are detailed on BPE's website: http://www.bpeng.org/10/0317731656532b.asp?DocID=295&MenuID=5.
38. Chris Nwachuku, "Why Workers Are Unhappy with Obasanjo's Economic Policies," *This Day* (Lagos), May 5, 2005.

or feared that rival groups would monopolize the proceeds. Political actors endeavored to block privatization as a bargaining tactic in resource competition.

The telecommunications sector provided a notable success in privatization and regulatory change. Abacha delayed reforms in this area, which forestalled citizens' access to wireless communications, the Internet, and independent media. The Obasanjo government revived the Nigerian Communications Commission as a regulatory body and commenced a lucrative auction of licenses for wireless telecommunications. With the opening of private markets for telecommunications, the country experienced a dizzying expansion of cellular services. The government carrier, NITEL, managed only 400,000 land lines in the entire country by 1999. Yet the cellular industry registered some ten million subscribers by 2004, after just four years of operation.[39] In addition, Internet access was opened to most of the country via satellite networks, and the government accelerated the approval of licenses for electronic media, leading to a proliferation of private FM radio and television stations. The key to success in reforming communications was for government to avoid direct confrontation with state enterprises, relying instead on the liberalization of markets to foster a parallel growth of private providers, who quickly eclipsed the government services. The opportunity for monopoly rents in the new private markets furnished additional resources for political disbursal.

The distinctive reforms in the communications sector highlighted not only the potential benefits of economic restructuring but also the continuing impediments to change in other critical areas of the economy. The electricity grid and the fuel system, both of which depended on badly decayed infrastructure, could not be renovated by circumventing older systems with new technology. These sectors did not promise the rapid, high returns of cellular services or broadcasting. Government-managed price controls on fuel and electricity deterred the entry of private investors. Prospective buyers were also put off by the uncertainties of cost recovery, especially in the power sector. Privatization proved infeasible in these areas without an overhaul of regulatory policies and procedures, as well as abolishing the monopolistic structure of markets. The bureaucratic constraints on state sector reform, along with the obstacles posed by rivalries over state capture, prevented critical restructuring that would facilitate economic growth.

39. Cletus Akwaya, "Nigeria's Telephone Lines Now 10 Million," *This Day* (Lagos), January 25, 2005.

Distribution and Violence

The desultory results of privatization and financial restructuring underscored a failure to revitalize the real sectors of the economy, which were
essential to economic diversification and employment generation. Politics
and economic competition were overwhelmingly oriented to the capture
and distribution of state-mediated rents. In the arena of democratic institutions and plural politics, communal rivalries escalated and became
increasingly destructive.[40] While none of the leading political parties was
dominated by a single ethnic group, in the early years of the new regime
constituencies gravitated toward particular parties and elite factions. Having garnered acceptance from much of the Yoruba community,
Obasanjo's presidency brought southwestern voters and elites to the ruling
PDP, largely dissipating the political strength of the Yoruba-dominated
Alliance for Democracy. The movement for the expansion of Shari'a law
was led by northern governors aligned with the All People's Party, which
accentuated political allegiances for that party among Muslims in the
"core" north. Igbo elites also became more assertive, leading to dissension
within the dominant PDP and a tentative set of alliances with elements of
both the ruling party and the APP. Rather than producing a clear shift in
political cleavages, however, these maneuvers embodied rivalries over
rents and state resources in a fluid terrain of competitive politics.

Contentious politics among elites were accompanied by more intensive identity-based mobilization at the popular level.[41] Ethnic unions and
vigilante organizations proliferated in the major cities, along with comparable groups organized along religious lines. The sources of contention
varied, from the application of Shari'a law in the northern states, to
resource control in the Niger Delta, to community security in cities such as
Lagos or Onitsha. In rural areas and several urban settings, self-identified
"indigenes" or natives mobilized against nominal "settlers" in matters of
land rights, political boundaries, and representation.

Communal mobilization frequently incited a security dilemma in
which rival groups entered a cycle of competitive organization and mutual
suspicion, frequently culminating in conflict. Politicians often encouraged
communal organizations and allied with these groups in order to generate
support or to intimidate opponents. The accentuation of ethnic and reli-

---

40. Ukoha Ukiwo, "Politics, Ethno-Religious Conflicts, and Democratic Consolidation in
Nigeria," *Journal of Modern African Studies* 41, no. 1 (2003): 115–38.

41. A good overview and analysis of communal mobilization is found in Tunde Babawale,
ed., *Urban Violence, Ethnic Militias, and the Challenges of Democratic Consolidation in Nigeria* (Lagos: Malthouse Press, 2003).

gious politics turned lethal soon into the new regime, leading to a proliferation of violence. In more than three hundred incidents throughout the
country, at least ten thousand deaths were recorded in the first four years
of civil rule, with informal estimates running higher. There was no overriding trigger or fault line in the tide of conflict, which encompassed ethnic, religious, community, and partisan divisions, as well as ubiquitous
criminal violence.[42] The government was ill-prepared to manage the turmoil and often worsened the situation through draconian action by security forces in such areas as the Niger Delta and the middle-belt states of
Benue and Plateau. By reducing the security of persons and property, pervasive instability further dampened economic activity and the propensity
for investment, especially in the leading urban centers. Economic malaise
and distributional tensions fed a pernicious cycle.

Credibility, Investment, and Performance

The change of government did little to improve the country's economic
performance. Notwithstanding Obasanjo's frequent overseas travels to
promote the country's prospects, the inveterate lack of government credibility was decisive in shaping behavior among foreign investors. Domestic
asset-holders faced tattered infrastructure, a dearth of credit, chronic
uncertainty of property rights, and few assurances for contracts.[43] In the
absence of a coherent economic program or significant institutional
change, investors found little reason to engage in this perennially risky terrain. The private sector converged around familiar strategies of rent seeking, speculative activities, and deals that promised quick turnover in liquid
assets. Without a growth of fixed capital, there could be no expansion in
productive segments of the economy. Given the stagnation of nonoil activities, global oil markets remained the key driver in economic performance.
The civilian administration was relatively fortunate that the economic picture was buoyed by high oil prices after 1999, which enabled nominal
growth rates of between 4 and 6 percent during Obasanjo's first term in
office. These favorable export returns, however, created a new rent-based
windfall, with familiar political and economic consequences. The revenue
surge alleviated perceived fiscal constraints and therefore abated the
domestic urgency for economic reform. As was evident in the earlier Sec-

42. A survey of conflict in Nigeria is provided in the report by the Institute for Peace and
Conflict Resolution, *Nigeria Strategic Conflict Assessment: Consolidated Report* (Abuja:
IPCR, October 2002).
43. For a lucid account of the institutional setting, see Pat Utomi, *Managing Uncertainty:
Competition and Strategy in Emerging Economies* (Ibadan: Spectrum Books, 1998), 306–9.

ond Republic, an influx of resources encouraged political disbursements and the scramble for spoils.

The controversial 2003 elections, which were marred by significant flaws, brought changes to the political scene and the policy context. Despite an entry of new parties just prior to the elections, the ruling PDP further strengthened its dominance of the political system. The governing party retained the presidency, increased its legislative margin, and captured a larger number of state governments. The renamed ANPP (arising from a party merger with the former APP) emerged as the leading opposition force, and, with the declining appeal of the AD, the political arena took on the contours of a two-party system. Obasanjo acknowledged some of the failings of the first administration and assembled a highly competent team of economic technocrats for the second term. Key appointments for the Finance Minister, the Central Bank governor, and officials in charge of the budget, procurement, and the federal capital brought together the best-trained and best-qualified economic team in Nigeria's postcolonial history. They soon elaborated a program of economic reform and restructuring, dubbed the Nigerian Economic Empowerment and Development Strategy (NEEDS), which encompassed macroeconomic policies, sectoral strategy, and institutional reform.[44] Deferring to domestic political concerns, the new economic team avoided a formal agreement with the IMF but instead sought a quiet accord with the Bretton Woods institutions over key policies and performance targets.[45] With a large turnover in the National Assembly, there were possibilities for better executive-legislative relations and improved performance on key policies. Nonetheless, institutional rigidities and inherited reputational problems hampered progress on economic reform. A buoyant oil price remained the main factor in improving the economic picture.

Political Transition and Institutional Change

The demise of the Abacha regime ended a damaging chapter of predatory dictatorship in Nigeria. The return of civilian rule, accompanied by promises of political and economic reform, suggested prospects for arresting the downward trajectory of recent decades. Nigeria's crisis-ridden transition was nonetheless encumbered by a lackluster economy, weak governance, and deteriorating domestic security. Some problems were undoubtedly

44. Reuben Yunana, "New Economic Agenda Predicated on 5% Growth Rate," *Daily Trust* (Abuja), August 8, 2003.

45. International Monetary Fund, *Staff Report for the 2004 Article IV Consultation* (Washington, DC: International Montary Fund), June 22, 2004, 6; accessed at http://www.imf.org/external/pubs/ft/scr/2004/cr04239.pdf.

linked to underlying structural issues and the legacy of earlier regimes, though factors intrinsic to civilian politics were equally important.

The fundamental challenges of reforming governance in a rentier state are made more difficult by a political context of polarized elites and weak democratic structures. As argued throughout, the main potential drivers of change reside in the development of critical institutions, the emergence of new social coalitions to sustain a reform agenda, shifts in the composition of political elites, and the incentives of leaders.[46] Having described the central changes in policy and performance that followed the transition to civilian rule, I turn to an analysis of these domains of reform, beginning with the sources of institutional inertia.

Civilian leaders inherited an institutional landscape debilitated by years of fiscal scarcity, neglect, and outright plunder by preceding regimes. Poor institutional design was also a prominent issue, especially in the areas of constitutional reform, federal structure, the civil service, and the legal system. Institutional deficits hampered efforts to promote economic policy reform and constituted a major obstacle to private investment in productive activities. Moreover, in spite of repeated pronouncements and cosmetic steps to stem corruption, malfeasance remained epidemic in the public and private sectors. The structure of corruption was competitive and largely unregulated, which escalated transaction costs and dissipated resources. Major state institutions reflected chronically weak capacities.

There were limited degrees of freedom for revitalizing institutions critical to economic growth. The peak institutions of economic management and the broader administrative apparatus were badly degraded apart from a few pockets of competence in the privatization bureau, the Central Bank, and regulatory agencies for banking and communications. There was a pressing need to restructure core state institutions by rationalizing staff and organizational structures, strengthening the authority of capable technocratic managers, and insulating administrative organizations from political pressures. It was also imperative to raise compensation levels sufficiently to enable the public sector to compete in labor markets and to dampen incentives for corruption.[47] The new government, inheriting a

---

46. The rubric "drivers of change" is borrowed from recent research by the UK Department for International Development (DFID). For a summary see "Drivers of Change," DFID Public Information Note, September 2004, http://www.grc-exchange.org/docs/doc59.pdf.

47. The sources of poor performance in the state sector are analyzed by Dele Olowu, Eloho Otobo, and M. Okotoni, "The Role of the Civil Service in Enhancing Development and Democracy: An Evaluation of the Nigerian Experience," paper presented at the conference "Civil Service Systems in Comparative Perspective," School of Public and Environmental Affairs, Indiana University, Bloomington, Indiana, April 5–8, 1997.

huge debt overhang and a depleted treasury, was hardly in a position to make such resource commitments.

It would be misleading to suggest, however, that fiscal constraints were the central or primary impediment to institutional change. There was actually a negligible effort to advance administrative reform in the first civilian term, with no policy framework to guide such efforts. Although Obasanjo expressed a desire to make civil service reform a priority in his second term, efforts to elaborate concrete programs were slow to materialize. The reasons for the inaction of the new government were not self-evident, as there were grounds to expect that civilian elites might be inclined to support governance reforms. The collapse of state capabilities certainly influenced the military's decision to accept a regime transition, implying that elements of the armed forces also hoped for better outcomes under civilian rule. Further, the new president was reputed to be an advocate of better governance as well as an anticorruption campaigner. Many segments of the political class acknowledged the need to foster a capable state as a foundation of development.

The structure of political incentives, however, worked against institutional reform. The political elite reflected a loose assembly of clientelist groups embroiled in contentious distributional politics. Institutional weakness was an asset for political actors in the competition over rents and patronage.[48] There was little motive for competing factions to increase the transparency or effectiveness of public institutions, which might curtail their outlets for securing resources. To be sure, uncertain channels of rent distribution meant that some contenders were excluded, yet there was a general incentive among political elites to preserve broad informal access to state-mediated rents. Further, pressures from various factions in the ruling party undermined the ability of the executive to guide institutional reform. As in the previous Second Republic, a surge of revenues early in the new civilian regime held out the promise of increased rents at the center, while disarray within state structures furnished multiple access points for rent seeking.

Rivalries over distribution also played out in the turbulent arena of federalism. Nigeria had long-standing constitutional provisions for the devolution of power and finances, which were repeatedly circumvented by

48. Patrick Chabal and Jean-Pascal Daloz discuss the "instrumentalization of disorder" in weakly institutionalized states; see Chabal and Daloz, *Africa Works: Disorder as a Political Instrument* (Bloomington: Indiana University Press, 1999). See also Jacqueline Coolidge and Susan Rose-Ackerman, "High-Level Rent-Seeking and Corruption in African Regimes: Theory and Cases" Policy Research Working Paper (Washington DC: World Bank, June 1997).

presidentialist regimes in a rentier state.[49] With the transition to civilian rule in 1999, the new constitution opened a host of pressures to redefine and legitimate a democratic federal system. The updated constitution was modeled on the 1979 constitution, which, despite the failure of its custodians in the Second Republic, was generally considered to be a sound expression of federalism. The succeeding document contained some obvious changes—notably an increase in the number of states from nineteen to thirty-six, with a corresponding proliferation of local governments—as well as a number of provisions that emerged through the murky process of drafting, revision, and review under military rulers.

The incoming civilian politicians carefully parsed the new constitution for opportunities to advance their various political agendas, and many found (or created) the openings they sought. Elites in the northern states were resentful over the central political bargain of the transition, which fostered a power shift from a northern Muslim executive to a southern Christian president, leading an ethnically plural party. A push for northern regional interests and Islamic assertion quickly followed the political transition, as a dozen northern governors advanced Shari'a law in their states. The southern responses to a new federal compact were markedly different. In Lagos State, the opposition governor embarked on an agenda of privatization that began with a contract with Enron to revive the state's battered electricity system. The governors of the Niger Delta pressed for delivery of the constitutional increase in revenue allocation and sought greater control over local development policies. Several other state leaders tested the boundaries of federal control, and the limits of their own prerogatives, in political confrontation with the center.[50]

There was an overriding irony in this contestation. Nigeria's federal arrangements offered a path from stagnation and inertia by providing for a diversification of economic strategy and governance in the country's disparate regions and communities.[51] Yet the struggles over federalism in effect became a distributional conflict over central revenues, undermining the diversification of the economy. From an economic vantage, the variety

---

49. The mechanisms of clientelist politics in democratizing states are discussed by Nicolas Van de Walle, "Presidentialism and Clientelism in Africa's Emerging Party System," *Journal of Modern African Studies* 41, no. 2 (2003).

50. On the disparate agendas of federalism, see Rotimi Suberu, "Democratizing Nigeria's Federal Experiment," in Rotberg, *Crafting the New Nigeria,* and John N. Paden, *Muslim Civic Cultures and Conflict Resolution: The Challenge of Democratic Federalism in Nigeria* (Washington, DC: Brookings Institution Press, 2005), especially chaps. 7 and 8.

51. The potential economic benefits of federalism are elaborated by Barry Weingast, "The Economic Role of Political Institutions: Market-Preserving Federalism and Economic Development," *Journal of Law, Economics, and Organization* 11, no. 1 (1995): 1–33.

of resources, economic structure, and institutional endowments among the regions provided strong potential for a decentralized approach to policy and management. The country's disparate industrial clusters, mineral deposits, and areas of agricultural potential furnished the elements of distinct regional economies and complementarities of production within a national market. In order to realize the vision of a diversified economy, however, federalism had to create outlets for the development of local policies, infrastructure, and the institutional underpinnings of investment. A few state executives in the southern regions did grasp the economic dimensions of federalism and sought to craft policies independent of the center.[52] Others, however, sought to advance parochial concerns or opportunistic personal agendas, to the detriment of their own states and any prospects for cross-regional alliances between the government and producer groups. Federalism once again proved to be a divisive skirmish over rents rather than a mechanism for institutional change or sectional accommodation.

Elites and Leadership

Leadership has played a critical role for good or ill in the policy process and institutional change. The shortcomings of leadership extend well beyond the presidency, encompassing the political elite and the nature of political recruitment in Nigeria. The president's idiosyncratic problems are less relevant than the overall context of leadership selection and the setting in which rulers operate. Three observations are relevant. First, the advancement of leadership in Nigeria remains limited by a set of veto players that do not lend support for a strong reformist executive.[53] Second, executives must contend with polarized, competitive elites who are disinclined to support a common agenda of economic policy and institutional change. Third, the nature of political society in Nigeria remains strongly oriented to distributional politics and rent generation, which reinforces the social dilemma at the center of the state.[54]

As a retired military head of state, Olusegun Obasanjo personified an

52. Some observers pointed to an emergent stratum of reform-minded governors arising from a younger generation of entrepreneurial politicians, who were focused on developing their states and building a support base predicated on performance. See World Bank, *State and Local Governance in Nigeria* (Washington, DC: World Bank, 2002).

53. See George Tsebelis, *Veto Players: How Political Institutions Work* (Princeton: Princeton University Press, 2002), and Andrew MacIntyre, *The Power of Institutions: Political Architecture and Governance* (Ithaca: Cornell University Press, 2003).

54. Coolidge and Rose-Ackerman, "High-Level Rent-Seeking and Corruption in African Regimes."

emerging class of former officers who have decamped to civilian politics. He was also an acceptable compromise candidate to crucial veto groups in 1998, including the departing military establishment and the northern elites who had held power for much of the postcolonial era. Their acceptance of his candidacy enabled the nascent PDP to attract funds and build an electoral machine through numerous clientelist networks. The transitional elections were contested largely by civilians, though former military figures, mainly from the Muslim north, have subsequently dominated the roster of presidential aspirants. In short, there has been little renovation of leadership in the new republic. While the current military hierarchy cannot directly influence political advancement, there is a clear proxy in the cluster of retired rulers and officers, along with a significant network of regional elites, who hold a de facto veto on the selection of leaders. These groups represent an implicit constraint on change.

It is not impossible to envision the emergence of an independent civilian candidate who might seek to pursue a reform agenda. The early years of civilian rule, however, demonstrated the impediments to building an elite coalition around economic restructuring. The economic technocrats brought into Obasanjo's second administration were not backed by a strong executive mandate or a wider political base and therefore remained substantially isolated within their respective ministries and organizations. The ministries were highly politicized, and the civil service extremely weak, lending few areas of organizational support for policy change. Factionalism and rivalries among the legislature and the party establishments further obstructed initiatives from the executive. In the absence of a strategic elite consensus, initiatives for change could not be effectively implemented or sustained.

The realm of political society[55] is crucial for the reproduction of elites and the selection of leaders. Nigeria's electoral rules, intended to discourage communal politics, have fostered relatively large multiethnic parties. Given the impossibility of succeeding in national political competition without a broadly dispersed electoral appeal, the leading parties have attempted to build diverse coalitions. Yet the parties are largely bereft of programmatic or ideological differences and are constructed mainly on the basis of patronage and implicit communal appeals. In the early years of civil rule, social polarization furthered this tendency. The opposition ANPP cultivated a strong base among northern constituencies, especially

---

55. The concept of political society, as distinct from civil society, is elaborated by Juan J. Linz and Alfred Stepan in *Problems of Democratic Transition and Consolidation* (Baltimore: Johns Hopkins University Press, 1996).

the populist governors who championed the spread of Shari'a law. The PDP assembled a more diverse group of notables and patronage networks yet remained loosely constituted, with much of the party's support fairly contingent. Leaders of the dominant party confronted a central strategic problem in stabilizing patronage relations and fostering a more consistent support base. The narrow coalitions of authoritarian regimes were supplanted, under civilian rule, by a hegemonic party encompassing contentious interests and factions. The dispersal of rents remained the central adhesive in the system, although distribution was weakly managed from the center.

Coalitions and Competition

Elite divisions were not the only constraint on institutional change: a counterpart coalition among popular groups proved equally elusive. Communal interests defined much of the political arena, emphasizing distributional issues in economic policy debates and institutional reform. Even as the pattern of mutual vetoes seen under the First Republic gave way to a more diverse and fragmented set of interests, ethnoregional factions continued to foster veto points throughout the political system, often leading to stalemate among contending groups. The inability of the ruling party or an alternative multiethnic coalition to break through this distributional stalemate has been an abiding constraint on change.

The revitalization of civil society opened political space for civic groups, community associations, and the media to address issues of economic performance and policy change. A limited though vocal segment of associations specifically mobilized around governance reforms. Such groups, however, were largely restricted to a few urban areas, and their professional membership did not have wider linkages to popular constituencies. Many elements of civil society agitated specifically for distributional concerns, often mirroring the fragmentation of elites.[56] Further, much of the Nigerian public was deeply skeptical or overtly hostile to economic liberalization and structural reforms. Acclimated by decades of rent distribution from the central state, civic associations often lobbied for special allocations or preferences rather than broad policy changes or improvements in public goods.

The rentier political economy was also evident in the activities of the private sector. Though some business groups pressed for improvements in

---

56. A discussion of populist pressures and the problems of reform coalitions is offered by Sam Amadi in "Nigeria: Must a Reformer Be," *This Day* (Lagos), November 6, 2004.

general public goods, many in the private sector continued to rely on collusive relations with state elites to compete for rents. A prominent segment of the corporate community was organized in the Nigeria Economic Summit Group (NESG), which sponsored a consultative process with public officials over a range of issues, from macroeconomic and sectoral policies to institutional reforms. Some of the perspectives of NESG toward enhancing private sector growth were echoed by older business associations including the Nigerian Association of Chambers of Commerce, Industry, Mines, and Agriculture (NACCIMA) and the Lagos Chamber of Commerce. Other groups, notably the Manufacturers' Association of Nigeria (MAN), lobbied to sustain state protection, subsidies, and rents. Different sectoral interests and the ethnic segmentation of the private sector undermined the effort to exert a collective voice for institutional change.

The External Dimension

Finally, it is important to observe the international dimension of attempted reform. Nigeria's political transition was undertaken at the nadir of the country's credibility in global markets. Years of economic mismanagement, arrears on debt, lurid tales of corruption, periodic sanctions, and conspicuous international activities by Nigerian criminal networks drove Nigeria to the margins of the international economy. Nonoil trade had not grown for a decade, and direct foreign investment was steadily retreating from the Nigerian market. Capital controls and local market conditions essentially ruled out any chances of portfolio investment. Moreover, Nigeria found itself in one of the most difficult economic neighborhoods in the world, a desperately poor region riddled with civil wars, and with few beacons of success to provide demonstration effects for regional states. Apart from international interest in the region's rising energy reserves, and intermittent attention to other resources such as timber and diamonds, the region was marginal to most global markets. Nigeria found it difficult to regain visibility or appeal, regardless of political change or policy reform.

Mixed signals and slow progress on reform deepened the challenges of credibility. President Obasanjo traveled widely during his first term in an effort to enhance Nigeria's visibility and reputation. Yet the lack of movement in such crucial areas as macroeconomic policy and privatization undermined the president's imprecations about Nigeria's potential. The country could not get a favorable hearing from the multilateral institutions on debt relief and was not made eligible for the formal HIPC process.

A scheme of debt reduction was eventually negotiated with the IMF and the Paris Club of bilateral donors toward the end of Obasanjo's second term, but it was not accompanied by new investment or portfolio flows. Apart from a regular stream of energy-related investments from foreign companies, investors remained aloof.

The Nigerian Conundrum

The collapse of predatory rule and the introduction of democratic reform dramatically altered Nigeria's political conditions. A large, plural elite entered competitive politics, complemented by diverse interests and civic groups. The new government confronted vocal public pressure for popular welfare, improved provision of public goods, and enhanced conditions for private economic activity. Important segments of the national elite (as well as many popular groups) clearly recognized Nigeria's central challenge in restructuring the state and the economy away from the syndrome of oil dependence and political rent distribution. Yet a reform agenda was contravened by the political incentives facing leaders and the corresponding strategies pursued by societal groups and organized interests. The leading impediments to change arose from the fragmentation of elites and the weakness of central institutions. Efforts to increase the role of technocrats constituted an important step, yet a small cluster of capable economic managers remained politically isolated and lacking in support from senior elites or effective institutional centers. The technocratic direction at the top of the political system was not accompanied by a growth coalition in the organized private sector, nor did reform elements ally to political parties or popular sectors. In the absence of these political catalysts for change, Nigeria's long-standing oil monoculture reinforced the path dependence of the economy. The economic structure furnished a weak basis for local production or entrepreneurship, as the private sector remained centered on rent seeking and collusive relations with state elites. Political leaders, for their part, were drawn to strategies of patronage and ad hoc rent distribution, rather than broader economic governance and growth. This remains the central political conundrum as a democratic Nigeria seeks economic revitalization.

Reprise: Democratization and Economic Reform

After three decades of divergent economic fortunes, Indonesia and Nigeria experienced abrupt political transitions in 1999 that produced seeming convergence in performance. In each case, regime change gave rise to institutional turbulence, escalating social conflict, and economic malaise. The apparent similarities in events, however, obscured underlying factors that led to different trajectories of reform and performance. Nigeria's chronic economic stagnation was aggravated by institutional weakness and a pronounced fragmentation of political and economic elites. Indonesia, also politically unsettled, nonetheless had a more stable institutional legacy, along with better coordination among policy elites and private sector groups. Prior institutional changes in each case gave rise to constellations of interest that produced varying outcomes under circumstances of democratic reform. Nonetheless, we confront similar analytical questions about the relative paths of these countries in circumstances of democratization and economic change.

Democratic transition can potentially have important effects on the course of economic governance, as noted earlier. Regime transitions create institutional changes that influence the patterns of decision making and accountability in the political system. Further, political liberalization opens the public sphere to civic associations and organized interests, permitting new groups and positions to engage the political process. This suggests that leaders are subject to greater pressures for transparency and the delivery of collective goods. As stressed throughout, the outcomes of political change are contingent on the character of leadership, the changing nature of support coalitions, the new institutional framework, and international linkages.

A number of structural conditions shape the context of reform in Indonesia and Nigeria. The legacy of authoritarian rule is especially salient, yielding weak institutions of accountability and lingering interests among rentier groups and clientelist networks. Social diversity also shapes the political arena, fostering an array of powerful distributional pressures from communal groups and sectional interests. Further, the centrality of resource exports in the political economies of both states remains influential. Resource windfalls create adverse pressures on macroeconomic management. Also, political authority is strongly linked to the distribution of rents, and asset control is concentrated through state ownership, political clientelism, and the narrow base of the economy. Finally, centralized political and fiscal systems aggravate distributional pressures, especially in resource-producing areas of the country.

The core challenges in these systems are to address major distortions arising from rentier regimes and clientelist rule. This largely depends on the ability of state authorities to furnish credible commitments for a wide array of private asset holders, in order to foster widespread investment and more dispersed economic power. Capable macroeconomic management is a basic condition of change, calling for delegation of policy authority to capable technocratic groups and efforts to strengthen peak agencies of economic management. Second, reforms aimed at reducing the fiscal discretion of rulers—notably measures for fiscal transparency, increased budgetary discipline, and reduced public sector control—can improve the delivery of collective goods and limit outlets for rent distribution. These changes are important in constraining clientelism and malfeasance, and reducing their growth-suppressing effects. A further direction of reform includes changes directed at productive investment in nonextractive activities. Rapid growth in productive segments of the economy will reduce the concentration of assets among state elites and rent-distribution networks, and may disperse the control of assets over the medium term.

Decentralization and fiscal reform are crucial strategic approaches to the distributional conflicts that threaten stability in democratizing states. Finally, selected international linkages can furnish important support for reform. Relations with multilateral institutions, regional governance structures, and policy advocacy networks (notably the Extractive Industries Transparency Initiative) could provide further inducements to political elites and national leaders to sustain reform agendas. Organizations such as the Asia Pacific Economic Cooperation (APEC) or the New Partnership for Africa's Development (NEPAD), with its peer review mechanism, are important external influences.

In terms of domestic political alignments, an important catalyst of change could emerge from new growth coalitions under democratic auspices. This entails the emergence of influential elements among the political parties who are committed to institutional reform, focused on economic restructuring, and motivated to build linkages with popular constituencies based on this agenda. The counterpart to a reform axis within the party system is a support coalition among business groups, civic activists pressing for improved governance, and popular sectors willing to support elements of a reform agenda such as fiscal transparency or anticorruption efforts. The size and diversity of independent business interests influences the potential for growth coalitions. While popular sectors in these countries are generally opposed to the program of orthodox reform, political crafting could bring in groups on the basis of selective policies.

These considerations should be weighed against the prevailing conditions of reform within these countries. Politically, Indonesia has shifted rapidly from a stable authoritarian system, circumscribed elites, and managed coalitions to a fragile democratic system with relatively plural elites and competitive coalitions. Important factors that guide economic recovery include the consensus within the state sector over technocratic guidance, along with a tentative convergence on economic strategy among major economic groups and the leading parties. Nigeria has moved from a factionalized and unstable authoritarian situation to an even more tenuous democratic regime, embodying polarized elites, a dominant party system, and fragmented competitive coalitions. There is little political consensus on economic policy, and the technocratic roles within the state are weak. This highlights the distinctive economic and institutional legacies of preceding regimes. Indonesia has experience with capable macroeconomic management, a comparatively sound infrastructure, nodes of institutional capacity, and a comparatively large domain of producers and investors in nonextractive areas of the economy. Despite a battered reputation in global markets, there is still considerable private sector engagement in Indonesia and a favorable neighborhood that offers economic benefits. Nigeria, by contrast, has little experience of stable macroeconomic policy, along with a decrepit infrastructure and debilitated state institutions. A small segment of economic actors engaged in productive activities have little weight in the political system. The country has for decades been marginal to most global markets, and the regional neighborhood provides few sources of economic assistance. Despite many likenesses, these countries encounter comparable challenges from what are, in fact, substantially different structural positions.

At present, the political incentives arising from rentier states and competitive clientelism foster obstacles to reform, especially in Nigeria. This is likely to persist under a scenario of high oil prices and abundant revenues. Both economies, however, are vulnerable to adverse shocks, since they are populous high absorbers of resource rents. As comparative experience suggests, crisis is frequently a necessary condition to induce major political and economic change.[57] Whether it is sufficient to encourage change is largely a political question. This analysis suggests that democratization in Indonesia and Nigeria offers new opportunities for policy innovation and institutional change, but these are attenuated by the effects of economic structure and inherited institutions.

---

57. Stephan Haggard and Robert Kaufman, *The Political Economy of Democratic Transitions* (Princeton: Princeton University Press, 1995).

CHAPTER 9

Conclusion

Indonesia and Nigeria in Comparative Perspective

This book offers a perspective on the political challenges of economic development. The problems of uneven development among regions and states have given rise to many questions about the conditions needed for sustained growth and competitiveness. Analyses of economic growth have increasingly centered on institutional factors, including the character of markets and the qualities of states in providing economic governance. The political conditions for institutional change, and the effects of different institutional arrangements on economic outcomes, provide central themes in understanding comparative economic performance. This study addresses these issues through a study of two comparable cases, Indonesia and Nigeria.

Among many important factors that influence relative economic performance, the conditions for private capital formation are clearly decisive. The ways that governments structure relations with private economic actors create the foundation for long-term economic performance. Growth and competitiveness are linked to market-supporting interventions by states that induce assets holders to commit to fixed capital in diverse areas of the economy. This entails coordination among state elites and private actors that enhances the calculability of economic affairs and focuses incentives for investment and entrepreneurship.[1] Close government-business relations can give rise to collusive dealings that suppress competition and restrict markets, fostering an inevitable tension between governance and opportunism. Despite such hazards, collaboration between the state and the private sector is needed for capital formation.[2]

---

1. Barry Weingast, "The Economic Role of Political Institutions: Market-Preserving Federalism and Economic Development," *Journal of Law, Economics, and Organization* 11, no. 1 (1995): 1–31; Thomas Callaghy, "The State and the Development of Capitalism in Africa: Theoretical, Historical, and Comparative Reflections," in Donald Rothchild and Naomi Chazan, eds., *The Precarious Balance: State and Society in Africa* (Boulder: Westview, 1988).

2. These problems are explored in Sylvia Maxfield and Ben Ross Schneider, eds., *Business and the State in Developing Countries* (Ithaca: Cornell University Press, 1997); Andrew

Institutionalist approaches to development generally emphasize the importance of credible commitments to private economic actors. This entails a set of guarantees by political rulers that can induce long-term investment in fixed assets, which are the basis for increased productive capacity. Secure property rights and reliable contracting are essential institutional bases for growth, often resting upon a stable rule of law. Increasingly, however, there is recognition that credible commitments may coalesce in circumstances of political uncertainty or institutional turbulence, where a broad legal and regulatory framework cannot be assumed. This leads to the general questions at the heart of this study: How are credible commitments furnished? How do such arrangements arise in adverse political or institutional settings? What factors sustain such commitments, and what circumstances undermine these assurances?

This analysis outlines a set of political factors that affect the emergence and sustainability of credible commitments. Political leadership, conditioned by particular sets of challenges and opportunities, is decisive in fostering (or undermining) institutional arrangements for economic growth. Coalitions provide another essential part of the analytical framework, since institutional arrangements embody particular bases of support. Elite coordination and accommodation with popular groups are integral strategies for the emergence of a stable growth compact. In addition, policy learning and other linkages from regional neighbors—embodied in a general "neighborhood effect"—influence states in different ways. Leadership, coalitions, and neighborhood influences shape the analysis of institutional change and economic performance in the cases considered here.

These themes and concepts have been applied to a structured comparison of Indonesia and Nigeria. The cases yield broadly applicable insights about the comparative politics of development. Both are populous countries that anchor their respective regions. They are communally and regionally diverse states, endowed with substantial natural resources—notably oil and gas—and each country was ruled by authoritarian regimes for three decades. In terms of size, diversity, resource wealth, and political regimes, Indonesia and Nigeria reflect attributes that are found in a number of other developing or transitional states, including Russia, Ukraine, Mexico, Brazil, South Africa, and Malaysia. Further, their strong similar-

---

MacIntyre, ed., *Business and Government in Industrializing Asia* (Ithaca: Cornell University Press, 1994); and David C. Kang, *Crony Capitalism: Corruption and Development in South Korea and the Philippines* (Cambridge: Cambridge University Press, 2002).

ities in terms of historical milestones and structural characteristics allow us to isolate particular political factors in institutional development, controlling for such broad elements as regime type, resources, social characteristics, and historical junctures.

The comparison of Indonesia and Nigeria reveals extraordinary paths during the past four decades, with elements of divergence and convergence. Beginning from very similar foundations, the two countries deviated sharply in the 1970s and 1980s, as Indonesia recovered from early economic crisis, successfully adjusted from the leading distortions of the resource windfall, and embarked on a period of sustained growth and competitive development. By the middle of the 1990s, Indonesia appeared as a promising economy with prospects of sustained high performance, an evaluation supported by the enthusiastic responses of international investors to the Indonesian market. Indonesia's dynamism was starkly contrasted by Nigeria's path from modest recovery after the civil war to the pathologies of the 1970s oil boom, through the postwindfall crash of the 1980s and the predatory decline of the 1990s. Nigeria's sustained decline pushed the country to the margins of the global economy as investment diminished, nonoil production withered, growth slowed, and poverty mounted.

At the end of the 1990s, however, the Indonesian economic debacle and the abrupt transition from authoritarian rule in both countries seemed to create a remarkable convergence, as they contended with the challenges of democratic development while grappling with economic disarray and widening social instability. On the economic front, diminished investment, capital flight, institutional turbulence, and political fragmentation combined to hamper recovery and suppress growth.

The apparent convergence, however, was transitory. The institutional foundations and social changes of the preceding three decades created different contexts for crisis management in Indonesia and Nigeria, and performance again diverged a few years after the tumultuous 1999 transitions. Indonesians embarked on significant institutional reforms, particularly in the constitutional arena, as the political system appeared to coalesce around a workable, if fluid, party configuration. The economy moved again toward encouraging growth, with substantial foreign investment and performance in nonoil segments of the economy. Nigeria had a far less promising trajectory. Nigerians were not successful in managing constitutional change or other institutional challenges, and the new civilian regime staggered through a sequence of flawed elections and volatile politics inside the dominant party. While economic growth was buoyed by high oil and gas prices, there was little activity in the nonenergy sectors of the economy, and scant impact on poverty or social provisions.

These changing fortunes raise parallel questions about the relative performance of each country: What factors account for Indonesia's distinctive economic vitality over a sustained period, and how can we account for the sudden collapse of the political and economic underpinnings of development? What are the sources of resilience in Indonesia's political economy? How can we understand Nigeria's contrasting evolution, and the recurring barriers to effective economic governance? Are there possibilities for change in the trajectory of the Nigerian political economy? A final comparative question is salient: Does the future portend closer parallels in the development of these countries under similar political and institutional conditions, or is there an element of path dependence that will restore a divergent course for each?

The questions may be answered at different levels. As a first cut, I note the distinctive orientations, strategies, and policy choices of elites in each country. Varying dispositions toward private capital and the global economy, as well as different propensities to adjust to economic shocks, are important elements in the story presented here. More fundamentally, I consider factors of leadership, coalition formation, and policy learning that gave rise to these distinctive policy regimes, reflecting the salient conclusions of the study about the political foundations of institutional change.

Strategy, Policy, and Performance

Indonesia and Nigeria display important variations in their responses to central challenges of development and economic governance. Elites in each country adopted different stances toward international markets and developed distinctive relationships among state officials and the private sector. The traditions of macroeconomic management also differ, as regimes in each country followed very different approaches to the problems of commitment and policy credibility. These factors highlight central distinctions among the cases during the long era of divergent performance, continuing through recent periods of adjustment and the transition to electoral rule.

Disposition toward the Global Economy

Indonesian and Nigerian leaders have had contrasting dispositions toward the international economy, varying among integration and insulation.

Indonesian policymakers have continually stressed a substantial degree of integration with the world economy, despite the strong nationalist impulses running through elite attitudes and public opinion. When the New Order regime confronted the initial economic crisis, they faced a large foreign debt and trade dominated by nonoil commodities. Indonesia's recovery depended upon improving the balance of payments, enhancing international competitiveness, and bolstering the country's general reputation. These concerns drew leaders toward relatively liberal macroeconomic measures. Although policy orientations wavered among the contentious pulls of nationalism and outward orientation, the foundations of an outward-oriented economy were preserved over the long term. Leaders sustained a realistic exchange rate, favorable incentives for many nonoil exports, and a manageable debt profile. At the same time, however, government took an interventionist approach to sectoral and microeconomic policies, favoring strategies of import substitution, trade protection, and state-led industrial development.

In the course of the 1980s and early 1990s, senior leadership responded to declining resources and balance of payments problems by turning decisively toward international markets. This direction was encouraged by the policy models of such neighbors as Singapore and Malaysia and facilitated by Southeast Asia's strengthening reputation in international markets. Indonesia's integration into global capital markets proved a crucial source of vulnerability during the Asian financial crisis, leading the Soeharto regime and some of his successors to flirt briefly with more inward-looking measures. Despite such policy vacillation, the fundamentals of sound macroeconomic policy have been sustained.

During most of the period considered here, Nigerian policymakers favored an inward orientation that insulated the economy from external competition and invited extensive political control of trade, investment, and currency. In the 1970s, growing petroleum exports eclipsed the country's revenues from agricultural commodities and solid minerals. Political leaders increasingly sought insulation from the global economy, motivated by economic nationalist views and the vision of fiscal autonomy fostered by the oil windfall. Nationalist policies included limitations on trade, foreign exchange, and ownership in the economy. Extensive state controls also furnished copious rents to political elites and facilitated ruling strategies of patronage and populism. These policies were economically corrosive as restrictive trade and investment regimes, overvalued exchange rates, and price discrimination against agricultural producers hindered production in nonoil sectors of the economy.

In the latter part of the 1980s, the Babangida regime belatedly sought to address some of these policy problems and pursue a measured opening toward the global economy. The initiatives soon gave way to inconsistent reform, domestic structural problems, and political reversals. In this respect, Nigeria mirrored the inconsistent policy movements and weak reform of other countries in the region, an outcome further influenced by West Africa's poor international reputation. Only recently, during the second term of President Olusegun Obasanjo, has there been a tentative shift toward economic opening and greater integration with external markets, though it is quite early to assess the effects of these policy changes.

State Relations with Private Capital

Another dimension of comparison is the state's relations with private capital, especially domestic entrepreneurs. Indonesia reflects a paradoxical divide between doctrine and behavior. Although statist preferences are expressed strongly in the national constitution, official discourse, and public opinion, political leaders have protected and even nurtured important elements of private capital. The New Order pursued an alliance among ruling elites, ethnic Chinese entrepreneurs, foreign capital, and selected *pribumi* actors. The regime provided inducements to a politically dependent segment of the private sector as an engine of growth.

Nigeria's contradictions play out in a different fashion. Compared with Indonesia, Nigerians hold fewer apparent inhibitions toward markets or the private sector. Antimarket sentiments are not prominent in public law or the stated attitudes of leadership, and a broad arena of private economic activity has been outwardly endorsed by all Nigerian regimes. Further, an impulse for entrepreneurship is evident through most segments of society. Notwithstanding the general acceptance of certain market values, political leaders have regularly impeded or penalized major segments of the private sector. Nigerian governments have acted at various times to constrain or expropriate foreign firms, domestic immigrant entrepreneurs, and selected ethnic or sectoral groups. State intervention has not been market supporting but has created obstacles to capital formation.

The distribution of assets and the structure of political competition in Nigeria undermine producer alliances between the state and private capital. The country's divisive ethnoregional politics give rise to fears about the uneven distribution of economic and political power. Sectional elites have consistently used political influence to bolster the fortunes of their own group while seeking to block the advancement of other ethnoregional segments. Nigerian governments have formally emphasized redistribution and balance among communal groups, though in reality ethnic patronage has served as the main channel for allocating resources. Consequently, a set of mutual vetoes among communal groups undermines the stabilization of property rights, impeding investment and commitment to fixed assets.

Elites in Indonesia and Nigeria have also varied in their response to private capital.[3] In both cases, collective action among business interests was relatively weak. Indonesia's New Order and the various rentier regimes that presided in Nigeria constructed coalitions among private cronies and allies based on the selective distribution of rents. Rulers were not generally confronted by industrial or professional groups who could lobby effectively for collective goods.[4] Yet Indonesian leaders were clearly more responsive to the exigencies of private capital, reflecting technocratic influences, the relative cohesion of state elites around a growth strategy, and the reflexive concerns of rulers about economic crisis. Nigeria's divided elites, locked in distributional contention and focused mainly on the dispersal of rents, were consequently less concerned with the overarching conditions for capital formation.

The Propensity to Adjust

Different orientations were most clearly evident in macroeconomic management. The leaders of each country showed different propensities to adjust to major shocks and economic crises. In Indonesia, the New Order regime attained power in the midst of economic and political turmoil. The leadership was preoccupied with economic instability, especially hyperinflation, along with slow growth and international isolation. The prominent role accorded to a core technocratic circle served to maintain focus on these problems throughout much of the regime's tenure. Until the crisis of 1997–98, the technocrats regularly prevailed on Soeharto for corrective action to restore macroeconomic balances and a degree of international competitiveness. Indonesian leaders showed a disposition for adjustment that was reinforced through successive shocks and episodes of

3. Jeffrey Winters emphasizes the Indonesian state's "structural reliance on capital" in *Power in Motion: Capital Mobility and the Indonesian State* (Ithaca: Cornell University Press, 1996), chap. 1; David Kang addresses much the same issue in his account of state and private sector elites as mutual hostages impelled toward cooperation in Kang, *Crony Capitalism,* 7. Kang's account recalls Oliver Williamson's model of "hostages" in contracting, in Williamson's *The Economic Institutions of Capitalism* (New York: Free Press, 1985), 168–69.

4. Andrew MacIntyre has documented how the atomistic, rentier character of the Indonesian business community began to change by the 1980s, as reflected in more effective lobbying efforts by organized industrial groups. This organizational capacity arose from earlier policies toward economic diversification, rather than providing a central catalyst of liberalization or improved governance. See MacIntyre, *Business and Politics in Indonesia* (Sydney: Allen and Unwin, 1990).

reform. Once again, influences of the neighborhood must be considered, as Indonesia had regional links to states that reflected sound macroeconomic policy regimes.

Nigeria's economic and political system fostered different policy orientations. The central upheaval in the 1960s arose from domestic sectional conflict rather than a generalized economic crisis. The experience of wartime economic management inclined government leaders toward more comprehensive state oversight of trade, foreign exchange, and fiscal affairs. Statist and nationalist economic policies were promoted by senior politicians and civil servants, who also set forth the central ideas guiding economic strategy. The petroleum windfall reinforced confidence in a planned and administered economy, while abundant revenues served to veil problems in productivity and competitiveness during the boom period. Political instability in the 1970s and 1980s fostered growing disarray in the economic bureaucracy. Also, decision makers experienced less flexibility in the face of rising fiscal commitments and increasing patronage demands. In consequence, Nigerian elites were dilatory in responding to external shocks, frequently divided on key policies, and generally reluctant to adopt adjustment measures. The prevalence of similar policy orientations throughout sub-Saharan Africa undoubtedly reinforced these policy choices.

Modes and Mechanisms of Commitment

Varying attitudes toward economic growth also impelled different approaches to the problems of commitment and policy credibility. For Indonesian leaders, commitment problems were addressed in a comparatively direct fashion. The Soeharto regime used three approaches to create inducements and encourage compliance. First were a series of formal, ex ante commitment devices. Two of the most important were the balanced budget rule, which imposed a measure of fiscal discipline, and the open capital account, which served both as a barometer of market stability and an exit option for asset holders. In addition, the government sought to bolster credibility through formal representations to donors and investors, especially through the Inter-Governmental Group for Indonesia (IGGI).[5] Key segments of the economic bureaucracy also pursued a close relationship with donors, which enhanced the government's reputation. Finally, ruling elites established patronage relations with key producers and investors—often through a direct stake in economic ventures—that served

5. These elements are detailed by John Bresnan in *Managing Indonesia: The Modern Political Economy* (New York: Columbia University Press, 1993).

to increase private confidence in government commitments. These arrangements broke down as succession problems loomed closer and Indonesia's integration with global markets increasingly exposed the weakness of domestic institutions in the financial, corporate, legal, and regulatory domains. Indonesian leaders have retained some of these commitment devices in the wake of Soeharto's regime, though political uncertainty and institutional change have made informal assurances of property rights less tenable. However, a legacy of commitment has sustained a considerable degree of productive investment and entrepreneurship.

In Nigeria, the commitment problem has eluded political leaders. The nature of the political system frames the setting for economic management. Divided and insecure governments have been unable to make authoritative commitments to economic policy or private holders of capital. The resource position and the context of choice for Nigerian elites also influenced the approach to economic oversight. Issues of credibility were not perceived to be significant through the 1970s, a period when growth was acceptable, revenue windfalls alleviated many fiscal problems, and international investors appeared willing (indeed eager) to enter the Nigerian market. Government leaders believed that state planning and fiscal policy, rather than the supply response of markets, were the essential levers of economic performance.

Contention over distribution among Nigerian political elites also inclined leaders toward discretionary control of resources. The need for discretion contravened any acceptance of ex ante constraints on policy. Statist military regimes, patronage-wielding politicians, and predatory autocrats all sought to maximize discretion, an approach that has persisted under the most recent period of civilian rule, with only tentative moves toward more institutionalized forms of commitment. The experience of both countries also reflects the influences of path dependence and regional reputation. Nigeria's record of capricious governance undermined the validity of stated commitments, while the poor reputation of West Africa deterred international markets. By the same token, Indonesia's record of reliability and its proximity to Asian successes enhanced the credence of new commitments.

The Comparative Politics of Economic Growth

In the opening chapter I outlined a set of general propositions about the political conditions for economic growth that were drawn from the central findings of this study. Returning to those ideas, I reflect on the comparative inferences of the book.

Leadership and Institutional Crafting

Countries with weak formal institutions may provisionally achieve substantial economic growth. This is an especially important conclusion, suggesting that political turbulence and weak institutional settings are not insuperable obstacles to advancing the economy. Such a finding is encouraging for countries at lower levels of development, states in transition to democratic market systems, or in situations of incipient and uncertain democratization. A fully elaborated rule of law is not a prerequisite for economic growth, though a sound institutional framework is clearly needed in order to sustain growth and competitiveness over the longer term. Where institutions are lacking, developmentally oriented elites may provisionally craft institutions to encourage growth and capital formation. Property rights and contracts can be guaranteed through ad hoc particular arrangements with producers and groups.[6] Such assurances are contingent upon growth-oriented leadership, a state that is sufficiently coherent to be able to deliver on ad hoc commitments, and a class or segment of asset holders who can readily respond to such inducements. While institutional crafting can be effective for significant periods of time (e.g., a matter of decades in the instances of Indonesia or China), this is an inherently unstable strategy that is vulnerable to abrupt political changes or economic shocks, as seen vividly in the case of Indonesia. Nonetheless, for states confronting the challenges of growth from a discouraging institutional position, the possibilities of informal arrangements hold some promise.

Methods of Credible Commitment

There is an inherent contradiction in attempting to craft growth-enhancing arrangements, since any ruler with sufficient discretion to guarantee property rights can also renege on such commitments.[7] The ability to furnish provisional guarantees to producers and other asset holders rests upon a set of special commitment devices that signal rulers' intent and create penalties for veering from policies. Such devices are available to most

---

6. This is a central finding from the historical experience of Mexico in the analysis by Stephen Haber, Armando Razo, and Noel Maurer, *The Politics of Property Rights* (New York: Cambridge University Press, 2003).

7. This point has been emphasized by Barry Weingast and Douglass C. North, "Constitutions and Commitment: The Evolution of Institutions Governing Public Choice in Seventeenth Century England," *Journal of Economic History* 49, no. 4 (1989): 803–32; Hilton Root, *Small Countries, Big Lessons: Governance and the Rise of East Asia* (Oxford: Oxford University Press, 1996); and Mancur Olson, "Dictatorship, Democracy, and Development," *American Political Science Review* 87, no. 3 (1993): 567–76.

leaders in either democratic or authoritarian settings. Although this study has highlighted the emergence of credible commitments in a nondemocratic setting under Indonesia's New Order, such institutional arrangements are not predicated on regime type. There is no inherent "authoritarian advantage" in furnishing credible commitments, as is evident from the long roster of nondemocratic regimes reflecting poor economic performance.[8] There are essential features of authoritarian developmental states, however, that can apply more broadly to an array of regimes and conditions. First, the delegation of economic policy to an effective technocratic team is essential for framing appropriate policies and signaling the government's intentions to private economic actors. The central role of technocrats in Indonesia's long economic success, and their diminished influence in the years just prior to the economic crisis, vividly illustrates the importance of these roles. Conversely, the intermittent role of technocrats in the Nigerian economic bureaucracy, and their political isolation, has been a significant source of poor economic governance.

Second, the introduction of ex ante lock-in measures can affirm incentives and ensure asset holders against arbitrary expropriation from unforeseen policy shifts. Such mechanisms may include a convertible currency, an open capital account, or rigid budgeting provisions. These policies worked for an extended period in Indonesia, though they must obviously be applied selectively in other settings. The Asian financial contagion vividly exposed the liabilities of opening the capital account, which can expose the economy to volatile capital movements. The general observation, however, is that credibility calls for commitment devices apart from the informal assurances of political leaders. Considered in this light, technocratic delegation can serve dual purposes of both signaling and lock-in. When technocratic clusters are sufficiently entrenched and politically insulated within a regime, they may provide added assurance against policy deviations.[9] Nigeria's capricious economic oversight, and the absence of commitment devices, has been integral to the country's economic stagnation.

Leaders, Elites, and Coordination

The comparison of Indonesia and Nigeria highlights the importance of developmental leadership in shifting the equilibrium of developing

8. Barbara Geddes, "Challenging the Conventional Wisdom," *Journal of Democracy* 5, no. 4 (1994): 104–18, and José María Maravall, "The Myth of the Authoritarian Advantage," *Journal of Democracy* 5, no. 4 (1994): 17–31.

9. The importance of technocrats in institutional crafting is emphasized by Mark Erick Williams, "Market Reforms, Technocrats, and Institutional Innovation," *World Development* 30, no. 3 (2002): 407.

economies toward productive accumulation. The stability of Soeharto's regime and his relatively consistent commitments to growth reveal a marked contrast to the sporadic tenure of Nigerian leaders and their strategies of clientelism, distributional politics, and economic predation. We are primarily interested in the sources of differing orientations among leaders. This study illuminates the sets of challenges and opportunities that draw leaders toward developmental or predatory approaches to rule. Economic crises, political upheavals, and security threats often impel rulers toward new strategies of economic governance. Economic failure creates an obvious need for reform, while the social dislocation accompanying an economic downturn may provide openings for greater policy experimentation.[10] Political turbulence and regime change confront new leaders with the difficulties of consolidating their ruling group and solidifying a popular support base. Rulers are often drawn toward developmental strategies in the face of strong external challenges or when confronted by domestic unrest driven by cohesive, class-based organizations. Broad-based growth can foster a new compact between the state and key constituencies while alleviating important sources of internal weakness.[11] In seeking to stem the political and economic turmoil of Sukarno's regime, Soeharto moved the New Order toward a developmental course. Through a strategy of economic stabilization and rapid growth, his regime sought to respond to the demands of the rural sectors and the urban poor that formed a base for the Communist Party as well as the large Muslim mass organizations.

Nigerian experience suggests that ethnic or communal fragmentation is more likely to impel rulers toward discretionary patronage and clientelist approaches to rule, which can quell challenges from particular segments while avoiding the problems of widespread class mobilization. Nigerian leaders faced equally significant crises arising from the breakdown of civilian rule and the civil war, yet they did not agree on a developmental strategy of rule. The oil windfall, coinciding with the end of the civil war, appeared to provide an easy outlet for addressing the distributional demands of Nigeria's competing communal groups. The nature of political competition and societal mobilization also drew leaders toward

10. Barbara Grosh, "Through the Structural Adjustment Minefield: Politics in an Era of Economic Liberalization," in Jennifer Widner, ed., *Economic Change and Political Liberalization in Sub-Saharan Africa* (Baltimore: Johns Hopkins University Press, 1994); Stephan Haggard and Robert Kaufman, *The Political Economy of Democratic Transitions* (Princeton: Princeton University Press, 1995).

11. Edgardo Campos and Hilton Root, *The Key to the Asian Miracle: Making Shared Growth Credible* (Washington, DC: Brookings Institution, 1996).

selective patronage and fiscally driven distributional politics. Leaders faced an ethnoregional balancing act that impelled ruling strategies under successive regimes.

The unity and coherence of regimes are also leading factors in the strategic behavior of leaders.[12] Indonesia reflects the opportunities for change in a situation of relative elite cohesion. Despite the ethnic diversity among Indonesian military and state elites, Soeharto was able to work with a mainly Javanese cohort and to gather them behind an economic plan. Further, the new leader effectively delegated economic policy to a circle of technocrats, a strategy that became increasingly familiar in comparable bureaucratic-authoritarian regimes in Asia and Latin America.[13] As Soeharto's position within the regime became more assured, the stabilization efforts of his senior economic team were increasingly effective, and the time-horizons of leaders expanded to accept a longer-term strategy of growth.

Among Nigerian leaders, we observe a very different set of circumstances. Four successive military rulers—Ironsi, Gowon, Murtala, and Obasanjo—came to power in situations of ethnic polarization often marked by violence. The democratic interregnum under the Second Republic (1979–83) was precarious from the beginning. Military and civilian elites were deeply divided and factionalized, and political uncertainty caused them to heavily discount the future. Divisions within these regimes created insecurity for rulers and hampered unity over an economic program. Nigeria's development plans were loose assemblages of projects and goals, framed by general appeals to nationalism and state-led development, and supported by populist largesse. Neither military leaders nor civilians identified a core circle of technocrats within the economic bureaucracy, and no regime furnished political cover for an economic team. The political calculus of rulers was shaped by the short-term exigencies of regime survival, providing little incentive to establish a developmental regime.

In the introduction, I also made the general observation that developmental states rest upon an organizational basis for elite coordination. In addition to securing general elite support, regimes that seek a durable reform compact must create alliances with essential producer groups. In fact, the compact usually extends beyond the elite level, since it is necessary to offer palliative sidepayments to others who may not immediately

---

12. Bruce Bueno de Mesquita, Alastair Smith, Randolph M. Siverson, and James D. Morrow, *The Logic of Political Survival* (Cambridge: MIT Press, 2003).

13. Guillermo O'Donnell, *Modernization and Bureaucratic-Authoritarianism* (Berkeley: Institute of International Studies, 1973).

benefit from core alliances.[14] These bargains can be secured in authoritarian situations by the military or a dominant party, and in democratic settings by political parties and consistent leadership. The bureaucracy also plays a role in asserting central rules and stabilizing the expectations of market participants. The central point is that successful developmental states have created institutional vehicles for coordinating the interests and incentives of private elites, and harmonizing them with state goals for investment and accumulation.[15] In the absence of such coordination, an atomistic domain of rent seeking is likely to prevail.[16]

The authoritarian-corporatist structure of the New Order illustrates one approach to elite coordination. The regime identified strategic producer groups among the ethnic Chinese community, foreign capital, and a coterie of *pribumi* entrepreneurs, and secured alliances with these segments. The ruling party, Golkar, and allied corporatist organizations regulated the political arena, containing the expression of interests and furnishing patronage to groups outside the inner circle.[17] With the collapse of the old regime a crucial question for Indonesia's incipient democracy is whether a new party or coalition can take on similar coordinating roles under democratic auspices. In addition to the challenges of crafting new coalitions, turbulence within the state also hampers reform. In the wake of the economic crisis, instability in the bureaucracy and regulatory institutions presents further impediments to regularizing expectations among market actors.

14. See David Waldner, *State Building and Late Development* (Ithaca: Cornell University Press, 1999), 37.

15. Gary Gereffi and Donald Wyman, eds., *Manufacturing Miracles: Paths of Industrialization in Latin America and East Asia* (Princeton: Princeton University Press, 1990); Sylvia Maxfield and Ben Ross Schneider, "Business, the State, and Economic Performance in Developing Countries," in Maxfield and Schneider, *Business and the State in Developing Countries,* 6–10; Waldner, *State Building and Late Development,* 47–39; and Atul Kohli, *State-Directed Development: Political Power, and Industrialization in the Global Periphery* (Cambridge: Cambridge University Press, 2004), 13–14.

16. This is emphasized by Peter Evans, *Embedded Autonomy: States and Industrial Transformation* (Princeton: Princeton University Press, 1995), 47.

17. Malaysia provides an example of an even more successful strategy of this type. Under Prime Minister Mahathir Mohamad the ruling UMNO party consolidated its dominance in tandem with a redistributive program, the New Economic Policy. Alliances with the ethnic Chinese minority and foreign capital were balanced by redistribution to the majority Malay community, under a de facto single party and a corporatist compact. See, for instance, Alasdair Bowie, *Crossing the Industrial Divide: State, Society, and the Politics of Economic Transformation in Malaysia* (New York: Columbia University Press, 1993), and Paul Lubeck, "Malaysian Industrialization, Ethnic Divisions, and the NIC Model: The Limits to Replication," in J. Henderson and R. Appelbaum, eds., *States and Development in the Pacific Rim* (Newbury Park: Sage, 1992).

Nigeria, as stressed throughout, is characterized by a lack of central coordination, yielding a collective action dilemma of fragmented competition over rents. The military and civilian political elites are each divided among communal groups and factions. Nigerians have not developed a genuinely national political party that can claim support from a significant cross-section of national elites and serve as a vehicle of broad economic interests. The country's divided and weak bureaucracy cannot play a coordinating role. A leading question for Nigeria, since the return of electoral rule, is whether a coalition of parties or interest groups can emerge to guide the polity toward a more coherent and productive vision of economic governance.

Distribution, Contention, and Growth

The problems of elite coordination are accompanied by challenges of distributional politics. Governments in culturally plural societies must pursue inclusive alliances with producers and popular sectors in order to secure growth compacts. Developmental regimes in these circumstances face a difficult balance between strong assurances to dynamic producer groups and the dispersal of benefits across wider elements of society.[18] Where benefits accrue to clients, cronies, or protected minorities, the resulting social tensions are likely to undermine growth compacts, making these arrangements inherently brittle. At the other extreme, there is a risk that expedient distributional politics will dissipate resources and prevent the concentration of capital and talent toward capital formation.[19] Ethnic balancing may foster social peace while impeding prospects for growth. The challenge is to favor entrepreneurs while assuaging distributional tensions.

The Indonesian experience highlights the limitations of narrow growth compacts. The New Order successfully fostered alliances with foreign capital and the ethnic Chinese minority, which served as an engine of growth for more than two decades. The regime made expedient sidepayments to *pribumi* business interests, and the expanding economy provided for a reduction of poverty, growth of the middle class, and selective government benefits to popular sectors. These avenues of redistribution, however, could not efface the resentment among the *pribumi* majority toward the Sino-

---

18. Zimbabwe is an especially strong illustration of how badly these arrangements may falter. The Mugabe regime's accommodation with white commercial farmers was offset by a general failure to promote growth in other segments of the economy, or to redistribute land and income among the black majority. Ultimately, Mugabe expropriated the commercial farmers in an attempt to alleviate distributional pressures from his populist base. The resulting economic collapse has shattered the country's economic prospects.

19. William Easterly and Ross Levine, "Africa's Growth Tragedy: Policies and Ethnic Divisions," *Quarterly Journal of Economics* 112, no. 4 (1997): 1214.

Indonesian minority, as well as pressures from labor, students, and Islamic groups, and tensions among Java and the outer islands. These stresses became more acute with time, as the narrow base of cronies and family around the regime generated increasing antipathy. The patrimonial nature of Soeharto's alliances limited the potential to expand the scope of beneficiaries or to provide more general market opportunities. The financial crisis ignited the distributional problems inherent in the regime's compact.

Where benefits are highly concentrated, coalitions for growth may be weakened. On the other hand, where pressures for distribution are widely dispersed, growth coalitions may not even be attainable. As I have noted, Nigeria vividly illustrates a situation in which mutual vetoes among segmented groups hinder the consolidation of property rights, showing the problems of building growth coalitions amid communal rivalries. Pressures for distribution among Nigeria's major ethnoregional groups drove leaders to pursue stability through tactics of recompense. These patrimonial strategies dissipated resources and subsidized consumption rather than investment. The inability of state elites to guarantee property rights, secure contracts, or regularize relations with entrepreneurial groups carried heavy costs for economic growth.[20] In the wake of authoritarian rule, some of these tensions could be diminished by new elite coalitions and efforts to revise Nigeria's federal structure. The political and institutional inheritance, however, is highly unfavorable to a growth compact.

Rents, Corruption, and Growth

Rent seeking and corruption are inefficient behaviors that generally suppress growth. There is increasing recognition, however, that some forms may be more corrosive than others. In the high-performing states of Asia, corruption and rent-seeking behavior have been compatible with sustained high growth; in sub-Saharan Africa and many other areas, collusive behavior is clearly linked with economic stagnation.[21] The comparison of

20. Pranab Bardhan has outlined a long-standing distributional syndrome in *The Political Economy of Development in India* (Delhi: Oxford University Press, 1984). He argues that India through the 1980s was caught between the pressures of distributional accommodation among plural elites, on the one hand, and the need to channel capital toward productive accumulation, on the other. A number of factors may have attenuated these problems in India, including strong economic interest groups, influential political parties, and a relatively capable bureaucracy.

21. Variations in the growth-suppressing effects of corruption are discussed by Andrei Shleifer and Robert W. Vishny, "Corruption," *Quarterly Journal of Economics* 108, no. 3 (1993): 599–617. For the Asian context, see Mushtaq H. Khan and K. S. Jomo, eds., *Rents, Rent-Seeking, and Economic Development: Theory and Evidence in Asia* (Cambridge: Cambridge University Press, 2000). On rent seeking and economic costs in Africa, see Charles M. DeLorme, D. R. Kamerschen, and J. M. Mbaku, "Rent-Seeking in the Cameroon Econ-

Indonesia and Nigeria highlights the varying effects of these syndromes under different political arrangements and macroeconomic contexts. Rent seeking and corruption were inveterate features of the political economy in both countries, yet these practices were organized very differently, with implications for economic performance.

In Indonesia, political influence over the economy gave rise to extensive rent seeking, especially among close allies of the regime. Administrative corruption was prodigious, as captured by the popular shorthand "KKN" (from the Indonesian words for "corruption, cronyism, and nepotism"), characterizing the operating style of the government and state agencies. These problems led to inefficiency, inequities, and wasted resources but nonetheless accorded with growth and capital formation. The availability of special preferences did not broadly undermine investment in production and actually facilitated some value-creating activities. Illicit or collusive gains were often reinvested in the local economy, rather than being siphoned abroad or into underground endeavors. Prominent members of the ruling circle and their associates reaped fabulous gains through protected markets and other rental havens, yet the regime loosely contained the scope, and sometimes the scale, of frankly illicit activities. A modicum of accountability was imposed under the New Order, as leading entrepreneurs and administrative agencies were expected to serve the ruler's goals for national development. Favorable macroeconomic conditions also helped to stem capital flight by furnishing local outlets for investment.

While emphasizing the growth-facilitating elements of the regime, it is equally important to emphasize the centrality of patronage, collusive relations among elites, widespread abuses of administrative discretion and public finance, and the distortions and inequities that resulted from these practices. The parlous conditions of public institutions, the banking system, and corporate governance in Soeharto's wake give ample testimony to the costs of the patrimonial capitalist system. The New Order was distinctive, however, in the degree to which rents and corruption were centralized and policed by the regime.[22] These practices were comparatively

---

omy," *American Journal of Economics and Sociology* 45, no. 4 (1986): 413–23; John Mbaku and C. Paul, "Political Instability in Africa: A Rent-Seeking Approach," *Public Choice* 63, no. 1 (1989): 63–72; and Emmanuel Ampofo-Tuffuor, C. D. DeLorme Jr., and D. R. Kamerschen, "The Nature, Significance, and Cost of Rent-Seeking in Ghana," *Kyklos* 44, no. 4 (1991): 537–59.

22. See Andrew MacIntyre, "Funny Money: Fiscal Policy, Rent-Seeking, and Economic Performance in Indonesia," in Khan and Jomo, eds., *Rents, Rent-Seeking, and Economic Development,* 266–67.

organized and stable, and operated under a leadership with developmental ambitions. Patterns of rent distribution and corruption have altered since the financial crisis and the collapse of the authoritarian regime. With less oversight by a central authority, these activities are more diffuse and opportunistic. Further, macroeconomic uncertainty has increased capital flight and reduced investment in fixed assets.

In Nigeria, the polarization of political elites and the weakness of central institutions gave rise to a more fragmented, competitive, and anarchic realm of rent allocation and corruption.[23] In the wake of the oil windfall, rents occurred in two forms: direct fiscal allotments derived from resource rents, and special access to protected markets. Different branches of government mediated different types of rents, creating a diffuse realm of lobbying and collusion. Corruption has imbued public agencies at all levels. Under authoritarian rule, the proliferation of states offered wide discretion to the military governors, who created personal fiefdoms, often with little supervision from the senior leadership. In civilian regimes, the added layers of elected officials multiply the points of access to state favors and resources.[24] In addition, civil servants and state enterprise managers frequently act within their own ambit, unaccountable to a broader hierarchy.[25]

The organization of the Nigerian state has fostered corruption and rent distribution in ways that are highly detrimental to economic development. Weak central authorities are generally unable to exercise surveillance of state organizations or personnel. With no accountability to a clear principal, state agents have a permissive setting for corrupt activities and few injunctions to provide official services. This has resulted in multiple, competitive pressures for corruption and rents, along with the theft of state resources and the neglect of formal duties.[26] Not only are public agencies arbitrary and venal, but they do not deliver effective outputs and are not held to standards of performance. Rather than confronting the problems of state weakness, governing elites have commonly utilized these conditions as an expedient means of distribution. Broad access to rents

23. Peter M. Lewis, "Economic Statism, Private Capital, and the Dilemmas of Accumulation in Nigeria," *World Development* 22, no. 3 (1994), and Tom Forrest, *Politics and Economic Development in Nigeria,* 2d ed. (Boulder: Westview, 1995).

24. Richard Joseph, *Democracy and Prebendal Politics in Nigeria: The Rise and Fall of the Second Republic* (Cambridge: Cambridge University Press, 1987).

25. Forms of corruption and rent distribution in the public sector are analyzed by Lewis, "Economic Statism"; see also Peter Lewis, "State, Economy, and Privatization in Nigeria," in John Waterbury and Ezra Suleiman, eds., *The Political Economy of Public Sector Reform and Privatization* (Boulder: Westview, 1990).

26. Drawing upon Shleifer and Vishny's distinctions in *Corruption,* 604–5.

and corrupt gains furnishes leaders with useful outlets for dispensing patronage. Political logic inclines leaders to favor policies and administrative measures that undermine the process of growth.[27]

The advent of democratic rule in Indonesia and Nigeria, however desirable from a political vantage, has also created new dilemmas for economic change. Political access points to state resources have expanded, politicians have increased the demands and avenues for patronage, and the new governments exercise weak control over party machines and elements of the bureaucracy. In recent years, both Indonesia and Nigeria have been ranked among the world's most corrupt states in comparative indices.[28] There is clearly a need to reduce absolute levels of corruption in these countries, although this analysis suggests that it is equally important to contain the unregulated and competitive elements of corruption. Reforms can reduce discretion through greater transparency and improved systems of surveillance and enforcement, while policy changes and institutional development can limit outlets for rent distribution. Viewed realistically, reform efforts are unlikely to produce dramatic reductions in levels of official corruption in the near to medium term. However, it may be possible in the near term to limit rentier activities and discipline corrupt dealings sufficiently to reduce the drag on growth.

The Dimensions of Reform

The future paths of Indonesia and Nigeria are much in question. The first civilian term after the transition from authoritarian rule revealed similar problems and trends in both states. Institutions were in turmoil in the wake of the old regime, while political elites were fragmented among parties, factions, and communal loyalties. Leadership proved uncertain and ineffectual, while important reform initiatives were blocked by legislative obstruction and competition for rents. Both economies languished as investment diminished, with growth rates generally below 5 percent despite highly favorable prices for resource exports. Widening poverty and accentuated tensions over distribution fostered social unrest, manifest particularly in communal violence and separatist movements.

27. On the tensions between political and economic logic, see Thomas M. Callaghy, "Political Passions and Economic Interests: Economic Reform and Political Structure in Africa," in Thomas Callaghy and John Ravenhill, eds., *Hemmed In: Responses to Africa's Economic Decline* (New York: Columbia University Press, 1994). Patrick Chabal and Jean-Pascal Daloz analyze the ways that rulers "instrumentalize" disorder and state weakness, in *Africa Works: Disorder as a Political Instrument* (Bloomington: Indiana University Press, 1999).

28. Transparency International, *Corruption Perceptions Index*, various years.

In both countries, however, second elections introduced governments with a stronger reform profile. Susilo Bambang Yudhoyono was regarded by many Indonesians as a capable figure outside the fray of self-dealing partisan politics, and his military background encouraged public expectations that he would firmly deal with security problems and the challenges of reform. In Nigeria, President Obasanjo was returned to office in a controversial election marked by widespread irregularities, although the general outcome was accepted by the public. Embarking on his second term, the administration attempted to invigorate reform through an overhaul of the economic team and a set of initiatives covering fiscal oversight, revenue transparency, bank restructuring, and anticorruption efforts. While these measures met with considerable public skepticism, the second Obasanjo administration showed a departure from the indecision and passivity of the first term, especially with regard to economic policy. However, elite divisions and weak state machinery remained, leaving uncertain the outcomes of reform.

When assessing the prospects for economic change in Indonesia and Nigeria, we can examine three important dimensions of change. These countries can be analyzed as resource-exporting states, embodying a common syndrome of economic and political distortions arising from energy exports. They can also be considered aspiring democracies with similar challenges of institutional development and political coordination. Finally, as multiethnic states they face abiding challenges of distributing resources and political power.

The Burden of Resources

Having discussed at length the syndrome associated with petro-states and the Dutch disease (chapter 3), I will briefly consider the political economy of reform in these resource-rich countries. Resource windfalls increase the fiscal autonomy and discretion of the central state. Burgeoning revenues also lead to the concentration of assets among rentier groups linked to political elites. These factors are commonly associated with low degrees of government accountability, limited economic diversity, limited independence of producer groups, and a narrow revenue base.[29] The structural

29. These factors are elaborated by Alan Gelb, "Adjustment to Windfall Gains: A Comparative Analysis of Oil Exporting Countries," in J. P. Neary and S. van Wijnbergen, eds., *Natural Resources and the Macroeconomy* (Oxford: Basil Blackwell, 1986); Terry Lynn Karl, *The Paradox of Plenty: Oil Booms and Petro-States* (Berkeley: University of California Press, 1997); and Richard M. Auty, "Economic and Political Reform of Distorted Oil-Exporting Economies," paper prepared for the workshop "Escaping the Resource Curse: Managing Natural Resource Revenues in Low-Income Countries," Center on Globalization and Sustainable Development (Columbia University Earth Institute, 2004).

conditions tend to reinforce patterns of rent seeking, authoritarianism, corruption, and economic volatility. Further, resource wealth is often associated with conflict, for at least two reasons. The concentration of rents generates intense struggles over political power and access to the state; and the local grievances of residents in areas of resource extraction often create restiveness.[30]

These structural problems are evident in both states under comparison, although many of the patterns in Indonesia have been attenuated by the adjustment and diversification pursued by the old regime. Assets are more widely dispersed in Indonesia, entrepreneurial groups can be independent and politically assertive, and the new government has generally sustained capable macroeconomic management. Nigeria's political economy is dominated by oil and gas revenues and the ensuing rent distribution from the central state. Political competition over rents and patronage has defined politics, and business groups have had limited influence on policy.

Resource-exporting states face two strategic issues of reform: diversification of the economy, which can disperse assets and deconcentrate power; and fiscal systems that reduce discretion and increase transparency.[31] These areas of change are crucial for addressing long-term structural problems of accountability, rent distribution, and volatility in petroleum-rich economies. Considering reform prospects in the two countries, Indonesia clearly retains advantages from earlier periods of high growth, having developed a substantial manufacturing base, supporting infrastructure, large sunk investments, varied mineral and agricultural exports, and a diverse business class with a base in productive activities. Nigeria, by contrast, confronts the most basic challenges in moving from an oil monoculture. However, governments in both countries face problems of credible commitment that can invigorate entrepreneurship and foster investment in nonoil activities. The pursuit of sound macroeconomic management is an important step toward broader restructuring. Macroeconomic policy has been more consistent in Indonesia, though Nigeria has moved toward improved oversight of currency, trade, monetary policy, and fiscal balances. The leading difficulties in each case are found in the domain of sectoral policies, where rent seeking and high levels of political discretion prevail. These regimes will have to craft new

---

30. Michael L. Ross, "How Do Natural Resources Influence Civil War? Evidence from Thirteen Cases," *International Organization* 58, no. 1 (2004): 35–67.

31. On the structural effects of economic diversification, see Thad Dunning, "Resource Dependence, Economic Performance, and Political Stability," *Journal of Conflict Resolution* 49, no. 4 (2005): 451–82.

alliances with producers and investors, with attention to particular sectors and industries. The formation of consultative groups and formal mechanisms for collaboration between firms and the public sector could provide avenues for commitment as well as policy guidance.[32]

Issues of fiscal management and accountability are also prominent. Indonesian and Nigerian administrations have recently sought to address the problems of opaque fiscal systems and excessive discretion in fiscal affairs. Both countries have increased transparency through more extensive and timely reporting of budgetary trends, which are increasingly monitored by parliament and civic groups. Nigeria has made significant efforts to rationalize fiscal management, including enhanced standards for reporting revenues and fiscal flows, maintaining external reserves, and organizing government procurement. A notable trend is the turn to international commitment mechanisms. The Extractive Industries Transparency Initiative, a UK-sponsored program that Nigeria has joined, creates a framework for both foreign companies and the government to report export proceeds, and it imposes requirements for tracking the use of revenues received by the state. Nigeria's leading position in the New Partnership for Africa's Development (NEPAD) encourages regional adherence to improved governance. The effort to build stronger controls and better reporting into the fiscal structure is a major departure from the neopatrimonial legacy of these states.

There are, however, countervailing trends that may limit reform. Rent-seeking interests continue to lobby for special preferences, to collude with state officials, and to resist institutional changes that increase transparency and reduce discretion. The parliaments of both countries have expanded budgets, delayed key legislation and regulatory changes, and engaged in widespread self-dealing with business elites. Similar practices can be found among other branches of government and the political elite. The most substantial challenge to reform is the movement of oil and gas prices, which have been on a sustained upward path. High resource revenues create a soft budget constraint, which diminishes the urgency of reform while reviving competitive pressures for rent distribution. The prospects for change are contingent on the ability of reform coalitions to act independently of revenue cycles and rentier pressures. Here too, Indonesia reflects advantages arising from a legacy of technocratic influence, strong macroeconomic oversight, and economic interest groups in the productive sectors of the economy.

32. Forms of consultation and coordination are analyzed by various contributors in Maxfield and Schneider, *Business and the State in Developing Countries.*

The problems of resource-related conflict and distribution are equally salient. Without addressing the full scope of challenges in the Indonesian provinces of Aceh and Western Papua, or Nigeria's Niger Delta, it is clear that fiscal restructuring is an important component of conflict management in these restive areas. Essential dimensions of state reform include improved allocations of revenues to resource-producing regions, increased transparency of revenue flows, greater administrative and fiscal autonomy for resource-producing regions, and improved performance of subnational administration. These structural and resource changes have the potential to address crucial sources of instability. The record so far has not been encouraging, as both regimes have employed heavy-handed security responses in these regions, while fiscal reforms and development initiatives have been slow to materialize. Nigeria has made some progress in the area of revenue allocation for states in the Niger Delta, while Indonesia has concluded a truce with Acehnese rebels that may facilitate a more permanent settlement. Neither government has moved toward a more comprehensive resolution of demands for distribution from resource-producing areas.

Democratic Dilemmas

I gave lengthy consideration to the problems of democratic transition and economic change in the two cases in chapters 7 and 8. It is sufficient to note here that challenges of democratization currently shape the political context of economic reform in each state. In the early years since the change of regime, both Indonesia and Nigeria have reflected comparable problems of building democratic institutions, stabilizing competitive party systems, fostering the accountability of rulers, and gathering ruling coalitions that can pursue an agenda of reform. As I have noted, the opening of democratic politics affords opportunities for shifting the incentives of rulers and the interests arrayed around economic policy and institutions. Organized business groups and civic organizations can play more assertive roles in pressing for changes in governance, while increased accountability to voters creates implicit (and often overt) demands for performance. Quite commonly, however, pressures for accountability and change in new democracies are offset by the influences of entrenched elites and collusive arrangements among government and business groups. Democratization is often a necessary condition for reform but rarely a sufficient basis for change.

Reform in Indonesia and Nigeria has been encumbered by the continued influence of traditional ruling segments and the powerful incentives fostered by structures of patronage and rent distribution. The major institutional innovation has been the introduction of constitutional provisions for competitive elections and full political and civil liberties. Beyond this foundation, Indonesians have moved more quickly to address basic flaws in institutional arrangements, passing a series of constitutional amendments and changes in the regulatory regime. In addition, Indonesia has experienced three full turnovers of incumbents and parties, two by election and one through impeachment. Formal provisions for military influence in politics have also been substantially curtailed. Despite these hallmarks of democratic change, traditional parties and elites continue to influence the political system in important ways. The former ruling Golkar party has emerged as a viable competitive force with a significant base, a well-developed national machine, and considerable resources. The military retains an implicit political role, as an institution and through the political activities of retired officers, including the current president. Many prominent cronies and rentier groups have been excluded from power, but the interests of major conglomerates and barons continue to find expression in the political system and the bureaucracy.

Nigeria has experienced presidential continuity in the first two terms following the transition, providing a basis for expanded executive authority in many areas. The party system has moved in an increasingly hegemonic direction. Nigerian political elites have introduced scant changes in political institutions, apart from a grudging expansion of the party system forced by judicial leverage. There has been only modest turnover among elites, as the ruling party and the leading opposition groups are heavily populated with veteran politicians and retired officers. In the second electoral term, the legislature experienced a major turnover of membership, allowing the entry of younger and less experienced participants. Along with changes in the states, there was further evidence of a generational shift in the composition of the political class. Despite such alterations, the Nigerian transition has afforded substantial continuity of clientelist networks and rentier groups, as there has been no major crisis to disrupt incumbent elites and few subsequent initiatives to reduce their influence. Government initiatives to investigate malfeasance and improve transparency have produced notable results, but there are inherent limits to political renovation in the context of a flawed electoral process and the growing dominance of a patronage-based ruling party.

How can we assess these crosscurrents of reform, and what are the implications for economic change? Turning to the analysis I have outlined, the central factors include trends in leadership, the nature of coalitions, and their effects on institutions for economic governance. Regarding leadership, there has been considerable change in Indonesia, following a comparable pattern seen in the Philippines and in Russia, where voters pursued a "flight to strength": after reform-oriented leaders proved ineffectual in securing economic recovery or public order, the public gravitated to candidates with a security background, drawn by the appeals of decisiveness and competence. It remains to be seen whether President Yudhoyono will prove more successful than international counterparts in managing change, but his emergence from a new party and his association with reform efforts as a cabinet minister under President Megawati signal an important shift in the character of leadership. In Nigeria, the Obasanjo administration has shaken loose the torpor and drift of the first term and has set out an array of measures to move policy and institutions toward a reform agenda. These initiatives, however, are still guided by the vagaries of individual choice and are not rooted in a more substantial institutional or political base. Whatever President Obasanjo's reform proclivities, his cohort generally represents an earlier generation of leadership and policy orientations. Nigeria provides little evidence that patterns of leadership selection or basic incentives for rulers have altered.

The evolution of the party system and the alliances that parties embody is a crucial aspect of changing coalitions. Indonesia's party system is comparatively fragmented, with a cluster of parties competing for a plurality in the electoral system and the legislature. The party system has been fluid, as some parties have declined rapidly, new competitors have emerged, and the fortunes of others have wavered. Further, Indonesia's parties display a degree of ideological variation, arrayed among Muslim-identified groups, more explicit Islamists, secular nationalists, and other tendencies. Nigeria's party system is far more concentrated, stable, and homogenous. The dominant PDP has increased its control of the central government and the states, and there are only a few parties with a presence in the national political arena, two of which have quite minor positions. There is scarcely any variation in ideology or programs among the parties, and they are structured mainly along the lines of personalities, communal alliances, and clientelist networks.

One approach to the questions of democratic reform is to assess the effects of institutional structure. Andrew MacIntyre has recently focused on the importance of institutional "architecture" in his comparative work on economic governance in Southeast Asia.[33] The comparison of Indonesia and Nigeria offers some perspective on this line of analysis. As MacIntyre observes, Indonesia has a mixed presidential-parliamentary system

---

33. Andrew MacIntyre, *The Power of Institutions: Political Architecture and Governance* (Ithaca: Cornell University Press, 2003).

and a dispersed and divided party constellation, a departure from the rigidly centralized system under Soeharto. In terms of institutional design, Nigeria embodies stronger presidential government and a more concentrated party system. One inference might be that this contrasting architecture would lead to less decisive governance in Indonesia and greater efficacy in Nigeria. Yet precisely the reverse is true: despite considerable division and obstruction, Indonesians have made greater progress in advancing constitutional change, restructuring regulatory institutions, and pursuing other needed legal and organizational reforms. Indonesian governments have also restored balance and consistency in macroeconomic management. Nigerians, in contrast, have been paralyzed by internal contention among political elites and hampered by a weak institutional legacy. This suggests that institutional design may be less influential than the way interests are arrayed within the political system. Informal arrangements of political influence trump structure, implying that institutions are an endogenous factor in development, reflecting underlying configurations of power, rather than an exogenous influence that constrains political actors.[34]

The party system is only one element of a broader set of coalitions that could emerge under democratic rule. The emergence of alliances between political authorities and producer groups will crucially influence prospects for improved economic governance. Organized business and sectoral associations, and their leverage with the major political parties, form an important locus of political change affecting the reform process. Other elements of a developmental coalition could include civic groups organized around the rule of law and anticorruption efforts. In addition, important pressures for change may arise from popular mobilization focusing on collective goods. The relative strength of such interests will shape reform propensities in Indonesia and Nigeria.

The development of core institutions associated with democracy, including the electoral system, the legislature, an independent judiciary, and the constitutional framework, is a central task in building the democratic foundations for economic growth. In the near term, I have argued that ad hoc arrangements may serve to accelerate growth and build confidence in markets. This can buy time for deeper institutional development, though it does not reduce the importance of an improved legal, administrative, and policy framework. A favorable scenario in these countries would be a moderate rate of economic growth accompanied by

---

34. Carles Boix, *Democracy and Redistribution* (Cambridge: Cambridge University Press, 2003).

longer-term institutional improvements in key areas of the political system and the economic bureaucracy. Should institutional deficits persist or worsen, however, provisional arrangements for property rights and invest- ment are likely to be extremely fragile.

Distribution and Communal Contention

A final consideration is the influence of communal contention and distri- butional politics on growth. The tensions and conflicts arising from com- munal divisions in these countries pose obvious challenges to political sta- bility and national integrity. An influential stream of literature has argued that plural societies have strong intrinsic obstacles to growth.[35] Pressures for distribution are not only destabilizing but also deplete the stock of resources that can be directed to growth-enhancing investments. Clearly, separatist pressures, religious conflict, ethnic rivalry, and the myriad demands for resources among communal groups foster basic challenges of governance for Indonesian and Nigerian leaders. Are there strategies for managing these tensions in ways compatible with stability and growth?

One solution lies in the area of institutional reform. Both countries have taken needed steps toward reducing political centralization and according greater fiscal and administrative autonomy to various commu- nities and regions. Indonesia's rapid decentralization in 2001, and Nige- ria's recurring efforts to renegotiate the arrangements of federalism, pre- sent two approaches to state reform. Though Indonesia's reforms have shown some promise, decentralization still carries potential risks that could aggravate sectional tensions and hamper growth. Low capacity and the emergence of alternate power centers under local strongmen could weaken central development strategies and sharpen disparities among regions or groups. Similarly, Nigerian efforts to renegotiate revenue distri- bution formulas and accord greater leeway to elected governors can assuage some of the problems of centralized policy-making and rentier relations between the capital and the states. Yet the truculent activities of governors in several Nigerian states, often strongly linked to the incidence of conflict, demonstrate the problems of developing federalism in circum- stances of weak institutions and concentrated fiscal resources. Despite such problems, the path to dispersed growth and distributional accommo- dation runs through these avenues of institutional change. The develop- ment of decentralization and federalism are central agendas for reform.

Apart from restructuring institutions, governments can take specific

---

35. See, for instance, Mancur Olson, *The Rise and Decline of Nations* (New Haven: Yale University Press, 1982), and Easterly and Levine, "Africa's Growth Tragedy."

initiatives to foster entrepreneurial groups and alliances with producers. These may encompass particular communal groups, since economic activities are ethnically segmented in both countries. Amy Chua has warned that favoritism toward "market-dominant minorities" will exacerbate tensions that jeopardize the stability of the democratic market system.[36] The violent antipathy toward Sino-Indonesians and numerous ethnic feuds in Nigeria certainly reflect the explosive convergence of economic inequality and communal difference. Yet this concern may be overdrawn: it is possible to develop the entrepreneurial capacities of particular groups while offsetting the risks of inequality and division. If different ethnically defined producer groups can develop interethnic economic linkages and complementarities, the promise of "gains from trade" can encourage new plural coalitions in a developmental project.[37] State elites can foster such plural alliances through direct support for particular activities and linkages, and through policy and institutional changes that encourage a more competitive and transparent market setting.

Ultimately, improved distributions are contingent upon growth. The objectives of economic expansion and redistribution can be served by encouraging broad-based investment in diverse areas of the economy. A vibrant economy provides the necessary foundation for expanding economic opportunities, channeling gains more broadly among communities and groups, and furnishing the state with resources to effectively pursue redistributive measures. All this brings us back to the animating idea of this book: the importance of institutional sources of growth and the political factors that encourage economic development. Institutional change is an uncertain, uneven, and incremental process. Institutional development is influenced by history, structural factors, and the choices of political actors and market participants. The historical course of development sets a pattern, but paths may be altered and new equilibria attained. The contingent factors in institutional and economic change compel our attention to conflict, strategy, and bargaining in the political sphere. Economic development rests upon politically negotiated institutions.

36. Amy Chua, *World on Fire: How Exporting Free Market Democracy Breeds Ethnic Hatred and Global Instability* (New York: Doubleday, 2002).

37. The potential for such interethnic economic cooperation is explored by Michael Watts and Paul Lubeck, "An Alliance of Oil and Maize? The Response of Indigenous and State Capital to Structural Adjustment in Nigeria," in Bruce Berman and Colin Leys, eds., *African Capitalists and African Development* (Boulder: Lynne Rienner, 1994). On the Malaysian case see Bowie, *Crossing the Industrial Divide.*

Bibliography

Aborisade, O., and R. J. Mundt. *Politics in Nigeria.* New York: Longman, 2001.

Aboyade, O. "Nigerian Public Enterprises as an Organizational Dilemma." In *Public Enterprise in Nigeria.* Ibadan: Nigerian Economic Society, 1973.

Adamolekun, Lapido. *Politics and Administration in Nigeria.* London: Hutchinson, 1986.

Agbaje, Adigun, Larry Diamond, and Ebere Onwudiwe. *Nigeria's Struggle for Democracy and Good Governance.* Ibadan: Ibadan University Press, 2004.

Agbese, Dan, and Etim Anyim. "The State Elections of 1991." In *Transition without End: Nigerian Politics and Civil Society under Babangida,* edited by Larry Diamond, Anthony Kirk-Greene, and Oyeleye Oyediran. Boulder: Lynne Rienner, 1997.

Agusto and Co. *1993/94 Banking Industry Survey.* Lagos: Agusto and Co., 1994.

Ajakaiye, D. Olu. "Impact of Policy on Public Enterprise Performance in Nigeria." *Nigerian Journal of Economic and Social Studies* 26, no. 3 (1984): 376–77.

Akanji, O. O. "Incidence of Poverty and Economic Growth in Nigeria." Paper presented to the Conference of the International Association for Official Statistics (IAOS) on "Statistics, Development and Human Rights," Montreaux, Switzerland, September 2000.

Ake, Claude. "How Politics Underdevelops Africa." In *The Challenges of African Economic Recovery and Development,* edited by Adebayo Adedeji and P. Bugemba. London: Frank Cass, 1989.

Akinsanya, Adeoye A. "State Strategies toward Nigerian and Foreign Business." In *The Political Economy of Nigeria,* edited by I. William Zartman. New York: Praeger, 1983.

Akinterinwa, Bola A. "The 1993 Presidential Election Imbroglio." In *Transition without End: Nigerian Politics and Civil Society under Babangida,* edited by Larry Diamond, Anthony Kirk-Greene, and Oyeleye Oyediran. Boulder: Lynne Rienner, 1997.

Akwaya, Cletus. "Nigeria's Telephone Lines Now 10 million." *This Day* (Lagos), January 25, 2005.

Alisjahbana, A. S., and C. Manning. "Survey of Recent Developments." *Bulletin of Indonesian Economic Studies* 38, no. 3 (2002): 277–305.

Alston, Lee J., Thráinn Eggertsson, and Douglass C. North. *Empirical Studies in Institutional Change.* Cambridge: Cambridge University Press, 1996.

Amadi, Sam. "Nigeria: Must a Reformer Be." *This Day* (Lagos), November 6, 2004.

Ames, Barry. *Political Survival: Politicians and Public Policy in Latin America.* Berkeley: University of California Press, 1987.

Ampofo-Tuffuor, Emmanuel, C. D. DeLorme Jr., and D. R. Kamerschen. "The Nature, Significance, and Cost of Rent-Seeking in Ghana." *Kyklos* 44, no. 4 (1991): 537–59.

Amsden, Alice. *Asia's Next Giant: South Korea and Late Industrialization.* New York: Oxford University Press, 1989.

———. "The State and Taiwan's Economic Development." In *Bringing the State Back In,* edited by Peter Evans, Dietrich Rueschemeyer, and Theda Skocpol. Cambridge: Cambridge University Press, 1985.

Amuwo, Kunle, Adigun Agbaje, Rotimi Suberu, and Georges Herault. *Federalism and Political Restructuring in Nigeria.* Ibadan: Spectrum Books, 1998.

Anderson, Benedict R. O'G. *Language and Power: Exploring Political Cultures in Indonesia.* Ithaca: Cornell University Press, 1990.

Andrew, Patrick. "World Bank Flays Cost of Abuja Stadium." *Daily Trust* (Abuja), December 13, 2001.

Anise, Ladun. "Political Parties and Election Manifestoes." In *The Nigerian 1979 Elections,* edited by Oyeleye Oyediran. London and Basingstoke: Macmillan, 1981.

Aoki, Masahiko, Masahiro Okuno-Fujiwara, and Hyung-Ki Kim. *The Role of Government in East Asian Economic Development: Comparative Institutional Analysis.* Oxford: Oxford University Press, 1996.

Ariyo, Ademola, ed. *Economic Reform and Macroeconomic Management in Nigeria.* Ibadan: Ibadan University Press, 1996.

Armijo, Leslie Elliott, Thomas J. Biersteker, and Abraham F. Lowenthal. "Economic Reform and Democracy: The Problem of Simultaneous Transitions." *Journal of Democracy* 5, no. 4 (1994): 161–75.

Arndt, Heinz W. *The Indonesian Economy.* Singapore: Chapman, 1984.

Arndt, Heinz W., and J. Panglaykim. "Survey of Recent Developments." *Bulletin of Indonesian Economic Studies* 2, no. 4 (1966): 1–35.

Arrow, K. "The Organization of Economic Activity: Issues Pertinent to the Choice of Market versus Nonmarket Allocation." *Public Expenditures and Policy Analysis: The PPB System,* vol. 1. U.S. Joint Economic Committee, 91st Congress, 1st session. Washington, DC: U.S. Government Printing Office, 1969.

———. "Towards a Theory of Price Adjustment." In *Allocation of Economic Resources,* edited by M. Abramovitz. Stanford: Stanford University Press, 1959.

Aryteetey, Ernest, and Machiko Nissanke. "Asia and Africa in the Global Economy." Paper presented at the UNU-AERC Conference, Tokyo, 1999.

Auty, Richard M. "Economic and Political Reform of Distorted Oil-Exporting Economies." Paper prepared for the workshop "Escaping the Resource Curse: Managing Natural Resource Revenues in Low-Income Countries," Center on Globalization and Sustainable Development, Earth Institute, Columbia University, February 2004.

———. *Patterns of Development: Resources, Policy, and Economic Growth.* London: Edward Arnold, 1995.

———, ed. *Resource Abundance and Economic Development.* Oxford: Oxford University Press, 2001.

———. *Sustainable Development in the Mineral Economies: The Resource Curse Thesis.* London: Routledge, 1993.

Ayida, Allison A. *Reflections on Nigerian Development.* Lagos: Heinemann, 1987.

Ayida, Allison A., and H. M. Onitiri, eds. *Reconstruction and Development in Nigeria.* Ibadan: Oxford University Press, 1971.

Babawale, Tunde, ed. *Urban Violence, Ethnic Militias, and the Challenges of Democratic Consolidation in Nigeria.* Lagos: Malthouse Press, 2003.

Baker, R., M. H. Soesastro, J. Kristiadi, and D. Ramage, eds. *Indonesia: The Challenge of Change.* Honolulu: East-West Center, 1999.

Bangura, Yusuf, and Bjorn Beckman. "African Workers and Structural Adjustment: A Nigerian Case Study." In *The Politics of Structural Adjustment in Nigeria,* edited by Adebayo Olukoshi. London: James Currey, 1993.

Barber, Karin. "Popular Reactions to the Petro-Naira." *Journal of Modern African Studies* 20, no. 3 (1982): 431–50.

Bardhan, Pranab. "The Nature of Institutional Impediments to Economic Development." In *A Not-So-Dismal Science: A Broader View of Economies and Societies,* edited by Mancur Olson and Satu Kahkonen. Oxford: Oxford University Press, 2000.

———. "The New Institutional Economics and Development Theory: A Brief Critical Assessment." *World Development* 17, no. 9 (1989): 1389–95.

———. *The Political Economy of Development in India.* Delhi: Oxford University Press, 1984.

Barro, Robert. *Determinants of Economic Growth: A Cross-Country Empirical Study.* Cambridge: MIT Press, 1997.

Bates, Robert H. *Markets and States in Tropical Africa.* Berkeley: University of California Press, 1981.

———. "Modernization, Ethnic Competition, and the Rationality of Politics in Africa." In *State versus Ethnic Claims: African Policy Dilemmas,* edited by Donald Rothchild. Boulder: Westview, 1982.

———. *Prosperity and Violence: The Political Economy of Development.* New York: W. W. Norton, 2000.

———. "Social Dilemmas and Rational Individuals: An Assessment of the New Institutionalism." *The New Institutional Economics and Third World Development,* edited by John Harriss, Janet Hunter, and Colin M. Lewis. London and New York: Routledge, 1995.

Berman, Bruce, and Colin Leys, eds. *African Capitalists and African Development.* Boulder: Lynne Rienner, 1994.

Bevan, David, Paul Collier, and J. W. Gunning. "Nigerian Economic Policy and Performance: 1981–92." Manuscript. Center for the Study of African Economies, Oxford University, May 1992.

———. *The Political Economy of Poverty, Equity, and Growth in Nigeria and Indonesia, 1950–86.* Washington, DC: World Bank, 1999.

Bhagwati, Jagdish N. "Directly Unproductive, Profit-Seeking (DUP) Activities." *Journal of Political Economy* 90, no. 5 (1982): 988–1002.

Bienen, Henry. *Armies and Parties in Africa.* New York: Holmes and Meier, 1978.

———. "Oil Revenues and Policy Choice in Nigeria." In *Political Conflict and Economic Change in Nigeria,* edited by Henry Bienen. London: Frank Cass, 1985.

Bienen, Henry, and V. P. Diejomaoh, eds. *The Political Economy of Income Distribution in Nigeria.* New York: Holmes and Meier, 1981.

Bienen, Henry, and Alan Gelb. "Nigeria: From Windfall Gains to Welfare Losses?" In *Oil Windfalls: Blessing or Curse?,* edited by Alan Gelb. Oxford: Oxford University Press for the World Bank, 1988.

Bienen, Henry, and Nicolas van de Walle. *Of Time and Power.* Stanford: Stanford University Press, 1990.

Biersteker, Thomas J. *Multinationals, the State, and Control of the Nigerian Economy.* Princeton: Princeton University Press, 1987.

———. "Reducing the Role of the State in the Economy: A Conceptual Exploration of IMF and World Bank Prescriptions." *International Studies Quarterly* 34, no. 4 (1990): 477–92.

———. "Structural Adjustment and the Political Transition in Nigeria." Paper presented at the Conference on Democratic Transition and Structural Adjustment in Nigeria, Stanford University, August 1990.

Biersteker, Thomas J., and Peter Lewis. "The Rise and Fall of Structural Adjustment in Nigeria." In *Transition without End: Nigerian Politics and Civil Society under Babangida,* edited by Larry Diamond, Anthony Kirk-Greene, and Oyeleye Oyediran. Boulder: Lynne Rienner, 1997.

Bird, Judith. "Indonesia in 1998: The Pot Boils Over." *Asian Survey* 39, no. 1 (1999): 27–37.

Bloch, Marc. *Feudal Society.* 2 vols. Chicago: University of Chicago Press, 1961.

Boix, Carles. *Democracy and Redistribution.* Cambridge: Cambridge University Press, 2003.

Boone, Catherine. "The Making of a Rentier Class: Wealth Accumulation and Political Control in Senegal." *Journal of Development Studies* 26, no. 3 (1990): 425–49.

Booth, Anne. *The Indonesian Economy in the Nineteenth and Twentieth Centuries: A History of Missed Opportunities.* New York: St. Martin's Press. 1998.

———. "Intergovernmental Relations and Fiscal Policy in Indonesia." In *Equity and Development across Nations,* edited by Christine Fletcher. St. Leonards: Allen and Unwin, 1996.

———, ed. *The Oil Boom and After: Indonesian Economic Policy and Performance in the Soeharto Era.* New York: Oxford University Press, 1992.

———. "Poverty and Inequality in the Soeharto Era: An Assessment." *Bulletin of Indonesian Economic Studies* 36, no. 1 (2000): 73–104.

———. "Survey of Recent Developments." *Bulletin of Indonesian Economic Studies* 22, no. 3 (1986): 1–26.

———. "Survey of Recent Developments." *Bulletin of Indonesian Economic Studies* 35, no. 3 (1999): 3–38.

Booth, Anne, and Amina Tyabji. "Survey of Recent Developments." *Bulletin of Indonesian Economic Studies* 15, no. 2 (1979): 1–44.

Borsuk, Richard. "Markets: The Limits of Reform." In *Indonesia beyond Suharto: Polity, Economy, Society, Transition,* edited by Donald Emmerson. Armonk: M. E. Sharpe, 1999.

Bourchier, David. "Habibie's Interregnum: *Reformasi,* Elections, Regionalism, and the Struggle for Power." In *Indonesia in Transition: Social Aspects of*

Reformasi and Crisis, edited by Chris Manning and Peter van Dierman. Singapore: Institute of Southeast Asian Studies, 2000.

Bowie, Alasdair. *Crossing the Industrial Divide: State, Society, and the Politics of Economic Transformation in Malaysia.* New York: Columbia University Press, 1993.

Bowie, Alasdair, and Daniel Unger. *The Politics of Open Economies: Indonesia, Malaysia, the Philippines, and Thailand.* Cambridge: Cambridge University Press, 1997.

Boyce, James K., and Leonce Ndikumana. "Is Africa a Net Creditor? New Estimates of Capital Flight from Severely Indebted Sub-Saharan African Countries, 1970–1996." Working Paper No. 5, University of Massachusetts, Department of Economics, 2000.

Bratton, Michael. "Civil Society and Political Transitions in Africa." In *Civil Society and the State in Africa,* edited by John Harbeson, Donald Rothchild, and Naomi Chazan. Boulder: Lynne Rienner, 1995.

Bratton, Michael, and Nicolas van de Walle. *Democratic Experiments in Africa.* Cambridge: Cambridge University Press, 1997.

———. "Neopatrimonial Regimes and Political Transitions in Africa." *World Politics* 46, no. 4 (1994): 453–89.

———. "Popular Protest and Political Reform in Africa." *Comparative Politics* 24, no. 4 (1992): 419–42.

Brautigam, Deborah. "Governance and Economy: A Review." Policy Research Working Paper. Washington, DC: World Bank, 1991.

Bresnan, John. *Managing Indonesia: The Modern Political Economy.* New York: Columbia University Press, 1993.

Buchanan, James M., R. D. Tollison, and G. Tullock. *Toward a Theory of the Rent-Seeking Society.* College Station: Texas A&M University Press, 1980.

Bueno de Mesquita, Bruce, and Hilton L. Root, eds. *Governing for Prosperity.* New Haven: Yale University Press, 2000.

Bueno de Mesquita, Bruce, Alastair Smith, Randolph M. Siverson, and James D. Marrow. *The Logic of Political Survival.* Cambridge: MIT Press, 2003.

Bureau of Public Statistics, Indonesia. *Export of Non Oil and Gas by Sector and Commodities, Indonesia, 2001–2002.* http://www.bps.go.id/sector/ftrade/export /table2.shtml.

Callaghy, Thomas. "Lost between State and Market: The Politics of Economic Adjustment in Ghana, Zambia, and Nigeria." In *Economic Crisis and Policy Choice,* edited by Joan Nelson. Princeton: Princeton University Press, 1990.

———. "Political Passions and Economic Interests: Economic Reform and Political Structure in Africa." In *Hemmed In: Responses to Africa's Economic Decline,* edited by Thomas Callaghy and John Ravenhill. New York: Columbia University Press, 1994.

———. "The State and the Development of Capitalism in Africa: Theoretical, Historical, and Comparative Reflections." In *The Precarious Balance: State and Society in Africa,* edited by Donald Rothchild and Naomi Chazan. Boulder: Westview, 1988.

Campos, Edgardo, and Hilton L. Root. *The Key to the Asian Miracle: Making Shared Growth Credible.* Washington, DC: Brookings Institution, 1996.

Campos, J. E. *Corruption: The Boom and Bust of East Asia.* Manila: Ateneo University Press, 2001.

Carey, John M. "Parchment, Equilibria, and Institutions." *Comparative Political Studies* 33, no. 6–7 (2000): 735–61.

CastleAsia. *Indonesian Business: The Year in Review.* Jakarta: CastleAsia, 2000.

Central Bank of Nigeria. *Annual Report and Statement of Accounts, 1992.* Lagos: Central Bank of Nigeria, 1993.

———. *Economic Policy Reforms in Nigeria: A Study Report.* Lagos: Central Bank of Nigeria Research Department, 1993.

———. *Perspectives on Economic Policy Reform in Nigeria.* Lagos: Central Bank of Nigeria, 1993.

———. *Annual Report and Statement of Accounts, 1994.* Lagos: Central Bank of Nigeria, 1995.

Chabal, Patrick, and Jean-Pascal Daloz. *Africa Works: Disorder as a Political Instrument.* Bloomington: Indiana University Press, 1999.

Chaudhry, Kiren Aziz. *The Price of Wealth: Economies and Institutions in the Middle East.* Ithaca: Cornell University Press, 1997.

Chazan, Naomi. "Africa's Democratic Challenge: Strengthening Civil Society and the State." *World Policy Journal* 9, no. 2 (1992): 279–307.

Chazan, Naomi, Peter Lewis, Robert Mortimer, Donald Rothchild, and Stephen John Stedman. *Politics and Society in Contemporary Africa.* 3d ed. Boulder: Lynne Rienner, 1999.

Chenery, Hollis. *Structural Change and Development Policy.* New York: Oxford University Press, 1979.

Cheng, Tun-jen. "Political Regimes and Development Strategies: South Korea and Taiwan." In *Manufacturing Miracles: Paths of Industrialization in Latin America and East Asia,* edited by Gary Gereffi and Donald Wyman. Princeton: Princeton University Press, 1990.

Chigbo, Maureen. "Obasanjo: Democracy Sans Dividend." *Newswatch* (Lagos), January 8, 2001.

Chirot, Daniel, and A. Reid, eds. *Essential Outsiders: The Chinese and Jews in the Modern Transformation of Southeast Asia and Central Europe.* Seattle: University of Washington Press, 1997.

Chua, Amy L. "Markets, Democracy, and Ethnicity: Toward a New Paradigm for Law and Development." *Yale Law Journal* 108, no. 1 (1998): 1–107.

———. *World on Fire: How Exporting Free Market Democracy Breeds Ethnic Hatred and Global Instability.* New York: Doubleday, 2002.

Civil Liberties Organization. *Annual Report on Human Rights in Nigeria.* Lagos: Civil Liberties Organization, 1992–1996.

Clapham, Christopher. *Private Patronage and Public Power: Political Clientelism in the Modern State.* New York: St. Martin's Press, 1982.

———. *Third World Politics.* Madison: University of Wisconsin Press, 1985.

Coase, Ronald H. "The Nature of the Firm." *Economica* 4, no. 16 (1937): 386–405.

———. "The Problem of Social Cost." *Journal of Law and Economics* 3 (1960): 1–44.

Cohen, Margot. "To the Barricades: As Economic Hardship Mounts, Student Protests Are Gaining Support from Other Segments of Society—and Starting to

Look Like a Nationwide Movement." *Far Eastern Economic Review,* May 14, 1998.

Colander, David C., ed. *Neoclassical Political Economy: The Analysis of Rent-Seeking and DUP Activities.* Cambridge, MA: Ballinger, 1984.

Coleman, James S. *Nigeria: Background to Nationalism.* Berkeley: University of California Press, 1958.

Collier, David, ed. *The New Authoritarianism in Latin America.* Princeton: Princeton University Press, 1979.

Collier, Paul. "Africa's External Economic Relations: 1960–90." *African Affairs* 90, no. 360 (1991): 339–56.

Coolidge, Jacqueline, and Susan Rose-Ackerman. "High-Level Rent-Seeking and Corruption in African Regimes: Theory and Cases." Policy Research Working Paper. Washington DC: World Bank, June 1997.

Cribb, Robert, and Colin Brown. *Modern Indonesia: A History since 1945.* London: Longman, 1995.

Crone, Donald K. "The Military and Development in Thailand and Indonesia: Patrimonialism versus the Market." In *Seeking Security and Development,* edited by Norman Graham. Boulder: Lynne Rienner, 1994.

———. "State, Social Elites, and Government Capacity in Southeast Asia." *World Politics* 40, no. 2 (1988): 252–68.

Crouch, Harold. *The Army and Politics in Indonesia.* Ithaca: Cornell University Press, 1978.

Cumings, Bruce. "Webs with No Spiders, Spiders with No Webs: The Genealogy of the Developmental State." In *The Developmental State,* edited by Meredith Woo-Cumings. Ithaca: Cornell University Press, 1999.

Dahl, Robert. *Polyarchy: Participation and Opposition.* New Haven: Yale University Press, 1971.

Dean, Edwin. "Noneconomic Barriers to Effective Planning in Nigeria." *Economic Development and Cultural Exchange* 19, no. 4 (1971): 560–79.

———. *Plan Implementation in Nigeria, 1962–1966.* Ibadan: Oxford University Press, 1972.

DeLorme, Charles M., D. R. Kamerschen, and J. M. Mbaku. "Rent-Seeking in the Cameroon Economy." *American Journal of Economics and Sociology* 45, no. 4 (1986): 413–23.

Denoon, David B. H. *Devaluation under Pressure: India, Indonesia, and Ghana.* Cambridge: MIT Press, 1986.

Deyo, Frederick, ed. *The Political Economy of the New Asian Industrialism.* Ithaca: Cornell University Press, 1987.

Diamond, Larry. "Class Formation in the Swollen African State." *Journal of Modern African Studies* 25, no. 4 (1987): 567–96.

———. *Developing Democracy: Toward Consolidation.* Baltimore: Johns Hopkins University Press, 1999.

———. "Nigeria in Search of Democracy." *Foreign Affairs* 62, no. 4 (1984): 905–27.

———. "Nigeria: The Uncivic Society and the Descent into Praetorianism." In *Politics in Developing Countries: Comparing Experiences with Democracy,* 2d ed., edited by Larry Diamond, Juan J. Linz, and Seymour Martin Lipset. Boulder: Lynne Rienner, 1995.

———. "Nigeria's Search for a New Political Order." *Journal of Democracy* 2, no. 2 (1991): 54–69.

———. "The Political Economy of Corruption in Nigeria." Paper presented at the 27th annual conference of the African Studies Association, Los Angeles, 1984.

Diamond, Larry, and Marc Plattner, eds. *Democratization in Africa.* Baltimore: Johns Hopkins University Press, 1999.

Dick, Howard. "Survey of Recent Developments." *Bulletin of Indonesian Economic Studies* 15, no. 1 (1979): 1–44.

———. "Survey of Recent Developments." *Bulletin of Indonesian Economic Studies* 37, no. 1 (2001): 7–41.

Diermeier, Joel M., Timothy Frye, and Steven Lewis. "Credible Commitment and Property Rights: The Role of Strategic Interaction between Political and Economic Actors." In *The Political Economy of Property Rights: Institutional Change and Credibility in the Reform of Centrally Planned Economies,* edited by David L. Weimer. Cambridge: Cambridge University Press, 1997.

Dixit, Avinash. *The Making of Economic Policy.* Cambridge: MIT Press, 1996.

Doner, Richard F. "Limits of State Strength: Toward an Institutionalist View of Economic Development." *World Politics* 44 (1992): 398–431.

Dore, Ronald. "Goodwill and the Spirit of Market Capitalism." In *The Sociology of Economic Life,* edited by Mark Granovetter and Richard Swedberg. Boulder: Westview, 1992.

Dudley, Billy. *An Introduction to Nigerian Government and Politics.* Bloomington: University of Indiana Press, 1982.

Dunning, Thad. "Resource Dependence, Economic Performance, and Political Stability." *Journal of Conflict Resolution* 49, no. 4 (2005): 451–82.

Durkheim, Emile. *The Division of Labor in Society.* New York: Free Press, 1984.

Easterly, William. *The Elusive Quest for Growth: An Economist's Adventures and Misadventures in the Tropics.* Cambridge: MIT Press, 2001.

Easterly, William, and Ross Levine. "Africa's Growth Tragedy: Policies and Ethnic Divisions." *Quarterly Journal of Economics* 112, no. 4 (1997): 1203–51.

Economist Intelligence Unit. *Indonesia Country Report, 3d Quarter 1999.* London: Economist Intelligence Unit, 1999.

———. *Nigeria Country Report.* No. 1. London: Economist Intelligence Unit, 1993.

Eggertsson, Thráinn. *Economic Behavior and Institutions.* Cambridge: Cambridge University Press, 1990.

Ellison, Christopher, and Gary Gereffi. "Explaining Strategies and Patterns of Industrial Development." In *Manufacturing Miracles: Paths of Industrialization in Latin America and East Asia,* edited by Gary Gereffi and Donald Wyman. Princeton: Princeton University Press, 1990.

Emmerson, Donald. "The Bureaucracy in Political Context: Weakness in Strength." In *Political Power and Communications in Indonesia,* edited by Karl D. Jackson and Lucien W. Pye. Berkeley: University of California Press, 1978.

———, ed. *Indonesia beyond Suharto: Polity, Economy, Society, Transition.* Armonk: M. E. Sharpe, 1999.

———. "Indonesia in 1990: A Foreshadow Play." *Asian Survey* 31, no. 2 (1991): 179–87.

Ensminger, Jean. *Making a Market: The Institutional Transformation of an African Society.* Cambridge: Cambridge University Press, 1992.

Esman, Milton. *Ethnic Politics.* Ithaca: Cornell University Press, 1994.

Evans, Peter. *Dependent Development.* Princeton: Princeton University Press, 1979.

———. *Embedded Autonomy: States and Industrial Transformation.* Princeton: Princeton University Press, 1995.

———. "The State as Problem and Solution: Predation, Embedded Autonomy, and Adjustment." In *The Politics of Economic Adjustment,* edited by Stephan Haggard and Robert Kaufman. Princeton: Princeton University Press, 1992.

———. "Transferable Lessons? Re-examining the Institutional Prerequisites of East Asian Economic Policies." *Journal of Development Studies* 34, no. 6 (1998): 66–86.

Evans, Peter, and James E. Rauch. "Bureaucracy and Growth: A Cross-National Analysis of the Effects of 'Weberian' State Structures on Economic Growth." *American Sociological Review* 64, no. 5 (1999): 748–66.

Evans, Peter, Dietrich Rueschemeyer, and Theda Skocpol, eds. *Bringing the State Back In.* Cambridge: Cambridge University Press, 1985.

Evensky, Jerry. "An Expansion of the Neoclassical Horizon in Economics: The Rent-Seeking Research Program Brings in the Nuances of Social and Political Control." *American Journal of Economics and Sociology* 47, no. 2 (1988): 223–37.

Fane, George. "Change and Continuity in Indonesia's New Fiscal Decentralisation Arrangements." *Bulletin of Indonesian Economic Studies* 39, no. 2 (2003): 159–76.

———. "Survey of Recent Developments." *Bulletin of Indonesian Economic Studies* 36, no. 1 (2000): 13–45.

Fane, George, and Ross H. McLeod. "Banking Collapse and Restructuring in Indonesia, 1997–2001." *Cato Journal* 22, no. 2 (2002): 277–95.

Federal Republic of Nigeria. *Second National Development Plan, 1970–74.* Lagos: Federal Government Printer, 1970.

———. *Structural Adjustment Program, July 1986–June 1988.* Federal Ministry of Information, November, 1986.

Feith, Herbert. "Politics of Economic Decline." In *Sukarno's Guided Indonesia,* edited by T. K. Tan. Brisbane: Jacaranda Press, 1967.

Fields, Karl. "Strong States and Business Organization in Korea and Taiwan." In *Business and the State in Developing Countries,* edited by Sylvia Maxfield and Ben Ross Schneider. Ithaca: Cornell University Press, 1997.

Firmin-Sellers, Kathryn. *The Transformation of Property Rights in the Gold Coast.* Cambridge: Cambridge University Press, 1996.

Folola, Toyin. *Violence in Nigeria: The Crisis of Religious Politics and Secular Ideologies.* Rochester: University of Rochester Press, 1998.

Forrest, Tom. "The Advance of African Capital: The Growth of Nigerian Private Enterprise." In *Alternative Development Strategies in Sub-Saharan Africa,* edited by Frances Stewart, S. Lall, and S. Wangwe. New York: St. Martin's Press, 1992.

———. *The Advance of African Capital: The Growth of Nigerian Private Enterprise.* Charlottesville: University Press of Virginia, 1995.

————. *Politics and Economic Development in Nigeria.* 2d ed. Boulder: Westview, 1995.

Forrester, Geoff, ed. *Post-Soeharto Indonesia: Renewal or Chaos.* Bathhurst: Crawford House, 1999.

Frieden, Jeffrey. *Debt, Development, and Democracy.* Princeton: Princeton University Press, 1991.

Garba, Joseph N. *Fractured History.* Princeton: Sungai Corporation, 1995.

Garnaut, Ross. "Survey of Recent Developments." *Bulletin of Indonesian Economic Studies* 15, no. 3 (1979): 1–42.

Geddes, Barbara. "Challenging the Conventional Wisdom." *Journal of Democracy* 5, no. 4 (1994): 104–18.

————. *Politician's Dilemma: Building State Capacity in Latin America.* Berkeley: University of California Press, 1994.

Geertz, Clifford. "The Integrative Revolution: Primordial Sentiments and Civic Politics in the New States." In *Old Societies and New States,* edited by Clifford Geertz. New York: Free Press, 1963.

————. *Negara: The Theatre State in Nineteenth Century Bali.* Princeton: Princeton University Press, 1980.

————. *Peddlers and Princes: Social Development and Economic Change in Two Indonesian Towns.* Chicago: University of Chicago Press, 1963.

Gelb, Alan. "Adjustment to Windfall Gains: A Comparative Analysis of Oil Exporting Countries." In *Natural Resources and the Macroeconomy,* edited by J. P. Neary and S. van Wijnbergen. Oxford: Basil Blackwell, 1986.

————. *Oil Windfalls: Blessing or Curse?* Oxford: Oxford University Press for the World Bank, 1988.

Gereffi, Gary, and Donald Wyman, eds. *Manufacturing Miracles: Paths of Industrialization in Latin America and East Asia.* Princeton: Princeton University Press, 1990.

Gerschenkron, Alexander. *Economic Backwardness in Historical Perspective.* Cambridge: Belknap Press of Harvard University Press, 1962.

Giddens, Anthony. *Central Problems in Social Theory: Action, Structure, and Contradiction in Social Analysis.* Berkeley: University of California Press, 1979.

Glassburner, Bruce, ed. *The Economy of Indonesia: Selected Readings.* Ithaca: Cornell University Press, 1971.

————. "In the Wake of General Ibnu: Crisis in the Indonesian Oil Industry." *Asian Survey* 16, no. 12 (1976): 1102–10.

————. "Political Economy and the Suharto Regime." *Bulletin of Indonesian Economic Studies* 14, no. 3 (1978): 25–50.

Glassburner, Bruce, and Alan Gelb. "Indonesia: Windfalls in a Poor Rural Economy." In *Oil Windfalls: Blessing or Curse?* edited by Alan Gelb. Oxford: Oxford University Press for the World Bank, 1988.

Gordon, David F. "Debt, Conditionality, and Reform: The International Relations of Economic Policy Restructuring in Sub-Saharan Africa." In *Hemmed In: Responses to Africa's Economic Decline,* edited by Thomas M. Callaghy and John Ravenhill. New York: Columbia University Press, 1993.

Gourevitch, Peter. *Politics in Hard Times: Comparative Responses to International Economic Crises.* Ithaca: Cornell University Press, 1986.

Granovetter, Mark. "Economic Action and Social Structure: The Problem of Embeddedness." *American Journal of Sociology* 91, no. 3 (1985): 481–510.

———. "Economic Institutions as Social Constructions: A Framework for Analysis." *Acta Sociologica* 35 (1992): 3–11.

Granovetter, Mark, and Richard Swedberg, eds. *The Sociology of Economic Life.* Boulder: Westview, 1992.

Greif, Avner. "Reputation and Coalitions in Medieval Trade: Evidence on the Maghribi Traders." *Journal of Economic History* 49, no. 4 (1989): 847–82.

Greif, Avner, Paul Milgrom, and Barry Weingast. "Coordination, Commitment, and Enforcement: The Case of the Merchant Guild." *Journal of Political Economy* 102, no. 4 (1994): 745–76.

Grindle, Merilee. *Challenging the State: Crisis and Innovation in Latin America and Africa.* Cambridge: Cambridge University Press, 1996.

———. "The New Political Economy: Positive Economics and Negative Politics." In *Politics and Policy Making in Developing Countries: Perspectives on the New Political Economy,* edited by Gerald M. Meier. San Francisco: ICS Press, 1991.

Grindle, Merilee, and John Thomas. *Public Choices and Policy Change: The Political Economy of Reform in Developing Countries.* Baltimore: Johns Hopkins University Press, 1991.

Grosh, Barbara. "Through the Structural Adjustment Minefield: Politics in an Era of Economic Liberalization." In *Economic Change and Political Liberalization in Sub-Saharan Africa,* edited by Jennifer Widner. Baltimore: Johns Hopkins University Press, 1994.

Grosh, Barbara, and Rwekaza Mukundala, eds. *State-Owned Enterprise in Africa.* Boulder: Lynne Rienner, 1993.

Haber, Stephen, Armando Razo, and Noel Maurer. *The Politics of Property Rights: Political Instability, Credible Commitments, and Economic Growth in Mexico, 1876–1929.* Cambridge: Cambridge University Press, 2003.

Habir, A. D. "Conglomerates: All in the Family?" In *Indonesia beyond Suharto: Polity, Economy, Society, Transition,* edited by Donald K. Emmerson. Armonk: M. E. Sharpe, 1999.

———. "State Enterprise: Reform and Policy Issues." In *Indonesia Assessment, 1990,* edited by Hal Hill and Terence Hull. Canberra: Australian National University, 1990.

Haggard, Stephan. *Pathways from the Periphery.* Ithaca: Cornell University Press, 1990.

———. *The Political Economy of the Asian Financial Crisis.* Washington, DC: Institute for International Economics, 2000.

Haggard, Stephan, and Robert Kaufman. *The Political Economy of Democratic Transitions.* Princeton: Princeton University Press, 1995.

Haggard, Stephan, and Steven B. Webb. *Voting for Reform: Democracy, Political Liberalization, and Economic Adjustment.* Washington, DC: World Bank, 1994.

Hall, Peter. *Governing the Economy: The Politics of State Intervention in Britain and France.* Oxford: Oxford University Press, 1986.

Hall, Peter A., and Rosemary C. R. Taylor. "Political Science and the Three New Institutionalisms." *Political Studies* 44, no. 5 (1996): 936–57.

Harbeson, John W., and Donald Rothchild. *Africa in World Politics.* Boulder: Westview, 1991.

Harbeson, John W., Donald Rothchild, and Naomi Chazan, eds. *Civil Society and the State in Africa.* Boulder: Lynne Rienner, 1994.

Harriss, John, Janet Hunter, and Colin M. Lewis, eds. *The New Institutional Economics and Third World Development.* London and New York: Routledge, 1995.

Hawes, Gary, and Hong Liu. "Explaining the Dynamics of the Southeast Asian Political Economy: State, Society, and the Search for Economic Growth." *World Politics* 45, no. 4 (1993): 629–60.

Hawkins, Tony. "An Urgent Need of Debt Relief." *Financial Times,* March 16, 1992.

———. "Why the Cap Did Not Fit." *Financial Times,* March 16, 1992.

Hefner, Robert W. *Civil Islam: Muslims and Democratization in Indonesia.* Princeton: Princeton University Press, 2000.

———, ed. *Market Cultures: Society and Morality in the New Asian Capitalist Economies.* Boulder: Westview, 1998.

Helleiner, G. K. "From Adjustment to Development in Sub-Saharan Africa: Consensus and Continuing Conflicts." In *From Adjustment to Development in Africa: Conflict, Controversy, Convergence, Consensus?* edited by G. A. Cornia and G. K. Helleiner. New York: St. Martin's Press, 1994.

———. *Peasant Agriculture, Government, and Economic Growth in Nigeria.* Homewood, IL: Richard D. Irwin, 1966.

Hellman, J. S. "Winners Take All: The Politics of Partial Reform in Postcommunist Transitions." *World Politics* 50, no. 2 (1998): 203–34.

Henderson, J., and R. Appelbaum. *States and Development in the Pacific Rim.* Newbury Park: Sage, 1992.

Herbst, Jeffrey. "The Structural Adjustment of Politics in Africa." *World Development* 18, no. 7 (1990): 949–58.

Hill, Hal. *The Indonesian Economy in Crisis: Causes, Consequences, and Lessons.* Singapore: ISEAS, Singapore, 1998.

———. *The Indonesian Economy since 1966.* Cambridge: Cambridge University Press, 1996.

———. *Indonesia's Industrial Transformation.* Singapore: Institute of South East Asia Studies, 1997.

———, ed. *Indonesia's New Order: The Dynamics of Socio-Economic Transformation.* Sydney: Allen and Unwin, 1993.

———. "Survey of Recent Developments." *Bulletin of Indonesian Economic Studies* 28, no. 2 (1992): 3–41.

Hill, Hal, and Terence Hull, eds. *Indonesia Assessment, 1990.* Canberra: Australian National University, 1990.

Hintze, Otto. *The Historical Essays of Otto Hintze.* Edited by Felix Gilbert, with the assistance of Robert M. Berdahl. New York: Oxford University Press, 1975.

Hollinger, William C. *Economic Policy under President Soeharto: Indonesia's Twenty-Five Year Record.* Washington, DC: United States–Indonesia Society, 1996.

Holman, Michael. "'Inconsistencies' in State Funds." *Financial Times,* March 16, 1992.

Horowitz, Donald. *Ethnic Groups in Conflict.* Berkeley: University of California Press, 1985.

Huntington, Samuel. *The Third Wave: Democratization in the Late Twentieth Century.* Norman: University of Oklahoma Press, 1991.

Hutchcroft, Paul. "Oligarchs and Cronies in the Philippine State: The Politics of Patrimonial Plunder." *World Politics* 43, no. 3 (1992): 429–34.

Ibrahim, Jibrin. "The Transition to Civilian Rule: Sapping Democracy." In *The Politics of Structural Adjustment in Nigeria,* edited by Adebayo O. Olukoshi. London: Heinemann, 1993.

Igbuzor, Otive. *A Critique of the 1999 Constitution Making and Review Process in Nigeria.* CFCR Monograph Series no. 1. Abuja: Citizens' Forum for Constitutional Reform, 2002.

Ihonvbere, Julius O. "A Critical Evaluation of the 1990 Failed Coup in Nigeria." *Journal of Modern African Studies* 29, no. 44 (1991): 601–26.

———. "Economic Crisis, Structural Adjustment, and Social Crisis in Nigeria." *World Development* 21, no. 1 (1993): 141–54.

Ihonvbere, Julius O., and Toyin Falola. *The Rise and Fall of Nigeria's Second Republic, 1979–84.* London: Zed Books, 1985.

Immergut, Ellen. "The Theoretical Core of the New Institutionalism." *Politics and Society* 26, no. 1 (1998): 5–34.

"Indonesia Shudders." *Economist* 347, no. 8067 (1998): 39.

Institute for Peace and Conflict Resolution. *Nigeria Strategic Conflict Assessment: Consolidated Report.* Abuja: IPCR, October 2002.

International Monetary Fund. *Letter of Intent.* Government of Indonesia and Bank Indonesia, *Memorandum of Economic and Financial Policies Medium-Term Strategy and Policies for 1999/2000 and 2000.* January 20, 2000. Available at http://www.imf.org/external/np/loi/2000/idn/01/index.htm.

———. *Staff Report for the 2004 Article IV Consultation.* Washington, DC: International Monetary Fund, June 22, 2004. http://www.imf.org/external/pubs/ft/scr/2004/cr04239.pdf.

Irwan, Alexander. *Financial Flows and the Environmental Strategy in Indonesia in the 1990s.* Washington DC: World Resources Institute, 1997.

Isumonah, V. Adefemi. "Southern Minorities, Hegemonic Politics, and Revenue Allocation in Nigeria." In *Nigerian Federalism in Crisis,* edited by Ebere Onwudiwe and Rotimi Suberu. Ibadan: Programme on Ethnic and Federal Studies, 2005.

Jackman, Robert W. *Power without Force: The Political Capacity of Nation States.* Ann Arbor: University of Michigan Press, 1993.

Jackson, Karl D., and Lucien W. Pye, eds. *Political Power and Communications in Indonesia.* Berkeley: University of California Press, 1978.

Jackson, Robert H., and Carl G. Rosberg. *Personal Rule in Black Africa.* Berkeley: University of California Press, 1982.

Jega, Attahiru. "Professional Associations and Structural Adjustment." In *The Politics of Structural Adjustment in Nigeria,* edited by Adebayo Olukoshi. London: Heinemann, 1993.

Johnson, Chalmers. *MITI and the Japanese Miracle.* Stanford: Stanford University Press, 1982.

Johnson, Colin. "Survey of Recent Developments." *Bulletin of Indonesian Economic Studies* 34, no. 2 (1998): 3–59.

Joseph, Richard A. "Affluence and Underdevelopment: The Nigerian Experience." *Journal of Modern African Studies* 16, no. 2 (1978): 221–40.

———. *Democracy and Prebendal Politics in Nigeria: The Rise and Fall of the Second Republic.* Cambridge: Cambridge University Press, 1987.

———, ed. *State, Conflict, and Democracy in Africa.* Boulder: Lynne Rienner, 1999.

Kahler, Miles. "External Influence, Conditionality, and the Politics of Adjustment." In *The Politics of Economic Adjustment,* edited by Stephan Haggard and Robert R. Kaufman. Princeton: Princeton University Press, 1992.

———. "Orthodoxy and Its Alternatives: Explaining Approaches to Stabilization and Adjustment." In *Economic Crisis and Policy Choice,* edited by Joan Nelson. Princeton: Princeton University Press, 1990.

Kang, David C. *Crony Capitalism: Corruption and Development in South Korea and the Philippines.* Cambridge: Cambridge University Press, 2002.

Karl, Terry Lynn. *The Paradox of Plenty.* Berkeley: University of California Press, 1997.

Keane, John, ed. *Civil Society and the State.* London: Verso, 1988.

Keefer, Phillip. "A Review of the Political Economy of Governance: From Property Rights to Voice." World Bank Policy Research Working Paper No. 3315, 2004.

Kennedy, Paul. *African Capitalism: The Struggle for Ascendancy.* Cambridge: Cambridge University Press, 1988.

Kenward, Lloyd R. "Survey of Recent Developments." *Bulletin of Indonesian Economic Studies* 40, no. 1 (2004): 9–35.

Kilby, Peter. *Industrialization in an Open Economy: Nigeria, 1945–1966.* Cambridge: Cambridge University Press, 1969.

Kingsbury, Damien. *The Politics of Indonesia.* Melbourne: Oxford University Press, 1998.

Kirk-Greene, Anthony, and Douglas Rimmer. *Nigeria since 1970: A Political and Economic Outline.* London: Hodder and Stoughton, 1981.

Klitgaard, Robert. *Adjusting to Reality: Beyond "State vs. Market" in Economic Development.* San Francisco: ICS Press, 1991.

Knight, Jack. *Institutions and Social Conflict.* Cambridge: Cambridge University Press, 1992.

Koehn, Peter. "Competitive Transition to Civilian Rule: Nigeria's First and Second Experiments." *Journal of Modern African Studies* 27, no. 3 (1989): 401–30.

———. *Public Policy and Administration in Africa: Lessons from Nigeria.* Boulder: Westview, 1990.

———. "The Role of Public Administrators in Public Policy Making: Practice and Prospects in Nigeria." *Public Administration and Development* 3 (1983): 1–26.

Kohli, Atul. *State-Directed Development: Political Power and Industrialization in the Global Periphery.* New York: Cambridge University Press, 2004.

———. "Where Do High-Growth Political Economies Come From? The Japanese Lineage of Korea's Developmental State." In *The Developmental State,* edited by Meredith Woo-Cumings. Ithaca: Cornell University Press, 1999.

Kraus, Jon. "Capital, Power, and Business Associations in the African Political Economy: A Tale of Two Countries, Ghana and Nigeria." *Journal of Modern African Studies* 40, no. 3 (2002): 395–436.

Krueger, Anne O. "The Political Economy of the Rent-Seeking Society." *American Economic Review* 64, no. 3 (1974): 291–303.

Kwik, Kian Gie, and B. N. Marbun, eds. *Konglomerat Indonesia.* Jakarta: Pustaka Sinar Harapan, 1993.

Ladipo, Adamolekun. *Politics and Administration in Nigeria.* London: Hutchinson, 1986.

Laitin, David. *Hegemony and Culture.* Chicago: University of Chicago Press, 1986.

Lancaster, Carol. "The Lagos Three: Economic Regionalism in Sub-Saharan Africa." In *Africa in World Politics,* edited by John W. Harbeson and Donald Rothchild. Boulder: Westview, 1991.

Landa, Janet Tai. *Trust, Ethnicity, and Identity.* Ann Arbor: University of Michigan Press, 1994.

Landes, David S. *The Wealth and Poverty of Nations: Why Some Are So Rich and Some Are So Poor.* New York: Norton, 1999.

Leftwich, Adrian. "Bringing Politics Back In: Towards a Model of the Developmental State." *Journal of Development Studies* 31 (1995): 400–427.

Lehman, Howard. *Indebted Development.* New York: St. Martin's Press, 1993.

Leonard, David. *African Successes: Four Public Managers of Kenyan Rural Development.* Berkeley: University of California Press, 1991.

Leonard, David, and Scott Straus. *Africa's Stalled Development: International Causes and Cures.* Boulder: Lynne Rienner, 2003.

Levi, Margaret. *Of Rule and Revenue.* Berkeley: University of California Press, 1988.

Lewis, Peter. "Development Strategy and Public Enterprise in Nigeria." In *State-Owned Enterprise in Africa,* edited by Barbara Grosh and Rwekaza Mukundala. Boulder: Lynne Rienner, 1993.

———. "Economic Statism, Private Capital, and the Dilemmas of Accumulation in Nigeria." *World Development* 22, no. 3 (1994): 437–51.

———. "An End to the Permanent Transition?" In *Democratization in Africa,* edited by Larry Diamond and Marc Plattner. Baltimore: Johns Hopkins University Press, 1999.

———. "Endgame in Nigeria? The Politics of a Failed Democratic Transition." *African Affairs* 93, no. 1 (1994): 323–40.

———. "From Prebendalism to Predation: The Political Economy of Decline in Nigeria." *Journal of Modern African Studies* 34, no. 1 (1996): 79–103.

———. "The Political Economy of Public Enterprise in Nigeria." PhD diss., Princeton University, 1992.

———. "Political Transition and the Dilemma of Civil Society in Africa." *Journal of International Affairs* 46, no. 1 (1992): 31–54.

———. "State, Economy, and Privatization in Nigeria." In *The Political Economy of Public Sector Reform and Privatization,* edited by John Waterbury and Ezra Suleiman. Boulder: Westview, 1990.

———. "State Structure, Elite Cohesion, and Economic Change: Nigeria and

Indonesia Compared." Presented at the annual meeting of the American Political Science Association, New York, September 1994.

———. "A Virtuous Circle? Democratization and Economic Reform in Africa." In *Pathways to Democracy,* edited by Calvin Jillson and James Hollifield. London: Routledge, 2000.

Lewis, Peter M., Pearl T. Robinson, and Barnett R. Rubin. *Stabilizing Nigeria: Sanctions, Incentives, and Support for Civil Society.* New York: Century Foundation Press, 1998.

Lewis, Peter M., and Howard Stein. "Shifting Fortunes: The Political Economy of Financial Liberalization in Nigeria." *World Development* 25, no. 1 (1997): 5–22.

Liddle, R. William. "Indonesia in 1999: Democracy Restored." *Asian Survey* 40, no. 1 (2000): 32–42.

———. "Indonesia in 2000: A Shaky Start for Democracy." *Asian Survey* 41, no. 1 (2001): 208–20.

———. "Indonesia's Democratic Opening." *Government and Opposition* 34, no. 1 (1999): 94–116.

———. "Indonesia's Threefold Crisis." *Journal of Democracy* 3, no. 4 (1992): 60–74.

———. "The Politics of Shared Growth: Some Indonesian Cases." *Comparative Politics* 19, no. 2 (1987): 127–46.

———. "Regime: The New Order." In *Indonesia beyond Suharto: Polity, Economy, Society, Transition,* edited by Donald Emmerson. Armonk: M. E. Sharpe, 1999.

———. "The Relative Autonomy of the Third World Politician: Soeharto and Indonesian Economic Development in Comparative Perspective." *International Studies Quarterly* 35, no. 4 (1991): 403–27.

———. "Soeharto's Indonesia: Personal Rule and Political Institutions." *Pacific Affairs* 58, no. 1 (1985): 68–90.

Liddle, R. William, and Rizal Mallarangeng. "Indonesia in 1996: Pressures from Above and Below." *Asian Survey* 37, no. 2 (1997): 167–74.

Light, Ivan, and Stavros Karageorgis. "The Ethnic Economy." In *The Handbook of Economic Sociology,* edited by Neil Smelser and Richard Swedberg. Princeton: Princeton University Press, 1994.

Lijphart, Arend. *Democracy in Plural Societies.* New Haven: Yale University Press, 1977.

Lim, Linda Y. C., and L. A. Peter Gosling. "Strengths and Weaknesses of Minority Status for Southeast Asian Chinese at a Time of Economic Growth and Liberalization." In *Essential Outsiders: Chinese and Jews in the Modern Transformation of Southeast Asia and Central Europe,* edited by Daniel Chirot and Anthony Reid. Seattle: University of Washington Press, 1997.

Lindauer, David L., and Michael Roemer, eds. *Development in Asia and Africa: Legacies and Opportunities.* San Francisco: International Center for Economic Growth, 1994.

Linz, Juan J. "Totalitarian and Authoritarian Regimes." In *Handbook of Political Science: Macropolitical Theory,* vol. 3, edited by Fred Greenstein and Nelson Polsby. Menlo Park: Addison-Wesley, 1975.

Linz, Juan J., and Alfred Stepan. *Problems of Democratic Transition and Consolidation.* Baltimore: Johns Hopkins University Press, 1996.

Lubeck, Paul. "Malaysian Industrialization, Ethnic Divisions, and the NIC Model: The Limits to Replication." In *States and Development in the Pacific Rim,* edited by J. Henderson and R. Appelbaum. Newbury Park: Sage, 1992.

———. "Restructuring Nigeria's Urban-Industrial Sector within the West African Region: The Interplay of Crisis, Linkages, and Popular Resistance." *International Journal of Urban and Regional Research* 16, no. 1 (1992): 6–23.

Luckham, Robin. *The Nigerian Military: A Sociological Analysis of Authority and Revolt, 1960–67.* London: Cambridge University Press, 1971.

MacIntyre, Andrew J., ed. *Business and Government in Industrializing Asia.* Ithaca: Cornell University Press, 1994.

———. *Business and Politics in Indonesia.* Sydney: Allen and Unwin, 1991.

———. "Funny Money: Fiscal Policy, Rent-Seeking, and Economic Performance in Indonesia." In *Rents, Rent-Seeking, and Economic Development: Theory and Evidence in Asia,* edited by Mushtaq H. Khan and K. S. Jomo. Cambridge: Cambridge University Press, 2000.

———. "Investment, Property Rights, and Corruption in Indonesia." In *Corruption: The Boom and Bust of East Asia,* edited by J. E. Campos. Manila: Ateneo University Press, 2001.

———. "Political Dimensions to Controversy over Business Conglomerates." In *Indonesia Assessment, 1990,* edited by Hal Hill and Terence Hull. Canberra: Australian National University, 1990.

———. "Politics and the Reorientation of Economic Policy in Indonesia." In *The Dynamics of Economic Policy Reform in South-east Asia and the South-west Pacific,* edited by Andrew J. MacIntyre and Kanishka Jayasuriya. Singapore: Oxford University Press, 1992.

———. *The Power of Institutions: Political Architecture and Governance.* Ithaca: Cornell University Press, 2003.

———. "Power, Prosperity, and Patrimonialism: Business and Government in Indonesia." In *Business and Government in Industrializing Asia,* edited by Andrew MacIntyre. Ithaca: Cornell University Press, 1994.

MacIntyre, Andrew J., and B. P. Resosudarmo. "Survey of Recent Developments." *Bulletin of Indonesian Economic Studies* 39, no. 2 (2003): 133–56.

Mackie, J. A. C. "Changing Patterns of Chinese Big Business in Southeast Asia." In *Southeast Asian Capitalists,* edited by Ruth McVey. Ithaca: Cornell University Southeast Asia Program, 1992.

———, ed. *The Chinese in Indonesia.* Hong Kong: Heinemann, 1976.

———. "The Indonesian Conglomerates in Regional Perspective." In *Indonesia Assessment, 1990,* edited by Hal Hill and Terence Hull. Canberra: Australian National University, Research School of Pacific Studies, 1990.

———. "The Indonesian Economy, 1950–1963." In *The Economy of Indonesia: Selected Readings,* edited by Bruce Glassburner. Ithaca: Cornell University Press, 1971.

———. "Tackling the 'Chinese Problem.'" In *Post-Soeharto Indonesia: Renewal or Chaos?* edited by Geoff Forrester. Bathurst: Crawford House, 1999.

Maier, Karl. "The Rise of the Moneytocracy." *Africa Report* (September–October 1992): 68–71.

Maja-Pearce, Adewale. *From Khaki to Agbada.* Lagos: Civil Liberties Organization, 1999.

Malley, Michael. "Indonesia in 2001: Restoring Stability in Jakarta." *Asian Survey* 42, no. 1 (2002): 124–32.

———. "Indonesia in 2002: The Rising Cost of Inaction." *Asian Survey* 43, no. 1 (2003): 135–46.

———. "Regions: Centralization and Resistance." In *Indonesia beyond Suharto: Polity, Economy, Society, Transition,* edited by Donald Emmerson. Armonk: M. E. Sharpe, 1999.

Manby, Bronwen. "Principal Human Rights Challenges." In *Crafting the New Nigeria: Confronting the Challenges,* edited by Robert Rotberg. Boulder: Lynne Rienner, 2004.

Manning, Chris, and Peter van Diermen, eds. *Indonesia in Transition: Social Aspects of Reforms and Crisis.* Singapore: Institute of Southeast Asian Studies, 2000.

Maravall, José María. "The Myth of the Authoritarian Advantage." *Journal of Democracy* 5, no. 4 (1994): 17–31.

Marks, Stephen V. "Survey of Recent Developments." *Bulletin of Indonesian Economic Studies* 40, no. 2 (2004): 151–75.

Matsuyama, Kiminori. "Economic Development as Coordination Problems." In *The Role of Government in East Asian Economic Development: Comparative Institutional Analysis,* edited by Masahiko Aoki, Masahiro Okuno-Fujiwara, and Hyung-Ki Kim. Oxford: Oxford University Press, 1996.

Maxfield, Sylvia, and Ben Ross Schneider, eds. *Business and the State in Developing Countries.* Ithaca: Cornell University Press, 1997.

Mbaku, J., and C. Paul. "Political Instability in Africa: A Rent-Seeking Approach." *Public Choice* 63 (1989): 63–72.

McCawley, Peter. "Some Consequences of the Pertamina Crisis in Indonesia." *Journal of Southeast Asian Studies* 9, no. 1 (1978): 1–27.

McDonald, Hamish. *Suharto's Indonesia.* Victoria: Fontana/Collins, 1980.

McKendrick, David. "Obstacles to Catch-Up: The Case of the Indonesian Aircraft Industry." *Bulletin of Indonesian Economic Studies* 28, no. 1 (1992): 39–66.

McLeod, Ross. "After Soeharto: Prospects for Reform and Recovery in Indonesia." Departmental Working Papers. Economics RSPAS: Australian National University, 2003. http://rspas.anu.edu.au/economics/ publish/papers/ wp2003/wp-econ-2003–10.pdf.

———. "Dealing with Bank System Failure: Indonesia, 1997–2003." *World Development* 40, no. 1 (2004): 95–116.

———, ed. *Indonesia Assessment 1994.* Canberra: Australian National University, Research School of Pacific and Asian Studies, 1994.

———. "Survey of Recent Developments." *Bulletin of Indonesian Economic Studies* 36, no. 2 (2000): 5–41.

McLeod, Ross H., and Ross Garnaut, eds. *East Asia in Crisis: From Being a Miracle to Needing One?* London: Routledge, 1999.

McMillan, John. *Reinventing the Bazaar: A Natural History of Markets.* New York: Norton, 2002.

McVey, Ruth. "The Indonesian Conglomerates in Regional Perspective." In

Indonesia Assessment, edited by Hal Hill and Terence Hull. Canberra: Australian National University, Research School of Pacific Studies, 1990.

———. "Overseas Chinese Entrepreneurship." *Asia-Pacific Economic Literature* 6, no. 1 (1992): 41–64.

———, ed. *Southeast Asian Capitalists.* Ithaca: Cornell University Southeast Asia Program, 1992.

Medema, Steven G. "Another Look at the Problem of Rent-Seeking." *Journal of Economic Issues* 25, no. 4 (1991): 1049–65.

Mehlum, Halvor, K. Moene, and R. Torvik. "Institutions and the Resource Curse." Working paper, Norwegian University of Science and Technology, August 28, 2002.

Meier, Gerald M., ed. *Politics and Policy Making in Developing Countries: Perspectives on the New Political Economy.* San Francisco: ICS Press, 1991.

Melson, Robert, and Howard Wolpe, eds. *Nigeria: Modernization and the Politics of Communalism.* East Lansing: Michigan State University Press, 1970.

Mietzner, Marcus. "From Soeharto to Habibie: The Indonesian Armed Forces and Political Islam during the Transition." In *Post-Soeharto Indonesia: Renewal or Chaos,* edited by Geoff Forrester. Bathurst: Crawford House, 1999.

———. "The 1999 General Session: Wahid, Megawati, and the Fight for the Presidency." In *Indonesia in Transition: Social Aspects of Reformasi and Crisis,* edited by Chris Manning and Peter Van Diermen. Singapore: Institute of Southeast Asian Studies, 1999.

Migdal, Joel S. *Strong Societies and Weak States.* Princeton: Princeton University Press, 1988.

Migdal, Joel S., Atul Kohli, and Vivienne Shue, eds. *State Power and Social Forces: Domination and Transformation in the Third World.* Cambridge: Cambridge University Press, 1994.

Moser, Gary. "The IMF and Nigeria, an Enduring Relationship." *This Day* (Lagos), April 15, 2002.

Mosley, Paul. "Policy-Making without Facts: A Note on the Assessment of Structural Adjustment Policies in Nigeria, 1985–1990." *African Affairs* 91 (1992): 227–40.

Mosley, Paul, Jane Harrigan, and John Toye. *Aid and Power: The World Bank and Policy-Based Lending.* Vol. 1. London: Routledge, 1991.

Mustapha, Abdul Raufu. "Structural Adjustment and Agrarian Change in Nigeria." In *The Politics of Structural Adjustment in Nigeria,* edited by Adebayo Olukoshi. London: James Currey, 1993.

Naim, Moises. "Fads and Fashions in Economic Reforms: Washington Consensus or Washington Confusion?" *Third World Quarterly* 21, no. 3 (2000): 505–28.

Nasution, Anwar. "Survey of Recent Developments." *Bulletin of Indonesian Economic Studies* 27, no. 2 (1991): 3–43.

Naya, Sieji, Miguel Urrutia, Mark Shelley, and Alfredo Fuentes, eds. *Lessons in Development: A Comparative Study of Asia and Latin America.* San Francisco: International Center for Economic Growth, 1989.

Neary, J. P., and S. van Wijnbergen, eds. *Natural Resources and the Macroeconomy.* Oxford: Basil Blackwell, 1986.

Nelson, Joan, ed. *Economic Crisis and Policy Choice: The Politics of Adjustment in the Third World.* Princeton: Princeton University Press, 1990.

———, ed. *Fragile Coalitions: The Politics of Adjustment.* New Brunswick: Transaction Books for the Overseas Development Council, 1989.

———. "The Political Economy of Stabilization: Commitment, Capacity, and Public Response." *World Development* 12, no. 10 (1984): 983–1006.

Nigerian Economic Summit Group. *Economic Action Agenda 2002.* Lagos: Nigerian Economic Summit Group, 2002.

"Nigeria Letter of Intent and Memorandum on Economic and Financial Policies of the Federal Government of 2000." Washington, DC: International Monetary Fund, July 20, 2000. http://www.imf.org/external/np/loi/2000/nga/01/index.htm.

Nore, Petter, and Terisa Turner. *Oil and Class Struggle.* London: Zed Press, 1980.

North, Douglass C. *Institutions, Institutional Change, and Economic Performance.* Cambridge: Cambridge University Press, 1990.

———. *Structure and Change in Economic History.* New York: W. W. Norton, 1981.

North, Douglass C., and Robert P. Thomas. *The Rise of the Western World: A New Economic History.* Cambridge: Cambridge University Press, 1973.

North, Douglass, and Barry Weingast. "Constitutions and Commitment: The Evolution of Institutions Governing Public Choice in Seventeenth Century England." *Journal of Economic History* 49, no. 4 (1989): 803–32.

Ntekop, T. J. "The Foreign Exchange Market in Nigeria." *Bullion* (Lagos) 16, no. 3 (1992).

Nwachuku, Chris. "Why Workers Are Unhappy with Obasanjo's Economic Policies." *This Day* (Lagos), May 5, 2005.

Nwolise, O. B. C. "How the Military Ruined Nigeria's Federalism." In *Nigerian Federalism in Crisis,* edited by Ebere Onwudiwe and Rotimi Suberu. Ibadan: Programme on Ethnic and Federal Studies, 2005.

Nwosu, Humphrey N. *Problems of Nigerian Administration.* Enugu: Fourth Dimension Publishers, 1985.

Nyatepe-Coo, Akorlie. "Dutch Disease, Government Policy, and Import Demand in Nigeria." *Applied Economics* 26, no. 4 (1994): 327–37.

Obi, Cyril I. "The Impact of Oil on Nigeria's Revenue Allocation System: Problems and Prospects for National Reconstruction." In *Federalism and Political Restructuring in Nigeria,* edited by Kunle Amuwo, Adigun Agbaje, Rotimi Suberu, and Georges Herault. Ibadan: Spectrum Books and IFRA, 1998.

O'Donnell, Guillermo. *Modernization and Bureaucratic-Authoritarianism.* Berkeley: Institute of International Studies, 1973.

O'Donnell, Guillermo, and Phillippe Schmitter. *Transitions from Authoritarian Rule: Tentative Conclusions about Uncertain Democracies.* Baltimore: Johns Hopkins University Press, 1986.

Ogbu, Chijuma. "Dangers of Another Delayed Budget." *Post Express* (Lagos), November 6, 2000.

Ojeifo, Sufuyan. "Clerk Indicts Senate on N650m Contracts." *Vanguard* (Lagos), July 25, 2000.

Ojewale, Olu. "Battle of the Elephants." *Newswatch* (Lagos), March 5, 2001.

Ojo, Emmanuel O. "The Military and Political Transition." In *Nigeria's Struggle for Democracy and Good Governance,* edited by Adigun Agbaje, Larry Diamond, and Ebere Onwudiwe. Ibadan: Ibadan University Press, 2004.

Ojo, M. O. "A Review and Appraisal of Nigeria's Experience with Financial Sector Reform." Central Bank of Nigeria, Research Department Occasional Paper No. 8, 1993.

"Okigbo Report Indicts IBB, Two Others." *Punch* (Lagos), May 16, 2005.

Olowononi, G. D. "Revenue Allocation and the Economics of Federalism." In *Federalism and Political Restructuring in Nigeria,* edited by Kunle Amuwo, Adigun Agbaje, Rotimi Suberu, and Georges Herault. Ibadan: Spectrum Books, 1998.

Olowu, Dele, Eloho Otobo, and M. Okotoni. "The Role of the Civil Service in Enhancing Development and Democracy: An Evaluation of the Nigerian Experience." Paper presented at the conference "Civil Service Systems in Comparative Perspective," School of Public and Environmental Affairs, Indiana University, Bloomington, April 5–8, 1997.

Olson, Mancur. "Dictatorship, Democracy, and Development." *American Political Science Review* 87, no. 3 (1993): 567–76.

———. *The Logic of Collective Action.* Cambridge: Harvard University Press, 1965.

———. *Power and Prosperity.* New York: Basic Books, 2000.

———. *The Rise and Decline of Nations.* New Haven: Yale University Press, 1982.

Olufemi, Kola. "The Quest for 'True Federalism' and Political Restructuring: Issues, Prospects, and Constraints." In *Nigerian Federalism in Crisis,* edited by Ebere Onwudiwe and Rotimi Suberu. Ibadan: Programme on Ethnic and Federal Studies, 2005.

Olukoshi, Adebayo. "Associational Life during the Nigerian Transition to Civilian Rule." Paper presented at the conference Democratic Transition and Structural Adjustment in Nigeria, Stanford University, August 1990.

———. *Crisis and Adjustment in the Nigerian Economy.* Lagos: JAD Publishers, 1991.

———, ed. *The Politics of Structural Adjustment in Nigeria.* London: James Currey, 1993.

Olukoshi, Adebayo, and Tajudeen Abdulraheem. "Nigeria: Crisis Management under the Buhari Regime." *Review of African Political Economy* 12, no. 34 (1985): 95–101.

Onishi, Norimitsu. "Nigeria Leader Amazes Many with Strong Anti-Graft Drive." *New York Times,* November 23, 1999, section A.

Onoge, Omafume F. "The Indigenisation Decree and Economic Independence: Another Case of Bourgeois Utopianism." In *Nigeria's Indigenization Policy.* Ibadan: Nigerian Economic Society, 1974.

Onosode, Gamaliel. *Three Decades of Development Crisis in Nigeria.* Lagos: Malthouse Press, 1993.

Onwudiwe, Ebere, and Rotimi Suberu, eds. *Nigerian Federalism in Crisis.* Ibadan: Programme on Ethnic and Federal Studies, 2005.

Osaghae, Eghosa. *Crippled Giant: Nigeria since Independence.* Bloomington: Indiana University Press, 1998.

Collective Action: Presidential Address, American Political Science Association, 1997." *American Political Science Review* 92, no. 1 (1998): 1–22.

———. *Governing the Commons: The Evolution of Institutions for Collective Action.* New York: Cambridge University Press, 1990.

Oyediran, Oyeleye, and Adigun Agbaje, eds. *Nigeria: Politics of Transition and Governance, 1986–1996.* CODESRIA book series. Basford: Russell, 1999.

Oyo, Remi. "President Obasanjo Cleans Up the Military." Inter-Press Service, June 13, 1999.

Ozanne, Julian. "Dealers Play for High Stakes." *Financial Times,* March 12, 1991.

Paden, John H. *Muslim Civic Cultures and Conflict Resolution: The Challenge of Democratic Federalism in Nigeria.* Washington, DC: Brookings Institution Press, 2005.

Pangestu, Mari, and Iwan Jaya Azis. "Survey of Recent Developments." *Bulletin of Indonesian Economic Studies* 30, no. 2 (1994): 3–47.

Pangestu, Mari, and Amar Bhattacharya. "Indonesia: Development Transformation and Public Policy." Washington, DC: World Bank, 1993.

Pangestu, Mari, and M. S. Goeltom. "Survey of Recent Development." *Bulletin of Indonesian Economic Studies* 37, no. 2 (2001): 141–71.

Panter-Brick, S. K. "From Military Coup to Civil War, January 1966 to May 1967." In *Nigerian Politics and Military Rule: Prelude to the Civil War,* edited by S. K. Panter-Brick. London: Athlone, 1970.

Pauker, Guy J. "Indonesia in 1980: Regime Fatigue?" *Asian Survey* 21, no. 2 (1981): 232–44.

Pearson, Scott R. *Petroleum and the Nigerian Economy.* Stanford: Stanford University Press, 1970.

Pempel, T. J. "The Developmental Regime in a Changing World Economy." In *The Developmental State,* edited by Meredith Woo-Cumings. Ithaca: Cornell University Press, 1999.

———, ed. *The Politics of the Asian Economic Crisis.* Ithaca: Cornell University Press, 1999.

Penn World Tables. Center for International Comparisons. Philadelphia: University of Pennsylvania. http://pwt.econ.upenn.edu/.

Penny, D. H., and Dhalan Thalib. "Survey of Recent Developments." *Bulletin of Indonesian Economic Studies* 3, no. 6 (1967): 1–30.

Pfeffermann, Guy P., Gregory V. Kisunko, and Mariusz A. Jumlinski. *Trends in Private Investment in Developing Countries.* Washington, DC: World Bank, 1999.

Pinto, Brian. "Nigeria During and After the Oil Boom: A Policy Comparison with Indonesia." *World Bank Economic Review* 1, no. 3 (1987): 419–45.

Popov, Vladimir. "Shock Therapy versus Gradualism: The End of the Debate (Explaining the Magnitude of Transformational Recession)." *Comparative Economic Studies* 42, no. 1 (2000): 1–58.

Powell, Walter, and Laurel Smith-Doerr. "Networks and Economic Life." In *The Handbook of Economic Sociology,* edited by Neil Smelser and Richard Swedberg. Princeton: Princeton University Press, 1994.

Prawiro, Radius. *Indonesia's Struggle for Economic Development: Pragmatism in Action.* Kuala Lumpur: Oxford University Press, 1998.

Przeworski, Adam. *Democracy and the Market: Political and Economic Reforms in Eastern Europe and Latin America.* Cambridge: Cambridge University Press, 1991.

―――. *States and Markets.* New York: Cambridge University Press, 2003.

Przeworski, Adam, and Henry Teune. *The Logic of Comparative Social Inquiry.* New York: Wiley-Interscience, 1970.

Putnam, Robert D. "Diplomacy and Domestic Politics: The Logic of Two-Level Games." *International Organization* 42, no. 3 (1988): 427–60.

Radelet, Steven C., and Wing Thye Woo. "Indonesia: A Troubled Beginning." In *The Asian Financial Crisis: Lessons for a Resilient Asia,* edited by Wing Thye Woo, Jeffrey D. Sachs, and Klaus Schwab. Cambridge: MIT Press, 2000.

Ramstetter, Eric D. "Survey of Recent Developments." *Bulletin of Indonesian Economic Studies* 36, no. 3 (2000): 3–47.

Redding, S. Gordon. *The Spirit of Chinese Capitalism.* Berlin: Walter de Gruyter, 1993.

Reid, Anthony. "Entrepreneurial Minorities, Nationalism, and the State." In *Essential Outsiders,* edited by Daniel Chirot and Anthony Reid. Seattle: University of Washington Press, 1997.

Remmer, Karen. "Theoretical Decay and Theoretical Development: The Resurgence of Institutional Analysis." *World Politics* 50, no. 1 (1997): 34–61.

Remmer, Karen L., and G. Merkx. "Bureaucratic-Authoritarianism Revisited." *Latin American Research Review* 17, no. 2 (1982): 3–40.

Reno, William. "Old Brigades, Money Bags, New Breeds, and the Ironies of Reform in Nigeria." *Canadian Journal of African Studies* 27, no. 1 (1993): 66–87.

―――. *Warlord Politics and African States.* Boulder: Lynne Rienner, 1998.

Report of the Coker Commission of Inquiry into the Affairs of Certain Statutory Corporations in Western Nigeria. Vols. 1–4. Lagos: Ministry of Information, 1962.

Report of the Tribunal Appointed to Inquire into Allegations Reflecting on the Official Conduct of the Premier of, and Certain Persons Holding Ministerial and Other Public Offices in the Eastern Region of Nigeria. Cmnd. 51. London: HMSO, 1957.

Report of the Tribunal of Inquiry into the Affairs of the Electricity Corporation of Nigeria for the Period 1st January, 1961 to 31st December, 1965, Comments of the Federal Military Government. Lagos: Federal Ministry of Information, 1968.

Ricklefs, M. C. *A History of Modern Indonesia since c. 1300.* 2d ed. Palo Alto: Stanford University Press, 1981.

Riggs, Fred. *Thailand: The Modernization of a Bureaucratic Polity.* Honolulu: East-West Center Press, 1966.

Rimmer, Douglas. "Development in Nigeria: An Overview." In *The Political Economy of Income Distribution in Nigeria,* edited by Henry Bienen and V. P. Diejomaoh. New York: Holmes and Meier, 1981.

―――. "External Debt and Structural Adjustment in Tropical Africa." *African Affairs* 89, no. 355 (1990): 283–91.

―――. "The Over-Valued Currency and Over-Administered Economy of Nigeria." *African Affairs* 84, no. 336 (1985): 432–46.

Robertson-Snape, Fiona. "Corruption, Collusion, and Nepotism in Indonesia." *Third World Quarterly* 20, no. 3 (1999): 589–602.

Robison, Richard. "Authoritarian States, Capital-Owning Classes, and the Politics of Newly-Industrializing Countries: The Case of Indonesia." *World Politics* 61, no. 1 (1988): 52–74.

————. *Indonesia: The Rise of Capital.* Sydney: Allen and Unwin, 1986.

————. *Power and Economy in Suharto's Indonesia.* Manila: Journal of Contemporary Asia Publishers, 1990.

Rodan, G., K. Hewison, and R. Robison, eds. *The Political Economy of South-East Asia: An Introduction.* Oxford: Oxford University Press, 1997.

Rodrik, Dani. *Has Globalization Gone Too Far?* Washington, DC: Institute for International Economics, 1997.

————. "The 'Paradoxes' of the Successful State." *European Economic Review* 41 (1997): 411–42.

Rodrik, Dani, and Raquel Fernandez. "Resistance to Reform: Status Quo Bias in the Presence of Individual-Specific Uncertainty." *American Economic Review* 81, no. 5 (1991): 1146–55.

Rogowski, Ronald. *Commerce and Coalitions: How Trade Affects Domestic Political Alignments.* Princeton: Princeton University Press, 1989.

Root, Hilton. *Small Countries, Big Lessons: Governance and the Rise of East Asia.* Oxford: Oxford University Press for the Asian Development Bank, 1996.

Ross, Michael. "How Do Natural Resources Influence Civil War? Evidence from Thirteen Cases." *International Organization* 58, no. 1 (2004): 35–67.

————. "The Political Economy of the Resource Curse." *World Politics* 51 (January 1999): 297–322.

————. "Resources and Rebellion in Aceh, Indonesia." In *Understanding Civil War: Evidence and Analysis.* Vol. 2, *Europe, Central Asia, and Other Regions,* edited by Paul Collier and Nicholas Sambanis. Washington, DC: World Bank, 2005.

Rotberg, Robert, ed. *Crafting the New Nigeria: Confronting the Challenges.* Boulder: Lynne Rienner, 2004.

Rothchild, Donald, ed. *State versus Ethnic Claims: African Policy Dilemmas.* Boulder: Westview, 1983.

Rothchild, Donald, and Naomi Chazan, eds. *The Precarious Balance: State and Society in Africa.* Boulder: Westview, 1988.

Rowen, S. Henry, ed. *Behind East Asian Growth: The Political and Social Foundations of Prosperity.* London: Routledge, 1998.

Rueschemeyer, Dietrich, and Peter Evans. "The State and Economic Transformation: Toward an Analysis of the Conditions Underlying Economic Transformation." In *Bringing the State Back In,* edited by Peter Evans, Dietrich Rueschemeyer, and Theda Skocpol. Cambridge: Cambridge University Press, 1985.

Rueschemeyer, Dietrich, Evelyn Stephens, and John Stephens. *Capitalist Development and Democracy.* Chicago: University of Chicago Press, 1992.

Sachs, Jeffrey, and Andrew M. Warner. "The Curse of Natural Resources." *European Economic Review* 45 (2001): 827–38.

Sahn, David, ed. *Adjusting to Policy Failure in African Economies.* Ithaca: Cornell University Press, 1994.

Samuels, Richard. *Machiavelli's Children: Leaders and Their Legacies in Italy and Japan.* Ithaca: Cornell University Press, 2003.

Sandbrook, Richard. *The Politics of Africa's Economic Recovery.* Cambridge: Cambridge University Press, 1993.

————. *The Politics of Africa's Economic Stagnation.* Cambridge: Cambridge University Press, 1985.

Sandbrook, Richard, and J. Oelbaum. "Reforming Dysfunctional Institutions through Democratization: Reflections on Ghana." *Journal of Modern African Studies* 34, no. 4 (1997): 603–46.

SarDesai, D. R. *Southeast Asia, Past and Present.* 4th ed. Boulder: Westview, 1989.

Scharpf, Fritz W. "Institutions in Comparative Policy Research." *Comparative Political Studies* 33, 6–7 (2000): 762–90.

Schatz, Sayre P. *Nigerian Capitalism.* Berkeley: University of California Press, 1977.

————. "Pirate Capitalism and the Inert Economy of Nigeria." *Journal of Modern African Studies* 22, no. 1 (1984): 45–58.

Schmidt, Steffan, Laura Guasti, Carl H. Lande, and James C. Scott, eds. *Friends, Followers, and Factions: A Reader in Political Clientelism.* Berkeley: University of California Press, 1977.

Schneider, Ben Ross. *Politics within the State: Elite Bureaucrats and Industrial Policy in Authoritarian Brazil.* Pittsburgh: University of Pittsburgh Press, 1991.

Schwarz, Adam. *A Nation in Waiting: Indonesia in the 1990s.* 2d ed. Boulder: Westview, 1999.

Schwarz, Adam, and Jonathan Paris, eds. *The Politics of Post-Suharto Indonesia.* New York: Council on Foreign Relations Press, 1999.

Shafer, D. Michael. *Winners and Losers: How Sectors Shape the Developmental Prospects of States.* Ithaca: Cornell University Press, 1994.

Sheahan, John. *Patterns of Development in Latin America: Poverty, Repression, and Economic Strategy.* Princeton: Princeton University Press, 1987.

Shleifer, Andrei, and Robert W. Vishny. "Corruption." *Quarterly Journal of Economics* 108, no. 3 (1993): 599–617.

Simanjuntak, Djisman S. "The Indonesian Economy in 1999: Another Year of Delayed Reform." In *Indonesia in Transition: Social Aspects of Reformasi and Crisis,* edited by Chris Manning and Peter Van Diermen. Singapore: Institute of Southeast Asian Studies, 1999.

————. "Survey of Recent Developments." *Bulletin of Indonesian Economic Studies* 25, no. 1 (1989): 3–29.

Siregar, R. Y. "Survey of Recent Developments." *Bulletin of Indonesian Economic Studies* 37, no. 3 (2001): 277–303.

Sklar, Richard. "The Nature of Class Domination in Africa." *Journal of Modern African Studies* 17, no. 4 (1979): 531–52.

————. *Nigerian Political Parties.* Princeton: Princeton University Press, 1963.

Sklar, R. L., and C. S. Whitaker Jr. "Nigeria." In *Political Parties and National Integration in Tropical Africa,* edited by James S. Coleman and Carl G. Rosberg Jr. Berkeley and Los Angeles: University of California Press, 1964.

Smelser, Neil, and Richard Swedberg, eds. *The Handbook of Economic Sociology.* Princeton: Princeton University Press, 1994.

Smith, Tony. "The Underdevelopment of Development Literature: The Case of Dependency Theory." *World Politics* 31, no. 2 (1979): 247–88.

Smith, William C., Carlos H. Acuna, and Eduardo A. Gamarra, eds. *Latin*

American Political Economy in the Age of Neoliberal Reform. New Brunswick: Transaction, 1994.

Soeharto. *Soeharto: My Thoughts, Words, and Deeds.* Jakarta: PT Citra Lamtoro Gung Persada, 1991.

Soesastro, M. Hadi. "The Political Economy of Deregulation in Indonesia." *Asian Survey* 29, no. 9 (1989): 853–69.

Soesastro, Hadi, and M. Basri. "Survey of Recent Developments." *Bulletin of Indonesian Economic Studies* 34, no. 1 (1998): 3–54.

Soyinka, Wole. *The Open Sore of a Continent: A Personal Narrative of the Nigerian Crisis.* Oxford: Oxford University Press, 1996.

Stallings, Barbara, ed. *Global Change, Regional Response: The New International Context of Development.* Cambridge: Cambridge University Press, 1995.

Stallings, Barbara, and Robert Kaufman, eds. *Debt and Democracy in Latin America.* Boulder: Westview, 1989.

Stein, Howard, ed. *Asian Industrialization and Africa: Studies in Policy Alternatives to Structural Adjustment.* Basingstoke: Macmillan, 1995.

Steinmo, Sven, Kathleen Thelen, and Frank Longstreth, eds. *Structuring Politics: Historical Institutionalism in Comparative Analysis.* Cambridge: Cambridge University Press, 1992.

Stepan, Alfred. *Rethinking Military Politics.* Princeton: Princeton University Press, 1988.

Stiglitz, Joseph. *Globalization and Its Discontents.* New York: W. W. Norton, 2002.

Suberu, Rotimi T. *Ethnic Minority Conflicts and Governance in Nigeria.* Ibadan: Spectrum Books Limited, 1996.

———. *Federalism and Ethnic Conflict in Nigeria.* Washington, DC: United States Institute of Peace Press, 2001.

———. "The Travails of Federalism in Nigeria." *Journal of Democracy* 4, no. 4 (1993): 39–53.

Suryahadi, Asep, Sudarno Sumarto, Yusuf Suharso, and Lant Pritchett. "The Evolution of Poverty during the Crisis in Indonesia, 1996–99." Policy Research Working Paper no. WPS 2435. Washington, DC: World Bank, 2000.

Teriba, O. "Development Strategy, Investment Decision, and Expenditure Patterns of a Public Development Institution: The Case of Western Nigeria Development Corporation, 1949–62." *Nigerian Journal of Economic and Social Studies* 8, no. 2 (1966).

Teriba, O., and M. O. Kayode. *Industrial Development in Nigeria: Patterns, Problems, and Prospects.* Ibadan: Ibadan University Press, 1970.

Thee, Kian Wie. "Indonesia." In *Industrial Structures and the Development of Small and Medium Enterprise Linkages: Examples from East Asia,* edited by S. D. Meyanathan. Washington, DC: World Bank, 1994.

———. "The Investment Surge from Asia's NICs into Indonesia." In *Indonesia Assessment, 1990,* edited by Hal Hill and Terry Hull. Canberra: Research School of Pacific Studies, Australian National University, 1990.

———. "Japanese Direct Investment in Indonesian Manufacturing." *Bulletin of Indonesian Economic Studies* 20, no. 2 (1984): 90–106.

———. "Reflections on Indonesia's Emerging Industrial Nationalism." Working Paper No. 41. Brisbane: Murdoch University Asia Research Centre, 1994.

Thorbecke, Erik, et al., eds. *Adjustment and Equity in Indonesia.* Paris: Centre of World Food Studies, OECD Development Centre, 1992.

Tilly, Charles. *Coercion, Capital, and European States, AD 990–1990.* Cambridge, MA: Basil Blackwell, 1990.

Timmer, Peter C. "Dutch Disease and Agriculture in Indonesia: The Policy Approach." Development Discussion Paper no. 490. Cambridge: Harvard Institute for International Development, 1994.

Tims, Wouter. *Nigeria: Prospects for Long-Term Development.* Washington, DC: World Bank, 1974.

Tollison, Robert D. "Rent-Seeking: A Survey." *Kyklos* 35, no. 4 (1982): 575–602.

Toye, John. "The New Institutional Economics and Its Implications for Development Theory." In *The New Institutional Economics and Third World Development,* edited by John Harriss, Janet Hunter, and Colin M. Lewis. London and New York: Routledge, 1995.

Transparency International. *Corruption Perceptions Index.* Various years. http://www.transparency.org/surveys/index.html#cpi.

Tsebelis, George. *Veto Players: How Political Institutions Work.* Princeton: Princeton University Press, 2002.

Turner, Terisa. "Nigeria: Imperialism, Oil Technology, and the Comprador State." In *Oil and Class Struggle,* edited by Petter Nore and Terisa Turner. London: Zed Press, 1980.

Unger, Danny. *Building Social Capital in Thailand: Fibers, Finance, and Infrastructure.* Cambridge: Cambridge University Press, 1998.

United Nations Conference on Trade and Development (UNCTAD). *Handbook of Statistics.* New York: United Nations, 2005.

Usman, Syaikhu. "Indonesia's Decentralization Policy." SMERU Working Paper. September, 2001. http://ideas.repec.org/p/eab/govern/123.html.

Utomi, Pat. *Managing Uncertainty: Competition and Strategy in Emerging Economies.* Ibadan: Spectrum Books Limited, 1998.

Uwazurike, P. Chudi. "Confronting Potential Breakdown: The Nigerian Redemocratization Process in Critical Perspective." *Journal of Modern African Studies* 28, no. 1 (1990): 55–77.

Van de Walle, Nicolas. *African Economies and the Politics of Permanent Crisis, 1979–1999.* Cambridge: Cambridge University Press, 2001.

———. "Elections without Democracy: Africa's Range of Regimes." *Journal of Democracy* 13, no. 2 (2002): 66–80.

———. "Neopatrimonialism and Democracy in Africa, with an Illustration from Cameroon." In *Economic Change and Political Liberalization in Sub-Saharan Africa,* edited by Jennifer A. Widner. Baltimore: Johns Hopkins University Press, 1994.

———. "The Politics of Non-Reform in Cameroon." In *Hemmed In: Responses to Africa's Economic Decline,* edited by Thomas Callaghy and John Ravenhill. New York: Columbia University Press, 1994.

Vatikiotis, Michael. *Indonesian Politics under Suharto.* London: Routledge, 1993.

Wade, Robert. "East Asia's Economic Success: Conflicting Perspectives, Partial Insights, Shaky Evidence." *World Politics* 44, no. 2 (1992): 270–320.

———. *Governing the Market: Economic Theory and the Role of Government in East Asian Industrialization.* Princeton: Princeton University Press, 1990.

Waldner, David. *State Building and Late Development.* Ithaca: Cornell University Press, 1999.

Wanandi, Sofyan. "The Post Soeharto Business Environment." In *Post-Soeharto Indonesia: Renewal or Chaos?* edited by Geoff Forrester. Bathurst: Crawford House, 1999.

Wardhana, Ali. "Economic Reform in Indonesia: The Transition from Resource Dependence to Industrial Competitiveness." In *Behind East Asian Growth: The Political and Social Foundations of Prosperity,* edited by Henry S. Rowen. London: Routledge, 1998.

Waterbury, John. *Exposed to Innumerable Delusions.* Cambridge: Cambridge University Press, 1993.

———. "The Political Management of Economic Adjustment and Reform" In *Fragile Coalitions: The Politics of Adjustment,* edited by Joan Nelson. New Brunswick: Transaction Books for the Overseas Development Council, 1989.

Waterbury, John, and Ezra Suleiman. *The Political Economy of Public Sector Reform and Privatization.* Boulder: Westview, 1990.

Watts, Michael. "The Popular Classes and the Oil Boom: A Political Economy of Rural and Urban Poverty." In *The Political Economy of Nigeria,* edited by I. William Zartman. New York: Praeger, 1983.

———. *Silent Violence: Food, Famine, and Peasantry in Northern Nigeria.* Berkeley: University of California Press, 1983.

———, ed. *State, Oil, and Agriculture in Nigeria.* Berkeley: Institute of International Studies, 1987.

Watts, Michael, and Paul Lubeck. "An Alliance of Oil and Maize? The Response of Indigenous and State Capital to Structural Adjustment in Nigeria." In *African Capitalists and African Development,* edited by Bruce Berman and Colin Leys. Boulder: Lynne Rienner, 1994.

Weber, Max. *Economy and Society.* 2 vols. Berkeley: University of California Press, 1978.

Weimer, David L., ed. *The Political Economy of Property Rights: Institutional Change and Credibility in the Reform of Centrally Planned Economies.* Cambridge: Cambridge University Press, 1997.

Weiner, Tim. "U.S. Aides Say Nigeria Leader Might Have Been Poisoned." *New York Times,* July 11, 1998, section A.

Weingast, Barry. "The Economic Role of Political Institutions: Market-Preserving Federalism and Economic Development." *Journal of Law, Economics, and Organization* 11, no. 1 (1995): 1–31.

———. "The Political Commitment to Markets and Marketization." In *The Political Economy of Property Rights: Institutional Change and Credibility in the Reform of Centrally Planned Economies,* edited by David L. Weimer. Cambridge: Cambridge University Press, 1997.

———. "Political Impediments to Economic Reform." Manuscript. Hoover Institution, Stanford University, October 1993.

Widner, Jennifer, ed. *Economic Change and Political Liberalization in Sub-Saharan Africa.* Baltimore: Johns Hopkins University Press, 1994.

———. "The Political Economy of Reform in Southeast Asia and Sub-Saharan Africa." In *Development in Asia and Africa: Legacies and Opportunities,* edited by David L. Lindauer and Michael Roemer. San Francisco: International Center for Economic Growth, 1994.

Williams, Gavin, and Terisa Turner. "Nigeria." In *West African States: Failure and Promise,* edited by John Dunn. Cambridge: Cambridge University Press, 1978.

Williams, Mark Erick. "Market Reforms, Technocrats, and Institutional Innovation." *World Development* 30, no. 3 (2002): 395–412.

Williamson, John, ed. *The Political Economy of Policy Reform.* Washington, DC: Institute for International Economics, 1994.

———. *The Progress of Policy Reform in Latin America.* Washington, DC: Institute for International Economics, 1990.

Williamson, Oliver. *The Economic Institutions of Capitalism.* New York: Free Press, 1985.

———. *Market and Hierarchies.* New York: Free Press, 1975.

Winters, Jeffrey. "Power and the Control of Capital." *World Politics* 46, no. 3 (1994): 419–52.

———. *Power in Motion: Capital Mobility and the Indonesian State.* Ithaca: Cornell University Press, 1996.

Woo, Wing Thye, Bruce Glassburner, and Anwar Nasution. *Macroeconomic Policies, Crises, and Long-Run Growth: The Case of Indonesia, 1965–90.* Washington, DC: World Bank, 1994.

Woo, Wing Thye, and Anwar Nasution. "The Conduct of Economic Policies in Indonesia and its Impact on External Debt." In *Developing Country Debt and the World Economy,* edited by Jeffrey D. Sachs. Chicago: University of Chicago Press for NBER, 1989.

Woo-Cumings, Meredith, ed. *The Developmental State.* Ithaca: Cornell University Press, 1999.

———. "The State, Democracy, and the Reform of the Corporate Sector in Korea." In *The Politics of the Asian Economic Crisis,* edited by T. J. Pempel. Ithaca: Cornell University Press, 1999.

World Bank. *Accelerated Growth in Sub-Saharan Africa.* Washington, DC: World Bank, 1981.

———. *Adjustment in Africa: Reforms, Results, and the Road Ahead.* New York: Oxford University Press for the World Bank, 1994.

———. *Indonesia: Stability, Growth, and Equity in Repelita VI.* Washington, DC: World Bank, 1994.

———. *Nigeria's Structural Adjustment Program: Policies, Implementation, and Impact.* Washington, DC: World Bank, 1994.

———. *State and Local Governance in Nigeria.* Washington, DC: World Bank, 2002.

———. *Sub-Saharan Africa: From Crisis to Sustainable Growth.* Washington, DC: World Bank, 1989.

———. *World Debt Tables, 1989–90: External Debt of Developing Countries.* 2d supp. Washington DC: World Bank, 1990.

———. *World Development Indicators.* Washington, DC: World Bank, 2005.

———. *World Development Report, 1991.* Oxford: Oxford University Press, 1991.

———. *World Development Report, 1994.* Oxford: Oxford University Press, 1994.

———. *World Development Report, 1997.* Oxford: Oxford University Press, 1997.

World Resources Institute. *World Resources 1994–95: People and the Environment.* Washington, DC: World Resources Institute, 1994.

Young, Crawford. *The African Colonial State in Comparative Perspective.* New Haven: Yale University Press, 1994.

————. *The Politics of Cultural Pluralism.* Madison: University of Wisconsin Press, 1976.

Yunana, Reuben. "New Economic Agenda Predicated on 5% Growth Rate." *Daily Trust* (Abuja), August 8, 2003.

Zartman, William I., ed. *The Political Economy of Nigeria.* New York: Praeger, 1983.

Nigerian Periodicals

Business Times	*Newswatch*
Concord	*Punch*
Daily Times	*Tell*
Financial Punch	*This Day*
The Guardian	*Vanguard*
New Nigerian	*The Week*
The News	

Indonesian Periodicals

Bisnis Indonesia	*Kompas*
Indonesian Observer	*Tempo*
Jakarta Post	

Index